# SPIRITS OF THE BORDER V:

# THE HISTORY AND MYSTERY OF THE LONE STAR STATE

By

## KEN HUDNALL

### AND

## SHARON HUDNALL

**Other Works by Ken Hudnall**

## FICTION

*Manhattan Conspiracy*
Blood On The Apple
Capital Crimes
Angel of Death

*The Darkness Series*
When Darkness Falls
Fear the Darkness

Even Paranoids Have Enemies

*The Estate Sale Murders:*
Deadman's Diary
Curse of the Dragon's Tooth

## NON-FICTION

*The Occult Connection*:
UFO's, Secret Societies and Ancient Gods
The Hidden Race
Men In Black

No Safe Haven: Homeland Insecurity

*Spirits of the Border*
The History and Mystery of El Paso Del Norte
The History and Mystery of Fort Bliss, Texas
The History and Mystery of the Rio Grande
The History and Mystery of New Mexico
The History and Mystery of Colorado
The History and Mystery of Arizona

The Veterans Practical Primer: Getting Your Benefits

The Northwoods Conspiracy

**SPIRITS OF THE BORDER:**
**THE HISTORY AND MYSTERY OF THE LONE STAR STATE**



**OMEGA PRESS**
An imprint of Omega Communications

For Information Address:

Omega Press
5823 N. Mesa, #823
El Paso, Texas 79912
Or
http://www.kenhudnall.com

FIRST EDITION

Printed in the United States of America

# TABLE OF CONTENTS

# FOREWORD

There are those who do not believe that there is anything after death. Then there are those who believe in reincarnation and life after death. Neither will be completely happy with this book, however, each will find a great deal of information to fascinate and baffle.

This book will cover all of the ghosts and hauntings of Texas except for the West Texas Area. The reason for this exception is that the first three books of the Spirits of the Border series were completely about the West Texas area. Thus to include these stories again here would be redundant. The three books, The History and Mystery of El Paso Del Note; The History and Mystery of Fort Bliss, Texas; and The History and Mystery of the Rio Grande are still available and can be easily obtained by the interested reader.

I hope you will enjoy this latest addition to the series.

Ken Hudnall

El Paso, Texas 2005

# PART ONE
## UNSOLVED MYSTERIES

# CHAPTER ONE

# THE STRANGE

Texas is the home to a number of very baffling mysteries. Humans developed only in the last 4 to 6 million years. This corresponds to our scientific knowledge today. But how does one explain the giant human footprints that were found in the bed of the Paluxy River in Texas? In fact, there have been many finds in the past 200 years do not match any known pattern.

In Oklahoma, USA, an iron cup was discovered in an ancient lump of charcoal rock. These bone segments were found in Colombia. They come from a rock plate which is more than 100 million years old. Are they human fingers? How do the fossilized fingers from the state of Texas fit into our view of the world? And who cultivated the fruit, the remnants of which were found in an Ecuadorian Monastery, 100 million years ago?  These are just some of the questions raised by discoveries that have received little in the way of publicity.

## SECRET WEAPON STASHES

With all of the attention being paid to Homeland Security, it might come as a shock to many to know that enough arms and ammunition to outfit a World War II era division were buried just north of Paris, Texas.

This unusual story actually began in 1940 when war clouds were becoming very clear to almost everyone who cared to follow the international news. Three Paris businessmen, Jim Caviness, Pat Mayse and R. Walter Wortham came up with the plan to convince the Army to establish a military base in Lamar County. There was no question that a military base would be a boon to the economic future of Paris.

After much behind the scenes negotiation, things began to look up for the establishment of a base, but it would take time to convince the powers that be. Then came the Japanese attack on Pearl Harbor and America was at war. On January 20, 1942, it was announced in the Paris news that the War Department would build a major military base in Lamar County. The military facility eventually constructed covered 70,000 acres. Camp Maxey[1], as the facility was called, was to become one of the largest wartime facilities in the continental United States.

Due to its size and the very versatile nature of this large facility, it was also decided that it would make a perfect Prisoner of War Facility for captured German soldiers. So in 1943, the first German soldiers were processed into the facility.  Eventually over 75,000 captured Axis soldiers were sent to Texas and over 5,000 Germans were sent to Camp Maxey to sit out the remainder of the war.

In addition to the P.O.W. Camp at Camp Maxey, the post was also used for the activation of new divisions to be sent to the war zones. One of these was the 49th Armored Division. Though originally one of the phantom divisions attached to General Patton's forces that the Germans believed was to invade Europe, it had been decided to actually bring this division to life for the planned invasion of the Japanese Home Islands.

Beginning in February 1945, trainload after trainload of equipment began to arrive at Camp Maxey to be used to equip the thousands of soldiers soon to arrive to become part of the newly formed 49th Armored Division. In addition to tanks, jeeps, half tracks, personnel carriers and field artillery pieces, heavily loaded supply trains also arrived containing tens of thousands of M1 rifles, Browning Automatic Rifles, pistols, Thompson submachine guns, hand grenades, bayonets, bazookas, mortars, radios and a small mountain of ammunition to be used by each weapon.

By the middle of the summer of 1945, the first of the soldiers assigned to this new Division began to arrive at Camp Maxey. It was anticipated that the Division would be at full strength by late March of 1946. However, before this could happen, the atomic bombs were dropped on Japan and the war ended. The 49th Division never had the opportunity to actually get into combat.

The end of a major war such as World War II created almost as many new problems as did the entry into the war. Now the Government was faced with disposing of a mountain of military hardware for which it had absolutely no use. If it simply dumped all of the tens of thousands of serviceable weapons and cars and trucks on the market, the prices would drop to very low levels and the companies that made weapons and cars and trucks would not be able to compete. Many would be forced to close their doors. This was a problem for which a solution had to be found before the country was drowned in a sea of military equipment.

It was finally decided that dispose of the equipment by simply leaving many military cars and trucks in Europe to be used by the post war administration or as replacements for equipment lost by the Allies. This became a taxpayer sponsored giveaway of tens of thousands of new and used cars and trucks. When it finally reached the point where the Allies could not take any

---

[1]The Camp was named after Confederate General Sam Bell Maxey.

more surplus US military equipment, a tremendous number of cars, trucks, tanks, canons and other assorted armaments were loaded on board ships, taken out to sea and dumped into the ocean. However, this did not deal with the problem of the mountains of munitions stored at stateside bases that could not be hauled out to sea and dumped.

In the case of Camp Maxey, in Mid-September 1945, camp officials and the Paris, Texas chamber of Commerce were notified that the camp would be deactivated as of October 1, 1945. The U.S. Army Surplus Administration moved quickly to dismantle the camp. Something had to be done with the mountain of munitions that had been shipped there for the 49th Armored Division. After some serious thought, long trenches were dug in the Texas prairie and these munitions were simply dumped in these holes and buried.

Into the ground went hundreds of tanks, artillery field pieces, cars and trucks as well as tens of thousands of new military weapons carefully packed in Cosmoline. To this day, these weapons have never been found, though there have been stories of hunters seeing the fronts of Sherman tanks sticking out of stream beds and a number of small arms being found[2]. Where are the weapons of the 49th Division? Perhaps some lucky treasure hunter will use his metal detector to find the tank of his dreams. Only time will tell.

## WEATHERFORD MONSTER

Weatherford, Texas is a peaceful community known for its rich texture of folklore and a long history of slightly differing accounts of a mysterious creature which haunts Lake Weatherford. There have long been stories about the Weatherford Monster, but it has been hard to get a good description of this creature since even most eye witnesses tend to disagree over what type of creature they've seen. A few of the reported accounts say the beast is the legendary Bigfoot, the hairy missing link ape-man mainly seen in the North Western United States.

However several accounts of the Lake Weatherford beast would cast doubts on it being a Bigfoot. For one thing the Lake Weatherford monster is mainly said to walk on all fours. A few people have even said that this creature is mainly hairless, and resembles a giant armadillo. But the most popular accounts report the beast as being a huge Bull with red glowing eyes and in at least two known cases, flames emitting from his nostrils.

Unlike some similar legendary creatures such as the Loch Ness Monster and the Yeti, there are no huge scientific research projects trying to prove or disprove the existence of the Lake Weatherford Monster. As of now it remains a local legend, a monster that brings more laughs than fear.

Sightings of the Weatherford Monster originated with the Indians who roamed the area which now makes up the community of Parker County. Their

---

[2] Chariton, Wallace O., Charlie Eckhardt and Kevin R. Young, <u>Unsolved Texas Mysteries</u>, Wordware Publishing, Inc., Plano, Texas.

legend told of a fire breathing bull that terrorized villages and killed several warriors until one young brave managed to stop the beast by piercing his heart with an arrow.

During the early summer of 1953 Texas was facing a terrible drought. The mayor of Weatherford, Jim Wright (a man who would later become Speaker of the House in the United States Congress) helped to negotiate the purchase of a small lake which was owned by the Texas and Pacific Railroad. This lake was located in the northwest quadrant of Weatherford.  The plan was to expand this small lake and turn it into a permanent water supply for the community.

After the area was cleared of underbrush, reported sightings of the monster started to increase. However a number of early accounts seem to be related to heavy alcohol use (at least that's how certain officials explained the events).  No real investigations were launched to explore these early claims.

In the early 1970s a couple of local monster hunters provided the world with a plaster cast of what they claimed to be the tracks of the Lake Weatherford Monster. The odd thing about these footprints proved to be the lack of a front right side track, leading many of those associated with the hunt to refer to the monster as "South Paw" and "Lefty". These men claimed that the monster's front paw must have been torn from its arm, leaving only a stump which it probably dragged along on the ground as it traveled.

As for the plaster cast of the remaining limbs, they were reported to resemble a giant crocodile's feet.  Needless to say, crocodiles are very rare in this part of the world. The plaster cast of these tracks were immediately met with cynical criticism and denounced as a hoax.

Reports of a phantom beast continued to increase.  But it wasn't until January 16, 2000 that the local news media decided to admit that something strange might exist, when The Weatherford Democrat ran a small article on page 6A of their Sunday Edition detailing the reports flooding in about the Lake Weatherford Monster. This article alone seems to give the local myth of the devil-water-cow a new amount of respect.

## DID LINCOLN FAKE HIS OWN DEATH?

There is a seldom told story that hold that President Abraham Lincoln faking his own death and fled to Weatherford, TX. It's a strange story which the older generation of Parker County citizens holds onto as a golden truth.

Weatherford, Texas is a small community located a few miles west of Fort Worth. It's a place known for its long history of rich folklore and mythology. Among the stranger tales to come out of this area is a legend about the United States President Abraham Lincoln.

The local belief is that President Lincoln faked his death in 1865 in order to start a simple life away from politics and his wife. Though this story flies in the face of established history, but before passing judgment let's review the whole story. The story that most of us have been taught is that President Lincoln was assassinated by an actor named John Wilkes Booth shortly after the Civil War had ended.

The official record says that Abraham Lincoln died on the morning of April 15, 1865. A hearse carried his body back to the White House around 9:00 A.M. The cavalry provided an escort to the procession which moved up 10th Street to G Street and then slowly to the White House. The temporary coffin of Abraham Lincoln was covered by an American flag and at the White House; the body of the President were placed in the Guest Room which was on the second floor.

There were nine men present for the autopsy. Among these were the Surgeon General Dr. Joseph K. Barnes, Lincoln family physician, Dr. Robert King Stone, Dr. Charles Sabin Taft, Assistant Surgeon

**Figure 1: The Only Picture of Alexander Hamilton**

General Dr. Charles H. Crane, Army Assistant Surgeon William Morrow Notson, General Rucker of the Army's Quartermaster Department, Lincoln's friend, Orville H. Browning, Army Assistant Surgeon (pathologist) J. Janvier Woodward, and Army Assistant Surgeon (pathologist) Edward Curtis. Lincoln's widow, Mary Todd Lincoln sent a messenger to request a lock of hair from the President's head (as if she needed proof that it was in fact her husband). The autopsy itself was done by Dr. Curtis and Dr. Woodward.

However some classrooms in Weatherford, TX have a different version of this event. Many local historians claim that the body examined by these men could not have been that of President Abraham Lincoln. Their problem with the official record of the Lincoln autopsy comes in the form of a man named Alexander (Billy Bob) Hamilton who lived in Weatherford from 1865 to 1881. The only known photo of Alexander (Billy Bob) Hamilton was taken in the spring of 1869 in Weatherford, TX and is reproduced above.

The strange theory coming out of Parker County, Texas is that Alexander (Billy Bob) Hamilton was in fact former President Abraham Lincoln. Like many men whose wife has become a royal pain, Lincoln wanted a divorce, but because he saw no way for a man of his public stature to end his marriage, President Abraham Lincoln decided to fake his own death and flee to Texas.

Changing his name to Alexander (Billy Bob) Hamilton, he took a job at a feed store. Clues to his true identity included his love of quoting from the Gettysburg Address (after all he wrote it ), his hat (it was just like the one Lincoln wore), and he went around telling everyone he was really President Lincoln and that he was sure sorry about that little war (The Civil War).

Was Alexander (Billy Bob) Hamilton just an ordinary man who had an uncanny resemblance to President Lincoln? Did he decide to use this resemblance as a prank on the citizens of Weatherford, maybe to the full extent of quoting lines from the Gettysburg Address? Would such a man then go as far as to claim that he actually was Abraham Lincoln? That would certainly be the logical conclusion, but things are not always so logical here in Weatherford.

The real controversy began several years after Alexander (Billy Bob) Hamilton had died, when a young C.L. Lennon first heard about the story. Lennon, a failed Baptists Preacher was intrigued by the tale and set out to learn more about it. The shadow of a conspiracy filled his mind.

Lennon devoted several hours a day to his research, interviewing members of the Parker County community, as well as attempting three trips to Washington DC, to try and find answers to the situation which he found so perplexing.

After committing a number of years to the painstaking study of this chapter in history, Lennon planned to publish his notes in book form, so that the public might have a greater understanding of the event. However Lennon's manuscript was rejected by every publishing house and editor he contacted.

Frustrated and heartbroken, Lennon decided he would have to use his own money to publish the book himself. But he was a man of limited funds, so he decided to organize a number of tent revival meetings around the Parker County area as a way to raise the cash he needed. The crowds that attended these revivals were treated to Lennon's sermons about the conspiracy, and how no God fearing man or woman should ever trust the federal government.

However all of Lennon's efforts would end up in tragedy. Shortly after the first pressing of his book began, a fire destroyed the subsidized publisher's printing press, along with Lennon's original manuscript and most of his research notes.

Shortly thereafter Lennon himself disappeared, with some people believing that the government kidnapped and murdered him because he was too close to the truth. However others simply think that Lennon skipped the country with the money he had earn from his heated government blasting revivals. Rumors persist to this day that a handful of books survived the fire, but no one has presented physical evidence of this.

## JOHN WILKES BOOTH ESCAPED

There seems to be something that attracts men with unusual pasts to come to the State of Texas. Most historians tend to agree that President Abraham Lincoln's assassin, John Wilkes Booth, died in Garrett's barn on April 26, 1865. However a number of troubling factors are tied to the autopsy and burial of Booth, leading a few people to actually claim that Booth didn't really die that night. Their theory is that Booth managed to escape and that the man who was shot in the barn was someone other then the President's assassin. When government officials discovered that they had killed the wrong man, they decided to cover up the truth and avoid the embarrassment of a controversy. When the trial of the other conspirators ended, most of the rumors about Booth escaping punishment began to settle down.

miles northeast of Houston. Hamilton is obsessed with the hairy, stinky creatures he says he has seen on four occasions and frequently has heard crying out to each other on his property. Hamilton saw his first Bigfoot when he was only five. He tells of it appearing at the window of his bedroom and motioning with its finger for him to come closer. His two older brothers speak of similar encounters.

"I think he may have been looking for an easy meal, and thought he could catch a child," Hamilton says. "Or maybe it was a female Bigfoot who had lost a baby and was trying to take a human away to replace it. I had no idea what it was. I thought I had seen the devil." Within a year, Bigfoot had driven Hamilton's family from its deep-woods homestead in Nacogdoches County. An unknown animal killed his pet calf. Monstrous screams in the night and loud banging on the house terrified his mother and aunt, he remembers. The family's perfectly good horse went crazy — Hamilton believes from terror — and could no longer be ridden.

"My dad was working offshore, and my mother called and told him he had better come move us out of there or she was going to do it herself. Bigfoot ran us away from our home." Hamilton took to sleeping with a sharp hunting knife in his hand, a tomahawk under his pillow and a baseball bat by his side. His mother would wake him by calling from the bedroom door, because she was afraid if she approached, he would attack.

"I wanted to keep my gun by my bed, but my parents wouldn't let me," he says.

At the time, Hamilton had no idea what he had seen motioning to him through the window. The East Texas backwoods are full of tales of monsters, demons and "haints." Now he's convinced he saw nothing more mysterious than a primate, a gorilla like creature as yet unrecognized and unclassified by science, but that a handful of scientists are sure exists.

Renowned primate expert Jane Goodall said in a September 27, 2002, interview with National Public Radio that she is certain Bigfoot exists, and is excited by the prospect that hair said to be from a Bigfoot came back from DNA testing as belonging to no known species.

"There are a lot of weird beliefs about Bigfoot, and I don't hold with none of them," Hamilton says. "He isn't from outer space. He ain't a shape-shifter. And he certainly isn't going to come in the house, sit in your La-Z-Boy, eat microwave popcorn and watch Perry Mason with you. It's a wild animal."

How could a large, hairy, smelly ape live for years undiscovered in the forests of East Texas? Though seldom far from a farm, a trailer or a man on horseback, parts of the woods are covered in brambles, vines and swampland that protect it even from experienced backwoodsmen like Hamilton.

This is where Bigfoot lives, Hamilton is convinced, sometimes ranging into more populated areas, as close to Houston as Conroe, to find food.

Tales abound in East Texas of a so-called Wild Man or Monkey Man who's tall and hairy like an ape and roams the swamplands. Hamilton wonders why a stream in Cherokee County, where a number of Bigfoot sightings have taken place, was named Monkey Creek. He is certain that it's because for many years a reclusive primate has remained hidden along its banks.

When Hamilton was eight, he saw a book on Bigfoot at a little country store and came to the conclusion that his family had been driven away from its home not by a monster but by a wild animal.

"I knew then and there that I was going to devote my life to hunting Bigfoot," he says. As a teenage boy, his interests strayed to easier excitements. The professional wrestling circuit later diverted him, and he flashed his smile weekly on Dallas television, as a wrestler sporting neon duds and shoulder-length, Mel Gibson-style hair. In 1988, he started a construction company.

"I had enough money where I could do anything I wanted to. So I started hunting Bigfoot," he says.

He has since put tens of thousands of dollars into the search, buying fancy cameras, infrared lights, high-powered pickups and guns that can kill a rhinoceros in one shot. Yes, he admits, he is afraid of Bigfoot.

"If he were at the end of the road, he could be over here and have you before you say, 'Don't do it to me, darlin'", Hamilton says. "They can run biped or quadruped. They are about eight feet tall and they kill deer by breaking their backs with their bare hands."

When on a research trip, Hamilton makes sure Bigfoot knows he is there by urinating around the edges of his campground, being sure to pee on trees that will hold the smell. He literally is trying to piss off Bigfoot.

"I'm saying, 'I'm the alpha male here.'"

Almost invariably, it works. The Bigfoot come out of the woods and howl and scream, tear branches from the trees and throw things at the tent, he says.

"After a while, I say, 'Enough of this.' I go outside and confront them. I can hear them howling, but they don't show their faces."

Once, when he ran into a Bigfoot just over the Louisiana state line, he said he was terrified as it let out a horrible stench, a smell Hamilton believes to be related to scents frightened gorillas emit as territorial warnings.

"I dropped my video camera, ran to the truck and came back with a shotgun, a rifle and a pistol. All the hairs on my body were standing up. I was nauseated for hours afterward. He definitely was trying to send me a message."

Interest in Bigfoot is increasing with the rise of the Internet, says Hamilton, who e-mails believers as far away as Australia, where the Bigfoot are known as Yowies. After experiencing frustration with some other Internet Bigfoot groups, he bought a book and taught himself HTML. He started his own site, the Gulf Coast Bigfoot Research Organization, in 1998. He posts sightings, hosts forums and leads camping trips into Bigfoot country. Members boast that they're willing to take polygraph tests regarding their sightings.

Despite their insistence that Bigfoot exists, there may be another explanation for some of the howling heard by them — it could be coming from skeptical locals.

Jesse Wolf, chief deputy of the Tyler County Sheriff's Department in Woodville, was asked about the authenticity of the claims made by Hamilton and his followers.

"The only Bigfoot around here is the one you're talking to," he said. Wolf, a former football pro for the Miami Dolphins, stands six foot eight and wears a size 17 shoe.

"I was born in 1952, and that's about the time when he comes around. If people have seen big footprints in their yard, it was probably me. The only difference is, Bigfoot ain't wearing Nikes."

Bigfoot hunters have had to face even more ridicule than usual since the December 2002 death of logger and Bigfoot hoaxer Ray Wallace in Seattle. When Wallace died, his sons revealed he had been playing pranks about Bigfoot since 1958, making tracks with giant carved feet, filming himself in a gorilla suit and cutting a record of Bigfoot sounds. He even offered to sell a Bigfoot to Texas millionaire Tom Slick and had to back out when Slick made a serious offer.

The announcement that Bigfoot was dead led to anger and disbelief among many who had grown up watching movies like The Legend of Boggy Creek. Los Angeles songwriter Danny Freyer, who has never had a Bigfoot encounter, responded in a bluesy swamp-rock song called Bigfoot Blues, that begins like this: "Well I still believe in Bigfoot / Don't care what they say / Still believe in apple pie, and the good ol' USA / Now they claim it was a hoax by a wise old fool / That those 16-inch footprints were carved with an iron tool / But we all saw the movie of a Bigfoot mama struttin' / Walking past the camera just like Dolly Parton / Well if it was a hoax then I want back my $5 / I swear at night in the woods I've heard them Bigfoot holler."

Freyer said it would be sad if Bigfoot were nothing more than a hoax.

"It is one of our American myths. I don't want to see it die out."

Hamilton's faith was unshaken by the disclosures about Wallace.

"I know it wasn't Ray Wallace hoaxing around our homestead back in 1969," Hamilton says. "If some guy shows up prancing around in a gorilla suit in these parts, he's going to have a hole put through him sooner rather than later."

Hamilton believes the scientists will step in after men like him have taken the risks.

"Some guy in a white lab coat isn't going to be the one to find Bigfoot," he says. "It's going to be guys like me that know the woods. I'm going to be the one to prove it. I have to touch one. I have to run my hands through its fur and touch its leathery face[3]."

---

[3] Mary Lee Grant, <u>Wrestling with Bigfoot</u>, Houston Press, 13 March 2003

# CHAPTER TWO

# UNDERGROUND MYSTERIES

In Texas there are almost as many mysteries underground as there are above ground. There have long been stories about races living in caves. The Indians who roamed the Texas prairies had many stories about these creatures.

Let us now examine reports of ancient subterranean excavations, the very reality of which presupposes the existence of scientifically-advanced races which reigned perhaps thousands of years ago, excavations that had apparently been constructed before the deluge and, in some cases, following it.

This fist account below appeared in the Oct. 1947 issue of 'AMAZING STORIES' science fiction/science fact magazine, pp. 171-172:

"Sirs:

"Norman Finley, a neighbor of a good friend of mine, told me about an experience he had which was rather unusual. He and a couple of other fellows were hunting down in the Big Bend country. I don't know whether you are familiar with the Big Bend or not, but there is no more wild or desolate area in the country. Rugged, mountainous, cut by canyons, there are innumerable parts of it which have never known the foot of man.

"It was in one of the most desirable areas that Finley and his companions found themselves. They had driven about ninety miles southwest of Marathon, Texas, a little town of about 700 people, at the foot of the Del Norte Mountains, 4000 feet high, and had then gone on afoot. The dirt road just petered out and they couldn't get their car further. They were hunting deer but had no luck. Just as they were about to call it a day, Finley spotted a mountain lion. He snapped a shot at it and knocked it over. But the lion just rolled over on his feet and started to leave those parts.

"Finley and the other fellows took after him, since it was obvious that he was wounded and not making very good time. They managed to keep him in sight for about a mile and were sure they had him when he ran into a box canyon.

The lion, however, started up a faint trail up one side of the canyon to a small cave they could see about a hundred feet from the floor of the canyon. They followed him up this trail, but when they got to the cave--there was no lion!

"The cave was one of those dished-out affairs that are so common in the southwest. Eroded out of the face of a cliff and cup-shaped. The only access to it was by that trail. But this cave was a bit queer. It had a sand floor and was just about big enough to park twenty cars in it. On the cliff edge was a low STONE WALL. This in itself was not too unusual, because such caves have sheltered Indians for thousands of years.

"The thing that did make it unusual was that in the rear of it was a perfectly round hole. It was obvious that the lion had ducked into this.

"They approached it rather cautiously and tossed some stones in it to see if they could stir him up. But there was no response. They could hear the stones rolling and bouncing down an incline and the sound just got fainter and fainter until it died away altogether.

"They then approached the hole and peered down into it. It was perfectly round--also it was about four or five feet in diameter. They couldn't see very far down it, but it appeared to descend rather sharply and at a steady gradient. The fellows gathered some dry grass from the canyon floor and made some torches. The incline of the bore was too steep for them to climb down so they tossed the torches down it. They just slid down further and further and disappeared into the gloom. They never did see or hear of the lion again.

"At first they thought they had stumbled onto some old Spanish mine workings. But there was no sign anywhere of a dump that always goes with a mine. By all rights there should have been some sign of the earth and rock that had come out of that hole--but there wasn't.

"When they inspected the hole itself more closely, they were amazed at its symmetry and at the consistency of the section of the bore as far as they could see down it. The fact that the bore was perfectly round puzzled them, too. If it was a mine shaft, it most certainly wouldn't have been round, but instead would have been flat on the bottom. The fact that the shaft extended straight and unwavering as a rigid pipe was cause for further amazement. Since the fellows had no rope with them, which would have been needed to descend the shaft, as well as lights, they scratched their heads awhile and then left.

"Finley wanted to go back with equipment and see how far down the shaft went and what was at the bottom of it. But ranchers are busy people and he never went back. In the meantime he got pretty well broken up when a horse threw him and he now lives in Fort Worth while he has someone else to run the ranch. We talked rather idly about having a look at his cave someday. He says he knows exactly where it is and could find that box canyon with his eyes shut. So far we haven't done anything about it. But we may either this summer or next when we get time to go down to Big Bend.

"Finley told me this story about a year before even you heard of Shaver so you can be sure he wasn't influenced by the 'Shaver Mystery.' In fact, I don't believe he has ever heard of the 'Shaver Mystery,' even to this day.

"E. Stanton Brown., Fort Worth 7, Texas."

Another letter, dated Jan. 1948, appeared in 'AMAZING STORIES' magazine also confirming that strange 'para-speleon' phenomena exists in the western part of Texas. However the artifacts described in the following letter seem to involve areas north of Big Bend, not far from the Guadalupe Mts. and the New Mexico border. Perhaps this account is a partial confirmation of a subterranean connection between areas BELOW the Big Bend of Texas and the Guadalupe range of southern New Mexico - northwestern Texas. Quoting from the letter:

"Sirs: "Since I have been an interested reader of AMAZING STORIES since my high school days (1929) when A-S was a bigger magazine, I feel like one of the family when I read the letters in the discussion pages. The temptation has arisen many times to write a letter to you concerning some hotly discussed matter, but something has always prevented me from getting at it. However, the October Issue pushed me too far, and here goes.

"The mysterious cave Mr. E. Stanton Brown spoke of in his letter is not exactly news to me. In 1938 a party of six of my friends and myself spent seven months in that area of Texas, and upper Mexico. We were testing an electronic instrument that we had developed, and needed lots of space and some mineral deposits for the various tests.

So, we got rather well acquainted with the Big Bend country, and the Figure 2 Ranch north of there. We arrived there in January and camped IN THE SIERRA BLANCAS, storing a lot of our equipment at the town of Van Horn. By March we had gotten deep into the rugged country and as I recall, it was about the middle of March we stumbled onto this cave (or a twin) that Mr. Brown speaks of in his letter. Everyone was so dumbfounded by it that we spent the better part of the rest of the month in making a thorough investigation.

We penetrated the shaft to a distance of 870 feet and at about 650 feet found some very finely executed writing on the right wall at eye level, IN WHAT RESEMBLES CUNEIFORM. At 800 feet one of the party fell over a cloth lying in the dust, and upon closer examination, it was found to be part of a blue shirt, of fairly recent manufacture; indicating that someone else had been this far in recent times. This and an empty pint whisky bottle dated 1897 was all we located to indicate recent occupation. Of course in a country where desperadoes such as Black Jack, Billy the Kid, etc., hid out where they could and the more solitary the better, such a find was not too surprising.

"At about 780 feet the floor dips more sharply downward and at near 900 feet progress is very hazardous due to moisture and increased slant downward. We carried rocks from the opening, and rolled them from the point where we could no longer walk, but they simply faded out with a rumble after a few seconds. We tried rolling flaming yucca stumps to see if, perhaps, we might determine more about the bore further on, but this proved to be futile, since the stumps burned poorly at best, probably due to bad air. It was very stuffy and hot after the first 300 feet from the opening. We held a powwow to try and figure out how we could go further down, but the only thing would have been lots of lariat ropes, or a long steel cable, and neither was available nearer than some 50 miles.

"If Mr. Finley had taken the time to go hunting up in the Figure 2 Ranch territory he might have run across another, and to me, more interesting cave than the Big Bend one. About 62 miles north from the town of Van Horn you go through the salt-flat country, where the Salt Wars of the old west occurred. Westward, some 8 or 9 miles from the road is the Apache Canyon country, and as rugged as anywhere on the face of the globe. In an offshoot of Apache Canyon to the south, is an almost impassable gash called Hell Canyon.

The walls of this canyon rise precipitously for at least 1000 feet and top out on Apache Peak on one side and an old Indian ceremonial ground on the other side. More desolate country would be hard to imagine. Coyotes and mountain lions are plentiful, and panthers no novelty. I have seen as many as 34 deer in a herd down below on the grassy ledge sloping down toward the canyon floor. Of course, further up toward the box end of the canyon it was much too rugged for deer, but a few mountain sheep are seen, (it was) in the wildest part of the canyon that the other cave was found, in fact we almost fell into it. The high grass about the opening hid the dished out entrance.

"We were at an elevation of approximately 7000 feet and going was tough, especially with a pack, and we had stopped to rest when one of the party remarked that it 'sounded hollow' when any of us talked. Of course, we all yapped away at the same time trying to figure if this was so, and sure enough it was. Further investigation located the hole some six feet to the left of where we had stopped. It was roughly oval in shape, some 30 by 18 feet; and bridged in the center the short way by a natural rock arch heavy enough to support an elephant.

In the center of the arch were 3 deep grooves caused we hazarded, by rope passing over the arch. We spent several hours in investigating the surrounding terrain to see if there might be any other entrances to the cave, but found none. It sloped sharply from the opening down about 200 feet, and then the bore disappeared, curving upward. We succeeded in getting down to the first level, by tying all our ropes together, and subsequently investigated a lot of it.

"Threading through the soil were long stringers of quartz, but oddly enough at the same time there were chunks of rock as big as a piano that were solid masses of seashells. Quite a lot of pottery both broken and whole, was found. The most interesting thing was, however, that the farther we went the colder it got.

"Also there was a sound of either rushing wind or water, which got louder the lower we went. We came upon two human skeletons not over 500 feet from the entrance, but they must have been very old, as the bones crumbled at the touch. Everything was covered with a deep dust after passing the bend and no indication of any living thing having passed there was ever noted. It was very dark and depressing, and the chill was very penetrating. When you consider that the outside temperature was near 100 degrees, you can imagine how we were dressed.

"We had three flashlights, one a five cell, and after a while it was all that was left that would give a decent light. Down at what we estimated as 1200 feet from the opening we came smack up against a smooth stone wall. That was it. The end. None of us would admit it was natural, it was too smooth and perfect, and look as we would we could not find a single flaw or crack in it. It was of a marble-like texture and some eight or nine feet high in the center and around eleven wide.

"By placing our ears to the rock surface THE ROARING ON THE OTHER SIDE BECAME MUCH LOUDER, AND THE ROCK WAS QUITE COLD TO THE TOUCH. There was natural marble near there, in Marble Canyon, where marble was once taken out in large quantities, and so the rock was native rock, I'm sure. Since the remaining light was all we had except matches, we voted to get back to the opening as soon as possible, and after a hard struggle upgrade we got back to daylight and held a conference. We decided to bed down and talk it over further the next day, as it was getting late.

"However, the next day we were inclined to look foolishly at each other and claim it was all our imagination thinking there was anything strange on the other side of the barrier, and it was just another one of those many caves in the country. Carlsbad is just 65 miles north of there, AND THE WHOLE COUNTRY IS NO DOUBT HONEYCOMBED UNDERNEATH.

"We finished our experiments and left, late in July but I have never been able to forget the caves, and THE ODD SOUNDS ON THE OTHER SIDE OF THAT BARRIER. Or for that matter, the barrier itself, for it was too perfect to be natural, I believe. Or, maybe I've just read too many AMAZING STORIES,' and am inclined to wild ideas. As the Mexicans say, Quien sabe?

"Some day I'm going to write you a ding-how Scientifiction on something-or-other, and then place it and my rejection notice among my souvenirs. Maybe then I can go on reading AMAZING STORIES in peace, without wanting to dash off a dinger.

"K. A. Gookin., Carmel Radio & Sound Service., Box 1865., Carmel, California."

It is unlikely that the writers of the two letters which we have just quoted would be able to be reached at the addresses given. We've merely given them as they appeared in AMAZING STORIES magazine in the late 1940's.

# PART TWO

## LOST TREASURES IN TEXAS

# CHAPTER THREE

# MONEY BENEATH YOUR FEET

There are those who believe that there is a veritable fortune to be hand by digging in the Texas Dirt. There are stories of outlaw loot, pirate hoards, buried or lost mines, gold and silver dumped into lakes and a host of other lost treasures. In this section we are going to look at some of the better known treasures.

## Padre Island

Recorded history of what we know as Padre Island begins in 1519, when Alonso Alvarez de Pineda sailed past the Isla Blanca (White Island) while charting the Gulf of Mexico for Spain. Pineda claimed giants inhabited the coast, and may have been referring to the Karankawa Indians, a tall people as feisty as longhorn steers. The "Kronks", as they were nicknamed, wintered on the mainland and spent the summer on the island, living on fish and clams. Early stories portray them as cannibals who ate flesh of still-living victims or roasted their foes over campfire. This may be a myth, or cannibalism may have been a practice they learned from Spanish shipwreck victims who devoured their brethren in order to survive. We will never know since the Karankawas are extinct.

By 1521, Hernan Cortez had conquered the Aztecs and gold and silver were being mined in Mexico and shipped to Spain. Numerous galleons laden with treasure and immigrants were blown off course to Padre Island, where they foundered on sand bars and the surf smashed their hulls.

In 1553, three ships suffered this fate and were abandoned by 300 passengers who swam to shore. After being stranded for 6 days, they were surrounded by over 100 Indians (presumably Kronks), who showered them with arrows. The castaways fled south to Mexico, but only 2 men of the 300 passengers survived the trip. Ironically, Spanish divers recovered half of the cargo of silver reales. Over the centuries, treasure hunters have found some of the gray coins that now, by law, belong to the state.

Such wealth afloat offered irresistible temptation to buccaneers who preyed chiefly on Spanish ships. Around 1800, the pirate, Jean Lafitte, who became an American hero of the War of 1812, ranged around Padre Island. Legend has it that he filled his casks with fresh water from a well dug just west of Laguna Madre. Today, the marked well lies in the quiet village of Laguna Vista, a short drive west of Port Isabel. (From Texas 100, turn right on Santa Isabel Blvd. in Laguna Vista, left on Taylor Ave., left on Fernandez and go to the end of the street).

In 1804, Padre Jose Nicolas Balli[4], a Catholic Missionary Priest, founded a settlement on South Padre Island called Rancho Santa Cruz where he raised cattle and horses. At the eastern foot of the Queen Isabella Causeway stands a bronze statue of Padre Jose Nicolas Balli clad in a cassock and clasping a crucifix in his right hand. In 1829, the year he died, Balli was awarded title to the Island by the Mexican government. His nephew, Juan Jose Balli, lived on the Island until 1853. Rediscovered in 1931, the site of Rancho Santa Cruz is known as the Lost City of Padre Island. Numerous Balli descendants still live in the Lower Rio Grande Valley.

After Mexico won independence from Spain in 1821, the Anglo settlers of Texas began wanting independence for themselves. Soon revolution swept into the Valley and Mexican troops massed at Matamoras. On April 21, 1836, Sam Houston's forces annihilated the Mexican army led by General Santa Ana in the Battle of San Jacinto, and the Republic of Texas was born.

Two residents of the new republic were notable castaways whose schooner ran aground on Padre Island. John Singer, brother of the sewing machine magnate, and his wife, Johanna, built a home of driftwood on the site of Rancho Santa Cruz in 1847. Singer was part of a famous family which was highly thought of as businessmen and inventors. His brother, Isaac, had created a fortune with his Singer Sewing Machine Company – but John was more of an adventurer and he was happiest when exploring the vast coastline of Texas.

In 1847, John Singer was in Port Isabel. He was on another of his adventures, traveling the waters of the Gulf of Mexico – this time his wife, four sons, and a hired hand were along for the ride. This would turn out to be a trip that would be remembered forever by the Singer family. Not long after they left the harbor at Port Isabel, sailing a three-masted schooner known as the Alice Sadell, the family started to encounter some bad weather. Although not an experienced seaman, Singer had traveled the region before and he was of the opinion that the storm would soon blow over. But as the winds got stronger and the waves begin to crash over the vessel, he decided that he must somehow make it to shore. The squall helped him with that decision, and the huge waves promptly lifted the boat and smashed it onto a deserted island.

_______________

[4] Padre Island is named after Padre Balli.

The family spent the night in the ship's cabin and the storm had ceased by sunrise. Singer, along with his hired hand, explored the narrow island where fate had cast them. And after some discussion they came to the correct conclusion that they were on Padre Island – a narrow strip of land which extends some 100 miles, along the coast, from the Mexican border to Corpus Christi.

Singer and his group were not the only ones who had wrecked at this place. It seems that over the years dozens of Spanish vessels, while transporting gold and silver from the rich mines in Mexico, had found themselves in the middle of violent storms which blew the crippled ships onto Padre Island. Many of the ships sank offshore and the tide would wash the wreckage onto the sandy beach. Many stories were told of pirates burying vast amounts of gold, silver, and other ill-gotten gains under the sands of Padre.

The Singer family had no idea that there might be a fortune buried under their newfound residence. Fact is, they soon fell in love with Padre Island and decided to make it their home. And when a rescue vessel finally came for them, they refused to leave and instead went to work to build a life in this tropical paradise.

They used the wood from the shipwreck to fashion a frame house and crude furniture. Mrs. Singer planted seeds and raised a garden. John made a small boat to travel back and forth to the mainland. He purchased cattle and had them delivered to the island. They fished and harvested other food from the sea. You might say life was going great for the Singers – but that was all to change when the children came across some Spanish coins during one of their beachcombing endeavors.

John and his family went on to find more gold coins and eventually they came across a wooden chest containing about $80,000 in jewelry and coins. According to legend, the Singers continued to find pirate's treasure and John became highly successful in the cattle business. Singer decided to keep the bulk of his loot in a large sand dune which he named "money hill" – the story goes that he would go to his secret dune and retrieve money when he needed it. Other accounts say that he also buried another cache between two small oak trees.

With the start of the Civil War, John Singer's fate changed again – and when Yankee gunboats appeared off the coast of Padre Island, he decided to move his family to the mainland where they remained until the war ended, four years later. When Singer returned to the island, he found his house had been torn down by the Union sailors and used for firewood. He also discovered that the place had been hit by a hurricane and when he searched for his "money hill," it was nowhere to be found – the storm had changed the entire landscape of the isle, as well as completely destroying the two small oaks that he used for landmarks.

The story of the John Singer's treasure ended in 1877, when he passed away. It is said that he died a pauper with no funds whatsoever – a far cry from the riches he had enjoyed while living in his Padre Island paradise – and today's treasure hunters are still searching for his lost gold.

Friction between Mexico and Texas did not end when the United States annexed the Republic in 1845. President James Polk sent troops to Texas under the command of General Zachary Taylor. In 1846, fighting broke out around Point Isabel (now Port Isabel), but the Americans prevailed there and later at Palo Alto, Matamoras, Reynosa and Monterrey. The Mexican War success propelled Taylor to the office of President of the United States.

In 1861, when Texas seceded from the Union, the federal Navy moved to blockade the Padre Island coast, hoping to stop the flow of Confederate cotton and European guns. Fighting continued on both land and sea throughout the war. The last battle took place in May 1865, a full month after Robert E. Lee surrendered to Grant at Appomattox, within earshot of South Padre Island at Palmetto Hill. Ironically, the Confederates beat the Yankees in the final battle of the Civil War, sending them back to nearby Brazos Island.

Many changes have occurred since the last battle was fought. In 1964, the Port Mansfield Gulf Channel was completed, which separated South Padre Island from Padre Island forever. In 1974, the 2.5 mile long Queen Isabella Causeway, the longest bridge in Texas, was completed, and paved the way for the development that you see today. When you cross the Causeway as a tourist, you may, like the Singers and Padre Balli, decide to stay. It is said, that once you drink water from the Rio Grande, you will always come back, whether for a visit, or a lifetime.


## Devil's Elbow

The unusual curve in Padre Island's shore-line which faces the Gulf of Mexico is so named because as early as the 16th century it had become notorious as a place where ships would run aground. Many of these ill fated ships carried large amounts of gold and/or silver[5].

As an example of the treasures waiting on the Gulf floor near Padre Island or hidden beneath its shifting sands consider the following ship wrecks:

- In 1811, a Spanish ship was sunk off Padre Island by the Pirate John Lafitte with half a million dollars in gold locked within its hold.
- In 1873, the steamer *S.J. Lee* sank off Brazos Santiago Pass with a hundred thousand dollars locked in its purser's safe.
- In 1874, the ship *Little Fleeta* carried $20,000.00 to the floor of the Gulf.
- In 1875, 3 vessels, the *Texas Ranger*, *Ida Lewis* and *Reine des Mers* were lost off of Padre Island with more than a half a million dollars locked within their holds.

If these treasures do not get your heart racing, then read on.

---

[5] Daly, Loraine and Pat Reumert, <u>The Padre Island Story</u>, The Naylor Company, San Antonio, Texas.

## Incan Treasure

Atahualpa, the Incan Ruler was captured by Pizarro and imprisoned in his own palace. As a ransom, the Ruler of this mighty nation offered to fill the room with gold and silver as high as he could reach. Pizarro agreed and over forty mule loads of treasure were delivered in a very short time. Pizarro broke his word and murdered Atahualpa before finding out where the rest of the treasure was hidden.

This vast treasure, estimated to be worth over sixty million dollars was spirited out of Peru and is believed to have been buried near the Salt Fork of the Brazos River in Stonewall County.

## THE LEGEND OF JOHN FLETCHER'S BURIED TREASURE[6]

A century ago, treasure tales were a dime a dozen in Southeast Texas although the most of them are extinct today. Many of them centered along the coastal streams and lagoons frequented by the buccaneers of Galveston Island. By 1900 every bayou and shell bank along the Sabine or Neches Rivers or Sabine Lake had its own tale of buried gold, but the Lafitte treasure tales, having been passed down orally, were never recorded and are lost to posterity today.

Less well known are the treasure tales that once thrived at inland points in Jasper, Newton and neighboring counties, but these stories were widely circulated around 1890. In Aug., 1891, a Jasper "Newsboy" story was reprinted in a Galveston paper, as follows: "There is a great deal of buried treasure in Jasper County which can easily be obtained by industrious digging. There is a peculiarity about these buried treasures. They are never found in the poor hills, but always in the rich creek bottoms. There is a chance for a fortune by digging."

The source of this wealth was always mule trains of gold and silver in the old Coahuila trade days of Spanish Texas. This trade was anchored in the east at Nachitoches, Louisiana and in the west at San Antonio, Texas, and Nuevo Laredo and Piedras Negras, Mexico. Between 1800-1820 robbers from the Neutral Strip of Louisiana often lay in ambush in Jasper and Newton counties in an effort to waylay the pack trains moving east, who carried bullion to pay for their hardware purchases at Natchitoches.

On Oct. 2, 1891 the Galveston "News" carried a reprint from the Colmesneil (TX.) "Times," entitled 'Mexican Treasure Tale.' It described the efforts of many gold seekers to unearth these fortunes, but apparently only one factual account of hidden wealth can be verified. In 1867, while workers excavated log pilings for a steamboat wharf at Stark's Landing, ten miles south of Newton on the Sabine River, "the diggers unearthed a deposit of silver bars, the

---

[6] By W. T. Block
Reprinted from Beaumont ENTERPRISE, January 2, 1979.
Sources: "A Hidden Treasure," Galveston DAILY NEWS, April 21, 1898, reprinted in Block, EMERALD OF THE NECHES, pp. 420-423, 478, 483.

aggregate weight of which was 214 pounds avoirdupois. Extensive digging followed, but no other deposits there were found." The same article carried a report of a primitive silver smelter around Stark's Landing where bullion was re-melted and cast into smaller bars or coins. But the main treasure tale of the region received notoriety in 1898 in the neighboring county.

Beneath some lonely creek bank in Jasper County, however, there may still rest one of the biggest treasure hordes imaginable -- 12 jack loads of Spanish silver and 30 jack loads of Spanish gold. At least that was the story believed by W. S. Glenn of Palestine, Texas, and his associates of the Palestine Prospecting Company.

The nucleus of the story stemmed from on old letter and a crudely-drawn map of the year 1816 which had been passed down through Glenn's family. His lineal and collateral ancestors, John, James, and Duke Glenn, had settled in Bevil's Municipality, now Jasper County, before the Texas Revolution. How the letter and map came into their possession was unknown. The letter follows:

<u>"Nolan's Trail, Nov. 17, 1816"</u>

"On the trail a deposit was made in the year 1813 by a company of twelve of us, who were captured by a hundred of Jackson's Cavalry. Nine of our squad were killed dead on the ground. There were three of us left who were carried to New Orleans and put in prison. One man died in prison. The fight (Battle of New Orleans) coming off, we were given our choice to go into the fight, and if we survived, we were to go free, or else stay in prison for life."

"We chose to go in the fight, and Nathan Perkins, the eleventh man, was killed in battle, which left me the only living man who knew where the deposit was made in 1813 on Nolan's Trail, leading from Natchitoches on Red River to San Antonio, running in a southwest direction from Red River."

"The deposit is in a small, clear-running little creek, which runs the year round, 15 or 20 miles west of the Sabine River. It was taken down the creek 160 yards and put under a waterfall. We could pass through the water and it would fall clear over us, a high backbone ridge making right up to the bank on the east side."

"The first capture was made on April 7, 1813, twelve mule loads of silver, and on the 26th of October, we captured thirty mule loads of Spanish gold, and between these, we captured five other small lots which we put in the same place just about where the ridge points up to the creek at the lower end."

"We were very careful not to mark the site. We always passed down to the place through the water so as to leave no sign. We never stayed around the place, but would pass there once in a while to see that all was all right."

"John E. Fletcher"

"Nolan's Trail" was also the name sometimes given to El Camino Real, or the King's Highway, which covered the route from Natchitoches, La., via

Gaines' Ferry to Nacogdoches and San Antonio. A southern and less often-traveled varient route of Nolan's Trail from Natchitoches crossed the Sabine River near Toledo Bend, at a point later known as Bevil's Ferry, and proceeded to LaBahia (Goliad).

The trail's name stemmed from the expeditions of Philip Nolan to capture wild horses in Texas. In March, 1801, Nolan was killed during a battle with Spanish soldiers, and the survivors, including Peter Ellis Bean, were later imprisoned in Mexico.

Fletcher's letter, with minor discrepancies, had two precedents from the early Texas histories of Henerson Yoakum and Homer S. Thrall, which certainly lend to it some aura of authenticity, and in turn inspired Glen and his associates, who were some of the leading businessmen of Palestine. Both events occurred between 1810 and 1814, a period when Natchitoches-based filibusterers were invading Texas, and the "Neutral Strip," between the Sabine and Calcasieu Rivers, was infested with robbers.

According to Yoakum, a pack train of Mexican traders arrived at the Lanana, "a small creek west of Los Adaes," about 1812, where they were met by Lt. Augustus Magee and two other soldiers, who were to lead the Mexicans across the Neutral Strip to Natchitoches. The pack train was attacked by bandits who robbed the Mexicans, later sending them back to Salitre Prairie near the Sabine, but during the melee, Magee escaped.

The latter soon encountered United States troops, who the following day attacked the robbers, killing many and capturing two who were later imprisoned in Natchitoches and New Orleans. According to Yoakum, the prisoners were later offered pardons if they enlisted during the War of 1812 against England.

Also in 1812, Magee and Bernardo Gutierres led an expedition of American and Mexican republicans (anti-Royalists) against Spanish Texas, and within a few months they captured both La Bahia and San Antonio. The Americans were soon disenchanted with Gutierres' cruel execution of Royalist officers, and when another Spanish army from the Rio Grande threatened to retake San Antonio in 1813, a number of Americans deserted and returned to Natchitoches. But before leaving, they sacked San Antonio and dispatched a number of pack trains of captured gold and silver toward the Sabine.

Magee died during the expedition, and his command was assumed by Col. Kemper. According to Thrall, the filibusterer's pack train of loot fell into the hands of robbers before reaching the Sabine Riber. Some of the American survivors of that expedition, including Capt. McKim, whose journal of those frontier adventures survives, Samuel Kemper, Warren Hall, Joseph Talor and Henry Perry, all of whom lived in the Neutral Strip, later joined the filibustering enterprise of Capt. James Long, or else pirated with Jean Lafitte on Galveston Island, or joined up with the robber bands along the Sabine River.

From the crudely-drawn map, which offered no creek names that he could identify, Glenn ascertained that Fletcher's treasure was buried on the creek which passed through his parents farm in Jasper County. There was no longer a waterfall there, as mentioned in Fletcher's letter, but there was a high ridge on the east bank as well as the remains of a creek dam, a mill trace, and the ruins of an early-day grist mill, which family traditions asserted, had belonged to Glenn's great grandfather before the Texas Revolution.

The meager evidence was sufficient to convince some of Glenn's friends and neighbors as well. They organized the Palestine Prospecting Company early in 1898, and the firm's directors read more like a list of conservative bank officers rather than those of a treasure-hunting enterprise. The president was the Hon. A. L. Bowers, who was also the mayor of Palestine and a division superintendent of the International and Great Northern Railroad. Vice president of the firm was A. F. Seymour, who was the local agent of the Pacific Express Company, and the secretary-treasurer was D. B. Thompson, who was likewise an official of the International and Great Northern.

The officers voted to raise $5,000 for operating expenses by selling 100 shares of stock at $50 a share, payable in three monthly installments by May 1, 1898. All shareholders were slated to share the profits, if any treasure were found, after one-fourteenth had been reserved as a royalty for W. S. Glenn.

During the summer of 1898, Glenn superintended the search for Fletcher's gold, utilizing some of the best treasure-hunting devices that were available as of that year. He hired a gang of laborers who slowly excavated every inch of the high ridge on the creek's east bank. By October, 1898, the firm's funds were totally expended, the search was called off, and so far as is known, no one else has continued the search for the 42 mule loads of Spanish gold and silver.

The exact location of the Glenn family farm and the name of the creek which passed through it are still unknown to this writer. And perhaps it is just as well, for he has no desire to trigger another gold rush, that is, a stampede of pot hunters, on some one's private property in Jasper County.

A check several years ago with Ms. Eulys Hancock of the county clerk's office revealed that there was no record of a grantee deed to W. S. Glenn for any farm in Jasper County during the 1890's. Of coourse, the family farm may well have been in estate status, or for some other reason, in some other person's name. Likewise, as late as 1914, there was no grantor's deed on file involving any land sale in Jasper County by W. S. Glenn, although there are many deed records on file for other members, near and distant, of the large clan of Glenn relatives.

And so the Fletcher treasure legend remains to the present day, virtually lost to posterity since the original telling in 1898. Glenn's evidence was sufficient to entice cautious and conservative businessmen, so possibly he failed because he identified the wrong creek. And who knows, perhaps on the east bank of Sandy, or Thickety Creek, or some other of the clear-running streams of Jasper County, a vast horde of Spanish silver and gold may still lie hidden, awaiting the shovel or pick which strikes it first.

## Treasurers of Castle Gap

Thanks to long-lived rumors of buried gold and hidden treasures at Castle Gap, a widely popular landmark visited by Indians, Spanish explorers and settlers through the centuries, local land owners have had their land peppered with unexplained holes by intruders for years.

Rumors of lost gold are as prevalent in West Texas as the weathered windmills hovering over the rugged plains. Lost mines, raided wagon trains and kingly treasures — all have found a place in the lore of West Texas. But the tales are especially rich near a historic Pecos River crossing, known as Horsehead Crossing, on the once broad Pecos River and to the east at Castle Gap.

That is mainly because Horsehead Crossing hosted one of the most passable areas of the river that came to be used by cattle drivers, wagon trains and military troops after the European conquest of the Americas, explained Midland author Patrick Dearen, who has written extensively on the subject.

Joe Allen, a local historian, says there are many different types of treasures people can find at Castle Gap and Horsehead Crossing. However, he warns that local landowners don't like people to treasure hunt on their property without permission. (Lara Meckfessel/Odessa American)

"Anytime you have that many people moving through in the area, treasure tales crop up. They are still digging holes there to-day," Dearen said.

"There's as many different versions of the treasure tales as there are treasures," Allen said, as he traced the numerous wagon ruts still visible through the mesquite and cat's claw spread across the plains near the Pecos River. "I'm not going to say it's hog-wash. There's too much that's been written about it - too much been said about it. There's truth behind every tale."

Treasure hunters have been digging holes at Castle Gap, on the border between Upton and Crane counties, for hundreds of years. They chase numerous rumors of lost treasure, including those supposedly stolen from Mexican Emperor Maximillian during his attempted retreat from a hostile populace; a horseshoe keg of gold rumored left by Forty-niners returning from California; a valuable Catholic cross and treasures allegedly hidden by Spanish explorer Vasquez de Coronado in 1540.

By far, the most popular treasure tale of Castle Gap is that of Maximillian's gold It is rumored that before Maximillian was put before the firing squad as the deposed emperor of Mexico in 1867, he attempted to smuggle his great wealth from the country. A band of loyal subjects were chosen to transport the treasure by oxcart to the port at Galveston. Along the way, the group is said to have happened upon a band of ex-Confederate soldiers. Out of fear inspired by the Apache stories the soldiers relayed, the king's band - who claimed to be transporting flour - asked the soldiers to escort them to the port.

It was at Horsehead Crossing where the soldiers supposedly first spotted the gold, Allen said. One account states the treasure was made up of gold and silver coins of Spanish, Mexican, American and Austrian origin.

"They first discussed the treasure at the river and plotted (at Horsehead Crossing)," said Allen. "But they attacked and killed them at the Gap." It was in the Gap where the soldiers were said to have buried the bulk of the treasure, taking with them only what they could carry.

The area's most well-known treasure hunter was former Crane resident Cliff Newland, who stated before his passing that Maximillian's gold had been discovered years ago. But other items are said to have been found at the Gap, including an Austrian dagger, a Spanish coin mold and assorted coins.

"When I first got a metal detector, I was worried people would take me for a treasure hunter," said Allen. "Treasure hunters are after only one thing, and that's treasure."

Castle Gap is a place were treasure hunters come to look for Mexican emperor Maximillian's gold and other lost treasures. (Lara Meckfessel/Odessa American)  But for collectors and researchers such as Allen, an item's value is in the history it holds.

"When an artifact is taken and sold, that artifact becomes meaningless. Because what makes it valuable is not that it is a mili-tary button, but when you can show who wore the button and when and where," Allen said. "That's what makes it valuable."

Perhaps it is the relative poverty of the land itself - a land disposed to drought and heat - that feeds the numerous treasure tales of West Texas. Perhaps, as the artifacts themselves suggest, there is some truth to the legends.

## **Treasure Rock of Jacksboro**

Every county in Texas has at least one treasure story, some have seven or eight. The Lone Star State might possibly have more treasure stories than any other state in the Union. They seem to crop up every time you talk to someone. Of all these stories, few are more puzzling than the tale of Jacksboro's treasure under a rock. It is one that only a few have known, and only one man has told. Even those living in Jack County may not have heard the strange tale.

Examining it with a skeptical eye, you might dismiss it as fabrication. Were it not for the fact that I got it firsthand from an old-time treasure hunter who actually talked and searched for it with someone directly related to the story, I, too, would have had my doubts. In spite of the puzzles and unanswered questions, there is a strong possibility that 1,000 $20 gold pieces lie beneath a large boulder, less than three miles from the Jack County Courthouse.

The story was told to me by the late Alford Gregory of Sweetwater, Texas. It seems that in the late 1870s, a group of bandits robbed a train near Denton, Texas. It was during this time that the legendary Sam Bass was recorded robbing a train in this area in 1877. They divided up the coins so no one horse would be packing too much weight and rode west, intending to hide out in the rugged confines of far west Texas where little law existed.

As soon as the robbers left the scene, the trainmen notified the local sheriff who quickly organized a posse and mounted them on the best horses available. Within an hour, the posse had found the bandits' trail and was gaining on them. The next morning, the bandits were in sight, and a few shots were fired at long range. Before the posse could catch up, the outlaws rode into the rugged hills and canyons just north of Jacksboro, Texas. Two of the possemen were sent into Jacksboro to recruit more men, while the rest stayed on the bandits' trail.

The hills in Jack County aren't exceptionally high, nor are the canyons deep, but they are numerous and thickly covered with blackjack oak, mesquite and thick, thorny brush. Visibility in this brush country is limited to only a few yards. The only way through most places is by game trails which twist and turn, often coming to an abrupt end. The bandits and their pursuers were slowed to a walk as they weaved their way in and out of the tangles.

Given a temporary breather, the outlaws decided to cache the money in order to lighten the load on their horses and increase their chance of escape. In a small clearing they spotted a jagged boulder about four or five feet high. One climbed atop it and looked around for landmarks. Just to the southwest he spied the top of the courthouse in Jacksboro and estimated the distance to be three miles. They had no idea they were that near a town but decided to bury their loot anyway. Several of them tossed their lariats around the boulder, wrapped the free end around their saddle horns and began trying to tip the rock on its side. They managed to tilt it enough so there was a gap of about two feet between its bottom and the ground.

The only one small enough to crawl under the boulder and secret the saddlebags was a boy of about 15 or 16. As was common at this time, the youngster was with the bandits looking for excitement and adventure. The wild life of banditry seemed much more attractive than milking cows and cleaning barns. The outlaws took him in, but due to his age, allowed him only to hold their horses during the train robbery. He wasn't even allowed to carry a gun.

The boy inched his way under the boulder, trembling each time the huge rock above him wavered. He shoved the bags as far as he could under the rock and scrambled out. The bandits then released the tension on their ropes and the rock settled back in place. The entire operation took only a few minutes.

They knew the posse was close behind so they wasted no time but coiled their ropes and rode a steep, twisting trail to the west, topped a low ridge and dropped down into an adjoining ravine.

It was a blasting, fiery ravine of death rather than a way out, for the posse was lined up on the opposite ridge and fired into the outlaws with a deadly effect. This posse was not a wild, undisciplined bunch as so often portrayed by movies and books, rather it was made up of seasoned plainsmen, ranchers and buffalo hunters who knew how to use a gun. Each shot scored a hit, and the entire battle lasted less than two minutes. The kid, who so longed for the wild life, was one of the first shot down. A lawman's bullet took him low down, in the right side. He slumped forward, across his saddle horn, unconscious. His horse, frantic from the thunder of guns, bolted into the brushy tangle. How the boy stayed in the saddle, no one knows. Once away from the thunder of guns, the horse apparently slowed and wandered for several hours, his unconscious burden still in the saddle.

In the meantime, the posse had effectively executed the remaining gang members, collected the bodies and returned to nearby Jacksboro. No one bothered to make an accurate count — they just assumed all were dead.

It is here the story raises some questions. If this were Sam Bass' gang, where was he? Did he escape, or was another gang using his name? That was common in the days of the West. A small gang wishing to gain fame often claimed to be another. In 1878, Sam Bass robbed four trains in succession. Another gang might have claimed to be Bass' to throw blame off themselves. At times, the newspapers or the victims themselves just assumed it was a famous outlaw who had robbed them. It was a lot more exciting to be robbed by Sam Bass than an unknown outlaw. At any rate, the gang was eliminated, and the youth with them was never connected. The money was never sought. Why?

The wounded boy was found later the same day by a young Indian who worked as a herder for a local rancher. The kid was lying beside a small stream, and his horse was grazing nearby. The Indian carried the kid back to the home ranch where the ranch owner nursed him back to health. This act of humanity was not uncommon during the time. It wasn't uncommon for a lone rancher to keep his mouth shut. Texas was still recovering from reconstruction, and many of those who went through the Civil War had hard feelings for law of any kind. Railroads and banks were considered more of a bane than a boon, for many a small rancher fell victim to their greed. If they got robbed, most small ranchers felt they deserved what they got.

When the youth recovered, he stayed on as a cowboy for the ranch. His taste for outlawry was completely gone. He told no one about his past except the Indian boy with whom he had become close friends. Even then, the kid swore his pal to secrecy. Only sketchy details to the cache site were given, but two gold coins were offered as proof. The boy and the Indian stayed partners for life, both working on the ranch, some 10 miles north of Jacksboro. The kid worked hard, stayed honest and eventually became foreman. He even married the rancher's daughter and inherited the property. The bandit boy became a solid, law-abiding citizen with only the two tainted gold pieces to remind him of his past. For all he cared, the remaining loot could sink into the soil beneath its rocky sentinel.

In the 1930s, the kid, now an old man, died. The Indian went one last time to pay his respects. He watched as the mortician dressed his friend's old body and again saw the massive scar on his back. Hiding tears, he turned and walked away.

Now, in his 60s, the Indian never returned to the ranch, but wandered from job to job, eventually ending up on a road crew in east Texas. It was on that road crew where Alford Gregory met the old Indian. He said the Indian could outwork him every day of the week. Young Gregory and the old man became fast friends. The younger listened while the older talked. It was during one of those late-night storytellings that the tale of the train robbery came out. Gregory listened, then in secret, made notes until he thought he had every detail down as it happened.

This wasn't Alford's first venture into treasure hunting. He had grown up following his father along many trails through west Texas in search of the golden dream. This one, however, offered him a chance to try his own luck at finding treasure.

Gregory quit his job and headed for Jacksboro. "Three miles, as the crow flies" were the old Indian's words. He also said, "You can see the top of the courthouse from the rock."

Alford Gregory drove the country roads, in all directions, looking for spots where he could see the top of the courthouse.

At each likely spot, he stopped and climbed to the hood of his old Ford so he could be on an approximate level with the rock the outlaws stood on. He found several places where he could see the top of the courthouse, but each location was a dead end. Either there was no rock nearby or it was the wrong height.

He drove the country roads because many of them followed the early trails, and he felt he would have a better chance of finding his treasure.

Perhaps he was right. On his last trip, he spotted a large, jagged rock that fit the description. It was in the middle of a small clearing. There was a ravine nearby that looked as if it could have been the battle site. The only reason he spotted it was that the area had recently been victim of a massive brush fire and much of the brush formerly obstructing view from the road had burned off.

"I never got to look around," Gregory said, "because when I crossed the fence and got to the rock, four big, old, mean dogs came after me. I didn't see it from the road, but there was a house about a hundred yards on the other side of the rock."

Gregory tried several times to get permission to search the area, but the landowner refused. Fortunately, for future treasure hunters, he did not give a hint of what might be there. He only said he was looking for "Spanish marks."

Alford Gregory might have had a better chance of finding this treasure had not Uncle Sam invited him to World War II.

That ended his treasure hunting until 1945. After he was discharged, he returned home, married and began to search for treasures in west Texas.

"I always meant to go back to Jacksboro," he said. "I never got to, and now it's too late." Gregory paused a moment, coughed and then went on. "I've got this lung cancer now, and I won't last much longer. No one else knows the story, so it's yours if you want it. Just remember, three miles northeast of the courthouse, as the crow flies."

The treasure: 1,000 $20 gold pieces was stolen in a train robbery near Denton, Texas. Today's value: up to $400,000.

How to find it:

1. Remember all property in this portion of Texas is private property. Trespass laws are severe. You must obtain permission of all landowners.

2. The cache is within a three-mile radius of Jacksboro, Texas, to the northeast.

3. Use topographical maps. Drive the back roads. Plot locations of all large boulders located in visible flat areas.

4. You might ask local ranchers about a ravine where a number of spent cartridges have been found. If so, you are close.

Sources:

Taped interviews made in 1987 and 1988 with the late W. A. Gregory of Sweetwater, Texas. This information was withheld, at his request, until after his death.

# THE SPIDER ROCK TREASURE

Hidden in the unforgiving earth of West Texas were clues: archaic clues etched upon buried rocks, stacked as artifacts upon other clues, or carved into rock walls. These centuries-old clues, placed to lead Spaniards back to their cache, eventually formed an intricate web which lured treasure seekers and captured them in its mystery. But the question still remains: Has the Spider Rock treasure ever been found?

Sometime between 1902 and 1910 three mysterious stones were discovered in three different Central Texas Counties by Dave M. Arnold and local land owners. All three discoveries sparked extensive treasure hunts, two of which were financed by Dr. Caleb Lafon Terrell of Haskell, Texas, until his death on May 8, 1909 . Each stone bore hieroglyphic symbols that have not yet been totally deciphered, even at this late date. (1)

Throughout the last century, into the current period, treasure hunters, a history professor, archeologists, ranchers, a lock smith, mechanical engineer, logistics specialists, a postman, authors, museum personnel and a long list of others have sought to unravel the purpose of the stones and interrupt their cryptic symbols. (2) Bill Townsley became interested in this Texas mystery in 1989, when George W. Copeland, (Ft. Worth, Texas), W.T. (Bill) Farmer (Mineral Wells, Texas), Tom Jones (Arlington, Texas), Raymond Boyle (Mineral Wells), Terry Hutson (Abilene, Texas) and Bob Odom (from Tennessee) were using heavy earth moving equipment northeast of Clyde, Texas, in Callahan County, near the site of the original 1902 discovery of the Clyde Spider Rock. (3)

A second stone was discovered between 1902 and 1905 near Aspermont, Texas, in Stonewall County, near the Salt and Double Mountain Fork of the Brazos River. Then about 1910 the third stone was discovered near Rotan, Texas, Fisher County, in the proximity of Gyp Creek. All three rocks bear some of the same symbols. As example, a spider web design is found on either the front or back side of all three stones. Cut along the edge of the Rotan Spider Rock is the numeral "94", the same appears on the Aspermont Spider Rock. "71" written as an Arabic numeral on the Clyde Spider Rock appears as a Roman numeral on the Aspermont Spider Rock. Capital "F"s appears on all three stones. The numeral "29" appears on both the Rotan and Clyde Spider Rocks, as do the letters "PO". "CXF" appears on both the Aspermont and Clyde rocks. (4)

Dr. Duane K. Hale, a Professor of History at Cisco Junior College, Abilene, Texas, interviewed C. Ormin Duke of Rotan, Texas, in October of 1971. Duke had in his possession a disc, he claimed, he had found in the 1960's near Kiowa Peak [pictured above]. Reporting in Treasure, Vol. 21 Number 2, February, 1990, Hale, Robert Kyker and Johnny Terrell write, "It (the disc) definitely linked the Clyde site with the Aspermont site, for on one side it had the Clyde map cut and on the other side it had the Aspermont map." (5) Reference 1991/92 Great Plains Journal (an annual interdisciplinary publication of the Institute if the Great Plains, Lawton, Oklahoma), Steve Wilson, Editor/Director, writes on page 82, "Neither etching on the copper disc is a duplicate of the stone maps, but are similar enough to cause one to ponder its purpose." Wilson says Dan Ferris (of Rotan, Texas) discovered the metal disc on the east side of Kiowa Peak in Stonewall County, Texas. (6) R. E. Sherrill, a Haskell, Texas business man and member of the Texas Folk-Lore Society recorded in 1924 the events of the 1907-1908 treasure hunt, "Nearly every man of that searching party of seventeen years ago was a friend of mine. At one time the party believed that they were within a foot or two of their treasure, but they feared to uncover it before they had made arrangements to take care of it... they wished, to entrust it to our private vault, where no one would suspect its presence." (7)

Of equal interest is a discovery made by rancher, B. Hendrix, who lived west of Knox City, Texas, in 1971. In the cedar breaks near his property B. Hendrix discovered a religious medallion that bore the date 1647. (The date is no longer legible. Dr. Hale surmises this is due to Hendrix having carried it in his pocket or billfold, for a period, after it discovery). (8) In September of 1998, Bill Townsley and George Copeland traveled from Ft. Worth, Texas, to O'Brien, Texas, to interview Vivian Hendrix (B. Hendrix's widow). Townsley, Copeland and Ray Penman (of Knox City, Texas) photographed the medallion. Printed on the artifact is "S.PATER BENEDICTVS. SILVESTCON SILF.". Ms. Hendrix told the trio, prior to her husband's death, he had given another medallion to an area priest. Ms. Hendrix could not remember what was depicted on that object, but did remember that one of the medallions had been found in a cave. (9)

In September of 1995, Bill Townsley located W. L. Duke (C. Ormin Duke's nephew). Although C. O. Duke was deceased, W. L. Duke put Townsley in contact Ormin's widow. Townsley learned from Mrs. Duke that her daughter, Joanne, still had the disc and it was stored in a safety deposit box in Abilene, Texas. For a little over two years, Townsley attempted to purchase the disc from the Duke family. In early November of 1997, David Auldridge (of Mansfield, Texas) telephoned Ms. Duke, and learned the family had decided to sell the disc. On 26 November 1997, Townsley met with Mrs. Duke and her daughter in

Abilene, Texas, where he purchased the mysterious artifact depicted with this article. (10)

We do not know what the three stones (the three Spider Rocks), found in Central Texas represent. We do not know who carved the intricate symbols depicted on them, nor do we know why someone would cut replicas of two of the stone maps (the Clyde map and the Aspermont map) on a disc a mere one-eighth-inch-thick and one and three quarters inches in diameter, then loose it or place it on the east side of Kiowa Peak (for centuries a historic landmark for travelers). Possibly the whole thing is a hoax, but it would certainly have taken a considerable amount of time for an individual or individuals to conceive and carry it out. Perhaps you have found a stone or metal artifact, located a document or have solved a piece of this puzzling Texas mystery.

Readers are welcome to communicate with the author by sending e-mail to Bill.Townsley@prodigy.net. Or you may write to him at the following address: Bill Townsley, 22500 Waterview Circle, Flint, Texas 75762 (c/o Floy Brown). If you wish, you may also direct correspondence to Ira Kennedy, editor www.texfiles.com.

# PART THREE

# GHOSTS IN WEST TEXAS

# ALPINE, TEXAS

Alpine is located in a wide valley in the foothills of the Davis Mountains in northwest Brewster County. Cattlemen lived in tents near their herds in the area between 1878 and 1882. The town began in the spring of 1882, when a few railroad workers and their families pitched their tents along a small spring-fed creek at the foot of what is now known as "A" Mountain. The railroad section was given the name of Osborne, and for a brief period the name Osborne was applied to the small community of settlers. The best of the springs was on a section belonging to Daniel and Thomas Murphy. The railroad needed control of the spring as a source of water for its steam engines, so it entered into an agreement with the Murphys to change the name of the section and settlement to Murphyville in exchange for a contract to use the spring. In November of 1883 the Murphys registered a plat for the town of Murphyville with the county clerk of Presidio County.

As the town grew the residents petitioned for its name to be changed to Alpine, and on February 3, 1888, the name of the local post office was officially changed. In 1888 a description of the town mentioned a dozen houses, three saloons, a hotel and rooming house, a livery stable, a butcher shop, and a drugstore, which also housed the post office.

## Sul Ross University

Called "Possibly the most underrated little university west of the Mississippi" by CBS's Dan Rather, Sul Ross State University in West Texas boasts a combination of small class sizes, an appreciation of both fine arts and the sciences and popular professional programs in a relaxed, friendly environment.

The university's name honors Lawrence Sullivan "Sul" Ross, the son of a pioneer Waco, Texas, family and a popular soldier, governor, educator and humanitarian. Founded in 1917 as a teacher college, Sul Ross continues to offer teacher education as one of its most popular programs. Others in high demand are business, criminal justice and agricultural and natural resource sciences. Sul Ross achieved university status in 1969. The university, comprising 647 acres in Alpine, Texas, boasts a beautiful 93-acre main campus of exquisitely-detailed buildings and enjoys perhaps the most temperate climate in the state. Its situation in the Davis Mountains overlooks the center of the city below, yet it remains within easy reach of many local stores and restaurants. The university also has a 468-acre working ranch that serves its animal science programs.

The university has three satellite campuses collectively known as Rio Grande College. Based on the Southwest Texas Junior College campuses in Del Rio, Uvalde and Eagle Pass, Rio Grande College offers junior, senior and graduate courses. Sul Ross State University and Rio Grande College are part of The Texas State University System, the largest college system in the state after the University of Texas and Texas A&M systems. It is also among those Universities that seem to have permanent students prowling their halls.

## Fletcher Hall.

Thomas J. Fletcher Hall is a two-story, co-ed facility housing 110 residents, with men on one floor and women on the other. Sophomore and older students are housed in this building. Fletcher Hall was originally known as Morelock Hall, but was remained in 1988 to continue the use of the name Fletcher in honor of Thomas Fletcher who was president of Sul Ross from 1917 to 1920.

There is a dormitory room that has showers & doors that operate on their own. A female apparition, who is believed to be named Beverly, has been spotted walking around late at night in a skimpy nightgown. During life she resided in room 308. Also, things end up missing even if the doors had been locked all day.

Residents of the Dorm have also reported waking up in the night and seeing strange apparitions at the foot of the bed. It is a belief among many students that whenever there is a mention of the "Fletcher Ghost", a door slams, there is a loud bang, someone screams, or some other jolting noise.

## Indian Lodge Resort

In the early '90s, there was a young lady who was living in Ft. Davis, Texas while going to college at Sul Ross State University. Ft. Davis has a rich history of spooky tales because it was founded from the Fort where many battles took place with Indians. This young lady worked as a waitress at The Indian Lodge Resort that was about three miles outside of town. It is a beautiful drive through mountains during the day, but really spooky at night.

On one particularly slow night at the lodge's restaurant, the employees kept noticing that the lights kept coming on in a room that was unoccupied that night. The employees would tell the front desk and they would send one of them to shut it off, but inevitably, the light would keep coming back on. This went on for hours.

The young lady in question was a complete neat freak and had just washed and vacuumed her car earlier in the day. And after work she would cash in any change that she received in tips into paper money so she would not be bothered with a lot of change.

As she was driving home that evening (through the mountains, alone) she kept hearing the sound of something metallic falling into the passenger seat beside her, onto the floor and hitting the console and gear shift areas between the two front seats. It was like it was falling from the roof of her car! It was all she could do to keep driving, but she later admitted that she was too afraid to stop and get out of her car in the mountains.

As soon as she came to a streetlight in town, she pulled over and got out. When her interior lights came on, she could see that there was change in the passenger seat, around my stick shift and on the floor board. She knew the change had to come from somewhere else, since her car was vacuumed that day and her own wallet was zipped. There was no other place in the car from which the change could have come. She knew she had a "visitor" riding in her car.

## BIG SPRING, TEXAS

Big Spring has long been known as the crossroads of West Texas. The ancient spring for which the town was named attracted prehistoric people, Amerinds, Spaniards, Mexicans and Anglos. The fascinating Comanche 'War Trail' to Mexico branched at the spring. Old tales are legion and photographic documentation is extensive. Early explorers and cartographers noted the 'big spring of the Colorado River'.

In 1839, Dr. Henry Connelly, a trader from Chihuahua, Mexico successfully led a huge caravan with a fortune in silver to Fort Towson, Oklahoma, stopping midway at the spring. U.S. Army Captain R.B. Marcy in 1849 lauded the beauty of the place and one of his Indian guides, Manuel, said that his brother-in-law died in a battle between Indians at the spring, fifteen years earlier. Official reports of Texas Rangers and U.S. Cavalry frequently mention the Big Spring.

### <u>Big Spring High School</u>

Big Spring High School is located at 707 E 11th Place, Big Spring, Texas, 79720. The residents of Big Spring had shown a desire for sound education even before there was a Howard county. This was proven by the creation of Big Spring Independent School district in 1901 and Howard College half a century ago. The earliest settlers of this area, around 1880 recalled that the first "school" functioned under a buffalo hide fly tenet, possibly at the historic big spring and surrounded by buffalo bone haulers' crude merchant tents, one of which may have passed as a saloon.

When Howard County was organized in 1891, one of the first actions was to provide a two-story frame building to house a school on the west side of the 300 block of Scurry Street on the condition it also would house court proceedings at various times until a courthouse could be built.

One of the areas of the Big Spring High School that is said to be haunted is the auditorium which is said to be haunted by a ghost named Harold. Harold was an employee of the school and fell from the catwalk while hanging up the lights. There is even a strange footprint on the ceiling. When people paint over the footprint, it reappears. Witnesses have also claimed to see Harold walking around backstage with a flashlight.

## Flight Line Prison

The Flight Line Prison facility was shut down many years ago, some say because of the mysterious occurrences. These occurrences started happening before the prison was even completely finished. Some building materials were stolen from the site so a guard had to be posted there. During the first night the control center got a frantic call from the guard asking for back up because he knew some one was out there he could hear them but he couldn't find them.

Upon response loud music could be heard in the mess hall, but as soon as the security personnel would open the door the music would stop. The entire facility was searched and no trace could be found of anyone. Guards were doubled up due to the fact that no one would go out there alone. However, in spite of the increased security personnel, strange noises, lights, and whispering reoccurred every night.

Then the prison was completed and staffed. A fire safety inspection, area shakedowns and an outer perimeter fence check was conducted every night. While doing these checks guards have reported seeing an old woman in the education wing that would walk the halls at night and give anyone she met a quick glance and then she would disappear. She would always leave behind a white powder everywhere she had been spotted.

The mischievous entity that haunts the mess hall will clank and rattle the pots and pans as well as move things about the facility. There is a shadowy figure that walks the living quarter wings and there is a small child who loves to scare the life out of anyone who so happens to be in the perimeter truck at that time. This small figure has appeared on several occasions in the back of the truck looking in at the passengers through the back window, or in front of the truck as the security personnel drive around. Even more unusual, it is said that this small figure has even decided to wake up several guards who dozed off by tapping them on the arm. The sudden appearance of this child has caused several wrecks from trying to swerve to miss him, rounds being chambered into their firearms, and on a couple of occasions caused guards to quit on the spot.

## Runnells Junior High School

Students of Runnels Junior High School report that if you approach the building after hours and peer through the windows you can see what appears to be a little girl. This small figure wanders the halls until school begins the next day. There are also the lights throughout the building that will come on and off by themselves.

## Center Point Road

Center Point Road is a road a little past the outskirt's of town. On foggy nights you can see a truck, but after a little while, it disappears. You can see its headlights and it looks solid. You can also feel like there's something in the backseat, staring at the back of your head. There's a bunch of old, abandoned houses dotting the sides of the road. Some residents say that some of those old houses are haunted.

# BLOOMING GROVE, TEXAS

Blooming Grove, also known as Gradyville, is on State Highway 22 and Farm Road 55 ten miles west of Corsicana in northwestern Navarro County. The town originated in a store established by R. J. Grady and Sam Andrews shortly after the Civil War. When a post office was established there in 1871, citizens met at the White Church Cemetery to choose a name for the community. The town was named either for a grove of blooming trees or for the son–Blooming Davis–of a Doctor Davis. After 1881 the community moved a mile north to be on the Cotton Belt rail line (officially known as the St. Louis Southwestern Railway) and merged with the community of White Church.

## Lone Oak Cemetery

If you travel outside of town and drive down an old dirt road, there is a small cemetery located about 2 miles down the road. Once you arrive at the Lone Oak Cemetery, if you switch off your engine and listen, you will hear what sounds like voices whispering. Sounds of someone or something gently hitting the barbed wire near the cemetery are also regularly heard.

# BRADY, TEXAS

Brady, the county seat of McCulloch County, is located on U.S. highways 87, 283, and 190, 115 miles northwest of Austin, near the geographic center of Texas. When the area was settled in the 1870s, the community was named Brady City after Brady Creek, which runs through town. The name was shortened to Brady when the town was incorporated in 1906. In 1787-88 Spanish explorer José Mares crossed the creek near the site of present Brady. Henry and Nancy Fulcher, the first settlers on Brady Creek, donated land for the town site in the mid-1870s.

## Soldiers Water Hole

There's a historical marker outside of Brady that is an old watering Hole used by soldiers during one of the many Indian wars in the area. According to local legend some soldiers, and the settlers they were escorting, were camping by the water hole one night and were attacked by Indians.

Being overwhelmed by surprise, the soldiers were unable to prevent the Indians from burning the wagons, stealing most of the horses and killing all of the women and children as well as many of the male members of the party.

And now if you go there at night, you can hear cries of people, also you can here arrows flying by as if shot at you, also on occasion you can see camp fire glows out in the woods. There is also a story of one your lady coming in contact with a figure from that event.

One night a group of friends were trying the legend out as they explored the area of the massacre. While the majority of the group were talking a couple of girls walked off on their own. When the girls were walking back one of the girls noticed that her friend had not said a word while walking, she would just nod her head to everything she would say. Then she heard her friends calling her from a distance. With a start, she realized that it was not her best friend walking with her, but an unknown figure that suddenly disappeared. Her best friend was still with the main group.

# CHRISTOVAL, TEXAS

Christoval, also known as Delong and South Concho, is on Loop 110, U.S. Highway 277, Farm Road 2084, and the South Concho River, twenty miles south of San Angelo in southern Tom Green County. It is supposedly named, in Spanish, for Christopher Columbus Doty, an early settler. A Christoval post office was established in 1889, and by 1901 the local school had forty-six pupils and one teacher. In 1914 Christoval had a population of 200, two general stores, and a newspaper, the Christoval Observer. The Panhandle and Santa Fe Railway ran through town. From that decade through the 1930s 10,000 persons attended the Baptist encampment on the South Concho annually, and mineral waters in Christoval attracted visitors and settlers.

## Residential Area

In one residential area, there is a paper boy who has somehow been able to come in contact with a ghostly Indian warrior and his family. This small family group has been seen by the paper-boy on several occasions, always in the early hours of the morning.

# COAHOMA, TEXAS

Coahoma, on Interstate Highway 20 ten miles northeast of Big Spring in east central Howard County, probably took its name from Coahoma County, Mississippi, which in turn derived its name from an Indian word meaning "red panther." Early names for the community included Signal Mountain and Signal Mountain Station, after a nearby hill. After the 1881 arrival of the Texas and

Pacific Railway in the area, Coahoma grew into a retail trade center and shipping point. Its residents built their first school in 1891, and Gertrude McIntyre was the first teacher. By the time its second school was built in 1904, the town had a post office.

## Coahoma Junior High Gym

The Junior High of Coahoma is supposedly built on land that is sacred to some of the early Native American tribes. There have also been stories that the school is actually built on an Indian burial ground. People have reported hearing the sounds of opening and shutting of doors, footsteps and mysterious voices in areas that are unoccupied.

During cheerleading practice about 15 or more years ago it was reported that the lights mysteriously, leaving the girls in almost total darkness. After a few moment of silence, they heard the sound of a car engine racing at high speed and they were suddenly bathed in the headlights of a vehicle that seemed to be racing directly at them. Though the girls ran, the sounds and lights seemed to chase them.

## COLORADO CITY, TEXAS

Colorado City, the county seat of Mitchell County, is on the Colorado River, Lone Wolf Creek, U.S. Highway 20/80, State highways 208 and 163, and the Missouri Pacific Railroad, thirty-eight miles east of Big Spring and twenty-three miles south of Snyder in the north central part of the county. It has been called the "Mother City of West Texas" for its early origin as a ranger camp in 1877 and for its prominence as a cattlemen's center. In 1881 the town was chosen county seat and acquired a station on the new Texas and Pacific Railway. Local ranchers hauled in tons of buffalo bones for shipment to the East and loaded their empty wagons with provisions purchased from pioneer merchant William H. "Uncle Pete" Snyder and others. When the town was granted a post office in 1881 Prince A. Hazzard became the first postmaster. Water was hauled to town from Seven Wells and elsewhere and sold at fifty cents a barrel. The first school, conducted in a dugout in 1881, was moved to a building the next year, and soon a new building was built.

## Ruddick Park

Ruddick Park on 7th St. is on Lone Wolf Creek and features a limited number of RV campsites, picnic shelters, grills, a swimming pool and a playground. In fact it has everything that a person could ask for, including a ghost. In this case, the ghost is that of a young woman who appears to be searching the river bank for her baby. It is said that the young woman buried her baby alive in order to please her mother.

# FORT DAVIS, TEXAS

The first Spanish expedition through what is now, Fort Davis came in 1583; a second group followed 100 years later. Few Americans had seen the Davis Mountains prior to end of the war with Mexico in 1846. After the war with Mexico, as west Texas settlements increased, and a wave of gold seekers, settlers, and traders came through the area, the need for a military post soon became evident. As raiding along the San Antonio-El Paso Trail became a way of life for Apaches, Kiowas, and Comanches. From 1859 to 1861, Butterfield Overland Stage Line and Mail Company coaches transported mail to California linking St. Louis, San Antonio, Fort Davis and El Paso. The route used by the company quickly became known as part of the Overland Trail with Fort Davis serving as a major stopping point.

Because of the inscriptions left on the giant cottonwoods by the Native Americans who traveled through here, the Fort Davis area was initially known to many immigrant parties as the Painted Comanche Camp or The Painted Camp on the Limpia. As the post grew, several settlements near and adjacent to the fort developed. The small nearby settlements along Limpia Creek boasted about 70 residents (Limpia means "clear or clean" in Spanish--and the water in the creek is still probably some of the cleanest in Texas). It became the town and took its name from the post, named after the then Secretary of War, Jefferson Davis, (later on he was to become the president of the Confederacy). With the outbreak of the Civil War, the Union abandoned Fort Davis. Briefly occupied by Confederate forces, then for the next five years the military post of Fort Davis lay abandoned.

In 1867, because of continuing bandit, Apache and Comanche raids along the Overland Trail the Army reestablished the post. African American troops of the Ninth U.S. Cavalry, one of two all black cavalry regiments organized in 1866 (later to be known by their designation by the Indians as "Buffalo Soldiers") immediately began construction of a new post just east of the original site.

After closing, the fort's dignified adobe and stone buildings slowly deteriorated under private ownership. In 1961, thanks to the efforts of the Fort Davis Historical Society and area residents Fort Davis was designated a National Historic Site, operated by the National Park Service. In 1963, the Fort Davis National Historic Site opened to the public year round except on Christmas Day.

## Fort Davis Historical Site

There are ghosts of several soldiers who are said to still carry out their duties at fort Davis. The hospital walls are said to change color, and others have claimed to have actually seen specters in several places.

## Fort Davis Hospital

There has been a "presence" felt in the hospital part of this fort, colds spots and a feeling of being watched.

# FORT STOCKTON, TEXAS

Fort Stockton, the county seat of Pecos County, is on Interstate Highway 10, U.S. highways 67, 290, and 385, and the Santa Fe Railroad, 329 miles northwest of San Antonio and 245 miles east of El Paso. It grew up around Comanche Springs, at one time the third largest source of spring water in Texas, and near the military fort founded in 1859 and named for Robert Field Stockton. Comanche Springs was a favorite rest stop on the Comanche Trail to Chihuahua, the Old San Antonio Road, the Butterfield Overland Mail route, and the San Antonio-Chihuahua freight-wagon road. The Confederates took possession of the fort at the outbreak of the Civil War but abandoned it the next year. In 1867 the army rebuilt the fort on a larger and more permanent basis to protect travelers and settlers from Indians. Until abandoned in 1886, the fort provided employment for freighters and laborers and a market for farmers, stockmen, and merchants.

## The Post Sutlery

A strange, dark figure of an apparition has been spotted near this old building. Locals call him "El Bulto" which means "the Figure". Many people believe that the figure is that of George "Coche" Garcia, who lived inside the old adobe Sutlery during the 1930s. He always dressed in black and loved to scare the locals.

Others say that the figure is that of Barney Riggs who was killed on the steps of the Sutlery when, after an altercation, he pursued his wife into the old building with intent of inflicting serious bodily harm. At the time, the old building was home to a friend of Barney's wife who tried to protect her from Barney. His own stepson is the one to kill him with one well placed shot.

Of course, still others believe that the figure dates from the 1918 Spanish Flu Epidemic when the old building was used as a hospital for those infected with the deadly disease. Those who died from this disease were buried out back of the building.

At another period in its existence, this old building served as a courthouse. Those tried here who were found guilty were then hung form a large tree growing directly behind the building.

In addition to "El Bulto" there have been a number of reports of lights moving inside the, now, deserted building. Some nights, the sounds of a struggle, including what sounds like China being smashed can be heard emanating from the old building.

# LAJITAS, TEXAS

Lajitas is located on F.M. 170 at the western edge of Big Bend National Park; the village name is Spanish for "flagstones," of which there are prominent outcroppings in the area. First became a village in 1915 when an Army post was stationed to protect Big Bend area from flamboyant Mexican bandit Francisco (Pancho) Villa.

Recent developments feature a modern motel and resort complex with golf course, river rafting, swimming pools, tennis courts, horseback riding, restaurant, and genuine-looking "frontier" building styles with plank sidewalks and hitching rails.

## Bad Lands Hotel

What was once a Cavalry Post and La Questa are now the unique lodging facilities of a multi-million dollar golf resort. Both have been recently renovated. These ruggedly luxurious guestrooms have stocked refreshment cabinets, refrigerator, twice-daily maid service, terrycloth robes, goose-down pillows and fast-access Internet connections and cable television. You will find the Badlands Hotel in the center of the western boardwalk and The Officer's Quarters, another place to stay, will be renovated in the future.

There are many stories that the Badlands Hotel was the site of terrible domestic violence that ended in a grisly murder. Strange noises have been reported here and many have seen what appear to be the ghosts of one or more women.

# LITTLEFIELD, TEXAS

Littlefield, the county seat of Lamb County, is on U.S. Highway 84, Farm Road 54, and the Santa Fe line in the south central part of the county. It was named for George W. Littlefield, who divided his Yellow House Ranch and formed a land company when surveys showed that the new Santa Fe line from Coleman to Texico, New Mexico, would pass through his land.

Arthur P. Duggan, husband of Littlefield's niece, helped to lay out land tracts and became sales manager. In 1913 the site became a station on the Panhandle and Santa Fe Railway, and a school, supported for several years by the Littlefield Land Company, was established. The developing community's population reached 250 in 1915, when the town also had a bank, several other businesses, and a library. Two years later the Lamb County News began publication there. Littlefield was incorporated in 1924, and by 1930 it had a population of 3,500, grain elevators, gins, a compress, and cottonseed oil mills.

## Lennox/Church School

In a small church house or what people would also call a school house, there is to be seen lights turning on and off when it is known that there is no one in the building. Those who have ventured close to the structure report that black shadows have been seen around the building. It has been said if you drive there around midnight you can see both the shadows and the lights being turned on and off.

# LOS CHISOS MOUNTAINS

The Chisos Mountains are the heart of Big Bend National Park in southern Brewster County. They extend twenty miles from Punta de la Sierra in the southwest to Panther Junction in the northeast. Among the highest peaks in the range are Emory Peak (7,835 feet above sea level), Lost Mine Peak (7,535 feet), Toll Mountain (7,415 feet), and Casa Grande Peak (7,325 feet). Shallow, stony soils on the mountains support a flora that includes Douglas fir, aspen, Arizona cypress, maple, ponderosa pine, and madrone.

The Chisos Mountains and the surrounding lowlands sit in a sunken block bounded on the northeast by the Sierra del Carmen and Santiago Mountains and on the southwest by the Sierra de Santa Elena. The mountains were pushed up to elevations of more than 5,000 feet above sea level by a great deformation during the Cenozoic era. During this uplift, however, formations from the Cretaceous period, between 66 million and 144 million years old, were also pushed up, and are still found occasionally high in the mountains.

In the eighteenth century the Chisos Mountains became the base of the Mescalero Apaches, who raided the Spanish settlements in Coahuila and Neuva Vizcaya, south of the Rio Grande. In 1747 Governor Pedro de Rábago y Terán of Coahuila led the first full-scale European expedition into the Big Bend. In the 1770s and 1780s Lt. Col. Hugo Oconór and Col. Juan de Ugaldeq led several campaigns against the Mescaleros, who had moved down into northern Mexico, and succeeded in driving them as far north as the Guadalupe Mountains. In the nineteenth century the Comanche Trail, used by Comanche raiding parties striking into northern Mexico, passed through the Chisos Mountains. By this time, however, white settlers, traders, and soldiers were also using the pathways through the mountains, and eventually cattle ranchers replaced hostile Indians as the primary occupants of the range. Since 1944 the Chisos Mountains have been part of Big Bend National Park.

Several explanations of the origin of the name of the range have been offered over the years. One held that Chisos means "ghost," and that the mountains were named for the ghost of the Apache chief Alsate, who hid in the mountains for a time. Another version was that Chisos was the plural of chis, meaning "clash of arms" (chischás in Castilian), since some reported hearing battle sounds at night in the mountains as the ghosts of Spanish soldiers returned to fight again. A third story was that Chisos was a corruption of the Spanish hechizos, "bewitchments" or "enchantments." The mountains were almost certainly named, however, for the Chizos Indians.

## Ghost Lights

Ghost lights, not unlike the Marfa Lights, have been seen throughout this area. Others have reported seeing figures moving in the darkness, though later investigations reveal no tracks.

## Ghostly Indian Maiden

Nearby lies Canyon de Brujas (Witch Canyon), often the site of moaning cries from an Apache maiden who is said to have drowned herself rather than be defiled by her white captors. The spirit of the maiden is said to wander the canyon in search of a way home to her Apache village. In the nearby towns of Study Butte and Terlingua, ghost stories abound. Once great mining villages, there are countless tales of haunts and evil spirits who plagued the minors here.

# MARATHON, TEXAS

Marathon is a thriving tourist destination along U.S. 90 with distinctive hostelries, restaurants, shops and galleries related to its location in the historic and picturesque Big Bend of West Texas. The area, and Big Bend National Park just 40 miles south of Marathon, was given the name because it is defined by the Rio Grande River's bend to the south, and then north again, as it flows to the Gulf of Mexico.

Marathon was named in 1882 by retired sea captain, railroad surveyor and local landowner Albion Shepard, who said the locale, a high desert basin surrounded by mountains, reminded him of the famous Marathon in Greece, from which runner Phidippides ran 26.2 miles to tell Athenians of their victory against the Persians in 490 BC. This feat gave rise to marathon races world-wide and Marathon now has its own certified marathon road race each year from Alpine to Marathon on a weekend in October.

## Captain Shepard's Inn

Captain Shepard's Inn is a fully restored 100 year old two story adobe home built by the town founder. It has private baths and nice porches. The carriage house at the rear of the main building is equipped with a kitchenette. Located at the corner of Avenue D & 2nd Street in Marathon TX this building also boasts of at least one ghost. There have been a number of reports of doors opening and closing when no one has been near them and quite often, guests see unexplained shadows.

## Gage Hotel

The historic Gage Hotel, located on U.S. Highway 90 was built in 1927, and renovated in 1980. The original brick building is a local landmark, now flanked by attractive additions. Furnishings are border style, reflecting Mexican and Anglo ranching heritage. Landscaped courtyard and grounds include a refreshing pool.

Guests in room 10 have reported hearing ghostly music and sometimes are awakened at night by a ghost tapping on their shoulder. When the unfortunate guest is roused from a sound sleep, there is never anyone else in the room. Some have reported hearing ghostly poetry recitation and seeing apparitions.

## MARFA, TEXAS

Marfa, the county seat of Presidio County, is at the junction of U.S. Highways 90 and 67 in the northeastern part of the county. It was established in 1883 as a water stop and freight headquarters for the Galveston, Harrisburg and San Antonio Railway. Reportedly, the wife of a railroad executive suggested the name Marfa from Fyodor Dostoyevsky's The Brothers Karamazov, which she was reading at the time. Marfa is in an area that has been called one of the last American frontiers. It is situated at an altitude of 4,830 feet above sea level in a semiarid region with many dry streambeds that the summer thunderstorms fill and further erode. To the north are the Davis Mountains, to the southeast the Chisos Mountains, and to the southwest the Chinati Mountains.

Marfa lies semi-protected within these escarpments on a great highland plain known as the Marfa Plateau. By 1885 Marfa had one or two saloons, a hotel, and a general merchandise store-Humphris and Company. Poker bets in the saloons were often made with deeds to town lots. At the St. George Hotel stayed drummers-traveling salesmen-who came by train, established their headquarters in the hotel, and from Marfa made stagecoach trips to Shafter, Fort Davis, Valentine, and Presidio to show their wares. Humphris and Company's store also contained the bank, the post office (established in 1883), and a restaurant.

In 1885 Marfa replaced Fort Davis as the Presidio county seat, and in July of that year the public records were moved from Fort Davis to Marfa. Since the southern border of Presidio County was the Rio Grande, during the Mexican Revolution the United States government in 1911 sent cavalry troops to Marfa; it also built canvas hangars there from which biplanes flew reconnaissance missions. The military presence in Marfa and Presidio County was continued and enlarged by the establishment of Camp Albert (later renamed Camp Marfa and then renamed Fort D. A. Russell). These installations were on the southwest edge of town. The Marfa population continued to grow, and in 1930 the town had 3,909 residents. During the 1940s the government stationed the Chemical Warfare Brigades in Marfa and constructed a prisoners of war camp nearby. World War II also saw the building of Marfa Army Air Field ten miles east of Marfa; it was an advanced flight-training base. The military presence boosted Marfa's population to a record high of 5,000 in 1945. Both military installations were closed the next year, however, ending a vital economic and cultural influence to the area.

## Arcon Inn B & B

The Arcón Inn is a gorgeous, two-story 19th century Gothic Victorian adobe home just a few blocks from the Marfa courthouse, at 215 North Austin Street[7]. "Arcón" is the Old Spanish word for "treasure chest." One look inside The Arcón Inn and you'll discover the name fits it just perfectly. The Arcón Inn is filled to the brim with art and antiques from many countries.

Parts of the Arcón Inn are like a virtual Spanish shrine, decorated with religious sculptures and paintings that look like they're straight out of some 17th century church. Marvelous mirrors, glowing chandeliers, countless angel figurines, elaborate wooden screens, and of course, a generous collection of treasure chests, are just a few of the intriguing items you'll find in the living and dining areas. And that's just downstairs!

Upstairs, the main house has two full baths and four bedrooms, each one lavishly decorated with antiques from the cities after which they are named. I stayed in the Paris Room, the smallest of the four. But the prettiest one was the London Room. (Apparently, it was Martha Stewart's favorite too--she stayed there once!) The Madrid Room, drenched in red, has two small twin beds and an outdoor patio. The Lima Room is the largest of the four, with a beautiful, king-sized canopy bed.

The Casita sits just behind The Arcon Inn and can accommodate up to eight people. This 1850's Spanish adobe cottage has two huge bedrooms, two private baths, plus a kitchenette, sitting room and private patio.

The great-grandfather, J.R. Blocker, of the current owner (who prefers to be called Mona) was a rancher who came to Texas in the 1800s from South Carolina. He later became a member of the first Texas Cattleman's Association. The owner's husband, Rodolfo Garcia Salazar y Lesdesma, has an equally historic lineage. Rudy's grandfather moved to Mexico from northern Spain. Later his family settled in Texas to escape the Mexican Revolution.

---

[7] Their website is http://www.bedandbreakfast.com/bbc/p150264.asp

Mona's son, Greg is a chef who doubles as an artist. His artistic talent created the marvelous metal sculptures that dot The Arcon Inn's landscape.

Mona calls Marfa "a magical place" and many of her guests at The Arcón Inn seem to agree.  Most agree that the Arcon Inn is haunted. The ghost that haunts the Arcon is a female, she has been named "Emmeline", is often seen gazing through the window of the north bedroom in her white dress.  Doors open and shut without human assistance and cold spots are felt.

## Marfa Lights

Over 75 local legends are known to exist about the origin of the Marfa Lights. As yet there is no definitive explanation for their occurrence. Marfa is the county seat of sprawling Presidio County, but it was not always that way. Back in 1850, when the County was first created by combining a Land District with a chunk of land from Bexar County, Marfa did not exist. In fact, only one or two small pockets of adobe buildings scattered along the Rio Grande constituted the only real towns for miles in any direction. Since the newly created county became the largest in Texas, it had to contend with government from neighboring El Paso County, which had all the population.

All that changed in 1854 with the United States and Mexican Boundary Survey, which established the International Boundary at the Rio Grande. That year, the U. S. Army built Fort Davis to protect the supply trains freighting between San Antonio and El Paso from the marauding Comanche and Apache Indians. It soon grew into the first real town in the whole County, and in 1875, because of its military and commercial connections, it became Presidio County's official county seat.

Six years later, Marfa sprang into existence as a water stop on the old Southern Pacific Railroad line between San Antonio and El Paso. Legend says that it was named after an exotic Russian heroine in the dime novel a railroad magnate's wife was reading as they passed through the area. Within two years, it had a population of about two hundred people---and six times as many cattle, horses, and sheep.

By the mid-1880's, the Indian Wars were winding down, and folks became suspicious that the military would abandon Fort Davis, which eventually did happen in 1891. They held an election in 1885 to move the county seat from Fort Davis, tucked away in the Davis Mountains, to the new town of Marfa, out on the prairie, some twenty-five miles south, only many of the residents of Presidio County cried fraud. They believed Alpine, forty miles east of Marfa, had just as much right to be the new county seat. The civilian population of Fort Davis was not very pleased with the election decision, either.

Back then, when most Texans were still wild and untamed, land feuds usually culminated in some kind of war. The county seat argument flared for two years---until the Alpine hierarchy snatched a huge chunk out of Presidio County for themselves. They called their new County, Brewster. A year later, Fort Davis mimicked Alpine and became the county seat of Jeff Davis County. The once giant, sparsely populated Presidio County thus became the fourth largest county by area---and possibly the smallest by population. Even today, it has just a little more than 6,500 residents. Marfa, the largest city in the County, boasts a whopping population of 2,500.

No one knows for sure just when the legendary lights were first seen flickering in the area. As early as 1840, wagon trains on the Chihuahua Trail reported seeing unexplained lights along the flats. But no one ever dared to investigate. The Trail ran eight hundred miles over the roughest country in North America, beginning at Ojinaga, Mexico, and culminating at Indianola on the Texas Gulf Coast. Apache Indians were everywhere, and to stray off the Trail meant flirting with death. There may be even older accounts still hidden in Mexican archives.

The first recorded Texan history occurred in 1883, when Robert Ellison off-loaded his cattle in Alpine and drove them west through the Paisano Pass toward his ranch forty miles away near Marfa. Camped at the base of the Pass, at a place now known as Mitchell Flats, he saw strange lights in the distance. He was looking southwest toward the Chinati Mountains, and he and his fellow cowhands thought they were looking at the flickering flames of Apache campfires. The lights appeared to be a few miles away and hovered just above the ground.

The unexpected lights alarmed the cowboys, who thought the Apaches were on the move, and they quickly doused their own campfires. But they determined to investigate the area in the daylight. After spending an uncomfortable night huddled under blankets for warmth on the cold desert floor, dawn found them on horseback, combing the area for any signs of an Indian encampment. They found none.

All day, the men searched along the base of the Chinati Mountains and the mesa between their camp and where the lights had been. They found no evidence that Indians had been anywhere in the area. No tracks, no doused campfires, no nothing. But the next night and the next after that, they again saw the strange lights. Cowboys kept seeing the lights night after night, week after week, and year after year. All attempts at identifying them went fruitless. Full of superstition, the cowboys finally decided the lights were not man-made and began calling them "ghost lights."

The lights really do defy all attempts at explanation. Attempts to locate their source always fail because they usually vanish when anyone tries to approach them. People hike, ride horseback, drive jeeps, and even fly helicopters and airplanes to follow the lights. Some have followed them as far as thirty-five miles. The lights always win. Searchers have never found campfires, buildings, tire tracks, footprints, or any other evidence that could explain the lights' sources. Some people even claim that the lights would reappear, after they had abandoned the search and were miles away looking back over their shoulders.

The lights can be seen in the southwest, across the Mitchell Flats near Chinati Mountain, from an official viewing point on Highway 90 between Alpine and Marfa. This viewing point was erected at the request of area ranchers, who became tired of curiosity seekers disturbing their cattle, and they had a right to complain. Just about every night, right before dusk, the parking lot fills up with spectators equipped with everything from binoculars, cameras, and camcorders to high-powered telescopes. And they are seldom disappointed. As the sun sets, the lights appear, coming in all sorts of sizes, which climb in the sky, then merge, split, or float back down. They change color, appearing green, yellow, blue, and sometimes orange. One minute they will be bright, then fade and disappear. They have even been reported between Paso Lajitas and San Carlos, Mexico, and the Federales, who patrol the road for smugglers, have been fooled into spotting what they thought were approaching headlights, only to have no vehicle ever appear.

One long-time resident of the area, Hallie Stillwell, reported she first saw the phenomenon when she was eighteen-years-old in 1916. Her home was in Alpine, but she taught school in Presidio. That small town of sun-baked adobe buildings squats in the shade of giant cottonwood trees lying along the Rio Grande about twenty miles south of Marfa. What were current events to Hallie turned out to be old stuff to the residents of Presidio. The town is more than three hundred years old, having been founded along with Ojinaga across the river in Mexico by the Spanish in the 1600's. Everyone knew of the lights. They had seen them in the winter, as well as the other seasons of the year, and nearly every night. The lights always appeared to be moving erratically around the Flats, winking and twinkling like fireflies in the night. This is one reason why most believers rule out car headlights as the cause. For one thing, there were not many cars in 1916 and none in the 1880's, when the first official recording was made.

Describing Marfa's mysterious lights is all but impossible. They appear as distant bright lights on the Mitchell Flats and are distinguishable from ranch lights and automobile headlights on nearby Highway 67, between Marfa and Presidio, by their aberrant movements and behavior. They appear and disappear, veering and cavorting suddenly in odd directions. One moment there might be one, and just as suddenly, it might split into two or three or more, dividing and merging at whim. They hover in mid-air and sometimes flicker like balls of fire. They might shoot straight up into the sky, or race madly to the left and right. The color is predominately greenish-yellow, but they also are white and shades of pastel. "I do not know how anyone could mistake them for car lights," reported one eyewitness in 1984.

The only thing certain about the Marfa Lights is that nothing is certain. As the town grew, the locals became accustomed to seeing the strange lights flickering in the distance and ignored them, but newcomers to the area remained intrigued. During the period of Pancho Villa, and also later in World War I, Army observers saw the lights and immediately jumped to the conclusion that they were some sort of spotlights set up to guide an invasion force into the United States from the south. The Army's recorded observations brought the lights to the attention of people outside the immediate area, but not enough to garner any real public interest. The legend just continued as "ghost lights."

It was 1943 when the mysterious lights were given a real boost in publicity. That year, the Army established a pilot training base in Marfa. Fritz Kahl, an airman at the base, who later stayed to run the Marfa airport, reported that when the airmen saw the lights for the first time, there was absolutely no vehicular traffic at night. In fact, fuel was rationed, and lights themselves were a phenomenon because there were no lights of any kind, not even on the local ranches. Kahl described seeing something that was totally foreign to anything in and around the air base. He said finding the lights' origins was like trying to catch a rainbow. When officials inquired of the phenomenon with the area residents, the locals simply said, "Yeah, we got ghost lights. So what?"

Over the years, explanations for the mysterious lights have ranged from ball lightning to St. Elmo's fire to dead Indians, ghosts, tricks, static electricity, combustible dust, bat guano, solar activity, electromagnetic energy, volcanic activity, biological luminescence, and UFO's. There's even the glowing jackrabbit explanation. Under that theory, the jackrabbits race across the desert with a coating of phosphorescent dust or glow worms clinging to their hides. In the absence of a more definitive explanation, legend and folklore have been known to sprout like tumbleweeds.

Fortunately, several of these theories can be discounted because they don't apply to the West Texas region. For instance, while jackrabbits are abundant, phosphorous is not, and volcanic activity in the area ceased about 30 million years ago. Also, although jackrabbits are known for their speed, they are not known to fly or outrun cars, and both pilots and motorists have reported being chased by the lights.

Still, the locals are convinced that there is more to the Marfa Lights than first meets the eye. Native superstition seems to confirm it. The Indians saw the lights long before any white man did. Their legends tell of the Great Spirit, who made the mountains in the area by throwing all the jumbled rocks left over from the creation of the stars, the birds and fishes, and the earth itself, into a huge pile in the middle of the leftover wasteland. The Devil then promptly claimed the rock pile and wasteland and turned it into hell, adding things that bite, sting, or prick. When anyone died in that hell, the lights became the spirits of the dead ones, who were thwarted in real life and forced to wander the desolate world in search of kith and kin. The locals who like this explanation also say that 'it is a hell of a place that the Devil has for hell.'

Other Native stories tell of the phosphorescent souls of brave warriors, betrayed by treachery or killed in battle, and doomed to roam the lunar-like landscape in search of justice or revenge. This has the classical advantage of perpetuating myth into legend. Still another ancient Indian tale came from the journal of O.W. Williams, grandfather of former Texas governor Clayton Williams. According to the elder Williams, the lights are the ghosts of the Apache war chief, Alsate.

Williams, who was a surveyor in Terlingua and other parts of the Big Bend in the 1880's, worked with a mostly Mexican crew from San Carlos, Mexico, located across the Rio Grande from the ghost town of Lajitas, Texas. One member of the surveying crew, Natividad Lujan, always told stories around the campfires, and Williams patiently recorded them in his journal. One morning, Williams called attention to the beautiful sunrise. Lujan promptly called it "the great spirit of Alsate" and regaled his rapt listeners with the story of the last Apache leader in the Big Bend. It seems that in the 1850's and 1860's, the Kiowas, Comanches, and Apaches maintained friendly relations with the townsfolk of San Carlos and Presidio, while at the same time raiding back and forth across the border into Mexico. Alsate, like most Apaches, grew up believing this way of life to be normal. He was of the Mescalero Apaches, also known in the Big Bend area as the Chinati or Rio Grande Apaches.

As Alsate grew into manhood, he became a great warrior and leader of his people. But, his depredations into Mexico made him hotly sought after by the Mexican Rurales. He and his tribe were finally caught and taken to Mexico City to stand trial. Throughout the trial, and no doubt also through the help of the earnest plea-bargaining from a close relative, he managed to talk himself free. He then led his tribe back to the Big Bend country, where he once again took up his thieving ways. He was caught again, only this time, he was taken to Presidio and executed. His tribe was taken into Mexico and scattered into slavery, by one's and two's, and the whole tribe was thus destroyed.

After a time, a sinister rumor began to creep across the old frontier of the Chisos Mountains and the Chinatis. Ranchers and cowboys talked of seeing the ghost of Alsate. It came in the form of flickering lights, and was seen in the old haunts of the Chinati Apaches. One man saw it rolling up a rocky slope, another saw it stationary on a promontory of the Rio Grande. It appeared often in the Chinati Mountains and could be seen as far south as the Chisos. The rumor finally became part of the folklore of the area---that the "lights that some people see" is the spirit of the dead Alsate.

Although mysterious lights can be seen all along the mountain range from the Chinatis to the Chisos, they are most constantly seen on the high desert plateau of Marfa. This has prompted many serious searches for the lights' source. The first such attempt appears to have been made by Walter T. Harris just before the turn of the century. He was an employee of the railroad, and with the help of several other employees, he used surveyor's methods of triangulation to plot the exact location of the night beacons. By his calculations, the lights were behind the Chinatis, "deep in Mexico, and impossible to be seen from the spot where we had taken our readings!"

An unscientific method was tried in the 1980's by Dallas journalist, Kirby Warnock. Warnock's family had settled in the Trans-Pecos region just north of Big Bend country more than one hundred years ago, and he first saw the lights in 1963, when he was eleven-years-old and his brother was eight. He and his brother decided that the reason no one ever got close to the lights was because they used motor vehicles, such as airplanes, jeeps, and cars. The two men thought that if they headed out on foot across the desert, they just might be able to sneak up on the lights.

One summer, they assembled their gear and a camera, and at dusk, started walking. They tried for four hours to get close to the lights, but it was like walking up to a mirage. The more they walked, the further the lights moved away. Warnock reported that he thought the lights were "trying to frustrate and thwart us. It was like they knew what we were doing and were teasing us by staying just a little ahead of us." It is a fact that distances are deceiving in the desert. The Warnocks could not tell if they were looking at a light as big as a tire or one as big as a cantaloupe. They just could not get close enough to get a good idea of how big the lights actually were.

Local lore also has a way of turning into local legend. Supposedly, during World War II, pilots training at the old air base dropped sacks of flour to mark the lights' location. It is a story that has been told so many times and in so many variations, that it long ago achieved the semblance of fact. But, Fritz Kahl disclaims it. He has been either instructing at or running the airport for the past forty years. If someone had flown out and dropped flour sacks, he would have known about it.

It was in March 1973 that the legendary lights got a big boost of publicity. Two visiting geologists appeared in the area to assess the likelihood of uranium deposits for a big corporation. While parked in their car on the Flats, they were startled by the sudden appearance of two similar balls of light. The lights were about one-half the size of a basketball, and they darted behind some bushes and in front of others, always hovering a few hundred feet away before they blinked out. Coming from the scientific community as it did, all sorts of people sat up and took notice. Theories begin to multiply tenfold.

It is a known fact that triboluminescence is light resulting from friction at the surface of certain crystalline materials, such as quartz, and quartz is abundant in the area. Under pressure, it creates an electric current called piezoelectricity. The current is capable of ionizing the air into visible luminosities. Piezoelectricity also might ignite gases escaping from sedimentary rock along fractures lines. The gas explanation is reinforced by the history of the Cienaga Mountains. Cienaga is Spanish for "marsh" or "swamp." In the past, the area was wetter and may have produced natural gas. Gas has been found in the Casa

Piedra area, south of Marfa, near the Cienaga Mountains. One pilot even reported a patch of phosphorescence the size of a football field, as he flew over the Mitchell Flats at night, and phosphorescent gases can produce luminescence without ignition. So, scientists argue, with the severe heating and cooling of the Earth's surface in the area, as well as seismic activity, might not there be all sorts of friction along the fault lines?

Locals really do laugh about all the scientific theories that crop up, especially since the lights appear to have minds of their own and do all sorts of crazy things which defy explanation. For instance, believers argue, cannot science be described in terms of either black or white…either it is or it isn't? How then does science explain all the shades of gray that the locals experience? There is absolutely nothing cut and dried about the lights. Some of the bizarre stories involve lights chasing or scorching cars, jeeps, and trucks. Some claim cars melt and their occupants disappear, go into shock, or turn into babbling idiots who are put away in sanitariums. There is even the tale that the lights are a government laser weapon project that went awry. Several years ago, the operator of a Marfa gas station had to make a delivery to Presidio late at night. It was close to midnight, as he drove through the Chinatis. "Suddenly there was this big blue ball of light a few feet off the road right in front of me," Hector Escobedo said. "I slammed on my brakes, but it did not move. I decided to keep driving, but it was so bright, I had to shade my eyes to see the road." The light stayed right in front of him for several miles, miles where the highway never once formed a straight line, as it twisted and turned around the rocks and peaks of the mountain pass. As suddenly as it came, it disappeared. "I was never so scared in my life. I do not drive through there at night anymore."

The case file contains thousands of reports from ordinary citizens just like Hector, who have seen the legendary lights. Even celebrities have gotten into the spirit. In 1955, when film crews were in Marfa making the movie Giant, which starred Elizabeth Taylor, James Dean, and Rock Hudson, James Dean mounted a small telescope on a fence post to better spy on the lights, should they suddenly pop up.

Because the phenomenon is so well-recorded and remains yet unsolved, there have been many serious investigations by individuals and small groups attempting to explain the lights. One of the best known, and recorded, came in March 1975. Don Witt, then a physics professor at Sul Ross University in Alpine, coordinated a monumental effort to locate the lights' source. Using the Sul Ross Society of Physics Students, the Big Bend Outdoor Club comprised of community members, and local pilots, short-wave radio amateurs, and a few outside professionals, Witt's group was positively unable to form any sort of solid conclusion. They did say, however, that sometimes the lights that people claimed were "Marfa Lights," were really artificial lights from area ranches or automobile headlights merely passing behind unseen obstructions along distant Highway 67, which winds through the Chinati Mountains between Marfa and Presidio.

The findings created an uproar in the otherwise sleepy little town of Marfa. Highway 67 was twenty-four miles away and well below the horizon, eyewitnesses pointed out. And even if the lights were headlights, it had to be traffic from Presidio to Marfa, or traffic moving left to right, since anyone going from Marfa to Presidio would show only taillights. Furthermore, they maintained, the lights also move from right to left which, if the scientists' theory were to be accepted, indicated a crazy person backing up on Highway 67 at a high rate of speed on a dark night on a treacherous mountain road in order to make the right-to-left kind of movements that the mystery orbs have been known to make. It was preposterous.

The eyewitnesses also ruled out the scientists' artificial "ranch lights" theory. With only one ranch in the area with only one spotlight---a spotlight easily recognizable to the naked eye and, therefore, discounted as a legitimate sighting---there was no way ranches played any role in the matter.

Then, a sighting occurred in 1985 which appeared to succeed in wiping out the car headlight theory...at least, that's the claim. Robert Black, a graduate student in geology at Sul Ross University, decided to climb Goat Mountain south of Alpine for rock samples. On the Saturday after Thanksgiving, he and a friend drove out a county road east of Marfa, parked their truck, and hiked in. It was early in the morning on an exceptionally warm day for the mountains at that time of year, and both men were dressed in light-weight clothing.

After collecting rock samples, Black's friend, who loved sunsets, commented, "This is going to be a beautiful sunset, isn't it. Look, the sun's going down." At that moment, Black realized that they had stayed longer on the climb than he had intended. They would have to really hurry to make it out before dark.

Breaking into a run, they spied the truck way off on the Flats, but distances are deceiving in the desert, and before they could reach the truck, the sun was down. They were on the west side of Goat Mountain, in the middle of the Mitchell Flats. Black says it best, "Anyone who knows the Marfa flats, knows that it is flat, featureless, and boring---no geological marker out in the sea of desert and really no way to find your way around, especially in the dark." The men wisely decided to spend the night where they were. To keep warm, they gathered creosote bushes for fires.

A little before midnight, as they huddled around the fires looking toward the north and northwest in the direction of Highway 90, their talk turned to the Marfa Lights. The men were right in the Flats, where the lights were normally seen, and they began to hope the lights would make an appearance. They didn't have long to wait. Shortly after midnight, they saw a "horizontal length of light that had a sort of dancing vibration movement." As the men watched in fascination, the "little beams of light danced up and down in a kind of wave formation, moved across, jumped straight up vertically, came back down, danced horizontally, then disappeared." They saw the lights four or five times that night.

Black's account was unusual because it was the first reported sighting of the lights from a location several miles south of Highway 90 and looking north toward Highway 90. The Chinati Mountains were to their backs. It ruled out any supposition of car headlights in the mountains as being the cause of the mystery lights. Since Black and his companion were between the Chinati Mountains and Highway 90, and the lights appeared between the men and the highway, skeptics were forced to rethink their previous positions.

There is even another recorded incident of the brilliant orbs communicating with one of the local ranchers. Mrs. W.T. Giddens of Sundown, Texas, reported that her father actually lived the adventure. According to her story, her father was up in the Chinati Mountains, looking for stray cattle, when a sudden blizzard struck. Darkness accompanied by howling wind and blowing snow, reduced visibility to near zero. He was unable to see his way home and had to feel his way along what he hoped was the right trail, fearing he would soon freeze to death if he did not find shelter.

Rounding an outcropping of rocks, the panicked rancher stopped dead in his tracks when some of the mystery lights suddenly appeared. Although he never explained how they did it, the rancher claimed the lights "spoke" to him, telling him he was three miles south of Chinati Peak, off course, headed in the wrong direction, and dangerously close to a steep precipice. He was advised to follow the lights---or die.

The lights led him to a cave that provided shelter from the raging storm. The smaller lights left, but the larger light remained with him until morning. According to the rancher, the light claimed they were "spirits from elsewhere and long ago."

When the rancher awoke the next morning, both the light and the storm were gone. As he headed toward home, he passed the outcropping of rocks and discovered that when the lights had intercepted him, he had been on the edge of a sheer cliff several hundred feet high. He had no doubts---the lights had saved his life.

In July 1989, scientists from McDonald Observatory on Mount Locke outside Fort Davis, and from Sul Ross University, decided to conduct another investigation into the lights. Included in the group were a professor of chemistry, Dr. Avinash Rangra, and an astronomer, Dr. Edwin Barker. With them were eleven other technicians and observers. Since the lights are most frequently seen near the Chinati Mountains from Highway 90, which runs east and west between Marfa and Alpine, the scientists decided they had best rule out any misidentification of headlights on Highway 67, which winds through the Chinati Mountains north and south between Marfa and Presidio.

A radio beacon resembling a red spotlight, visible in front of the peaks, was used as a guide. In order to prevent the misidentification of headlights, two marker lights were placed at the borders of Highway 67, where it enters and leaves the mountain range. These marker locations were manned by two technicians with radio equipment. Any lights spotted outside the markers, which the scientists could not explain, would be identified as the ghostly phenomena.

The investigators used special cameras and night-viewing equipment. At midnight, an unknown light appeared past the right marker light in the middle of the empty Mitchell Flats. Contacting the technician at the marker by radio indicated there was no traffic on Highway 67. The ghostly globe was recorded on a video camera. Observers were certain the light did not come from a man-made source. It disappeared and came back and faded again.

Doctor Rangra confirmed that something of natural origin was occurring over Mitchell Flats outside Marfa, but he did not know what. All he could say for certain was that it was not man-made. Doctor Edwin Barker agreed. People were seeing real activity in the atmosphere, but how to explain it? One scientist thought the lights might be refracted starlight. Another believed them to be illuminous gases produced by small earthquakes. But the fact is, every one of the scientists in the investigation were not sure and could only say for certain that it is a natural phenomena as yet unexplained by science. "Ha," the locals snorted, "we already knew that."

So, what are the mysterious Marfa Lights? Who knows? Theories are as prolific as the skeptics are to the theories. There are some who think the lights are caused by swamp gas escaping from underground pockets and igniting. Well...maybe. Only there has not been a swamp in that part of Texas for thousands, perhaps millions of years. What about St. Elmo's Fire? Possibly, but not very likely. Saint Elmo's Fire only occurs when conditions are absolutely perfect. The Marfa Lights, on the other hand, are seen year-round in all kinds of weather and under all sorts of different atmospheric conditions. This seems to also rule out ball lightning.

According to another theory, the lights might be a by-product of what is referred to as the Novaya Zemlya effect, which was first noted by the explorer Willem Barrents in 1597. Unlike the normal temperature inversion layer, which forms a distinct reflective boundary between warm and cold layers of air, the Novaya Zemlya effect may involve several different layers or slices of atmosphere. This means that a locomotive headlight between Ojinaga and Chihuahua, Mexico, could bounce back and forth between varying layers of air and be seen as far away as Texas' official "Marfa Lights" viewing site, located ten miles east of Marfa on Highway 90. In a strange sort of way, this seems to corroborate the Walter T. Harris surveying party's conclusion conducted at the turn of the century, as well as adding credence to the refracted starlight theory. The only real problem with the Novaya Zemlya effect is that the lights appear even on cloudy nights, which cannot possibly be considered atmospheric reflections.

The real truth is that no one really knows for sure what causes the Marfa Lights. The legends surrounding them just continue to expand, as more and more research proves nothing. For the people of Marfa, who have grown up with the lights, no explanation is necessary. They have them, and they mean to keep them.

An interesting anecdote was recorded by researcher Dennis Stacy in 1989. It seems that Dr. Ray Hauser of Hauser Laboratories in Boulder, Colorado, wrote The Marfa Independent with an unusual request. He offered one dollar for each used car air filter (up to ten) used in the area south of Marfa. The filters had to have at least a thousand miles of wear and tear. Hauser wanted to analyze the dust in the filters to see if there might be a connection between the lights and the chemical composition and behavior of certain dust-clouds. According to Stacy, "the idea sounds completely cock-eyed, until one remembers that accumulated dust in grain elevators is capable of tremendous explosive ignition."

## MONAHANS, TEXAS

Monahans is at the intersection of Farm Road 18 and Interstate Highway 20, thirty-six miles southwest of Odessa in northeast Ward County. The town was named for Thomas John (Pat) Monahan, who dug the first water well between the Pecos River and Big Spring at Monahans in 1881 and selected the site for a water tank, around which a ranch supply point later developed. The town was originally called Monahan's Well. The Texas and Pacific Railway reached the site in August 1881. A post office was established at Monahans in 1883, and in 1900 James R. Holman opened the Monahans Hotel, a landmark for prospectors and land agents. Growth was slow. A public school was begun in 1898; the following year thirty-six students attended. The precinct that included Pyote and Monahans had 222 residents in 1900; by 1905 Monahans itself had an estimated population of eighty-nine. In 1910 the precinct had a population of 378, two churches, and several businesses. Monahans did not begin to grow more rapidly until the opening of the nearby Hendrick oilfield in 1926. The town was incorporated in 1928, and Fred G. Gipson was elected the first mayor. In 1929 the Texas-New Mexico Railway completed tracks from Monahans to Lovington, New Mexico, to handle the increasing transportation demands of the oilfields. By 1930 the population had increased to 816. The 1930s were boom years.

### Monahans Sandhills State Park

More than 400 years ago, Spanish explorers were the first Europeans to report the vast hills of sand. Man was present in this area as far back as 12,000 years ago. Later, various Indian tribes used the area for temporary campgrounds and a meeting place, finding game, abundant fresh water beneath the sands, acorns, and mesquite beans available for grinding into paste with their stone tools. The area remained a favorable environment for Indians until the 1880s, when the Texas and Pacific Railroad selected Monahans as a water stop between the Pecos River and the town of Big Spring. In the late 1920s, oil production began in the area, now commonly known as the Permian Basin, and today Monahans is a marketing center for more than 800 square miles of oil and cattle country. With about 39-hundred acres of sand dunes, some up to 70 feet high it might seem hard to believe that anyone could have ever called what is now Monahans Sandhills State Park home. But 200 years ago Native Americans walked these very dunes, and some say they never left.

"That's the theory that it's the Indians that were known to encamp here in the area are, wandering through the sand."

Park manager Glen Korth says on any given day, if the wind blows just right, you will find what folks at the park call sand ghost trails out on the dunes…

"Indentions on the ground that kinda look like footprints and if it's a heavy wind it looks like little figures walking across the sand…"

Whether the markings are in fact ghosts from the Native Americans who lived there is anyone's guess, but before you write off the phenomenon Glen offers this little extra bit of history about the park…

"There are several Indian burial grounds at this park from the various tribes who had encampments here at the park

"I get goose bumps and the hair on my arms pulls back…I really have no explanation…"

Mysterious footsteps are al most commonplace at Monahans Sandhills State Park. Legend has it that the visitor center was built on the site of a 19th-century Comanche burial ground In 1967, two boys who were digging near the building unearthed a skeleton, giving credence to the story of the burial ground.

Staff members at the Monahans Visitors Center report hearing doors open and close by themselves and occasionally they report hearing the slamming of doors that were already closed. Mysterious shadows come and go, with no explanation. Staff members routinely hear the sounds of a heavy object falling, but never find any explanation.

A new employee, having been told of these phenomena, thought her coworkers were pulling her leg until the day she was alone in the office and heard a woman scream just outside the building. She ran out to help, but found no one; she searched the perimeter of the building until the screams subsided, but never found the frightened woman.

## Monahans High School - Auditorium

Monahans High School is located at 809 S. Betty Avenue, Monahans, Texas. It was in the Auditorium of this school that a young girl, in a fit of depression, allegedly hung herself. A number of people have reported walking into the auditorium and seeing the shadow of a body hanging from a rope. Others say that it is in the basement that the spirit can be seen and felt. Somewhat mischievously, the spirit of the dead girl is known to go through the costumes storied in the basement and she hides in strange places to scare the unsuspecting persons who have a need to go to the basement.

# ODESSA, TEXAS

Odessa, the largest town and county seat of Ector County, is the chief shipping point for the surrounding livestock area as well as a center for the oil and gas industry. Located at 31°51' north latitude and 102°22' west longitude in the heart of the vast oil-rich area known as the Permian Basin, it is 321 miles west of Fort Worth and 280 miles east of El Paso on the Texas and Pacific Railway. U.S. highways 80 and 385 and Interstate Highway 20 are the major transportation links. The warm dry climate and 300 days of sunshine per year make it a haven for retirees from the colder climates. Situated at the hub of West Texas, Odessa traces its founding to the extension of the Texas and Pacific Railway across the South Plains in July 1881, and to a real estate promotion by the Odessa Land and Townsite Company. Used as a water stop by the railroad, Odessa was supposedly named by railroad workers who thought the area resembled their home in Odessa, Russia. In 1885 C. W. Rathburn became the first postmaster of the newly established post office. The actual platting of Odessa took place in 1886; 300 acres of the original town site are now at the center of the city's downtown. Odessa became the county seat when Ector County was formally organized in January 1891. In 1927 it incorporated as a city and elected its first mayor, S. R. McKinney.

## Odessa High School

Odessa High School is located at 1301 Dotsy Avenue, Odessa, Texas. The story goes that a drama student, whose name was said to be Betty, who attended the high school talked her boyfriend into shooting her, and now she haunts the auditorium wearing a white dress.

Further research shows that there was a student who died whose name was Betty. Betty, her real name was Elizabeth, was a student back in the 60s. After an argument, it is said that her boyfriend took her out to a stock pond around Notres and shot her. He weighed her body down and dropped her in the pond. However, he was the primary suspect in the disappearance of the young woman. The following day he was questioned by police and it is said that he confessed. After the confession, he showed the police where he dumped her body. In spite of her killer being caught, Betty haunts the auditorium, still around the theater that she enjoyed in life.

## Ector JR. High

Ector Jr. High School is located at 809 E. Clements, in Odessa. Back in the 1960s it used to be a high school. At that time, the school employed a man on its janitorial staff who was somewhat mentally slow. The students always teased the janitor about his lack of perceived intelligence. This teasing caused the janitor great embarrassment and finally, one day he climbed up to the balcony in the auditorium and hung himself. Now, many students have said that they have seen him walking around the balcony and in the stage area.

## Insane Asylum

There is an old hospital on the Westside of town that has a very noticeable Spanish design. A number of the patients confined in this Asylum killed themselves in this place and it has been said that at late at night their spirits still wander that hallways looking for their doctor.

Many times figures have been seen in the dimly lit hallways and many of those living in Odessa have been frightened by sounds emanating from the building of figures seen in or about the building. The police have boarded up the windows and the doors, but some teenagers broke in and started a fire. It is said that if you drive by late at night you might be able to see a light glow from the upstairs windows.

# OLTON, TEXAS

Olton, on U.S. Highway 70 and Farm Road 168, twenty miles northeast of Littlefield in northeast Lamb County, was settled around 1900 by Harry Baughn, T. F. Brown, and Luther Williams on state land surrounded by the C. C. Slaughter ranch. As the first town in the county, it became the county seat when the county was organized in 1908. In 1903 A. B. Powell started the first store and post office in his home three miles from the present town site; he named the community for either a son or an early preacher. The post office changed location in 1904, 1905, and 1908. In 1908 it was moved to T. F. Brown's home, an old Slaughter ranch windmill. The Burro school, so named because a herd of burros froze to death beside it in a blizzard, was established in 1903 and moved to Olton in 1908.

## The Trees

There is an area of dense forest on the outskirts of town where witnesses report hearing drums that sounded like Indian war drums. There have also been reports that as the witnesses listened to the mysterious drums that a white mist rose up around the car in which they where sitting.

# PECOS, TEXAS

The entire downtown section of Pecos (Pay Cuss) is intact, with only one building gone due to a fire. At the north end of the main street is the railroad station. It's easy to spot - just look for the Union Pacific caboose in the middle of the street. Next to the caboose is the headstone for Clay Allison, a notorious gunfighter who may have "died with his boots on" but actually his head was crushed

**Figure 2 Reeves County Courthouse in 1960.**

by his own wagon.

As hard as it is to believe - the town of Pecos was once East of the Pecos River. The popular slogan "West of the Pecos" wouldn't work very well if the town of Pecos was east of the river. A Mr. George Knight who owned the land gave a small portion for a depot and a little more for good measure to the Texas and Pacific Railroad who laid tracks in 1881. The evolution of the name was Pecos Station, then Pecos City and finally the simple utilitarian Pecos. After going through so many changes, they weren't about to change it when their portion of Pecos County became Reeves County in 1883. They got a post office in 1884 and a bad reputation for violence shortly thereafter. We'd like to point out that the reputation had nothing to do with postal employees.

The name Pecos even evolved into a verb like "Shanghai". To "Pecos" a man was to ambush him, steal his horse and money and roll his body off a riverbank (which didn't have to actually be the Pecos River to qualify). Even though things have quieted down today, having Clay Allison's grave in back of the Orient Hotel (itself riddled with bullet holes) testifies to the town's legendary wild-west past. During WWII Pecos Army Air Field was opened and the population of the town reached 6,500. The city nearly doubled its population in the 50s from 8,000 to 14,000.

## Reeves County Courthouse

The current courthouse is not the original one built in 1886 rather it was built in 1937. However, sometimes, spirits remain at the location, though the building is changed. That well may be the case here. There have been a number of reports of footsteps heard on the 3rd floor or descending the stairs, even though witnesses can see that there is no one there. Shadowy figures are seen by many in their peripheral vision late at night.

## Barrio Santa Rosa

It has been reported by many that late at night, next to the railroad tracks in front of the Santa Rosa Church, you can hear a women sobbing down the street. This sobbing is also accompanied by the sound of her high heel shoes as she slowly walks towards you.

## Bessie Haynes Elementary

Located at 800 E 11th St, Pecos, TX, it is said to be haunted by a builder that was on the school roof when she fell through and died. So they named the school after her. However, there were few female builders at the time that this school was built.

However, there is no doubt that the school is haunted and that the ghost is a female. Many people have seen her wondering the halls, and heard her in the girls' restroom. Also many lights have gone on and off with no explanation. The hauntings seem to be centered on the girls' restroom.

## Lamar Middle School

According to local legends, a few years ago, a boy was swinging in one of the swings on the school playground. Accidentally, he fell out of the swing and landed on his head. As a result of his injury, he died. Now a certain time between September and December the swing from which the little boy fell will swing by its self and it will look like someone is swinging on it, but the other swings are still and quiet. This will normally happen on a calm day.

## Pecos Elementary

Pecos Elementary School is closed now. Some say it is partly because of the unexplained occurrences. There have been a number of reports of unexplained voices and strange apparitions that are seen and heard on the roof and in the girls' bathroom. Custodians also report that late at night children are heard playing on the deserted playground.

# PRESIDIO, TEXAS

Presidio is on the Rio Grande, Farm Road 170, and State Highway 67 eighteen miles south of Shafter in southern Presidio County. The surrounding area is the oldest continuously cultivated area in the United States. Farmers have lived at Presidio since 1500 B.C. By 1400 A.D. the area Indians lived in small, close-together settlements, which the Spaniards later called pueblos.

The first Spaniards came to Presidio in 1535, when Álvar Núñez Cabeza de Vaca and his three companions stopped at the Indian pueblo, placed a cross on the mountain side, and called the village La Junta de las Cruces. On December 10, 1582, Antonio de Espejo and his company arrived at the site and called the pueblo San Juan Evangelista. By 1681 the area of Presidio was known as La Junta de los Ríos or the Junction of the Rivers, for the Río Conchos and the Rio Grande join at the site. About 1760 a penal colony and a military garrison of sixty men were established near Presidio.

In 1783 Juan Sabeata, the chief of the Jumano Indian nation, reported having seen a fiery cross on the mountain at Presidio. The settlement then became known as La Navidad en Las Cruces. In 1830 the name of the area around Presidio was changed from La Junta de los Rios to Presidio del Norte. In 1849 a Comanche raid almost destroyed Presidio, and in 1850 Indians drove off most of the cattle in town. A post office was established at Presidio in 1868, and the first public school was opened in 1887. In 1930 the Kansas City, Mexico and Orient Railway reached Presidio, and the town incorporated.

## Fort Leaton

Ben Leaton had been a scalp hunter for the Mexican government before coming to this spot on the Rio Grande in 1848 and building a massive fortress. These adobe walls have seen bloodshed and violence, the perfect scenario for ghost stories. Ben Leaton died in 1851. His widow married Edward Hall, a local customs agent, and the Halls made their home in the adobe fort.

Some time after marrying Leaton's widow, Hall borrowed a large sum of money from Leaton's old partner, John Burgess, using the fort as collateral. Hall failed to repay the loan and Burgess foreclosed, but Hall refused to leave. Frontier justice being what it was, Burgess allegedly had Hall murdered in one of the rooms of the fort. The Burgess family assumed ownership of the fort.

Soon after moving in, Burgess did an odd thing: he converted the room in which Hall had been murdered into a chapel, complete with an altar. Did John Burgess-a man with no qualms about taking whatever action he deemed appropriate-suffer a guilty conscience? Or did Edward Hall's ghost return and demand retribution?

John Burgess supposedly died at the hands of Bill Leaton-Ben Leaton's son and Edward Hall's stepson-in 1875. The Burgess family abandoned the fort in 1926, but the huge adobe structure's presence continued to be felt in this small community. Workers in the area often reported seeing an old woman in a rocking chair in the kitchen. Mrs. Hall or Mrs. Burgess, perhaps, watching over her home? The vague figure of a man matching Edward Hall's description also has been seen in the room in which he was murdered. Even today, staff and visitors occasionally hear chains rattling in the granary, as though some long-ago horsemen were removing the harnesses from their horses.

According to one legend, a horseman was caught in a sudden thunderstorm near Fort Leaton around the turn of the century. As he tried to pull his cape around his shoulders, a clap of thunder startled the horse. The horse bolted, but instead of being thrown clear, the rider's foot was caught in the stirrup and he was dragged along behind the horse. The rider's body slammed into a sharp boulder and he was beheaded. If you believe that ghosts linger in the places in which they died suddenly, watch carefully if you find yourself near Fort Leaton during a sudden thunderstorm: reports persist of a headless horseman in a black cape that can be seen riding a white horse around the compound.

During the period Fort Leaton was abandoned, its rooms served as temporary shelter for homeless families in the area. An elderly couple visited the site recently, and told Superintendent Luis Armerdariz they had set up housekeeping in two of the fort's rooms when they were newly married in the late 1920s. Among their meager furnishings were some wooden crates they used as shelves for their dishes. The couple said that after they retired for the night, they would hear dishes crashing to the floor and breaking, as if the crates had been pushed over. When they went to check, everything was fine. This occurred night after night, and became so unnerving that the couple soon sought other quarters.

Rumors circulated for decades that Ben Leaton had buried gold under the floor of one of the rooms. Throughout the years that the structure stood abandoned, treasure hunters dug for the nonexistent gold. The result was a deep pit that eventually filled with garbage. When the Texas Parks and Wildlife Department acquired Fort Leaton in 1968, one of the first jobs was to clean out the pit. The local workers who were hired for the job were about halfway into the pit when they became terror stricken. Both claimed to feel something pulling them into the hole. They abandoned the work and the fort and never returned, not even for their paychecks.

## SEMINOLE, TEXAS

Seminole, Texas was named after local Indian watering holes. The County was named after signer of the Texas Declaration of Independence James Gaines. Seminole was made the County Seat of Gaines County when it was organized in 1905. However Seagraves was the county's most populated town until 1950.

The first bank was opened in 1906. Bank robbers didn't find out about it until 1912. As soon as they did they robbed it. In 1914 the population was about 300 people. For five years Seminole enjoyed a rail connection to Midland. This proved unprofitable in 1923 and the railroad (The Midland and Northwestern) suspended operations. The same year, Seminole had their worst fire, destroying a good portion of downtown.

### Shafter Lake

There is a place known as Shafter Lake in between Seminole and Andrews. It is known to have been an Indian Burial grounds. It is said that if you go there at night and park just off the road by the large rocks and flash your lights three times you will see an apparition of a woman carrying a lantern dressed in a white flowing gown coming towards you. You can also hear the sounds of drums at the site.

## SHAFTER, TEXAS

**Figure 3: Shafter Mine About 1890**

Shafter is on Cibolo Creek and U.S. Highway 67, at the east end of the Chinati Mountains eighteen miles north of Presidio in southern Presidio County. Its history is closely tied to silver mining. There is evidence that the Spaniards prospected for valuable ores in the area during the early 1600s, but Shafter became a mining town only after September 1880, when John W. Spencer, a freighter turned prospector, found silver ore there. Spencer showed an ore sample to Col. William R. Shafter, commander of the First Infantry Regiment at Fort Davis, who had it assayed. When small amounts of profitable silver were found, Colonel Shafter interested two army friends, Lt. John L. Bullis of the Twenty-fourth Infantry and Lt. Louis Wilhelmi of the First Infantry, in a land deal on the acreage surrounding Spencer's strike.

In October 1880 Colonel Shafter and his partners asked the state to sell them nine sections of school land in the Chinati Mountains near the site of Shafter. Colonel Shafter requested two sections in his name and two in his wife's. Wilhelmi filed for three sections. Because Bullis already owned many acres of West Texas land in his name, he applied for two sections in his wife's name

## School Building

People that have explored the older part of the School building have reported that they heard unexplained whispering. It has also been reported that people in the newer part of the building have heard ghostly footsteps of at least two children, and there have been occasional unexplained electrical disruption. The old building is currently being converted into a private home.

# STERLING CITY, TEXAS

Sterling City, the county seat of Sterling County, is on the North Concho River at the intersection of U.S. Highway 87 and State Highway 158, forty-three miles northwest of San Angelo and forty-two miles southeast of Big Spring in the east central part of the county. It was named in honor of W. S. Sterling, an early buffalo hunter and Indian fighter in the area, when it became the county seat in July 1891. As virtually the only community in the sparsely populated county, Sterling City progressed in pace with the influx of settlers coming from Cummins, a mile east.

The town site was donated in January 1891 by R. C. Stewart and surveyed and platted in February by H. B. Tarver. By June a hotel and several businesses were in operation and S. R. and Frank Ezell had established the Sterling Courier. A post office was established later that year. The first school was built by 1892, and the first cotton gin in the county was erected in 1895. In 1896 the community had 300 residents, eight businesses, and three churches. The Santa Fe Railroad provided service in 1910 but was later discontinued. Sterling City was noted for its windmills, which at one time numbered 150. By 1914 the community had two banks, two hotels, other businesses, and a population of 900.

## Landmark Hotel

The Landmark Hotel has been a home to travelers for many years. It has also had some employees who have remained long after they should have gone on to better things. Years after her death, there is a ghostly telephone operator that still calls the payphone in the cafe downstairs. Unexplained footsteps have been reported throughout the hotel, and mysterious business records would turn up in odd places.

## TERLINGUA, TEXAS

Terlingua started as a simple Mexican village on Terlingua Creek just north of the Rio Grande. The name Terlingua is a corruption of Tres Lenguas or three languages (tongues) that were spoken by the inhabitants of the village.

When mercury-bearing ore was discovered in the 1800s, a mine was opened and the tent village of the laborers and miners appropriated the name Terlingua. The village became known as Terlingua Abajo, or "Lower Terlingua".

At the turn of the century there were about 300 workers and they had their own post office. By 1905 the population was over 1,000 and when the mine closed in 1910, the post office moved 10 miles east, keeping the name Terlingua.

The cemetery at Terlingua is still maintained (somewhat), although the miners buried here are probably mostly forgotten to their families. Its primitive and barely decipherable system of grave identification and handmade markers make it a rather picturesque photo opportunity for some people. Frequent mowing is not a problem in Terlingua.

### Perry House

**Figure 4: The Perry House**

Howard E. Perry, founder and president of the Chisos Mining Company, was an autocratic, single-minded industrialist whose sole aim was to reduce expenses and maximize profits. Extremely secretive, wary of everyone and responsible to none but himself, he was totally incapable to changing his policy or adapting new techniques. He capped a miserable career in 1940 by firing without notice his manager of 25 years. In 1942 the company closed down. An unidentified female apparition has been seen wandering the halls of the house of the former cinnabar mining magnate.

# PART FOUR

## GHOSTS OF THE TEXAS PANHANDLE

# AMARILLO, TEXAS

The first European to set foot in the wide-open spaces of what is now known as the Texas Panhandle was Francisco Coronado. He passed through in 1541, some 79 years before the Pilgrims landed at Plymouth Rock, in search of gold and land for the Spanish Crown[8].

In the 19th century cattlemen, buffalo hunters and adventurers pushed west in search of a new life and Amarillo was settled in 1887. The name Amarillo, which means yellow in Spanish, was adopted because of the color of the subsoil in the channel of Amarillo Creek. In the early days, most houses were painted yellow in honor of the name.

The first county courthouse was built in 1888 and the Amarillo Hotel followed in 1889. The Texas Rangers administered the only law until 1899 when the City Council incorporated to govern the fledgling city of 925 acres and 1,442 citizens. The population grew to 9,957 in 1910 when Amarillo wrote its own charter and became the first town in the Southwest, and fifth in the United States, to adopt the Commission-Manager form of government.

## Ghost Lights

Between Amarillo and Tascosa, the ghost lights were first reported in the earlier half of this century.

## Gebo's, 2500 E. 3$^{rd}$, Hereford, Texas

This well known establishment was once a Bonanza Supermarket back in the 1980's, before Gebo's opened their second store. A number of people maintain that an employee was the Bonanza supermarket called Bonanza was killed in the meat department one night.

Now there are a number of stories of the ghost that haunts Gebo's. Employees maintain that it is this ghost that moves items and misplaces them at night. The situation has gotten so bad that employees try to avoid night inventory. No matter how neat things are left each night, in the morning, things are always out of place. Lots of employees have seen what the ghost has done.

---

[8] http://texas.allinfoabout.com/cities/amarillo_history.html

## Tradewinds Airport , 2 miles south of Amarillo, Texas.

Tradewinds Airport is located in the southern part of the City. Rumor has

**Figure 5: Tradewinds Airport**

it that back when the place was a private air strip, a woman caught her husband with his mistress in their private plane and killed both of them. Overcome with remorse at what she had done, the wronged wife then committed suicide. This would explain the distinct smell of perfume, which comes and goes (even in the strongest breeze).

At times, strange lights (like a plane gearing up) can be seen coming from an abandoned hanger. From this same area the sounds of two people arguing have been heard, but there is no one there.

## York Tire Co., 714 E. 10th Ave., Amarillo, Texas

Montie Townsend, the York Tire Company's assistant manager, said he first encountered the ghosts after he went to work for the company almost five years ago. "When I first came to work here, we'd unload a truck and stack the tires in the back. The next day, the stack would be knocked over," Townsend said. "... Finally, I spoke to them and told them to quit knocking over the tires or else. They didn't do it again."

Townsend said almost all of the company's 15 employees have had some sort of an encounter, from hearing footsteps behind them to seeing shadows move out of the corners of their eyes.

"One day, I saw a person walking by, counting his change. He was wearing a gray uniform like the Westinghouse elevator repair people used to wear. ... He walked into the break room like he was going to get a Coke, and I went to see if he needed any help finding anything," Townsend said. "But nobody was there."

The three-story building was constructed in the 1920s, and Townsend knows of at least one death inside its walls - an elevator repairman who fell down the length of the elevator shaft.

"At one point, I think they brought in some people to check the building out, and they said there were several presences here, seven or eight different entities. I thought, 'Pshaw, right.' But then, I saw the guy with the change."

## <u>Summit Elementary School, 9<sup>th</sup> Avenue and Florida Street</u>

In Amarillo's own version of "A Nightmare on Elm Street," there is a story that four boys attending Summit Elementary School were allegedly slaughtered in the boiler room by the school janitor. Visitors to the now-closed school, located at Northwest Ninth Avenue and Florida Street, swear they hear the voices of children playing and, if they happen to be inside the building looking out through the windows, see swings on the playground swaying without a breeze - even though there are no swings on the playground.

Legend even suggests that the ghosts will cause your car to go nuts should you drop by for a visit: Doors will lock or unlock themselves, the windows will roll up or down, and the radio will turn on.

## LUBBOCK, TEXAS

Lubbock, the county seat of Lubbock County, is located at the approximate center of the county (at 33°35' N, 101°51' W) at an elevation of 3,256 feet above sea level. The city, the largest on the South Plains, is on Interstate Highway 27, 327 miles northwest of Dallas and 122 miles south of Amarillo. Lubbock was founded as a part of the movement westward onto the High Plains of Texas by ranchers and farmers. More directly it was the result of a compromise between two groups of town promoters, one led by Frank E. Wheelock and the other by W. E. Rayner. In the fall of 1890 these groups abandoned their settlements, known respectively as Old Lubbock and Monterey, and agreed on December 19 of that year to combine into the new settlement. In 1876 the county had been named for Thomas S. Lubbock, former Texas Ranger and brother of Francis R. Lubbock, governor of Texas during the Civil War. As early as 1884 a federal post office called Lubbock existed at George W. Singer's store in Yellow House Canyon, in the northern part of the present-day city.

## Broadway Avenue

There is a sort of strip shopping center on Broadway Avenue that has a couple of bars and a few stores. The building was a hotel at the turn of the century, and there are several restless spirits who continue to haut the location.

## Television Station

There is a television station in Lubbock where it is said that the ghost plays with faucets, clears throat, and tells people to, "Slow down."

## O.L. Slaton Junior High School, 1602 32nd St. Lubbock, TX 79405

O.L. Slaton Junior High School is a two-story building that houses both a large and small gymnasium. The band room and the field house are separate from the main facility. The school was built in 1947 with two new wings added in 1997, and, at the same time, the office was renovated and a new teachers' workroom was added. O.L. Slaton has three computer labs, and most classrooms have at least one computer accessible to teachers.  The lab computers are Internet-ready, and most of the classroom computers are wired for Internet access. The school adopted a new mascot in 2000, renaming itself the O.L Slaton Knights.

It has been said that a substitute teacher killed himself. Every now and then you will see light go one and off and hear strange noises. Also, the light is in the theater, and the ghost has also been known to make the stage lights shake violently from time to time. Supposedly, it has tried to push people down the stairs a few times. As for the identity of the ghost, it was supposedly a teacher who died near the theatre when it was being built.

## Texas Tech University, 2500 Broadway, Lubbock, Texas

Texas Tech University is a teaching and research institution offering bachelors, masters and doctoral degrees. It is located in Lubbock with an enrollment that is approximately 24000 living students and a number of dead ones as well.

## Beta Theta Pi Fraternity House, Delta MU Chapter

On the evening of August 8, 1839, when eight young men - all students at Miami University - secretly held the first meeting of their newly-founded society: Beta Theta Pi. Locally, the Delta Mu chapter was founded at Tech, February 21, 1970.

**Figure 6: Beta Theta Pi Fraternity House**

The fraternity was not much older than most of its members when it was put to the ultimate test. With the outbreak of the Civil War, communication with the nine chapters south of the Mason-Dixon Line became impossible. And Beta Theta Pi, like the rest of the nation, split into two camps - both in philosophy and in war. But, in a testament to the strength of its fraternal bond, Beta Theta Pi was the only Greek organization to revive every chapter after the war. One such chapter was made up of twelve young men from both the Union and Confederate Armies. Among these soldiers-turned-students was Horace Lurton, Cumberland 1867, who would later be named an Associate Justice of the Supreme Court.

As both the first fraternity founded west of the Allegheny Mountains and the first to locate a chapter west of the Mississippi River, Beta Theta Pi earned a reputation as a pioneer. In fact, Beta is the oldest member of the University of Florida Greek system. It was this pioneering spirit, together with our emphasis on scholastic achievement, that made it the first social fraternity to establish higher academic standards for our chapters than our host schools require of them as students, and why more than 80 Betas have been Rhodes Scholars.

In fact, the Beta roll reads more like a "Who's Who" than a fraternity roster. From founder Charles Hardin, Miami 1841, Governor of Missouri; to Sam Walton, Missouri '40, founder of Wal-Mart; to astronaut Joe Allen, DePauw '59; John Turner, British Columbia '49, former prime minister of Canada; slugger Mike Schmidt, Ohio '71; and actor George Peppard, Purdue '52; the rolls are full of men who have made significant contributions in their respective fields...and beyond.

Many accounts have been reported of ghost sightings in the Fraternity House since it has been built recently. Pledges report that during pledge-ship, there were many sightings of male ghosts watching them through the windows and have been reported to haunt certain date parties whispering to the girl dates that their date is gay. One certain pledge said that a 5th year senior alumni has had strange behaviors towards the pledges and has been seen at night wandering the lodge talking to shadowy male figures.

## Geosciences Building

Folks claim that the third floor of the Chemistry/Geosciences Building at Texas Tech University is home to the ghost of a cleaning lady who was killed at night when she caught a student stealing a biology final exam. She mostly appears during final exams, students say, as a disembodied head seen through a window. Supposedly there is a big bloodstain on the floor where she was killed.

There have only been occasional sightings of a full body apparition. It is said that during the night of the Tech Carol of Lights, you can see an image in the top center window standing there looking out just as all the lights surrounding Memorial Circle are turned off.

## Horn/Knapp Dining Hall

The Horn/Knapp Dining Hall is one of the main dining facilities for University Students. There is a storage room that many people do not know about on the third floor of this heavily traveled building. There is no fourth floor, just a small attic. A little boy is said to have died on the third floor and you can now hear him throwing a ball down the stairs. Sometimes he will knock on the door if you knock first.

## Ranching Heritage Center

Officially dedicated on July 4, 1976, the Ranching Heritage Center is comprised of a 12 acre outdoor exhibit of 31 historic structures, dating from the 1830's to about 1917, with the structures having been moved to the current site from locations throughout the state and authentically restored in order to depict the history of farming and ranching in the West Texas area[9]. These buildings show the evolution of ranching, and many of the structures originate from famous ranches that played decisive roles in the development of modern ranching such as the 6666, the Matador, the XIT, and the King ranches.

The two story house at the Southwest end of the complex has been reported to have a white female in one of the upper windows. The police have responded to the reports of the female and have checked the building only to find it empty. The female is believed to be the wife of the rancher that built the house.

## Thompson Hall

Thompson Hall is now the student health center, but once it was where Gross-Anatomy was located for its med school until the University built a separate building for the med school. There are rumors that it was used for the morgue at one time also. There are reports of seeing people on floors that are locked and electronically monitored when no one had opened the doors. The lights will go out and sometimes turn on when you are directly under them.

---

[9] http://www.lib.utexas.edu/taro/ttuua/00086/tua-00086.html

The elevator opens in front of the security kiosk, and ghostly footsteps exit the elevator, walk past the kiosk, and down the hall. Doors have also been known to slam shut, and footsteps are heard on upper floors when no one is in the building.  A lady, dressed in a nurse's uniform, looks out a fourth floor window overlooking the main entrance.

## The Water Tower

On the coldest night of the year you can often see what looks like 5 or 6 young men on the top catwalk which goes around the water tower. They appear up there all night as if they are spending the night. It is always the coldest night that year, so you can't predict in advance when that may be. The first reported sighting was about 1949 or 1950 and seen almost every year since when observed. There is no knowledge as to who they are.

## Texas Tech University

Spirits on this campus are not just confined to the buildings. One professor has reported seeing the partial apparition of an incredibly deformed entity in one of the parking lots.

## Holden Hall

Ghostly chemistry professor continues to tutor students having problems with chemistry in Holden Hall.

## Museum of Texas Tech University.

In the Museum at Texas Tech University, locked doors open themselves and slam shut before the disbelieving eyes of the security guards who just locked them.

# ACUFF, TEXAS

Acuff is on Farm roads 40 and 789 ten miles east of Lubbock in east central Lubbock County. The town is said to have been named for Michael S. Acuff, who reportedly arrived in the area in February 1891. Other early settlers were the Thomas Acuff, L. O. Burford, and Jim Brown families. Acuff's first school was constructed in 1902. It was a wooden structure built from lumber hauled in from as far away as Amarillo or Big Spring. A six-room brick schoolhouse was built in 1924, and in 1925 Acuff was designated an independent school district. However, by 1942 the community's children were attending the Roosevelt school, and by 1947 Acuff was a part of the Roosevelt district. The Lubbock International Dragway is located near Acuff[10].

---

[10] http://www.tsha.utexas.edu/handbook/online/articles/AA/hna6.html

## Roosevelt High School

Accepting its first class in 1942, the building that houses this school is old and has many stories of odd happenings associated with it. In the Roosevelt High school auditorium a dark figure is seen seated in the audience during play rehearsals. During the actual performance, the figure is gone, but there is an unseen presence backstage amongst the actors. Props that were missing suddenly appear. Costumes that were damaged suddenly are fixed.

Backstage in a dark passageway a seemingly malevolent spirit tries to cause harm to unescorted females as they walk through. No male has felt it, but the females, who have passed through it, feel it. It is usually just a feeling of anxiety to pass through, but there were occasions where the spirit became more forceful. The spirit will not let some girls pass from one end to the other, leaving them trapped in the darkness. A couple of girls have actually felt something grab their arms in the dark. They emerged from the passageway with unexplained bruises.

It is thought that the spirit of a young girl who died in the basement of the high school is said to still roam the hall. Janitors who are down there at night have heard the screaming of a young girl and also heard footsteps running the length of the hall back and forth. The spirit of an elderly man has been seen and felt in an upstairs computer lab. He is said to leave breath marks and fingerprints on the window of the door before he disappears.

# ANDREWS, TEXAS

Andrews, the seat of Andrews County and the only incorporated town in the county, is on U.S. Highway 385 thirty-four miles north of Odessa. The town, like the county, was named for Richard Andrews, the first man to die in the war for Texas independence in 1835. The town began around 1908 with a general store and a schoolhouse. There were only eighty-seven people living in the county, most of them ranchers. A post office was established in 1909, and Andrews became the county seat in 1910 after a spirited contest against Shafter Lake; in 1911 residents built their first courthouse.

## Andrews Middle School

There are number who say that when you go to Andrews Middle School after dark you can park your car at an angle with your headlights illuminating the front of the school. According to those who have done this, at this point you should see a shadow that spells out " Thirteen ". It is said that this was the tag drawing that a young boy would also use to mark those areas he had been to. Allegedly, he chose the tag thirteen because that was his birthday. It was also the date of the day he died.

## Shafter Lake

Just north of Andrews, Texas, west of Highway 385, is the original location of the county seat of Andrews County, Shafter. It was named after a Confederate general of the same last name. The town was almost completely wiped out by a smallpox epidemic around the turn of the last century, possibly sometime before 1910. Up until about ten years ago, the cemetery where the victims were buried was located on the near edge of the small lake (which comes and goes as it pleases), but the bodies were moved and reentered elsewhere.

There is also a legend that a "lady in white" haunted the graveyard, possibly the reason for its removal. Sometime during the fall of the year, you may also see a troop of Confederate soldiers and their horses galloping across the lake, usually during a full moon. Most think it is General Shafter and his men, who did patrol that area before it was settled, trying to escape Comanche Indians pursing them. By the way, the lake wasn't (and isn't) always there. It just appeared sometime in the forties. The water is very salty, not good for anything, and there is no explanation for its being there at all.

# RANSOM CANYON, TEXAS

As of the census of 2000, there are 1,011 people, 404 households, and 338 families residing in Ransom Canyon. The population density is 470.3/km² (1,213.1/mi²). There are 412 housing units at an average density of 191.7/km² (494.4/mi²). The racial makeup of the town is 95.25% White, 0.40% African American, 0.20% Native American, 0.40% Asian, 0.00% Pacific Islander, 2.57% from other races, and 1.19% from two or more races. 4.85% of the population are Hispanic or Latino.

### Hauntings

There have been a number of hauntings reported from this relatively small town. In the 1880s Apache and Comanche Indians kidnapped white settlers and held them for ransom in this small canyon. The spirits of two twin girls and their mother have been seen near the town's lake. Legend claims that the woman, fearing what would happen to her daughters, drowned them in the lake and then killed herself.

A woman dressed in white walks the area where the modern entrance is. She can be seen in the early morning hours walking up and down the area. The ghost of a deceased cleaning woman was spotted climbing out of a manhole on a Ransom Canyon street in the early morning hours.

A skeleton was witnessed in a college dorm in the Ransom Canyon area. This ghost is very active in this area as there have been many other sightings of this particular ghost. The ghost of a civil war soldier was seen snooping in people's mailboxes around midnight in Ransom Canyon. The ghost of an old lady carrying a rifle was spotted playing a piano in a Ransom Canyon home. The ghost spoke of revenging a murder. Finally, the ghost of a young air force pilot was witnessed trying on shoes in a Ransom Canyon house. Other sightings of this ghost have also been reported.

# ABILENE, TEXAS

Abilene is in the northeast corner of Taylor County. It is situated 1,708 feet above sea level on generally flat terrain. The city is connected east-west by Interstate Highway 20, U.S. Highway 80, and State Highway 36 and north-south by U.S. highways 83, 84, and 277. Reflecting its beginning as a railroad town site, Abilene is bisected by the Texas and Pacific tracks, which run east-west.

Abilene owes its beginning to the Texas and Pacific Railroad and a group of ranchers and land speculators. Before the coming of the railroad, the Abilene area had been sporadically inhabited by nomadic Indians and United States military personnel and later by buffalo hunters and ranchers. By the 1870s the Indians had been driven out, and cattlemen began to graze their herds in the area. Taylor County was organized in 1878, and Buffalo Gap was designated the county seat. When the Texas and Pacific Railway began to push westward in 1880, several ranchers and businessmen-Claiborne W. Merchant, John Merchant, John N. Simpson, John T. Berry, and S. L. Chalk-met with H. C. Whithers, the Texas and Pacific track and town site locator, and arranged to have the railroad bypass Buffalo Gap. They agreed that the route would traverse the northern part of the county and consequently their own land, and that a new town would be established between Cedar and Big Elm creeks east of Catclaw Creek. C. W. Merchant apparently suggested the name Abilene, after the Kansas cattle town.

## Fort Phantom Hill

Located in Jones County, Texas, Fort Phantom Hill is one of the most pristine historic sites in the Lone Star State. Built in the early 1850s to protect the westward moving pioneers, the historic site not only provides today's visitor with a rich historical view of the past, but is also said to be extremely haunted.

In 1849, the federal government sent Captain Randolph B. Marcy to explore the vast region to the north and west of Austin to establish a route through the area. Long inhabited by the warlike Comanche Indians, the area was known as the Comancheria. The purpose of Marcy's exploration was to establish a safer passage for immigrants headed to the California gold fields. As a result of Marcy's recommendations, a cordon of forts, including Fort Phantom Hill, were established on the new route through the Comancheria.

Acting on orders from General Persifor F. Smith, Lieutenant Colonel John J. Abercrombie arrived at the Clear Fork of the Brazos River with five companies of the Fifth Infantry on November 14, 1851. His first impression was not a good one, as a wet snowstorm blew in killing one teamster, and twenty horses, mules, and oxen that froze to death. Also Abercrombie found, much to his dismay, that the site had neither wood for construction nor suitable water for the men and the animals. Though he sent word of the poor conditions the orders were unchanged and construction on the fort began.  What was unknown to both Smith and Abercrombie is that the fort was being built at the wrong location. Smith had just recently taken command from his ailing General who had been supervising the construction of the forts along the route.

The plan had been to build the fort at a site in Coleman County but Smith, unfamiliar with the area, changed the locale to the Clear Fork near its junction with Elm Creek.  This decision affected the post's future as the fort was built in an area with inadequate water and building timbers to supply the needs of new garrison.

Stone was brought in from Elm Creek about two miles south of the fort and oak logs for the officers' quarters and hospital had to be brought in by ox wagon from as far away as forty miles. The guardhouse, magazine and commissary storehouse were built entirely of stone, but the other buildings were built in an adobe style.

Fort Phantom Hill was never officially named. Rather, it was simply referred to as the "Post on the Clear Fork of the Brazos."  There are two legends about the origin of the unofficial designation Phantom Hill, the first of which is that the hill rises sharply from the plains when approached from a distance, but seems to level out as it is approached, vanishing like a phantom. The second account is that of a nervous sentry who fired on what he thought was an Indian on the hill.  The investigation that followed failed to discover the presence of any Indians, and one of the troopers suggested that the man had seen a ghost.

Life at the fort was difficult for the soldiers as Elm Creek was often dry, and the waters of the Clear Fork were brackish. Early on, an eighty-foot-deep well was dug near the guardhouse, but even it was not always reliable. More often than not, it was necessary to haul barrels of water in wagons from a spring about four miles upriver from the post. Because of the lack of water a post garden could not be toiled, leading to a shortage of vegetable in the men's diet.  As a result the soldiers began to suffer from scurvy, fevers, dysentery, colds and pneumonia. Desertions at the fort were said to have been common due to the monotony and loneliness at the isolated fort.

One member of the garrison, Lieutenant Clinton W. Lear wrote a letter to his wife in Fort Washita that described it this way:

*"When I say to you that we have a beautiful valley to look upon, I have said everything favorable that could be said of this place.  We are camped in a grove of blackjack two or three hundred yards from the creek which is alt. Everybody is disgusted.  Like the Dove after the Deluge, not one green sprig can we find to indicate this was ever intended by man to inhabit.  Indeed I cannot imagine that God ever intended for white man to occupy such a barren waste."*

Although the isolated fort was vulnerable to attacks, its garrison had only peaceful encounters with the Indians, including the Comanches, Lipans, Wichitas, Kiowas, and Kickapoos. Because its occupation was relatively uneventful, the fort was abandoned on April 6, 1854. At the time of its evacuation, the Indian menace had been curbed due to the establishment of reservations on the upper Brazos and the Clear Fork to the northeast.

As the troops marched out of Fort Phantom headed toward El Paso, the looked back to discover the fort was in flames. The event was blamed on the Indians or Confederate troops, but many said that it was the members of the garrison, because of their distaste for the post, who set the fire.

In 1858 the remaining structures of the fort were repaired and utilized as a way station the Southern Overland (Butterfield) Mail Stagecoach Line. During the Civil War, Colonel James B. (Buck) Barry and some of his units used Fort Phantom Hill as a base of field operations. Beginning in 1871, the fort served as a subpost of Fort Griffin, near the site of present Albany, Texas.

After the Indian Wars subsided, a town grew up around the fort ruins. In 1876-77, it was a buying and shipping point for buffalo hides. By 1880, Fort Phantom had a population of more than 500 and was made the Jones County seat the following year in May, 1991. However, that was a short lived title, as the county seat was moved just six months later in November to nearby Anson, Texas.

The Texas and Pacific Railway routed its tracks through Abilene, fourteen miles to the south. A letter written to the San Antonio Express in 1892 commented that Fort Phantom contained nothing but "one hotel, one saloon, one general store, one blacksmith shop, and 10,000 prairie dogs." In 1928, John Guitar of Abilene, Texas purchased the property. In 1969, his grandson, Jim Alexander, also of Abilene, deeded the property to the Fort Phantom Foundation to ensure its long-term preservation.

<u>Hauntings</u>

As to the hauntings of the Fort, its name alone suggests that it would only make sense that the place would be alive with spirits from the past. Several legends exist that the place is haunted by restless Indians of frontier times, who continue to stalk their ancient grounds during the night. Another says the fort is haunted by an innocent man who was wrongly hanged near the fort. After his life ended at the end of a rope, his accusers are all said to have died in mysterious ways.

A former Abilene psychic, who visited the fort, said that he suddenly saw the old officers' quarters change into its former complete structure, where he found himself in the parlor. There, two men in officer's uniforms stood before him. One man was said to have been tall and thin, while the other was a red haired short man with piercing eyes. As the psychic stood there in fright, the men glared at him, seemingly unhappy at his intrusion. When he turned to flee, the apparitions and the restored building faded.

The nearby Lake Fort Phantom Hill is also said to be haunted by a watery spirit who is familiarly called the "Lady of the Lake." This phantom woman is said to have been seen numerous times, the first of which almost 150 years ago, long be the lake even existed.  Dressed in a light-colored long gown or robe the watery ghost is said have been seen wandering aimlessly around the lakeside.  Others who have seen her described the apparition as floating over the lake, sometimes carrying a lantern and surrounded by a bluish glow.

Who is this restless spirit?  The answer to this question provides as many legends and the spirit herself.  The first legend says she was the wife of a pioneer who built a small cabin in the woods that are now filled with Lake Phantom.  In the midst of the dangerous Comancheria, the cabin was often attacked by Indians.  To protect themselves the couple made a pact that no one would enter the cabin without first speaking a secret password.  If the code word wasn't given, they were to shoot anything or anyone that tried to enter.  One day when the man had gone out hunting he was ambushed by Indians as he approaching his cabin.  Injured, he managed to escape and began clawing at the door to his cabin.  Forgetting about his password or unable to say it, his wife shot him before he cleared the stoop.  According to legend, the forlorn woman continues to wander the lake, cursed for eternity for killing her husband.

A second legend says the when a couple were to meet at a church near the lake in the mid 1940s to exchange wedding vows, the groom never arrived.  After hours of waiting and sure that he would not have left her standing at the altar, she begged authorities to look for her groom.  The next morning he was found dressed in his finest suit floating in a boat in the middle of the lake.  Though the man's face bore and expression of severe pain, doctors could not determine the cause of death.  Some say the spirit was the bride searching for her fiancé's killer.

A third legend places the spirit at a much later date in the early 1980s.  According to this tale, a young woman and her lover agree to mete at the lake for an evening of romance.  However, when the young man arrived he was enraged by a rumor he had heard about her and the two began to quarrel. The disagreement grew worse ending in the man drowning her in the lake. In this version, it is the murdered woman who wanders the lake.

Finally, if you were to ask anyone of Hispanic descent, they would most assuredly tell you that the ghostly woman is that of La Llorona, who is often seen about the lakes and rivers of the southwest.

In any event, there have been literally hundreds of sightings throughout the years of the Lady of the Lake, who seemingly doesn't keep her excursions only at lakeside.  She has also said to have been seen at a nearby cemetery as well as along a dirt road called Lover's Lane.  One couple sighting her at Lover's Lane described her as walking along the road; however, when she grew closer, they could see that the apparition had not eyes.

Other strange phenomena around the lake include the sounds of screams, moaning, gunshots and rapping upon vehicle windows.  Others report smells of decaying flesh, perfume and roses. Dogs at the lake have been noticed to go into unprovoked snapping and barking at seemingly invisible visitors.

## The Anson Light

The Anson light is actually just one light (bluish in color) and if you try to drive towards it goes away. Turn the car around so that it is facing the cemetery. Then flash you headlight 3 times. This is in keeping with those who say that this light is held by a woman who died long ago but still looks for her children. She lived near the cemetery and as she watched for her children to come home at night she would flash her lantern and they would flash back to let her know they where coming. There is, in fact, a cemetery off the highway and you take the dirt road down to the crossroads.

It is not uncommon to see road kill near this cemetery.  There have been a number of reports of people switching off their car engines as they waited for the light and when they went to start their cars, the engine was dead. A lot of people have claimed that it's just lights from the highway, but then how can a light from the highway approach within fifty feet of someone near the cemetery?

## Taylor County Expo Center,  1700 Hwy. 36, Abilene, Texas 79602

The Livestock Barn, which also includes the Griffin Arena, contains 600 cattle ties, 400 sheep and swine pens, a show arena, wash racks, excellent sound system, newly remodeled restrooms and office space for livestock show officials. Equipped with a portable concession stand, this building is ready for any type of livestock event.

What surprises most is that this ultra modern facility also comes complete with its own ghosts. Visitors and workers have reported hearing strange footsteps, voices and noises late at night, when there has been no one else around. For a fun time, go check out the cow barn.

## The Travel Lodge Motel

Three connected rooms in this Travel Lodge Motel are haunted. In one of the rooms the light in the bathroom will flicker on and off throughout the night (the switch is sideways, making a loud clicking noise). In another room a specter plays with the visitors belongings. It likes to use their credit cards, money, and driver's license to play a game of poker under the bed. In the last room during the hours of 12 and 2:30 a foul smell is present in the room, which is said to be the same spirit that likes to play with the lights and belongings.

There was also a case where a mysterious man wearing all green and a cap that concealed all of his face except for his red beard was seen working in the office in the early morning hours; the next day it was discovered that no men were employed at this motel, yet he had a set of keys and checked in customers. There were no other employees at the establishment at the time.

# ALBANY, TEXAS

This postcard of a town is on the West Texas/Panhandle border. The Albany Chamber of Commerce is in the old railroad depot, a proper bookstore on the square, restored Aztec Theater and Art Center in the Old Jail. 1883 Courthouse has clock and bell. Albany Guide published twice a year to correspond with the County's two major events: The Fort Griffin Fandandle (last two weekends of June) and hunting season. If every small town was like this, we'd never stay home.

## Rail Road Tracks

The legend that is told here is that many years ago there was a wreck on the nearby railroad track and it killed a number of children. Today, late at night if you switch off your vehicle while parked on the tracks and put baby powder on the bumper of your car, later you will see hand prints from the children trying to push your car across the tracks.

# ANSON, TEXAS

Eighteen miles southeast of Hamlin, at the junction of US-180, sits Anson, named in honor of Dr. Anson Jones, the last president of the Republic of Texas. Anson was also a stop on the legendary Butterfield Stage U.S. Mail route that ran between St. Louis and San Francisco from 1858 to 1861, but these days it feels more like a stage set for The Last Picture Show, with handsome blocks of brick-fronted buildings forming a square around the stately Jones County Courthouse at the center of town. Anson is still a center for the local cotton industry, but its main claim to fame is the Cowboys' Christmas Ball, described in an 1890 poem by William Lawrence "Larry" Chittenden and recently re-awakened by the involvement of country-folk singer Michael Martin Murphey, who did a Christmas show there in 1995.

## Anson Lights

The story was covered by the television series Unsolved Mysteries several years ago. Many residents from Anson and the nearby town of Abilene have gone to witness these phenomenal lights. The cemetery is located going towards the country. The lights are viewed by driving down the dirt farm road equivalent of about a half mile or more. As you drive closer to the cemetery towards the lights they disappear.

As locals tell it, one night during the Depression a young mother ran frantically along the road searching for her missing child, slipping in icy ruts as she stumbled through the cold winter darkness. She never found her little one; the child had wandered away from the house and was presumed to have frozen to death. The mother's spirit still searches for her child, holding her lantern high to light her way in the dark night.

## Haunted Bridge on the outskirts of town

An old metal bridge in the outskirts is supposedly haunted by some hanging victim. It is extremely loud if you drive on it and if walked upon footstep can be heard underneath and wind blowing on one side yet be calm on the other.

# BORGER, TEXAS

Borger, at the junction of State highways 136, 152, and 207, in south central Hutchinson County, was established by and named for A. P. (Ace) Borger, who was reputed throughout Oklahoma and Texas to be a shrewd town promoter. In March 1926, after the discovery of oil in the vicinity, Borger and his partner, attorney John R. Miller, purchased a 240-acre town site near the Canadian River in the southern part of the county. Within ninety days of its founding, sensational advertising and the lure of "black gold" brought over 45,000 men and women to the new boomtown. In October the charter incorporating the city of Borger was adopted, and Miller was elected mayor. By that time the Panhandle and Santa Fe Railway had completed a spur line to Borger, a post office had opened, and a school district had been established. J. D. (Big Heart) Williams set up the first hamburger stand in Borger on the three-mile-long Main Street, where a hotel and a jail had also been erected. Telephone service and steam-generated electricity were available by the end of 1926. Before wells were drilled, drinking water was provided in tank wagons.

The ranchers John R. Weatherly and James A. Whittenburg, hoping to cash in on the boom, established two rival town sites, Isom and Dixon Creek, next to that of Borger. Later these were incorporated into the Borger city limits, as was the oil camp of Signal Hill to the northeast. In November 1927 a fire destroyed the Dixon Creek Oil Company refinery, causing more than $60,000 worth of damage.

## Hutchinson County Museum, 618 N. Main, (Borger, Texas) [11]

The door was locked to the Hutchinson County Museum in Amarillo as the Museum was officially closed. The only people inside were several members of the Friends of the Museum who were discussing fund raising. A sudden noise came from another room as the meeting was about to begin.

"It sounded like some fellow was in the other room whistling," says Museum director Ed Benz. "There were seven other people there who heard the same thing I heard."

---

[11] http://www.weird-wi.com/ghostwatch/feb2001.htm

Several went to investigate, but found the place was empty. "So we all came back and had a big laugh – it was just the museum ghost."

Despite their laughter, the Friends had been unnerved by the sound, and within ten minutes "we all kinda nervously left." Benz claims many paranormal events have taken place in the Museum.

"Some people have told me that ghosts come in with some of the artifacts. Other people have said there was so much humanity and population on Main Street in the 1920s that it leaves some kind of electrical energy. It was a pretty wild place back then; who knows what was left behind." Some skeptics have dismissed the ghosts as wind rattling around the old building. But when Benz heard seven footsteps and chains dragging across the wood floor, it raised goose bumps and the hair on the back of his neck, making him a believer. "They are like friendly ghosts. None have really been bad ... just kind of freaky. The lights will go out for no reason. The alarm has gone off. ... Some staffers have actually heard voices speak to them."

The sound of someone clearing their throat, non-functioning electronic displays starting up, sounds of spurs hitting the floor as if someone invisible was walking, radios playing by themselves, strange voices, and a painting that just appeared on the wall of the cellar have also been reported.

## Morley Movie Theater

The Morley Movie Theater has been around a long time. It was built as a protection theater, never having had live acts as did so many of the old theaters. No one seems to know where the ghost came from, but there is no question that there is a spirit that haunts this silent building. The "Morley" ghost's appearances may be responsible for this theater failing 3 times.

## Plemons Bridge

There is a ghost town called Plemons that is located just a little ways outside of Borger. Plemons, way back when, used to be a fairly good-sized town, but then the Spanish Flu epidemic hit in about 1916 and a large number of residents died from this deadly virus.

To get to Plemons, a visitor has to cross an old, rickety bridge. Several people have died on that bridge. Some of them died when their cars mysteriously ran off the bridge and drowned in the Canadian River below. Others died because of the Ku Klux Klan. The Klan used to have their secret meetings down by the river, and according to legend, the Klan killed several black men by hanging them on the bridge or drowning them.

There is another story about a teenager who died on the bridge because he was drinking and driving really fast on the old, dark country road that leads up to it. The turn from the bridge came up sooner than he thought and he crashed into the steel beams. One of those beams busted through the windshield, right into the driver's head, nearly decapitating the driver.

There are a number of other stories that I have heard about this old rusted span across the Canadian River. One story holds that if you drive across the river real slow with your lights turned off that the ghosts that haunt the bridge would communicate with the driver by making the lights of the car flash on and off in Morse Code. There was one young lady who claimed that she had seen this phenomenon up close and personal. She said her car lights started flashing and a guy who was riding with her knew Morse Code. The lights, he said, were blinking this message: "D-E-A-T-H/D-E-A-T-H" over and over. It freaked her out and she gunned the engine and got out of there.

It is also said that if you walk across the bridge, strange people will try to pull you down underneath it.

## BUFFALO GAP, TEXAS

In ancient days, great herds of buffalo favored this gap in the Callahan Divide, a few miles south of present-day Abilene, and it soon became a favored camping place for native peoples. As settlement approached, U.S. soldiers patrolled and skirmished in the area. Hide hunters and cattlemen arrived in the 1870s.

After the Indians and the buffalo passed into history, settlers came to the gap, drawn to its abundant water and good grazing. A new town called Buffalo Gap arose, the first capital of Taylor County. A county courthouse, a two-story limestone structure combining a courtroom and a jail, was completed in 1879. In the following years, the face of the area changed rapidly. Soon, steel rails criss-crossed the once-wild land, horsepower no longer meant horse-drawn wagons, and motor cars churned up dust once trod by shaggy bison and Indian ponies. The county seat was moved to the new city of Abilene in 1883. Buffalo Gap's history is described in detail in the Handbook of Texas.

Buffalo Gap Historic Village originated as a historical site in 1956. Ernest Walter (Ernie) Wilson purchased the courthouse building and established a small historical museum of Indian and Western artifacts. Wilson, a well known lawyer, historian, churchman, and rancher, eventfully brought in two other Taylor County structures, the Hill House and the Knight/Sayles Cabin.

### Old Buffalo Gap School

On the site of this old school building, in the 1800's a farmer accidentally shot and killed his wife. Overcome with remorse at what he had done, he went insane, burning down their house and taking his own life. Now it is said that anyone who is in the school can hear the dead woman's favorite possession, a mantle clock, going "tick-tock, tick-tock".

## CACTUS, TEXAS

Cactus began in 1942 as an Ordnance plant run by the Chemical Construction Company for the government. The facility was huge – with 16 sections of land being purchased to house the workers. It was one of the largest in the country. Completed in 1943 – the main product was ammonium nitrate. Other facilities opened to take care of ammonium nitrate production and Shell Union Oil Company began an aviation fuel facility in early 1944. Other changes were made after the war – the largest being the plants absorption by Phillips Chemical in 1948. The post office was opened that year for the 2,000 people who remained in the area, but over the years the population declined to where there were only 898 people in the early 80s.

### <u>Cactus City Park</u>

Some kids were playing basketball in the Cactus City Park the ball rolled on to the street. One of the kids ran after the ball without noticing that a car was coming. The car hit him and now it is said that the little boy is heard every single day crying and mourning that he never will grow out of this misery.

## CANYON, TEXAS

Canyon, located in Randall County, is at the junction of U.S. Highway 60 and Interstate Highway 27, near the center of Randall County and southwest of the old T Anchor Ranch headquarters[12]. In December 1887 Lincoln Guy Conner surveyed and settled at the site. He laid out the town in the spring of 1889, his dugout serving as home, general store, and post office. A. L. Hammond established the second business and a blacksmith shop, and suggested the name Canyon City, after nearby Palo Duro Canyon, when Conner refused to have the settlement named after himself. When Randall County was organized in July 1889 Conner's home was the voting place for that precinct, and Canyon City was chosen as the county seat.

Lumber for commercial buildings was hauled from Quanah by mule-drawn freight wagons. A temporary, two-room frame building served as a courthouse, where church services and other community gatherings were held. Conner established the town's first real estate office and built the Victoria Hotel. Beginning in August 1890 several newspapers, the Echo, the Keystone, the Headlight, and the Battleship, appeared briefly. In 1896 Mrs. R. W. Morgan began publishing the Stayer; George A. Brandon renamed this paper the Canyon City News after buying it in 1903. The first telephone line reached Canyon City from Amarillo in 1896.

---

[12] http://www.tsha.utexas.edu/handbook/online/articles/CC/hec1.html.

## **Panhandle Plains Museum, 2503 4<sup>th</sup> Avenue, Canyon, Texas 79015**

Hattie Anderson moved to Canyon, Texas in 1920 to teach history at West Texas State Normal College. She was captivated by what she found. It was an historian's dream - a bustling city on the grow, eager young college students preparing to be teachers and a significant number of the area's original settlers still actively involved in ranching, farming, and business[13].

In early 1921, Miss Anderson, L.F. Sheffy (the head of the college's history department), seven other faculty members and about thirty students organized the Panhandle-Plains Historical Society. Their goal was to collect and preserve the history, both human and natural, of the region. They also began soliciting support for their efforts in the form of Society memberships.

Since 1921, Hattie Anderson's dream of preserving the region's history has grown into the supporting organization for the largest history museum in the state of Texas. Approximately 100,000 guests visit the Panhandle-Plains Historical Museum each year. On the campus of what is now West Texas A&M University, the Museum has more than a million artifacts, ranging from the Comanche Chief Quanah Parker's eagle feather headdress to collections of historic New Mexico and Texas art.

Hauntings

No one knows why Sarah Jane lurks in the east annex at the Panhandle-Plains Historical Museum. But, for at least the past three decades, some museum employees have seen the apparition[14].

An account printed in the summer/fall 1989 issue of a West Texas State University magazine quotes Ann Bacon's experiences as campus custodial worker. Bacon recalled seeing a spirit that she said identified herself as "Sarah Jane" as early as 1975. A young woman in her 20s, Sarah Jane was always spotted near an early 20th century horse-drawn war ambulance in the museum's east annex. When spotted, she was wearing a long, full calico dress and had reddish-brown hair and frequently was swinging a bonnet by the ribbons, according to several accounts.

"Evidently Miss Bacon asked (Sarah Jane) if there was something she could do to help her, but there was never an answer," Vanderpool said.

There is also an old ambulance-wagon that sits in the middle of the car/wagon room. The ghostly woman known as "Sara Jane" is sometimes seen standing near the ambulance, and several visitors have experienced headaches, feelings of panic, and the smell of blood as they pass by the old vehicle.

## **Home at 902 Fifth Avenue**

Bill Green, curator of history at the Panhandle Plains Historical Museum, hasn't seen Sarah Jane, but he believes in ghosts. In fact, he says that his own

---

[13] http://www.panhandleplains.org/about/society_info.php
[14] http://getout.amarillo.com/content/getout/102904_getintospirit.shtml

home is haunted. Green's Canyon home, built in 1906, is located at 902 Fifth Ave., formerly Evelyn Street. He bought the home in 2001 and met the ghost, or ghosts, shortly thereafter.

He believes the ghost is that of Myrtle Cartwright Park, wife of Canyon banker David Ayers Park, for whom the home was built. Myrtle was one of two daughters of Dr. J.W. Cartwright, one of Amarillo's first physicians.

In the summer of 1909, she was in the cellar washing utensils after milking the family cow one evening. "She reached up to turn on the light bulb and was electrocuted instantly and fell dead in her husband's arms," Green said.

Green had been in the home only a few days when he heard a noise, as though someone was walking around in the house. At first, he thought the noise might have been caused by someone who had been staying in the formerly vacant home.

He spent an hour looking in every corner, closet and cubbyhole with a flashlight. He found nothing, but after he returned to bed, he still heard noises. Later, he confirmed that one previous owner also had seen an apparition of a woman sitting in a chair in the home. But Green's roommate has lived there a few years and never seen or heard the ghost.

Still, Green sees signs of Myrtle in unexplained openings or closings of doors in the night, as though someone has walked through the home. "We just laugh and say 'Myrtle's been up to it again.' It's fun. I don't mind ghosts at all. I believe there are spirits around us, and she's a friendly ghost," Green said.

## West Texas A&M University Lobby

The West Texas A&M University Lobby is known to be haunted a girl got murdered there a while back. It is haunted by a young lady who walks in the dorms and in the halls of the dorms. She has also been seen on the elevator. Also to be said there is one dorm room that has they say like an underground thing that leads all over the dorms. At midnight if you park your car at the Wal-Mart parking lot you will see a light go on and the girl will be standing there looking out the window. Also if you live in the dorms you will smell popcorn popping at 12:30.

## West Texas A&M University Stafford Hall

For years, the women of Stafford Hall at West Texas A&M University have claimed the dorm is cursed with a ghost. Some stories claim a girl was murdered in the dorm's H wing. Others say a loner committed suicide there. Neither story, apparently, is true, but the urban legends live on in stories passed down via the Internet and through speech Professor Trudy Hanson's storytelling class.

Hanson, who assigns students in the class to tell the story frequently, said the presence has been seen both in the form of a person and in the form of an unidentifiable shape. "There is no back story about why there would be a presence there," she said. "We don't have a story that would explain what that presence might be."

Freshman Marie Dominguez has lived in the dorm for only a few months, but already, she has felt that presence. Dominguez said she sometimes gets a strange, cold feeling and sees shadows that she can't quite make out at night. Whether it's a ghost or all in the imagination, Dominguez said just living at Stafford Hall can be eerie. "It's scary here," she said.

# DUMAS, TEXAS

Dumas, the county seat of Moore County, is at the junction of U.S. highways 87 and 287 in the center of the county. It was named for Louis Dumas, president of the Panhandle Townsite Company in Sherman, who purchased railroad survey lands in the Panhandle. In January 1891 Dumas and his associates formed the Moore County Townsite Company and platted the town on a site some five miles south of South Palo Duro Creek. The first building housed the company office, a hotel, a general store, and the first post office. James C. Wilson served as first postmaster and was followed by John F. Patterson, who opened a general store later that year. The following year Moore County was organized, and Dumas was elected county seat. By then several lots had been sold and a courthouse erected. The first school was constructed in 1892 on the block west of the courthouse.

## <u>Dumas Jr. High</u>

In the North Gym at Dumas Jr. High there was a group of JR High girls practicing Volleyball. After practice everyone left except this one girl. No one came to pick her up so she decided to go back into the gym to wait for her ride. The janitor, seeing that she was alone, went into the gym and attacked the girl. She struggled and finally, he stabbed the girl and then himself. If you are in there by yourself you can hear the girl screaming for help and the janitor laughing at what he was doing.

# EARTH, TEXAS

Earth, Texas is a small farming community located approximately 70 miles northwest of Lubbock, 90 miles southwest of Amarillo, 45 miles west of Plainview, and 40 miles east of the Texas/New Mexico line. State Highway 70 and Farm Road 1055 intersect at the only stop light in this northwestern Lamb county town. Established in 1924 by William E. Halsell, Earth was first called "Tulsa," but the postal authorities rejected this name. Although it is not clear how the name Earth was chosen, most people believe that a local resident, O. H. Reeves, suggested the name "Good Earth" because of the fertile soil in the surrounding area. However, the name was shortened to Earth and a post office was established on May 25, 1925.

The community continued to grow and many businesses emerged. The town's population hit its peak in 1980 at 1,512. This economic growth was due, in part, to the development of irrigation on the farms and the establishment of Plant X, an electrical plant three miles south of Earth.

## Earth High School

Many Students that have attended Earth High School have been killed over the years in car accidents. It is believed that some of them, possibly along with a teacher that was killed in a car wreck, may haunt the gym, the auditorium, and the band hall. If you go into the gym alone, you can hear people talking in the girls' locker room. No one wants to go into the auditorium alone, because the janitors have reported hearing the same ghostly sounds every day while cleaning. It's so bad that they now turn a radio up full blast just so they won't have to hear it.

# EOLA, TEXAS

Eola is a small agricultural community first settled in 1898 on vast Midwest Texas ranch lands of Concho County. Original name of Jordan changed in 1903 with establishment of post office. Name, taken from nearby creek, is Indian for "good returns from blowing wind."

## Old Middle School

The Old Middle School is now closed, but according to the story, some children died when a boiler blew up. Many people who have gone into the school since that time have gotten a weird feeling when walking through it. During Halloween the school is sometimes opened up as a haunted house. During the setups and the "haunted tours" a number of truly weird things have happened such as doors slamming and footsteps being heard.

# FLOYDADA, TEXAS

Floydada was established by M.C. Williams in 1890. Floydada is designated county seat in an election against Della Plain. The County's namesake was Dolphin Ward Floyd, who died at the Alamo. At one time the town's name had been Floyd City. There are at least three versions on how the Ada was added: "Some claim the new name was meant to be Floydalia and was garbled in transmission to Washington; others say it was a combination of the county name and that of donor James Price's mother, Ada; still another version is that it was named for Caroline Price's parents, Floyd and Ada."

## Lamplighter Hotel

In Floydada, two spirits, Floyd and Ada, haunt the Lamplighter Inn. Ada smells of lilacs; Floyd smells of Old Spice. Apparitions have been spotted here. They also have window shades that won't stay put and ghostly noises.

Michelle Ruddell is the current new owner of the old hotel, having bought the old building at an auction. According to a news story I read, she plans on making it into a Women's Christian Job Corps office called The Maker's Mansion.

According to folklore, the old Commercial Hotel[15] in Floydada, built in 1912, is home to two ghosts, Floyd and Ada. A pair of man's legs has been seen running up the stairs, and a woman dressed in 1930s-era clothing also has been seen, the story goes. According to legend, a past owner got up one morning to find that a table had set itself for lunch. Others have reported feeling cold breezes during periods there was no wind outside. Finally, there have been reports of whistling being heard coming form the upstairs area when it was known that there was no one upstairs.

# HEREFORD, TEXAS

Hereford was born on September 1, 1898. Troy Womble was given the honor of being called the first resident. His photograph was made on March 3, 1898, as he stood in the door of his dugout which was located 40 yards west of what is now Highway 385 and 10 feet south of the present railroad track. The town took the name from the registered Hereford cattle brought in by L. R. Bradly and G. R. Jowell from Hereford, England.

## Victorian House

There is a Victorian style house in Hereford that has long had the reputation as being haunted. Visitors and tenants report hearing mysterious music, ghostly steps and voices. Often those in the house detect cigar smoke and there have been a number of reports of moving objects. All of these unusual happenings are attributed to "Jack".

## The Tower

The Tower is said to be haunted. The haunting is alleged to stem from an incident that occurred here where several men killed a young boy. According to the story, they took him out there to the Tower where they said there were going to go be a party. Looking for a good time, the boy went with them. The story is to be that when they got out there with the boy they chopped him up and ate him.

The police apprehended these men and they were eventually convicted of murdering the boy. Now it is said that when you drive out there while you are

---

[15] AKA The Lamplighter

driving along the paved road to the Tower, you will be enveloped in a cloud of dust. If you drive on through the cloud and arrive at the tower, if you roll your window down, you will hear terrible screams that are alleged to be the screams of the young boy calling for help.

No one has yet entered the tower. But there is also another past to this tower. Hereford was a war ground they fought here and they say that the tower was where they kept the prisoners.

## KALGARY, TEXAS

Kalgary is on Farm Road 261 fifty-five miles southeast of Lubbock in southeastern Crosby County. It began around 1905 as Spur, when E. P. Swenson started selling parcels of his vast 437,670-acre SMS Ranch. It then became known as Watson, for early settler Richard Watson Self. To accommodate the growing number of children in the area, the Watson school was constructed in 1907 with Rae Nichols as the teacher. A post office opened at the community in 1911, closed from 1913 to 1925, and was permanently discontinued in 1955.

The name of the community was changed from Watson to Kalgary in 1927, when it was discovered that a second Texas community was named Watson. Kalgary had a population of ten in the early 1930s. The community reached a peak in 1940 with a population of 100, three stores, and a gin. The Kalgary school district, known as Self County Line, began consolidating with that of Crosbyton in 1949, and after the local school burned in October 1952, no further classes were held in the community. In 1980 and 1990 Kalgary reported a population of 140.

### Stampede Mesa

According to the story, in the fall of 1889 the area was a frequent stop for trail herds. The area was good for the tall grass, the water and a high place to spot trouble for some distance away. For one trail boss trouble came in an unexpected fashion. The men had accidentally driven their herd through the property of a farmer and had driven his cows up the Mesa with their own. The Farmer arrived on a scrawny white mare and demanded his cows back.

There was no argument with that, they had no use for his cows, which were just as skinny and malcontent as both the farmer and his horse, but they did have a problem when he also cut out some of their cattle and began to drive them away. An argument ensued that the trail men were too tired and hungry to endure. The old farmer was instructed to come back at daybreak when the sun was up and he had a "better chance of seeing things" the cowboy's way. Cursing bitterly the farmer, embarrassed not only by being caught stealing but also in having to leave his own stock, rode his old scrawny horse back down the Mesa.

The men gratefully ate and prepared to sleep. Their rest was to be short lived for in the night the cattle stampeded. Incredibly, since they seem to be driven away from the North and heading south, they headed straight for the steepest part of the canyon. Every man knew his job and did his best but when the sun came up that morning two men and hundreds of steers lay dead at the bottom of the canyon. Men who had witness the beginning of the stampede claimed to have seen the old Farmer and his white mare driving the cattle toward the cliffs edge.

The Trail Boss decided to let the punishment fit the crime. He had the Farmer dragged up the hill, his hands tied, his eyes blindfolded and then ordered he be tied to his likewise blindfold horse and driven off the edge of the Mesa. Of course this is not the end of the story. The Farmer still blindfolded and tied to his horse has been seen countless times. And word began to spread from cowboy to trail driver not to camp on Stampede Mesa lest your herd or your men share his fate as he would try to drive men, horse, and steer over the cliff where his body had been left to rot. A number of people have reported seeing a Ghost herd and a single rider on Stampede Mesa.

# LEVELLAND, TEXAS

Levelland was literally once the home on the range where the buffalo roamed and the antelope played. But by the beginning of the 20th century, enterprising ranchers and farmers were beginning to transform the area's boundless sea of grass into cattle ranches and crop production. One enterprising entrepreneur, C. W. Post, the cereal king, wanted to go further. He bought the Oxsheer Ranch with the idea of developing a town site. For some reason he did not pursue it, but the town site he had selected eventually became the county seat, first known as Hockley City. However, when the post office discovered there was another town in Texas by the same name, the enterprising women of the county took one look at the uninterrupted landscape and came up with the name of Levelland.

That was in 1921, and a general mercantile store and the city's first church and school first popped up. Levelland got a boost in 1925 with the arrival of the railroad, and the 1920s saw the explosion of farms throughout the county. During the 1930s, oil was discovered in Hockley County, ushering in a new industry and a new era for the area.

Today, Hockley County is the fifth biggest producer of oil in Texas and celebrated its billionth barrel of oil drilled in 1982. The county is also the fifth largest producer in Texas of cotton. A number of business related have sprung up which depend on the economic strength of the two major industries. Levelland is the heart of this agricultural and oil producing region, which includes a number of historic ranches, such as the Spade and Mallett Ranches.

## Phantom Ambulance

The phantom ambulance is generally seen on FM 1490 just outside of town. Many people who have no prior knowledge of the legend have pulled over for this ambulance which comes roaring toward them. Most witnesses who have agreed to talk about it say that when the ambulance reaches the witness, it simply vanishes. Because it is one of the old-fashioned kind many mistake it for a patrol car in their rearview mirrors.

## Rural Health Clinic

As much of Texas is rural, there have been many health clinics established in small out of the way areas for the local inhabitants. Many of the doctors and nurses who staff these facilities are dedicated to the care of those in the area. At one rural health clinic near Levelland, there is a story that an old nurse died during her shift. Though medical care was immediately available, she did not report that she was feeling bad. Now many patients and staff members report seeing the old nurse walking the halls of the clinic, as she continues to carry out her duties. She is especially diligent about checking on patients.

## Levelland High School, 704 11th St, Levelland, TX 79336

The story is told that a group of seniors were telling ghost stories one evening during a rehearsal in the School Theater and someone said that a student had died in the auto mechanic department in the mid 1990s. At this point an argument erupted over whether or not the story was real and finally it was decided that they could go to the school janitors who would surely have seen a ghost if there was one about.

According to the janitors, the story was true that a boy had died there. He was electrocuted; and that someone had died in the gym as well when the school was being built. They had seen a tall man dressed in black wondering the halls. A teacher's husband had seen a girl in the library and then two cheerleaders said they heard the sound of little feet chasing them in the library one night.

These same students then decided to track down the ghosts that haunted the school so every evening a group of these students, in company with the janitors would patrol the corridors of the school. They filmed these ghost hunts with a video camera and for several nights found nothing. Finally, on one patrol, one of the students reported hearing piano music that the rest of the group did not hear. However, at the time, no one saw anything.

However, when the students later replayed the tape of that night, they saw a man at the end of the hallway, wearing a white shirt. The piano music could also be heard on the tape. Unfortunately, never again were they able to catch anything on camera, nor hear anything out of the ordinary.

# MATADOR, TEXAS

Matador, on U.S. Highway 62/70, State Highway 70, and Farm Road 94, thirty-one miles east of Floydada and thirty-two miles west of Paducah in central Motley County, was named for the Matador Ranch, which was established in 1879 at Ballard Springs. A ranch post office named Matador opened in 1886 before the town existed. When the county was organized in 1891 Matador was designated county seat after Matador Ranch manager Henry H. Campbell laid out a town site and encouraged cowboys to set up one-day businesses to meet the General Land Office requirement that a county seat have twenty commercial enterprises. Campbell was the county's first elected judge, and cowboy Joe Beckham was the first sheriff.

## US HWY 70

Though much of it unconfirmed highway 70 between Matador and Paduca, TX has a lot of deadly history. Many car accidents have occurred in this area. Since the nearest hospital being over 80 miles away many accident victims do not survive. Driving through at night along this stretch of highway can also give you a complete sense of dread.

Some drivers have claimed that on the highway they became very agitated wondering if what they were feeling was real. Some even found themselves wondering if they were alive or dead. Paranoia is the strongest emotion felt here. Many of these drivers have also claimed to see lights and refractions coming from the Matador Cemetery. This desolate highway has very little to offer in the way of peace. It however has much to offer in the way of death.

# MIDLAND, TEXAS

Midland, the county seat of Midland County, is on Interstate Highway 20, U.S. Highway 80, State highways 158, 191, 349, the Missouri Pacific Railroad, and numerous county and local roads, twenty miles northeast of Odessa and thirty-nine miles southwest of Big Spring in the north central part of the county at 32°00' north latitude and 102°10' west latitude[16]. The elevation is 2,779 feet. Midland Draw runs through the northern section of the city limits. In late June 1881 the Texas and Pacific Railway, which was building its line between Dallas and El Paso, established Midway Station, a section house, halfway between those two cities.

The first permanent resident was Herman N. Garrett, who moved to Midway from California with a herd of sheep in 1882. Over the next two years a number of other ranchers moved into the area, and a post office was granted on January 4, 1884, when the area was still attached to Tom Green County. Because other towns in Texas were already named Midway, the site was renamed Midland to get the post office. In early 1884 an Ohio real estate firm bought land at the site, established the Midland Town Company, and began to promote the settlement across the Midwest. The company drilled three water wells and held a successful land auction; by early 1885 there were 100 families living at the site. When Midland County was organized in March 1885, Midland became the

---

[16] http://www.tsha.utexas.edu/handbook/online/articles/MM/hdm3.html

county seat. A new courthouse was built by January 1886; later that year Baptist and Methodist churches were established in the town, and Midland's first school was opened. Before long the town's newspaper, the Midland Gazette, was promoting Midland as "the Queen City of the South Plains."

## Museum of the Southwest, 1705 W. Missouri Ave Midland, Texas 79701

The Museum of the Southwest, Midland, Texas is one of the country's most interactive and imaginative blends of art and science, and features an Art Museum, Children's Museum, and a Planetarium. It is a cultural center for all ages and interests.

The Museum of the Southwest is housed in the historic Turner/Thomas House Mansion, originally built in 1934. The Turner/Thomas Mansion, on the National Register of Historic Places, was the first of many homes designed by architects for oil barons. The 50,000-square-foot complex now serves as an ornate setting for traveling exhibitions and permanent collections of art focusing on the Southwest. The original owner of the house was murdered, now there are reports of strange banging and general spookiness in certain parts of the historic old home.

# PAMPA, TEXAS

Pampa, the county seat and largest town in Gray County, is at the junction of U.S. highway 60 and State highways 70, 152, and 273, in the northwestern part of the county. The site, once owned by the Francklyn Land and Cattle Company (later White Deer Land Company), was designated as a station on the Southern Kansas Railway in the summer of 1887. The first resident was Thomas H. Lane, the railroad section foreman, who settled his family in a half-dugout near the boxcar station, which was known initially as Glasgow and then as Sutton. Because of confusion with Sutton County, railroad officials asked George Tyng, manager of the White Deer Land Company, to select a new name for Sutton. After his first suggestions were rejected by the chief engineer, Tyng submitted the name Pampa because the place resembled the pampas of Argentina, which he had earlier visited. The post office opened in 1892 with Lane as postmaster.

Tyng constructed Pampa's first frame building as the White Deer Land Company boardinghouse. This building later was leased to the Matador Ranch as a headquarters and then sold to Alfred Ace Holland, who made it the town's first hotel. As early as December 1, 1889, Tyng had recommended that the White Deer Land Company establish a town at the Sutton station. In 1898 Russell Benedict, associate of trustee Frederic Foster, came from New York to investigate this possibility.

## Worley Hospital

Oil money spawned the Worley Hospital so that the newly created wealthy residents would have first class medical care. However, time does not respect man's accomplishments and Worley Hospital was abandoned many years ago. It lies empty and silent in the middle of downtown Pampa. The historic building has been broken into several times, and graffiti covers the wall.

There are a number of manifestations that are said to occur within the walls of this building. There is an incinerator on the third floor that shakes violently when opened. There is usually a distant female scream immediately after opening it. However, the eeriest room in the building is the nursery. It is always extremely cold, and surprisingly it is the only room in the building that has not been touched by vandals. Several other unusual noises are generally heard in this area as well.

# PLAINVIEW, TEXAS

The County was named after John Hale, who fell at San Jacinto. Plainview is named after no person, but the unobstructed view of the countryside. Hale County was formed in the country's centennial year, before there was any community. In 1888 there were enough people to organize and declare Plainview the county seat[17].

The railroad came in 1907 and then they hit on the idea of tapping into the underground water which was (and is) abundant. An east-west railroad (Fort Worth and Denver) joined the north-south Santa Fe, and the rest as they say is history.

## Old Hilton Hotel

Though there are those that say that the Hilton Hotel in Plainview was the first one that Conrad Hilton built to carry his name, this is not true. The first Hilton Hotel named after Conrad Hilton was actually built in El Paso, Texas. The Old Hilton in Plainview has been closed down for many years, but the place is not empty, as it is said to be haunted. Several rooms still have the curtains hanging in the windows that have been seen moving even though no one is in the building.

There is also a rumor that the place was broken into by Satanists. They were said to have performed ceremonies to call forth demons, which are now trapped there. There is even a story about Room 529. It is said to have an open Bible lying in the floor. If you enter the room, the air suddenly turns icy and the pages in the Bible begin to turn.

Interestingly enough, some of the hauntings in that haunted hotel are also taking place in the El Paso Hilton, which is also empty. Curtains have been seen

---

[17] http://www.texasescapes.com/TOWNS/Plainview/Plainview.htm

moving when no one is in the building and some have seen faces staring down at them from empty rooms.

## Wayland Baptist University, 1900 W 7th St, Plainview, 79072

The oldest university in continuous existence on the High Plains of Texas, Wayland began as the dream of pioneers who respected the life-altering value of education. In 1906, the Staked Plains Baptist Association received and acted upon a proposal to establish a school. Dr. and Mrs. James Henry Wayland offered $10,000 and 25 acres of land, if the Association and the citizens of Plainview would raise an additional $40,000. The Association and the city accepted both the proposal and the challenge and in 1908 applied for a charter from the State of Texas for the Wayland Literary and Technical Institute.

Construction began on the first two buildings on the Plainview campus in 1909 and Dr. I. E. Gates became president of Wayland, which was then literally only "a hole in the ground." Although the main administration building was incomplete, classes began in September 1910 in adjacent Matador Hall, even before its glass windowpanes were installed. From primary grads through junior college, 241 students enrolled that first term in the school whose name was changed the same year to Wayland Baptist College.

This university has the second oldest parapsychology school in the country. The Plainview campus of Wayland Baptist University is haunted. At least that's what some alumnae believe, including history professor Estelle Owens. The history professor told the story of young woman, perhaps 20 years old, who was obsessed with succeeding as a musician. This former music student (cause of death uncertain) continues to rehearse day after day.

## Gates Hall, Wayland Baptist University

Named for Dr. I. E. Gates, Wayland's first President, the three-storied Gates Hall was once the tallest building in Plainview. Its cornerstone was laid on July 4th, 1909. The building has been used for practically every conceivable thing connected with college life. For years the third floor was used for a men's dormitory and later a women's dormitory. For a while, there was an apartment which was occupied by such personnel as the

**Figure 7: Gates Hall**

President and faculty members. The area now occupied by administrative offices was the library until Van Howeling Library (now Education Building) was built in 1956. Today Gates Hall houses almost all the administrative offices, numerous classrooms, and the offices of two academic divisions. It continues to symbolize the strength and style of Wayland Baptist University.

However, there are many that believe that Gates Hall may be haunted as well. There have been a number of reports of doors opening and shutting on their own and dark, shadowy figures have been spotted roaming the hallways.

## Coronado Jr. High, 2501 Joliet St, Plainview, TX

A little boy died at Coronado Jr. High School and it is reported if you walk down the hall by the Gym alone you can here what sounds like a basketball bouncing on the floor, but if you investigate, you will find that there's no one there. If you are alone, near the stage you get the felling that's some one is watching you and, if you listen closely, you can hear what sounds like voices whispering.

## Masso's Department Store

Across from the courthouse there is a store that is named Masso's it used to be a photo shop at the turn of the century. The Masso's the owners of the store used to live upstairs there and had their western store downstairs. They said that they were ran out by weird stuff happening like they would leave and come back and furniture would be moved. So they moved out and used the upstairs for storage. But they still heard weird stuff happening like furniture moving around.

## Plainview High School Agricultural Building

**Figure 8: Plainview High School**

In the early 1980's some student's were in the auditorium of the Plainview High School Agricultural Building practicing for a school play and, during this practice, there were some other students on the top balcony putting up ornaments for the play. After everyone one left, one student stayed to finish the decorations and later that night killed himself by hanging him self from the top balcony. Since that time a ghost named Herkie is said to haunt the school auditorium.

Under the auditorium are said to be some big tunnels that have been used by students to enter and leave the building with no one being the wiser. According to the story, about 2 weeks after the death of "Herkie" some kids were skipping class, hanging out in the tunnels and got caught. Instead of stopping when told they ran into the tunnels, going deeper in them. School officials waited and waited for the students to come out but they didn't, so finally they went in after them. Deep in the tunnels they found the bodies of the students that they had been chasing. The students were found to have had their throats cut back all the way to where the knife hit the bone.

Police went into the tunnels, searching for the killers, but they found that a short way past the bodies, that particular tunnel reached a dead end. It was their belief that if someone in the tunnels wanted to exist, then they would have had to come out the front where officials had been waiting. Who or what killed the students remains a mystery to this day, but current students report that they can still hear the ghosts of those that were murdered screaming, "HELP" and begging "PLEASE DONT KILL ME".

## Plainview High School - Athletic Department

One day after school in the Plainview High School Athletic Department the football players went straight to practice, after football practice they had to lift weights. One of the football players was bench pressing by himself with no spotter and apparently tried to lift more weight than he could handle. When trying to pick it up he couldn't control the weight any longer and the weight fell right on his throat. He tried to call for help but the weight had caused such an injury to his throat that he couldn't talk or even breathe. About 20 minutes later the coaches found him dead. It is said that when no one else is in the weight room you can hear the weights moving and you can hear the man screaming and sometimes see the guy walking across the room with his head down.

# POST, TEXAS

Post, the county seat of Garza County, is on the Santa Fe Railroad at the junction of U.S. highways 84 and 380, east of the Caprock escarpment near the west central part of the county. The town began under the name Post City in 1907 as a colonizing venture of cereal manufacturer Charles William Post, who sought to develop a model town. He purchased 200,000 acres of ranchland and established the Double U. Company to manage the town's construction. The company built trim houses and numerous structures, which included the Algerita Hotel, a gin, and a textile plant. They planted trees along every street and prohibited alcoholic beverages and brothels. The Double U. Company rented and sold farms and houses to settlers. A post office began in a tent during the year of Post City's founding. Two years later the town had a school, a bank, and a newspaper, the Post City Post. The railroad reached the town in 1910. The town changed its name to Post when it incorporated in 1914, the year of C. W. Post's death.

## The Town

The small town of Post is haunted by C.W. Post, the founder of the town and of the mega million dollar cereal company that still bears his name. Police officers while patrolling at night enforcing the curfew law have seen a person walking down the main street and around a corner. When the officers speed up to catch up with the person, the figure vanishes or walks around corners and no trace of him is found. The local museum was an insane asylum in which Post reportedly killed himself and is said to be haunted too.

# ROBY, TEXAS

Roby is a quiet farming community, described as being very friendly and community oriented. Cotton is the mainstay of farming in the area. Roby was made the county seat of Fisher County in 1886 and became incorporated in 1915. It is the second largest town in Fisher County. It has an elementary school, a junior high school and high school. The city has a park, community center, rodeo grounds, swimming pool and baseball park. It remains a center of commerce for the county. Rotan and Roby are 10 miles apart on State Highway 70.

## Fisher County Jail

The Fisher County Jail is not old enough to be called historic, but it has been around for a few years. According to both staff and inmates, there is an inmate here that does not appear to be human, or even living. The ghost has made himself known to inmates through various forms of physical contact. Inmates have reported the spirit touching them, throwing things, flushing toilets, and just making noise. He has even been seen by the sheriff, who was somewhat shocked to say the least.

On one occasion, the ghost lit a stove for a jailer. The origin of the spirit is unknown, but it is believed to perhaps be the ghost or ghosts of a sheriff and deputy that were murdered by an inmate in 1927.

# SANTA ANA, TEXAS

Santa Anna is at the intersection of the Atchison, Topeka and Santa Fe Railway, U.S. highways 283, 67, and 84, and Farm Road 1176 eight miles southeast of Coleman in southeast central Coleman County. The town was named for the twin mountains located just north of the community, which were in turn named for Santa Anna, a Comanche chief. The peaks served as a landmark to early surveyors and settlers. Camp Colorado, occupied by the United States Army from 1857 to 1861, was ten miles north of the site. Texas Rangers were also stationed in the vicinity and used the peaks as an observation post.

L. V. Stockard, the first railroad agent, built a two-story rock store, and residents used the upper floor as an assembly hall and theater. Church groups of several denominations held services in the schoolhouse. Santa Anna developed as a cattle shipping point and as the chief marketing town for the eastern part of the county. By 1884 the town had two general stores, a drugstore, and a blacksmith shop. Among prominent early residents was John Riley Banister, a Texas Ranger and county sheriff, and his wife, Emma Banister, who became the first woman sheriff in Texas after her husband's death. Santa Anna was hit by a tornado in 1893 that destroyed five houses.

## Santa Ana High School Auditorium

A number of years ago a girl fell from a balcony in the Santa Ana High School Auditorium during a play. Whenever there is a play in that auditorium, a dim light can be seen from the balcony above the stage itself. Investigations will reveal that there is nothing in the balcony area that will cause a light such as was seen. Dressing room doors open and close by themselves and there are cold spots in the dressing room area. It is a tradition that the students bring the spirit of the dead girl flowers before every play to insure a safe performance.

# SHALLOWATER, TEXAS

Shallowater is on State Highway 84 and the Santa Fe line, twelve miles northwest of Lubbock in Lubbock County. As early as 1909 J. C. (Jim) Bowles, whose ranch was adjacent to the site of what is now Shallowater, persuaded Bob Crump, a member of a ranching family, to help form a town site company and attract a railroad to go through the area. Land was purchased for the town site on May 18, 1909. A school was built at that time. After Santa Fe railroad officials received a bonus from rancher George W. Littlefield of the Yellow House Ranch, negotiations were finally completed.

The originators of the plan, and other interested individuals, formed the Ripley Town site Company, which was named after a Santa Fe railroad official and was incorporated on May 22, 1909. The company decided to name the new town Shallowater to attract settlers. On June 26, 1913, a celebration was held to note the founding of the town and completion of the railroad. By the time the town was established, the ranching industry in the area was waning and many of the large ranches were being divided into smaller lots for farmers. Cotton became an important cash crop.

During the 1920s Shallowater grew rapidly, and the town had a hotel, a lumberyard, and various filling stations, grocery stores, cotton gins, drugstores, barbershops, garages, blacksmith shops, and other businesses. Several churches and schools were also built. A county park with a clubhouse was established, a public well was constructed, and a real depot building was built to replace the boxcar the town had been using for years. From 1920 to 1922 the railroad station was known as Pacita.

## Banshee

Tales of banshees are normally associated with Irish legends. The banshee, from ban (bean), a woman, and shee (sidhe, a fairie), is an attendant fairy that follows the old families, and none but them, and wails before a death. Many have seen her as she goes wailing and clapping her hands. The keen (caoine), the funeral cry of the peasantry, is said to be an imitation of her cry.

When more than one banshee is present, and they wail and sing in chorus, it is for the death of some holy or great one. An omen that sometimes accompanies the banshee is the coach-a-bower (coiste-bodhar), an immense black coach, mounted by a coffin, and drawn by headless horses driven by a Dullahan. It will go rumbling to your door, and if you open it, according to Croker, a basin of blood will be thrown in your face. These headless phantoms are found elsewhere than in Ireland. In 1807 two of the sentries stationed outside St. James's Park died of fright. A headless woman the upper part of her body naked, used to pass at midnight and scale the railings. After a time the sentries were stationed no longer at the haunted spot. In Norway the heads of corpses were cut off to make their ghosts feeble. Thus came into existence the _Dullahans_, perhaps; unless, indeed, they are descended from that Irish giant who swam across the Channel with his head in his teeth[18].

However, there are a number of stories that there are Banshees in Texas as well. The banshee's screams have forewarned of impending doom to farmers and ne'er-do-wells. One of the banshee's victims reportedly haunts the area where his car overturned. A black, hooded figure has also been seen nearby.

## SNYDER, TEXAS

Snyder, the county seat of Scurry County, is at the junction of U.S. highways 84 and 180, eighty-seven miles southeast of Lubbock in the central part of the county. It had its beginnings in 1878, when a buffalo hunter and trader, William Henry (Pete) Snyder, a native of Pennsylvania, built a trading post on the banks of Deep Creek. Other hunters were attracted to the post, and a colony of buffalo-hide dwellings grew up around it. These dwellings, as well as the occasionally dubious character of their inhabitants, gave the town its first names, "Hide Town," and "Robber's Roost." In 1882 Snyder drew up a town plan and invited immigration.

### Snyder Coliseum

One day a child was chasing a bat down one of the corridors of the Snyder Coliseum, not paying attention to his surroundings, fell from the top of the stairs. He tumbled down a full flight of the steep stairs and broke his neck. Now, many visitors report that they have seen this boy running around the top of the building.

## STANTON, TEXAS

Originally called Grelton, Stanton was just a spot next to the Texas and Pacific Railroad tracks when it came through in 1881.

What is now Stanton, was settled in 1881 by German Catholics, who originally named the town Marienfeld (field of Mary). Stanton is the seat of

---

[18] from "A Treasury of Irish Myth, Legend, and Folklore", Ed. W.B. Yeats

Martin County, which was organized in 1884. The town's name changed in 1890 to honor Abraham Lincoln's Secretary of War, Edwin M. Stanton.

In 1882, the Carmelites opened a monastery in Stanton; the monks left in 1894 and the Sisters of Mercy established a convent boarding school that educated 2,000 students until most of the school was destroyed by a tornado in 1938. Abandoned structures remain on North Convent Street. The city is a cotton, agribusiness, and oil center.

## St. Joseph's Monastery

On August 15, 1881, Father Anastasius, three other members of the Carmelite Order, and Adam Konzqv moved to Grelton, a place at the end of a railway line being built by the Texas and Pacific, 280 miles west of Fort Worth. On August 29, 1881, Peters celebrated the first Mass in the area. Before long he petitioned the Texas and Pacific Railway to change the name of Grelton to Marienfeld; the site is now Stanton, Texas. On October 25, 1881, the priests completed a wooden church, which they named St. Joseph's.

More priests were expected from Kansas, and in the fall of 1882 the Carmelites began erecting a two-story adobe building to be used as a school for boys and as a monastery for candidates to the priesthood. Father Boniface instructed the priests, and Father Anastasias was in charge of the church, the monastery, and spreading the faith to other places. The area assigned to the Carmelites included much of West Texas and southeastern New Mexico. Only the largest settlements could support churches, and in smaller towns Mass was celebrated in the homes of parishioners.

St. Joseph's Monastery is haunted by the spirit of a Priest who hung himself after being accused of a crime. There have been many reports of lights being turned on and off inside the empty Monastery buildings at night. Some even say they have heard the sound of babies crying in the night. There have long been rumors that the bodies of a number of infants were supposedly buried under the convent.

## Sisters of Mercy Convent

In 1894 a group of nuns of the Sisters of Mercy arrived and opened the Convent and Academy of Our Lady of Mercy. The school was for many years the only Catholic academy between Fort Worth and El Paso, attracted students from all of West Texas. The convent and monastery also served as a base for mission

**Figure 9: Sisters of Mercy Convent**

activities. While the priests traveled regularly to Big Spring and Midland and occasionally to towns as far away as New Mexico to say Mass, the nuns opened schools and hospitals in Big Spring, Pecos, Menard, Fort Stockton, and Slaton. The Convent is also supposedly haunted by weeping nuns who may well have been the mothers of the babies said to have been buried beneath the building.

# SWEETWATER, TEXAS

An oasis with sweet water amid bitter-tasting gypsum streams, Sweetwater has always been a place to rest one's head and weary feet. Long before the settlers and ranchers arrived, the Kiowa Indians named the site "Mobeetie"--which was their word for "sweet water." The town of Sweetwater was declared the seat of Nolan County on April 12, 1881, though not a single building of any description existed at the location. The city of Sweetwater was later incorporated in 1902. The building of the railroad and depot launched the city into a new chapter of growth.

In 1876, Bat Masterson, 22, stole Melvin King's girlfriend, Molly Brennan from him. When King found them together one night in a saloon here, he opened fire on Bat. Molly threw herself in front of Bat to protect him, but a bullet passed through her body, killing her instantly, and lodged in Bat's pelvis. But as he fell, Bat fired back and killed King. Bat suffered a slight permanent limp from his wound, and forced him to walk with the aid of a cane.

During World War II, Avenger Field was once home to the Women Air Force Service Pilots (WASPs), who flew U.S. Army airplanes on a variety of missions. By mid-1944, however, as the demand for pilots began to slacken, pressure from men in the U.S. Congress forced the program to close by refusing to re-appropriate their funding. The program was officially disbanded on Dec. 7, 1944--the third anniversary of the attack on Pearl Harbor.

## Sweetwater High School,  1205 Ragland Street, Sweetwater, Texas

There seem to be a number of spirits residing at the Sweetwater High School. Unexplained footsteps are heard on stage in the auditorium while cold spots are felt by players on the gridiron. There is also a playful ghost that runs through the downstairs part of the school. Light footsteps are heard on the steps leading to the upper areas and this playful spook has been known to lock the doors to teacher's rooms.

## Sweetwater Lake

Sweetwater Lake is a 630 acre lake created in 1930, located on Bitter Creek and Cottonwood Creek in Nolan County, 45 miles west of Abilene and about 5 miles east of Sweetwater. The maximum depth is said to be about 45 feet. The water is normally clear to stained, with a normal visibility of up to 4 feet. This visibility actually works to make the mystery surrounding the lake even more baffling. Many nights, residents living near the lake, as well as visitors have reported seeing mysterious orange lights floating across the lake. In spite of several attempts, no one has been able to determine what causes the lights.

## Texas Movie Theatre, 114 East Broadway, Sweetwater, Texas

The hauntings in the Texas Movie Theater cause a bit of trouble for the staff. Cash has been known to disappear and then reappear in the cash register, making balancing at the end of the day almost impossible. There have also been a number of strange noises, unexplained voices & apparitions seen and heard about the theater.

# TURKEY, TEXAS

Turkey is at the intersection of State Highways 86 and 70, on the Burlington Northern line in the southwestern corner of Hall County. The community, probably first settled in the early 1890s, was initially called Turkey Roost, for the wild turkey roosts once found on nearby Turkey Creek. In 1892 a Methodist Episcopal congregation was organized at the home of W. M. Cooper. The town name was changed to Turkey in 1893, when a post office was established there in the dugout of Alfred P. Hall, the first postmaster. Later John M. Gist became the postmaster and served until 1895, when the post office was discontinued.

In 1900 the Turkey post office was reopened, and by 1906 a school district had been established and a chapter of the Woodmen of the World had been organized. A town plat was officially recorded in 1907. By 1914 about 250 people were living in Turkey, which included a bank, a hotel, a general store, and two groceries. A newspaper, the Turkey Gobbler, began publishing in 1919. When Turkey incorporated in 1926, Jess Jenkin became the first mayor, and G. Katzkie and J. B. Miller were elected as aldermen. Turkey is best known as the home of Bob Wills, the King of Western Swing. Raised "down between the rivers" outside the town, Bob Wills was a barber in Turkey in Ham's Barbershop during the 1920's. In the early 1930's, he formed the Texas Playboys band and ushered in a new era of country-western music called Western Swing.

The Bob Wills Foundation purchased the Turkey School buildings. The City Offices, Public Library, Senior Citizens Room, and Bob Wills Museum are located in the former grade school building. The Foundation has built a Bob Wills Monument and adjacent to it is the Bob Wills Park. The park includes a trailer area, camping area, picnic area, and a playground.

## Hotel Turkey, 3rd & Alexander  Turkey, Texas 79261

The Hotel Turkey was built in 1927 to provide lodging for railroad travelers and salesmen, and has continued to operate since that time. Hotel Turkey now operates as a bed and breakfast. There are a number of stories that staying at the Hotel Turkey can get you more than a good night's sleep.

The ghost of a cowboy checks into the hotel on stormy nights and leaves rumpled bed sheets in one of the rooms as a sign that he was there after he mysteriously disappears.  There has been a recent ghost sighting of a slightly different sort reported by the Hotel Turkey not long ago. A young guest in her 20s woke up in the night to see a figure standing in the doorway between the bedroom and bathroom. "He was waving his arm back and forth with a lantern, like an engineer or a trainman would do," says Suzie Johnson.

Johnson isn't sure whether she believes all the stories. "What is real to one person maybe the next person doesn't comprehend it. I will say I have heard noises upstairs ... but the next day there will be no indication of anything being moved or anything to indicate someone was there."

# PART FIVE

## GHOSTS OF CENTRAL TEXAS

# AUSTIN, TEXAS

Home of the state capitol, the city of Austin is named after the "Father of Texas" Stephen F. Austin. Austin brought the first 300 settlers from the United States of America to help the Mexican government "tame" the frontier. Rich in history, Austin is also rich in ghost lore.

Austin hasn't always been the bustling city that it is today, nor has it always been named Austin. This gentle bend in the Colorado River had many residents and visitors long before the first cornerstone was laid. For hundreds of years, nomadic tribes of Tonkawas, Comanches, and Lipan Apaches camped and hunted along the creeks, including what is now known as Barton Springs. In the late 1700s, the Spanish set up temporary missions in the area. In the 1830s the first permanent Anglo settlers arrived and called their village Waterloo.

In 1839, tiny Waterloo was chosen to be the capital of the new Republic of Texas. A new city was built quickly in the wilderness, and was named after Stephen F. Austin, "the father of Texas." Judge Edwin Waller, who was later to become the city's first mayor, surveyed the site and laid out a street plan that has survived largely intact to this day. In October 1839, the entire government of the Republic arrived from Houston in oxcarts. By the next January, the town's population had swollen to 856 people.

By the 1880s, Austin was becoming a city. In 1888, a grand capitol building, advertised as the "7th largest building in the world," was completed on the site originally chosen in the 1839 plan. Funded by very creative financing involving the famous XIT Ranch, the building remains a central landmark on the Austin skyline. It has also, of course, remained the center of one of the city's most prominent industries—government.

## B Side Bar/Bitter End Bistro & Brewery

This fashionable eating place is located at 311 Colorado St., Austin, Texas. The Bitter End is a bistro and brew pub that has been serving up fine food and beer in the Warehouse District for over eight years. The restaurant is actually a refurbished warehouse, which may account for some of the odd happenings. The Bitter End's kitchen offers an eclectic mix of contemporary cuisine fusing elements of Southwestern and Pacific Rim, Continental and Caribbean, with the feel of down-home cooking, our menu is sure to offer something for everyone.

**Figure 10: Entrance to the Bitter End.**

Not only do the diner crowds like the ambiance, but apparent so do those who should long ago have passed on. A number of patrons and staff have reported seeing dark figures moving between the bar area and the bathroom. One night, when the manager was alone and closing the bar, he suddenly found that all of the bar stools that had been carefully pushed under the bar were mysteriously pushed a couple of feet away from the bar.

## Bertram's Restaurant & Bar

This well known restaurant was located at 14th and Guadalupe. The 145 year old building used to be a general store and the ghost of the former owner doesn't seem to want to leave. However, from my research it was not the ghost that killed Bertram's but the small portions and high prices. The Clay Pit opened in the same building.

## Carrington's Bluff

**Figure 11: Carrington's Bluff**

The fashionable Carrington's Bluff Bed and Breakfast is located at 1900 David Street, Austin TX. The Main House, built in 1877, sits on an acre of tree-covered bluff above Pease Park in the center of Austin. Just inside the front door, the spacious dining room is the perfect place to relax after breakfast and enjoy the garden view, get cozy by the fireplace with the newspapers, or catch up on work.

However, keep in mind that you may not be the only one to be enjoying the ambiance of the historic old home. There is a TV without a remote that has been seen to turn on and off, and one guest reported that he got his hair shampooed by the ghost!

## Clay Pit, 1601 Guadalupe St, Austin

The Clay Pit opened in the same 145 year old building occupied by Bertram's Restaurant & Bar. To understand the hauntings, it is necessary to know the history of this historic old building. Rudolph Bertram[19] arrived in Austin in 1853 and began a trading post. In 1872 Bertram purchased the building at 1601 Guadalupe. In 1880 he began a wholesale grocery business, saloon and general store (1st floor) that served Austin for decades. The family living quarters were on the second floor[20].

There have been some examinations of this old building that have revealed some very interesting results. In the basement there is a tunnel that led to a brothel that was located next door. Austin had several brothels in what was officially classified in City documents as the First Ward, bordered by the river and Guadalupe, Colorado, and Fifth Street. Everyone else called it "Mexico", or, more commonly, "Guy Town". Many brothels had tunnels leading to them so the more "high-toned" male citizenry wouldn't be seen visiting. Their clients were city council members, legislators, students from the university, and businessmen who tacitly supported business in Guy Town through their continued patronage.

Several occurrences of strange "party like" noises have been reported coming from the upstairs dinning room in the nearly 150 year-old building. When the restaurant staff would walk up stairs to investigate the source of the noise, upon their arrival, the noises would suddenly stop.

Witnesses have also seen the apparition of a small child on the second floor. Exactly who the small child is remains unknown. However, looking at the records of possible deaths near or around the building, Bertram had a young son die in the family of typhoid fever.


## David Grimes Photography Studio 500 E. 5th Street, Austin, Texas

The David Grimes Photography Studio was formerly located at 503 Neches. This building also houses one of the most historically intriguing cases of paranormal activity. A psychic, reportedly without knowing the building's history, once said she heard a black man laughing there, amused, she said, that he had become his own client. Records show that the building was once owned by a black undertaker named Nathan Rhambo, who opened a funeral home there around 1915 and was murdered in 1932.

The murder, blamed on a young black man who police said was out to rob the wealthy Rhambo, threw the city's black community into an uproar (see "Killer Reputation," above). Does Rhambo carry on in his old shop because he has something to say about the circumstances of his murder[21]?

---

[19] (1829-1892)

[20] Interestingly enough, the town of Bertram was named for Rudolph Bertram.

[21] Austin Chronicle, Shades of the Past, January 26, 2001.

There is also the apparition of an elderly woman that has been seen here, a remote control car has operated by itself, and the ghost split a glass in half, while the owner was holding it.

## Driskill Hotel, 604 Brazos Street, Austin, Texas

Colonel Jesse Lincoln Driskill built the Driskill Hotel with monies he

PICA 05041, Austin History Center, Austin Public Library

earned as an entrepreneur dealing in cattle, real estate, and investments. Built in 1886 as the showplace of a cattle baron, The Driskill Hotel in Austin, Texas stands as a landmark of Texas hospitality. Austin's legendary luxury hotel occupies a dynamic site in the city's business district, convenient to the capitol building, convention center, entertainment district and other key destinations.

The lobby of the Driskill sets the initial tone of comfort and elegance with three-story columns framing a marble floor and stained-glass dome ceiling. Guests select from 188 rooms and suites distributed between the Historic Wing - with soaring ceilings, elaborate woodwork and balconies- and the Traditional Wing, built in 1929 and featuring art deco styling and the colors of the Texas Hill Country.

The palatial Driskill Hotel is also said to house more ghosts than can be listed here. Sightings are reported in the hotel to the present day, including that of a former housekeeper, Mrs. Bridges, in a long Victorian dress who appears to be still fussing with flower arrangements in the lobby, a longtime resident from the turn of the century, Mr. Lawless, who checks his pocket watch on the elevator, and a woman who carries shopping bags into a fourth-floor room where a wealthy Houston woman committed suicide in the early 1990s, after her fiancé canceled their wedding. Colonel Driskill himself still smokes cigars and turns on the lights in upper floor guest rooms. The deceased daughter of a senator bounces a ball and giggles down the grand staircase.

"Suicide Bride #1" has been spotted in the balcony level ladies' room - peering under stalls. "Suicide Bride #2", who only recently died in the hotel, has been seen emerging from the elevator on the fourth floor of the traditional side - arms loaded with packages. The elevators are the focus of all kinds of paranormal activity. The Driskill is probably Texas' most haunted hotel.

Guests and visitors also claim that they hear people playing upstairs. They also claim that they feel something touching their face and arms. Some people even say that they see figures in their windows and sitting in chairs. On the 3rd floor of the Driskill Hotel in one of the hallways there is a painting of a little girl holding flowers, witnesses report when they all looked at the picture a weird sensation came over them. It was like something was lifting up the heels of their feet. It was like a tingling sensation that caused their equilibrium to be off for the next few hours.

Finally, the flirtatious ghost of a Texas man is said to haunt the top floor of this majestic hotel where he entertained his lady friends. The old elevator still makes calls to that floor for no reason, and female guests have reported the playful spirit in several rooms on that floor. The rock group Concrete Blonde encountered his presence when they stayed at the hotel on a road tour.

## Fado Irish Pub

Located at 214 West 4th Street, Austin, the building once housed the Capitol City Playhouse Theater[22], and doesn't every theater have at least one ghost? Activity may have stopped, now, though, since it's now Fado Irish Pub.

However, for many years it was believed that malevolent inhuman spirits haunted the Capital City Playhouse. These spirits delight in moving furniture, playing with lights, and hiding objects when most needed. Other said that it was merely an energetic ghost that haunted the theater. The unidentified spirit rearranges furniture, moves stage lighting, and displaces small personal items.

## Governor's Mansion

The Texas Governor's Mansion located at 1010 Colorado was built in 1856. From 1845 to 1856 the Governors didn't have a "suitable residence". In 1854 the Texas Legislature appropriated $14,500 for construction of a permanent residence for the Governor of Texas. A Greek Revival Style building was chosen and designed by Austin master builder Abner Cook, (1814-1884). The bricks used to build the Mansion came from a clay pit on the Colorado River which produced the buff-colored bricks. Abner Cook owned the clay pit as well as the sawmill in Bastrop which supplied the pine lumber from the area forest. Construction was completed on June 14, 1856.

---

[22] The original building was actually a converted warehouse.

The mansion was built by the fourth governor of Texas, Elisha Pease, but the best known ghost to haunt the Governor's Mansion is Governor Pendleton Murrah's nineteen year old nephew, who committed suicide in his bedroom in 1864. The lovesick lad put a pistol to his head when a niece of Mrs. Murrah refused his hand in marriage. The nephew was found sprawled in a guest bedroom, a bullet through his head. As the story goes, the blood from the suicide was never even cleaned from the walls until 1870, because Murrah fled Texas shortly thereafter as Union troops advanced.

That wing of the mansion was thereafter dreaded by housekeeping staff and visitors, who complained of doors opening on their own, cold breaths, and frightful moans[23]. Afterward, servants refused to enter the room, which they said was haunted by the boy's anguished spirit.

No one could sleep in the ice cold room because of unexplainable banging sounds, so Governor A.J. Hamilton had it sealed after the Civil War. It was re-opened in 1952 and the muffled sobbing of the heartbroken boy can still be heard, especially on Sundays, the day on which he tried to end his misery.

**Figure 12: The Governor's Mansion**

The Houston Bedroom in the mansion is said to be haunted by none other than Sam Houston, the third governor of Texas. The statesman's shadow lurks in the corner of the room. His restless spirit was encountered by both the wife and daughter of Governor Mark White in the 1980s.

Some ghost stories recall an Austin we can scarcely conceive of: a log cabin settlement reduced to desperate rations in the gloomy final days of the Civil War, when cornmeal mush was served at Texas Gov. Pendleton Murrah's inauguration.

---

[23]Austin Chronicle, Shades of the Past, January 26, 2001.

## The Hideout Coffeehouse & Theatre

Located at 617 Congress Ave in Austin, the Hideout Coffeehouse & Theater is well known to be haunted. In fact, one of Austin's ghost tours starts at this location. Faucets turn on and off, locked gates open, and the main breaker was tripped during renovation for no apparent reason.

## HighLife Cafe

The Highlife Café is located on 7th Street just north of Austin's famous 6th Street. The building was constructed in 1872 and has served as an office and hotel for the New Orleans stagecoach. In 1886 a single woman with several children, Fanny Davis, purchased the building and opened a boarding house. The currant occupants believe she may be the ghost that has appeared on four occasions, or responsible for the numerous mischievous events that take place regularly. An apparition appears in both blue and white. A stereo system has turned itself on. Also, a mysterious light show appeared during a bachelor party.

## Inn at Pearl Street

Located at 809 W. Martin Luther King Blvd, the Inn at Pearl Street is a bed-and-breakfast establishment in a Greek Revival Style home close to the University of Texas. It's known as one of the most romantic B & Bs in Austin. The Inn underwent a renovation, during which time there was no electrical power. That didn't stop lights from flashing on and off, according to reports.

A long-ago owner of the home, Stella Snider, is thought to be one of the apparitions that has been reported. Some have claimed to see a woman, believed to be Stella Snider, carrying a child out of one guest room into another, while others have allegedly seen the same woman rocking a child in a rocking chair. Lights have come on even during periods of time when there was no power to the building.

## Jensen Auditorium

Jensen Auditorium is located on the campus of the University of Texas Campus, Austin. Pianist and Professor Dallis Franz still visits with the students even though he has been deceased for some years.

## Littlefield Building

The Littlefield Building has been an Austin Cornerstone Since 1912[24]. In 1910, banker and entrepreneur George Littlefield demolished the Ziller Building in order to erect an office building that would house his American National Bank, which was then located in the adjacent Driskill Hotel. The Littlefield Building became the financial center of Austin and was the height of opulence when it opened. It originally sported a roof garden for evening soirees until his friendly

---

[24] www.austinpostcard.com/lhistory.htm, courtesy of Phoebe Allen.

competition with the eight-story Scarbrough Building across the street led Littlefield to enclose the roof garden, adding one more story to its original eight. For a short time, its nine stories gave the Littlefield Building the distinction of being the tallest skyscraper between New Orleans and San Francisco.

The Littlefield Building was among the most prestigious and modern structures of its day. Purchased by Merit Texas Properties in December of 1999, the Littlefield Building lies on the northeast corner of Sixth Street and Congress Avenue. Austin is fortunate that the present owners of both the Littlefield and Scarbrough Buildings take pride in their history as we move toward their 100th anniversaries as cornerstones of Austin's downtown business district and its two downtown National Register Historic Districts.

Recognizing the wealth inherited by the area's widows and daughters, Littlefield designed a separate, ladies' banking department with female tellers. A "lady attendant" watched over an exclusive waiting room furnished in solid mahogany. Littlefield's first female vice president went on to become the president of the National Banking Association. [The bank, after a series of changes, is incorporated by today's Bank One, Austin.] The Littlefield Building quickly established itself as Austin's leading financial center. Today it is still the hub of the business activity it inspired.

Two solid bronze doors were installed at the corner entrance of the American National Bank in the Littlefield Building in 1911. Texan Daniel Webster sculpted the plaster models for the doors in a shack on South First at Barton Springs Road and sent them to Tiffany's in New York where they were cast in bronze using the lost-wax technique.

Heads of Longhorn steers were cast as handles. Bas relief scenes in the six panels of the doors depict cattle drives, cattlemen said to be uncles of Littlefield's banking partner, and grazing scenes reminiscent of Littlefield's Yellow House Ranch in the Panhandle. After the doors were installed, Littlefield noticed that his LFD brand was missing and hired someone to chisel the brand onto the cattle.

The doors, measuring 10'4" high by 6'9" wide and weighing two-and-a-half tons, were moved to the Congress Avenue entrance in 1918, and when the bank moved in 1954, they were removed and placed in storage. [13] In 1960 the doors were donated to the University of Texas Academic Center for use in the new undergraduate library. Since 1975, they have been on display at UT's Ashbel Smith Hall on Seventh Street at Colorado Street, two blocks from their original site.

George Washington Littlefield died on November 10, 1920, and is buried in Oakwood Cemetery between his wife and his life-long servant, Nathan Stokes. However, there are those who say that George Washington Littlefield never left his beloved building. Elevators in this historic building operate by themselves and then quit for no reason. Mysterious footsteps are heard on upper floors at night when no one is there. Is George Littlefield still keeping an eye on what takes place inside the walls of the building he put his heart and soul into?

## Neill-Cochran House

**Figure 13: The Neill-Cochran Mansion**

When Union troops arrived in Austin, they camped along the banks of Shoal Creek, which flooded and created a yellow fever epidemic. The dying soldiers were boarded at a mansion still standing today at 23rd and San Gabriel, and many were buried on the grounds. The house was later purchased by Col. Andrew Neill, a Texas Revolutionary War veteran, who died there in 1883 (It's now known as the Neill-Cochran House).

Neighbors used to report that Neill could still be seen riding his horse in the yard, or even having tea with Gen. Robert E. Lee on the balcony. And on chilly nights, footsteps are said to echo in the streets near the house, perhaps the distant echoes of soldiers' boots[25].

Constructed in 1853 this house on the UT campus has been reporting ghost sightings for as long as anyone can remember. During the Reconstruction Era following the Civil War a yellow fever epidemic swept through Austin and the building was used as a temporary hospital. Many of the people who died were buried on the school grounds.

## Paramount Theatre for the Performing Arts

Dating back to before World War I, the Paramount Theatre at 713 Congress Avenue is just down the street from the State Capitol and well worth taking the time to go see.

In years past it has been home to vaudeville, silent movies, and Broadway hits. Today the fare is usually classic movies but there are also plays, musical theatre, and the occasional star-studded major motion picture premiere. It is also home to strange lights that are seen in the projection room, and one employee reported an "old hag" experience there. Perhaps the spirits of deceased actors still walk the boards at the Paramount.

---

[25] Austin Chronicle, Shades of the Past, January 26, 2001.

## Speakeasy's

Speakeasy's Alley opened for business in 1997 in the historic Kreisel Building in Austin's famed Warehouse District. In the last 8 years of operation, Speakeasy has become one of downtown's signature places to sit back, relax and listen to live music with friends. The alley-way entrance is a nod to heroes of the prohibition era and the popular Rooftop Terrace is known for the totally-worth-it climb up 59 stairs to the best view downtown Austin has to offer.

Along with the music, keep your ears open for other sounds caused by things not of this world. For example, the front doors bang, followed by the sound of someone rushing up the stairs, then there is a loud knocking on the walls followed by a scream. Sometimes the ghost cuts to the chase and only the scream is heard by itself.

## State Capitol Building

One of the first tales of ghosts in Austin appeared in print in 1898. This story related the saga of a famous Texas scout and his stolen Comanche bride.

**Figure 14: State Capitol Building**

According to legend, these two are said to have died together on the grounds of the original Texas Capitol, at Eighth and Colorado. The father of the girl slew the scout in revenge for taking his daughter from the tribe, and she in turn thrust a knife through her own heart, falling over her lover's body. For decades afterward, witnesses claimed the tragic couple still wanders the grounds at night.

Built over a three-year period between 1885 and 1888, the Texas Capitol has been a host to many historic events. Within its walls great American's shaped a State and a Nation. It's not a wonder that some of their spirits remained within its wall to this day.

On the 30th day of June in 1903 at about 10:00 am, while serving as state comptroller, Robert Marshall Love (1847-1903), was shot at his desk in the Capitol by W. G. Hill, a former employee of the state comptrollers department. His last words were, "I have no idea why he shot me. May the Lord bless him and forgive him. I cannot say more." He died several hours later in Austin and was buried at Tehuacana his home town.

Today's Capitol is under constant watch by the Capitol police department. Nothing moves within the Capitol walls without being seen by an officer. Cameras have recorded the image of a man dressed in a business suite dating back to 1903 standing near the old comptroller of public accounts office. Several visitors have reported a "nice man-- dressed funny" to the visitor's desk on the first floor. Officers have reported walking up to a man on the second floor, east wing during off hours and as they approach the man he turns and walks through a wall.

Others report someone watching them while on tour at the Capitol and have noticed an oddly dressed man starring down at them from the second floor. Some reported the man has spoken to them as they walked by him. Saying "Good Day" and as they turn to reply he is gone.

Many believe the spirit is the man who was suddenly killed while serving Texas almost one hundred years ago. On your next visit if you see a nice man dressed in clothes from an older period, and if you have a chance, ask him. The apparition of a suicide from the 1980's has been also been seen on the rotunda.

## **Austin State School**

The Austin State School, in Austin, Texas, is a ninety-five-acre residential and training facility for adults with developmental disabilities. It is administered by the Texas Department of Mental Health and Mental Retardation. In 1991 the school had a staff of 1,505, more than two-thirds women, which served about 460 individuals at the west Austin campus and 615 in a fourteen-county region extending south and west of Travis County; about 315 of the off-campus population were under age three. Most campus residents had severe or profound retardation or multiple disabilities.

In 1915 the Texas legislature passed a bill to establish the state's first facility for the retarded, some of whom had been housed at the Austin State Lunatic Asylum until then. Two years later the State Colony for the Feebleminded opened on Austin's outskirts with an initial admission of sixty-five females, ages six to forty-nine. In 1925 it was renamed Austin State School. Dr. John Bradfield, superintendent from 1917 to 1936, faced severe shortages in dormitory space and in personnel trained to teach persons with developmental disabilities, but he worked to build a residential training program.

By 1927 a school building, for academic and vocational training on-site, had been added to the facilities. More capable residents were assigned by sex to domestic or farming chores. Beginning in 1930, adult clients also manufactured mattresses and brooms at the campus and assisted in the butcher shop, which provided meat for all state institutions in the area. In 1934 many male residents of Austin State School were moved to the school's new farm on the eastern edge of Travis County, to work in dairy, poultry, and truck farming. This farm, originally called Austin State School Farm Colony, was separated from the Austin school and renamed Travis State School in 1957.

With the farm serving only men and boys until 1973, Austin State School continued to house mostly women and children. Because Bradfield, like most people of his time, thought that persons with mild or moderate retardation easily gravitated toward promiscuity and criminal behavior, he believed that closed, sex-segregated institutions were the most appropriate permanent homes for them. Therefore, during the 1930s and early 1940s, the "colonies" were managed restrictively. Buildings generally were kept locked, employees lived on-site, and residents' families had minimal access during visits.

There are old several buildings in which employees have had sightings and heard mysterious sounds. One of the old buildings, now condemned, was built over a very old cemetery. The cemetery was originally for the patients that died there in the early part of this century. Recently, a coffin is said to have popped out of the ground right next to one of the condemned buildings. Staffers have experienced a number of apparitions and ghostly sounds in this area.

## The Tavern

The Tavern is located at 12th and Lamar and is said to be haunted by the ghost of a prostitute named Emily. According to the history of this establishment, Niles Graham wanted to open a pub. His choice of location was in Austin at 12th and Lamar. However, his timing however was bad. The year was 1921, and a new law called Prohibition meant no spirits and therefore he could not have a pub. So his dream was altered, the store modeled after a German public house, was transformed into a grocery store. Later the Grocery was moved next door and The Tavern became a restaurant.

**Figure 15: The Tavern**

At this point in the story there is some disagreement as to what happened next. There are those who say that during the "Roaring Twenties" a speakeasy? No one knows now or if they do have the facts they are keeping the information to themselves. But perhaps less then legal activities during those decades could account for the interesting and hard to explain activities that occur in the restaurant these days.

Some also say that the Tavern is haunted. There is a spirit that has been seen to walk through the kitchen and up the stairs. Patrons swear that televisions kept in the bar allowing current day patrons to watch sports and local news have the channels switched by an invisible entity. A figure of a little girl is often seen in the window before she vanishes from sight. A woman referred to as "Emily", possibly the child's mother, though others say she was a prostitute, is also seen frequently before she too is gone in the blink of an eye.

There are also rumors that murders were committed in this building. The most often told tale would have us believe that young Emily had a less than savory occupation. One night in the early forties a fight broke out between two men. Emily and her little girl were caught up in the middle of the brawl and neither one lived to tell their story.

## University of Texas Tower

Until Whitman undertook his shooting spree in Austin, Texas, public space felt safe and most citizens were utterly convinced they were comfortably removed from brutality and terror. After August 1, 1966, things would never be the same. Whitman's story stands out for many reasons, not the least of which

being that it features a co-star—the University of Texas Tower, from which he fired almost unimpeded for 96 minutes. The Tower afforded Whitman a nearly unassailable vantage point from which he could select and dispatch victims. It was as if it had been built for his purpose. In fact, in previous years Charlie had remarked offhandedly to various people that a sniper could do quite a bit of damage from the Tower.

The Tower is big—307 feet tall. It is a shorter building than the nearby State Capitol, but it stands taller as it is built on higher ground. The 307-foot tall UT Austin Tower, designed by Paul Cret of Philadelphia, was completed in 1937. Through the years, the Tower has served as the University's most distinguishing landmark and as a symbol of academic excellence and personal opportunity. It opened in 1937 and by 1966 it attracted roughly 20,000 visitors a year, most of whom wanted to take in the spectacular view of Austin from the 28th floor observation deck.

**Figure 16: University of Texas Tower**

What is not well known is that Whitman is not the first tragedy associated with this well known monument. The first death associated with the tower came during its construction; a worker slipped and fell twelve floors in 1935. There was another accidental death in 1950. There were also suicides in 1945, 1949 and 1961. Despite these tragedies the Tower stood as a beloved symbol of Texas pride and expansiveness, the figurative heart of the surrounding campus and city.

Then from July 31 to August 1, 1966 Charles Whitman went on a rampage that resulted in the deaths of 17 people, including himself. On the night of July 31 he murdered his mother in her apartment, and in the early hours of August 1 he stabbed his wife to death. By 12 noon on the 1st he had made his way up to the observation deck of the tower and began to open fire on the South Mall. Fatalities occurred on the South Mall, by the Computation Center to the east of the Tower, on The Drag section of Guadalupe, and inside the Tower itself. At 1:24 pm Whitman was shot to death by Austin PD and DPS officers, ending the massacre. In 1975 the Observation Deck was closed to the public due to the number of suicides. It was reopened in September 1999 with high fencing and metal detectors.

However, not even the best security can stop the spirits that seem to find the Tower a suitable home. Now, the lights have been known to turn themselves on when the building is vacant, but they will turn off again if guards ask Charlie to behave.

## West Lake Hills

This story takes place at The Eanes-Marshall Ranch in the West Lake Hills section of Austin. The peace and tranquility of this upscale section of Austin is haunted by 2 horses pulling a rider less wagon and seven other distinct ghosts. The house now serves as a studio for local artist Bruce Marshall. He is known for his paintings of the Civil War. One evening when attempting to contact any of the nine reported ghosts, 3 psychics fell to the floor unconscious.

## Zachary Scott Kleburg Theater

The Zachary Scott-Kleburg Theater located 1510 Toomey Rd is long said to be haunted by a number of unidentified spirits. There has also been a lot of poltergeist activity, as well.

## Austin Pizza Garden

Austin Pizza Garden, located at 6266 W. Highway 290 is a family-owned restaurant. It took over the long stone building near the intersection of William Cannon Drive and U.S. 290 West. It has turned out to be a good location for a restaurant, too. However, in addition to a good location, they also took over the care and feeding of several spirits as well. Long before the Pizza Garden moved into this location there were stories of facing appearing and disappearing in the walls.

## Central Market

Located at 4001 N. Lamar, the Central Market site is on a portion of the land that was formerly the site of the Austin State School. There are several buildings that have had sightings and sounds by staff members. This old place was built over a cemetery where patients that expired in the early part of this century were buried. But recently to show proof that this never took place a coffin popped out of the ground right next to one of the condemned buildings. As of April 2005,the school has been torn down. If there was any evidence of the bodies, they have been removed.

## Bedicheck Middle School

The Bedicheck Middle School is located at 6800 Bill Hughes Rd, Austin, TX. According to the story Billy, a student, was playing the part of the Phantom in the play Phantom of the Opera. He was on the new catwalk in the auditorium and the rope that he was holding slipped, he fell, and hung himself. Now Billy is said to push students off the catwalk, and also to help them remember their lines.

## Crockett High School

Located at 5601 Manchaca Road, Austin, Texas, Crockett High School has long been rumored to be the home of ghosts. According to students, there is a little girl that roams the basement of the school. It is said that she is lost and looking for her family. At night by the big gym when teachers work late that you can hear a little girl crying as she walks up and down the halls, searching for her lost loved ones.

## Garrison Park

Garrison Park is located on Manchaca Road next to Crockett high school. It is said that if you drive down the road that takes you around the park you can see kids playing on the basketball court and also see people putting flowers on the graves in the graveyard that is in the back of the park before the football field. There are 3 graveyards in this graveyard that have historical significance.

If you try to approach the kids on the basketball court or the people in the graveyard, they will slowly fade away.

## Harris Park

The family began to see objects moving above them at night, heard loud thumps in their attic, and every time the husband would come near his wife he'd feel an odd force pushing him away. They went around looking for old historical facts and information about their house. They found out that in 1985 a little girl named Doan was abused by her uncle and was raped by her cousin. She was later murdered by her uncle for telling her mother about it so now the family believes that she hovers around protecting any girl that is touched by a male.

## Home Depot at Brodie Lane and US 290

This Home Depot Store is said to be haunted by a Ghost referred to by employees as "Fred". There is said to be a turn of the century grave yard nearby which may be "Fred's" permanent home. People have reported seeing human figures in the outdoor garden section of the store long after the store is closed and all employees have left for the day.

A visitor to the site thinks this may be her father. She states, *"My father was a "craftsman" carpenter as some people call it and he built a lot of things around Austin and loved nothing better than to make things in his shop which was our garage. People would see the garage door open and stop to talk to him and he would help anyone who needed anything made. He was 74 when he died in his shop doing what he loved. He left me and my Mom in debt and a rundown house so we could only afford a cremation. I am a big believer that people should be buried where their happy doing what they loved. So me and my friend took my dad to home depot on Brodie, mainly the garden section because there were people around. I let my father's ashes go there because he had a love for making things and helping people. His name is Herbert, nick name Herb. I am a little freaked out about this because I wanted to do right by him by placing him where he loved to shop and run up his home depot credit card! He is bald and short and Blue eyes, has always walked very fast so if someone sees him tell them not to be afraid just ask him for help and he will find it."*

## Jacob's Hill

There is a bridge on a road beyond I-35 to the East, off of Wells Branch Parkway. If you put your car in neutral and turn the engine off, your car will roll across the bridge. Supposedly the ghosts of two children who were killed by their father around this area push your car away from their dangerous dad.

## Landon Lane

The family living at this location began to see objects moving about them at night, and heard loud thumps coming from their attic. Additional facts and information on their house can not be found as they do not wish to have the curious invading their privacy.

## Logan's on 6th street

Logan's on 6th Street is said to be haunted by a ghost that died when the building was a coffee plantation refinery and now glasses swing by themselves, doors swing open and a loud cackling can be heard on the second floor in the middle of the night.

## Metz Elementary School

The corridors of the old Metz Elementary School located at 84 Robert T. Martinez, Jr. Street that were once filled with bustling activity of hordes of children stood quiet and dark. School posters and lunch menus had been replaced by graffiti. The men who walked the hallways were not teachers, but contractors sent to demolish the old school.  Metz Elementary was no longer needed and would be demolished. Such is the gratitude of man.

Metz Elementary opened in 1916. That same year the school board decided that Spanish-speaking children should attend a separate school. The Board felt that the children would learn better if they had lessons in Spanish as well as English. Up until that time the Mexican-American community in Austin had not formally protested any action taken by the Board, but in this matter many from the neighborhood most affected appeared before the School Board to disagree with the decision. The proposed school

**Figure 17: Metz School**

would be several miles away making going to and from difficult for the children and their parents, there was also a concern that if the Spanish-speaking students were segregated they would not have the same opportunities as those children who spoke English. While the Board never formally backed down from its position, Spanish-speaking students who attended the nearby school, Metz Elementary, were never asked to leave or to attend the other school, and after a period of time the matter was quietly dropped.

Metz Elementary faithfully and tirelessly served the community through the better part of eight decades, but by 1989 the school was considered too small to meet the growing needs of the surrounding neighborhood. The decision was reached to tear down the structure and build a new and bigger school in its place. The crew who arrived to do the work did not anticipate any problems, on the surface there appeared to be nothing difficult about demolishing the crumbling structure, but as they would find from the first day, someone or something wanted to make the job almost impossible. They would have continual problems. The old dilapidated building was not as empty as it looked.

The first strange thing was the sound of children's laughter after the workmen had assured themselves that the condemned building was empty. Then they saw writing on the blackboards when no one had been nearby and saw figures vanish into the restrooms, but when they chased after the small figures, the rooms were empty. Equipment, which had been running perfectly before reaching the site, began to break. Bulldozers and trucks stalled out for no discernable reason and even workmen's watches would suddenly stop running while they attempted to bring down the school's walls.

Understandably men begin to quit, or just not show up for work, but the construction company that had won the bid refused to give in to supernatural pressure. They continued trying to work even as strange accidents began to plague them. After a workman was fatally injured in a wall collapse, Torres Construction Company contacted a Catholic priest who performed an exorcism another clergyman was brought in to bless the building. However, shortly afterward, one of the owners was killed when a wall "exploded" on him.

In spite of it all, the work was finally completed, nearly six months behind schedule. But that may not be the last of the ghosts. Foreman Joe Torres transplanted a tree from the site to the front yard of his daughter's home. Now, people claim to hear the voices of children coming from that tree.

The odd occurrences made national news and the Metz School Mystery has been puzzled over by the curious nationwide. A new school stands almost in the same spot as the old Metz Elementary and now fulfils the same role in the community as the first smaller school did for so long. Perhaps the ties to the neighborhood and the school are so strong, some students never really leave.

## Omni Hotel - downtown

The world famous Omni Hotel located at 700 San Jacinto Blvd, Austin has its own resident ghost. According to the story, a man committed suicide by jumping from balcony and fell to his death. His name was Jack and since he never paid his room his name still stays in the computer log in stays.

Night maids have said to hear him in his room still moving around when the rooms not occupied and guests also report noises in his room at night.

## Richard Moya Park

There is an old bridge by the Richard Moya Park that people say is haunted by ghosts. The bridge is closed because it is very old, but people still risk it for the chance of seeing these ghosts.

## Spaghetti Warehouse

The place for spaghetti in Austin is the Spaghetti Warehouse located at 117 W 4th St, Austin. Along with some excellent spaghetti, you can also get a big dose of ghost. There would seem to be a number of ghosts occupying these quarters.

It is said that the second floor of this building is the most haunted. This was where the employees break room was. As some employees would walk up the stairs to the break room, they would hear strange noises coming from above them. Some of them were so terrified; they refused to go up there.

A former worker at the spaghetti warehouse in Austin, reports there have been numerous occasions when the lights begin to flicker on and off throughout the restaurant. The basement though is where a lot of the employees don't like to go because of the fact it has a strong presence of someone watching you that sends chills down your spine. A young boy has been reported by several employees laughing and running in the direction of what are now the rest rooms. It's anyone's guess who the boy is or why he stays at the restaurant.

The building was once a brothel in the very famous red light district of Austin called "Guy Town" in the late 1800s. It's also next door to the haunted Bitter End's B Side, 311 Colorado. Could the child have died during an out break of yellow fever or perhaps he belonged to a prostitute and died mysteriously?

## Raymond Mansion

An aching melancholy for a doomed era perhaps helped popularize a vision once reported at the Raymond Mansion on West Sixth Street a few decades after the close of the Civil War: At night, a young woman in a ruffled, rose-colored gown descended the stairs into the arms of a Union soldier who galloped up to meet her. The story reported in the news was that a real-life Union sympathizer did fall in love with a woman who lived there, but he could not find her when he returned home from the war.

## St. Edward's University

When Bishop Claude M. Dubuis of Galveston learned of Mrs. Mary Doyle's intention to leave most of her 498-acre south Austin farm to the Catholic Church to establish an "education institution," he invited the Very Rev. Edward Sorin, Superior General of the Congregation of Holy Cross to Texas.

Father Sorin surveyed the beauty of the surrounding hills and lakes, and a year later following Mrs. Doyle's death, founded a Catholic school. Father Sorin called it St. Edward's Academy in honor of his patron saint, Edward the Confessor and King. In the fledgling institution's first year, 1878, three farm boys made up the student body and met for classes in a makeshift building on the old Doyle homestead.

In 1885, the president, Rev. P.J. Franciscus, took the academy to a new level by securing a charter, changing its name to St. Edward's College, assembling a faculty, and increasing enrollment. That same year, Father Peter J. Hurth became president.

In the spring of 1903, a mysterious fire destroyed the majority of the Main Building, but it was restored by the fall. In 1922, the Main Building sustained damage from a tornado that caused significant damage all over the campus.

In 1925, St. Edward's received its university charter. Most of the personnel were Holy Cross priests. In the mid-1940s, the university underwent instant growth as many veterans sought to take advantage of the G.I. Bill. A progression of energetic presidents transformed the university over the next 20 years, increasing enrollment, faculty and capital assets. Women arrived at St. Edward's in 1966 as students for Maryhill College, a coordinate institution. By 1970, Maryhill was absorbed and St. Edward's became co-educational.

## Doyle Hall

Doyle Hall was constructed in 1960 and was the home of male students during the time of enrollment. In recent years, it has been a women's hall. In the fall of 2005, it will house 128 students in its 67 rooms: 92 men on two floors and 36 women on the 3rd floor. Doyle Hall was named in remembrance of Mrs. Mary Doyle, an Austin native, who left most of her 498 acre farm in South Austin to the Catholic Church to establish an "educational institution" which became St. Edward's University. All female dorm - Haunted by a nun ghost. She's nice though. Some times the showers will turn on by themselves and you'll hear someone taking a shower but when you step out, the rest of the showers are dry as if no one was there at all.

## Mary Moody Northern Theatre

The Mary Moody Northern Theater has become a part of Austin Culture over the years. However, it also has made a name for itself as a haunted theater. There have been a number of reports of a shadow of a young man who committed suicide being seen a number of time. He hung himself by the sandbag ropes and it is said that if you listen closely, not only can you see the shadow of the body swinging across the stage (even when the ropes are missing) but you can hear the creaking of the rope.

## Premont Hall

Premont Hall is primarily an all male dorm. The spirit of a former RA still haunts the dorm. During spring break, he came back early and the next morning he slipped and fell in the showers and died instantly. Due to the holidays, he was one of the few students in the building, so he was left lying on the shower floor for a week before anyone found his body. Now, in order to gain attention, he slams doors and windows and turns on all the showers at once.

## Littlefield Home

A beautiful example of eclectic Victorian architecture, and a building rich in history, the Littlefield Home sits stubbornly on the west side of campus, refusing to alter its charmingly 19th century aspect or defer to the prevailing Spanish Renaissance style of the surrounding University. It is something of an anomaly on a campus that is surging into the future with new construction and excitedly embracing advanced technology[26].

---

[26] Randall, Key, *Littlefield Spirit Lives On*, University of Texas at Austin Student News Paper, May 16, 2005.

Built in 1893 for $50,000 by a Southern cattle baron, banker, Confederate officer and generous campus benefactor named George Littlefield, the home, at the time, was only one on a street full of pretty and imposing Victorian houses. Austin was thriving, and larger-than-life businessmen like Littlefield could comment upon their status—much as individuals do today—with tangible evidence such as architecture. Now it is the lone remaining example of those grand Victorian mansions.

Major Littlefield was a strong and outspoken Southern gentleman, and the Littlefield Home carries the weight of his boldness and confidence well. Victorian design was not about discretion, understatement or restraint, and the home, tastefully, seems to swirl and flutter with scrollwork and columns and a profile filled with a variety of turrets, leaping spires, dormer windows and finials.

A deep, generous veranda sweeps around the home and is surrounded by intricate iron grillwork and studded with stately, blue-gray marble columns. Wide, pale marble steps, shot through with veins of black, lead up to the veranda, which is mosaic-tiled, and a low stone fence encloses the generous skirt of lawn upon which the house sits.

As is the case with most fine examples of Victorian architecture, the effect is that of a full, lacy, asymmetrical expanse that carries just enough detail, in danger of toppling over like an ornate wedding cake if even one more dollop of icing is applied.

With all of its beauty and stateliness, it was, no doubt, a very cheerful and lively home when the Littlefields lived there. It was situated on the edge of the original Forty Acres, as the campus was called, and the Littlefields, who had no children, could sit and watch the students stroll by in the evenings or as they made their way to class.

Ghost tales about the home abound, and their variety is exceeded only by their vagueness. One common strain in most of the stories is Alice Littlefield, Major Littlefield's wife.

Some say that Major Littlefield locked Alice up in the attic when he was away so she would not be grabbed by Yankees who might be strolling by and oblivious to the fact that the Civil War was over. According to lore, while languishing in the attic she was assaulted by bats, and her shrieks of terror reverberate in the mansion to this day. Others say that the ghost of Alice can still be heard banging out a chord or two on the old piano on the first floor.

Some accounts paint Alice as a melancholic, depressive, agoraphobic woman who slowly and quietly went insane later in life. Others stress her deep concern for her husband's welfare and her fears for his safety when he was away. Her ghost is said to restlessly roam the attic, peering out the windows, watching for his return.

Some have seen the small round window in one of the attic turrets shuttered at times and at other times not. That window is accessible only if one climbs to the empty attic and crawls through a small hole to access the interior of the turret.

Although the first floor of the home is unoccupied and is usually as quiet as, well, a tomb, Resource Development Special Programs staff use the second floor for office space. At times, the staff members feel they are not alone in the rambling old house. With the requisite sense of humor about their abode, they relate anecdotes about occasional brushes with the mystifying and unexplainable.

Ruth Stone, senior event planner, said that one winter holiday, upon returning after vacation, they found two candelabrums from the fireplace mantle in the middle parlor lying on the floor, several feet away from the fireplace. No one had been in the home during the winter holiday and the candelabrums had been on the mantle before the staff's departure for vacation.

Stone also said that when she brought her four year-old granddaughter to the home, the first words the child uttered upon entering the mansion were, "Someone dead is here."

Maria Aleman, an event planner, said that one day, after staying late at work, Aleman's 8 year-old granddaughter snuggled up to her and commented that "granny smells like a ghost."

Most staff members agree that there are moments when a distinct sense of unease settles over them in the home and heartily concur that they do not relish being the first to arrive in the morning and do not care to be in the home alone or in the evenings.

"For some reason, leaving the home is much scarier than coming into it," says Carol Sablan, event planner. "Sometimes I feel like running rather than walking out, and I become afraid that maybe the door won't open, and I'll be trapped in here."

Sablan said that her young son also felt "creeped out" when he visited the house and told her, "I really, really don't like it here."

Wandering through the first floor of the home on a quiet afternoon, it can seem a little bit bereft and abandoned, but the house has served a number of practical purposes since Alice Littlefield died in 1935 and the home was donated to the university.

During that 67 years it has housed, at various points, the Austin and University of Texas Centennial Office, the Music Department, the Navy R.O.T.C. (who used the attic as a firing range and placed a cannon on the lawn) and Resource Development. The first floor of the home also is used today for special presidential functions.

During George Littlefield's life, he left his fingerprint all over the campus, showing his love for the university and also his wish to be remembered. He started the Littlefield Fund for Southern History and gave $225,000 toward the purchase of the John Henry Wrenn Library. He provided funds for the Littlefield Memorial Fountain and the six flanking statues south of the Main Building. He erected the Alice Littlefield Dorm and donated $500,000 (which had grown to $1 million by the time it was needed) toward the construction of the Main Building. And he wielded influence on the Board of Regents from 1911-20.

Maybe the best thing that the Littlefields left, though, was a little more lore and tradition for a campus that loves its colorful history. So when you stroll by the Littlefield Home, think of its Victorian beauty and its generous former residents. Don't think of ghosts. After all, Alice doesn't live here anymore...

## Treasury Department

The building located at 208 E 10th St, Austin, was thought to be a staid office building housing the financial arm of the Texas State Government. However, its history was to be anything but staid from an attempted robbery at the end of the civil war to being overrun with spirits, those that work in this Building have led an exciting life.

Employees report seeing chairs move without explanation. They also say that they can hear their names called but when asking fellow employees, they find out no one called them. A lot of unusual occurrences have also taken place in the building's library.

## Austin-Travis County MHMR Center - CARE Program 1633 East 2nd

There is a story that a woman that worked at the MHMR center had a most unusual experience one night. According to the story, the woman and her co-worker were cleaning up one night, and they started to open two doors that led into an area that needed to be cleaned. However, no matter how hard they tried to open the doors, something was holding the doors shut and they knew that they were the only two people in the whole building.

She said when the two of them finally pried the doors open, there was some furniture moved around in front of the doors. In addition, the place was getting remodeled, and when they started to refurnish the basement, they found those big wrist chains similar to those used in the movies to chain people to the walls The workers also found some mouthpieces of the type that were put in people's mouths to protect their teeth from breaking when they received the electric shock treatment.

# ALEXANDER, TEXAS

Originally called Harper's Mill - a post office was granted in 1876. According to the Handbook of Texas the name change occurred in 1881 when the Texas Central Railroad came through. The railroad platted the town after purchasing the land from W. C. Keith in 1880. Alexander expanded briefly, but growth diminished when the railroad reached Stephenville in 1889. In 1890, Alexander had a population of 381 where it remained through 1900.

The town had 200 people in 1940 and the post office closed sometime before 1970. A cemetery is shown inside the city limits of Alexander on the TX Dot map of Erath County.

## McDow's Hole

It is said that there is a headless woman that walks the creek bed with her head in one arm looking for her baby. The story goes that she, her husband, and their baby lived in a small house nearby in the late 1800's. Her husband left her and the baby in the house while he was out farming. While the family was home alone, Indians came in killed the wife and threw the baby into the creek. Now cars stall while passing this spot, many hear the sounds of banging on the outside of their cars and there have been a number of reports of a ball of light chasing passersby.

# AQUILLA, TEXAS

Aquilla, Texas is located in Hill County, Texas and began as a result of the railroad being built. The Old mill and a library are all that remains of the original town. The, main street has vanished altogether. As of the 2000 census, the city had a total population of 136.

## Lavanot

There is a really old cemetery, called Lavanot, back in the woods marked by a historic marker. In spite of the marker, you must still go through a field to get to it. Once you get to the cemetery, there is an opening in the trees were you can see into the field around you. If you flash your lights toward that opening then you'll see this 18 wheeler-diesel (without a trailer) coming right at you. If you don't leave right then it will come to you.

## Trains on the invisible railroads

There used to be a railroad track here. A long time ago the city burnt down twice because of the trains throwing sparks, so they decided to just take up all the rails. Well every now and then around 12:00 midnight you can here the train. Residents say it's so loud that it will wake you up from a dead sleep! You can see the light on the front and hear it blow its whistles! But it never stops it just goes right through town.

# BALLINGER, TEXAS

Ballinger is at the junction of U.S. highways 67 and 83 and State Highway 158, thirty-six miles northeast of San Angelo in south central Runnels County. The Colorado River and Elm Creek converge there, and the Atchison, Topeka and Santa Fe Railway run through the town. Ballinger was established when the Gulf, Colorado and Santa Fe Railway built westward out of Brownwood in 1886. Runnels City, the original county seat, campaigned for selection as the new railroad terminal but could not compete with the superior water supply offered at the future site of Ballinger, five miles to the south.

The town was originally called Gresham and then Hutchings (in honor of Santa Fe stockholders Walter Gresham and John H. Hutchings); it was officially named in honor of William Pitt Ballinger, a Galveston attorney and stockholder of the Gulf, Colorado and Santa Fe. Rapid growth and opportunity brought a boomtown atmosphere, attracting a crowd of drifters, fugitives, gamblers, and ruffians to the town's nine saloons and gambling halls. Stagecoach robberies were not uncommon. By 1888, however, the railroad extended to San Angelo, the overland stage business ended, and new, permanent settlers came to the land.

## Fort McKavett

Originally called Camp San Saba because it overlooks the headwaters of the San Saba River Valley, Fort McKavett was established by five companies of the Eighth Infantry in March of 1852 to protect frontier settlers and travelers on Upper El Paso Road. The camp was later renamed for Capt. Henry McKavett, killed at, the battle of Monterey on September 21, 1846. The fort was abandoned March 1859 and reoccupied April 1868. By 1880, the fort was no longer needed and was finally abandoned June 30, 1883.

Fort McKavett was once called by General William T. Sherman "the prettiest post in Texas." It is said that in the early 1900s a west-bound family stopped-over here with their sick daughter. The child died during the night, and the family pressed on without her. Her spirit is still sensed here. Also found here is the ghostly voice of a First Sergeant who is still carrying out his duties. He has been heard on the parade ground "talking to" (aka "shouting at") his troops.

Several years after the incident, a family living at the fort heard a knock on their door late at night. The caller was a young girl dressed in turn-of-the century clothing. "Follow me!" she cried, and ran toward the barracks. The family ran after her; it was far too late for a child to be out by herself. But when the girl reached the barracks, she disappeared into the wall and no evidence of the child could be found in side the building. Several people who lived at the fort prior to the 1970s reported similar experiences.

David Bischofhausen, superintendent at Fort McKavett State Historical Park, has never seen the little girl in turn-of-the-century clothing but he has a healthy respect for the past he lives with every day. One winter morning several years ago, Bischofhausen was in his office at the fort's old hospital when he heard someone wearing heavy boots walking back and forth along the porch. Knowing no one was in the park at the time, he went out to check but found nothing. When he returned to his office, the heavy footsteps resumed.

Another time, the superintendent was working at his home near the park when he heard "a voice like a first sergeant talking to his troops." The far off voice was in the vicinity of the park, and Bischofhausen went to investigate. The voice got louder as he got closer to the parade ground. "He was really on a tirade," said Bischofhausen. But as the superintendent approached the parade ground the voice faded. It started again when he retreated.

## Mission San Clemente

Mission San Clemente was a temporary mission established by the expedition of Juan Domínguez de Mendoza while it was camped on a river named the "Glorious San Clemente," from March 16 to May 1, 1684. Interpretations of Mendoza's route have placed the mission variously on the Colorado River west of Ballinger (Herbert Eugene Bolton), near the confluence of the Concho and Colorado rivers (Carlos E. Castañeda), and on the South Llano River (Jesse W. Williams).

The most recent study, by Seymour V. Connor, locates the mission on the San Saba River west of Menard. After calculating the approximate location of the mission, Connor discovered in the vicinity the remains of a massive stone ruin that matched Mendoza's description. Excavation in 1968 uncovered remarkably few items, suggesting that the site, although requiring significant manpower for its construction, was occupied only briefly. During their six-week stay at San Clemente the Spaniards were joined by 2,000 to 3,000 Indians, most of who were baptized by the two priests accompanying Mendoza. After several attacks by the Apaches from the north and the Salineros from Nueva Vizcaya, the Spaniards abandoned the mission.

Despite the desire of Mendoza and Father Nicolás López to return and establish a permanent mission, the appearance of the La Salle expedition on the Texas coast in 1685 persuaded the Spanish government to concentrate its energies in East Texas instead. A number of witnesses have reported see a grisly Indian attack replayed here, as if it were a movie and the mission was the screen.

## Rheem Air Conditioning Building

This building that houses the Rheem Air Conditioning Company occupies a site that used to be a saloon. Local history reports that this location is where a man named Isaiah was gunned down. Many believe that it is Isaiah's spirit that now moves things, walks around, and once, before the Rheem Air Conditioning Company occupied the building, he slapped a customer who voiced a doubt about his existence.

## Texas Grill

Located across from the Coppini Cowboy Statue on the courthouse square, Ballinger has the incredibly cheap and always packed Texas Grill, open 24 hours at the corner of US-83 and Hwy-67. What few visitors realize is that this popular eatery is also haunted. Many have heard ghostly footsteps and strange apparitions have been reported here.

## Texas Burger House

While the Texas Grill has long thrived, the Texas Burger House faded away. This place used to be a bustling restaurant but due to a sudden loss of sales the restaurant closed down. It is said that the ghost of the man that started this business haunts the second floor of the place. The building has now been turned into a Mexican Restaurant and the second floor is now used as a storage place but some of the employees said they get a cold felling when entering the second floor.

## BANDERA, TEXAS

Bandera is on State Highway 16 fifty miles northwest of San Antonio in east central Bandera County. A town site plat for the settlement, designated county seat at the formation of Bandera County in 1856, was filed with the first county commissioners' court that year by John James, Charles DeMontel, and John Herndon. The site, on a cypress-lined bend of the Medina River, had been occupied by Indians, then by white campers making shingles. The town and county were named for nearby Bandera Pass. The founders formed a partnership in 1853 to build a town and water-powered lumber mill. They recruited immigrant workers from Upper Silesia by way of the Polish colony in Karnes County (see poles). These workers arrived in 1855, and each family received purchase rights to town lots and farmland. The presence of the United States Cavalry at Camp Verde after 1856 encouraged increased activity and settlement.

### Bandera Pass

According to a book in the Kerrville Library Bandera Pass is one of the most haunted places in Kerr County. Bandera Pass is some Hills that separate Kerr County and Bandera County. Bandera Pass has its own ghost lights that nobody can explain like those of Marfa and Anson. The lights are believed to be that of spirits that are protecting a lost Treasure that settlers hid from Indians back in the 1800's. Bandera Pass also has a Headless Horseman who rides from Bandera Texas to Center Point Texas. He is a Mail carrier who got his head cut off by Apache Indians his fate is to ride for eternity looking for his head. Bandera Pass also has a ghost wagon of settlers that were murdered by Apache Indians. These settlers now ride on certain nights and cut thru local ranchers pastures. People have reported seeing all of these three in the surrounding area. All of this is in the Kerrville area.

## BANGS, TEXAS

Bangs is on U.S. highways 67 and 84 and the Santa Fe Railroad six miles west of Brownwood in west central Brown County. The town was named for its location in the Samuel Bangs survey. In 1886 a post office was established there, and in 1892 Bangs had eight businesses and a population of fifty. A school was begun that year. In 1900 the population was 136.

By 1915, when the town incorporated, Bangs had 600 residents and twenty-one businesses, including four churches, a bank, and a weekly newspaper.

The following year a water system was installed, and natural gas was piped into the community in 1920. The Bangs Independent School District, formed in 1927, eventually consolidated nine other school districts. Highway 67 was built through the town in 1932. After World War II several additions added new housing units to Bangs. Brownwood began supplying Bangs with filtered water in 1946. In 1963 a new high school was built, and passenger train service ended for the community in 1965. In 1973 Bangs became home to the controversial New Testament Holiness Church, led by David Heze Terrell, who also ran World Ministries, Incorporated, of Dallas. Bangs slowly grew to a population of 1,214 in 1970 and 1,716 in 1980, then declined to 1,555 inhabitants in 1990.

## Wilson Home

After witnessing a bizarre murder-suicide that took place inside this home, many have reported seeing strange lights and apparitions moving about the house.

# BELTON, TEXAS

Belton, the county seat of Bell County, is on Nolan Creek at the junction of Interstate 35 and U.S. highways 81 and 190, near the geographic center of the county. The area was first settled in the late 1840s. When Bell County was established in 1850 the small settlement of Nolan Springs, named for adventurer Philip Nolan, was chosen as county seat and renamed Nolanville. Col. Henry B. Elliot surveyed the area, and E. Lawrence Stickney made a plat of the town. The town was laid out on the Shelbyville plan, with a large courthouse square as its focus. The post office was established as Nolanville in October 1850. In December 1851 the Texas legislature incorporated the town and changed the name to Belton, after Bell County.

## University of Mary Hardin Baylor

The University of Mary Hardin-Baylor originated in 1845 in Independence as the Female Department of Baylor University. For the first 133 years it had the distinction of being called the oldest college for women west of the Mississippi. In 1971 it became coeducational. It has never merged with any other college, and continues to operate under its original charter. Baylor University, chartered under the Republic of Texas in 1845, fulfilled the purpose of the Texas Baptist Education Society of the Union Baptist Association to provide Christian education for its sons and daughters. Section six of the charter stipulated a Preparatory Department and a Female Department along with the provisions for the males. For the first six years all students were taught by the same faculty in the same building, although parental preference for separation of the sexes probably was met by scheduling separate classes.

In 1851 a step toward the separation of colleges came through the insistence of the second president, Rufus C. Burleson, that the sexes be separated.

In 1851 Burleson took the male students to a building on an adjacent hill and left the female students in the old frame building of Independence Academy with Horace Clark as principal. In 1855 the Female Department moved into a stone building built to Clark's design: the tall stone columns of the Female Department building are all of Baylor that stands today in Independence.

## Pressor Hall

The ghost of a girl who was killed by her boyfriend haunts this University. The top floor of Pressor Hall has been converted to storage due to unexplainable events like hearing a piano playing, elevator doors closing and opening, and the sound of footsteps. A campus police officer refuses to enter the building but will only lock the building from the outside because of the phenomena he witnessed here. It is said that you can see her in the window as you walk by at night. Many students have actually come in to close contact with this ghost.

## Wal-Mart

This Wal-Mart store, located at 603 East Central Avenue, is said by 3rd shift staff to be haunted by the apparitions of a woman wearing a Wal-Mart uniform and a small boy. Additional information reveals that there have been two separate sightings of these spirits by night shift workers.

In one case, a night time manager was walking by a toy aisle and saw a woman with a Wal-Mart smock on stocking the shelves. It suddenly dawned on the manager that no one was supposed to be in that area so she stopped and went back to the aisle where she had seen the young woman, however, the mysterious woman was nowhere to be found. On a different occasion a night associate was in the receiving area and turned to find a little boy standing near her. She then heard a peculiar noise behind her and glanced back, she saw nothing. When she looked back at the little boy, he was gone.

# THE COLONY, TEXAS

The Colony is by Lake Lewisville near the intersection of State Highway 121 and Farm Road 423, eight miles east of Lewisville, fifteen miles northeast of the Dallas-Fort Worth International Airport, and twenty-four miles north of downtown Dallas in southeastern Denton County. It is named after the Peters' colony. The Colony is on the site of the Hedgcoxe War of 1852, in which armed settlers raided and burned the office of the Texas Emigration and Land Company. The community was established as a housing development by Fox and Jacobs, Incorporated, on some 3,000 acres in 1973.

## Crider Road

At the site where a 3-story mansion, known as the Crider House, recently burned (the mansion was the site of serial murders), screams can still be heard, and people often see apparitions. The three-story mansion, which burned down at the beginning of 1999, was said to be without ownership for ninety-nine years. Allegedly, a serial killer used this house as his killing ground and over the years was said to have murdered over 1,000 men and women in this home. Many reported hearing screams and seeing flashing lights and ghosts when driving down Crider Road. The house was so scary that it was never really thoroughly searched.

## COMAL COUNTY, TEXAS

Comal County (L-15) is located in south central Texas on the divide between the Blackland Prairies and the Balcones Escarpment. Its largest city and county seat, New Braunfels, is twenty-nine miles northeast of San Antonio and forty-five miles southwest of Austin. The county's center lies at 29°48' north latitude and 98°17' west longitude. The county comprises 555 square miles of prairie and Hill Country terrain. The eastern quarter, below the Balcones Escarpment, is gently rolling grass and crop land ranging in elevation from 600 to 750 feet above sea level. The Blackland Prairie soil of this section is loam with clay subsoils and is well suited for cultivation.

### The Devil's Backbone

The Devil's Backbone is one of the West's most widely known haunts. The Devil's Backbone covers nearly 4,700 acres of Texas hill country that stretches from San Antonio to Austin. This massive plot of land is held in high regard as both a sacred place among Native Americans and a cursed and haunted place among those who have witnessed its paranormal attributes.

A group of men staying in a cabin on the range during a cattle drive were awakened in the middle of the night by the sound of nearby horses. Fearing the theft of their herd, the men raced outside, only to find a band of ghostly riders dressed in Civil War uniforms riding by the cabin. In a matter of seconds, the riders had disappeared. When the cattlemen examined the area around their cabin, they found no traces of the ghostly riding party. There were no hoof marks, no trampled foliage, and no sign of any horse other than their own.

Many witnesses claim that they have seen the apparitions of Native Americans. Hunters in the area report being trailed by the ghostly Indians. Apparitions dressed like Benedictine Monks have been seen on the many trails that wind through the area. A bar located near the beginning of one such trail also has its share of ghosts. Aptly named "The Devil's Backbone", the bar is haunted by two ghosts. The first, the spirit of a man who was shot and killed in the bar during its rowdy times in the Old West turns lights on and off, rearranges furniture, and knocks over drinks and chairs.

The second ghost, said to be that of a Native American, appears in the restrooms and on the bar's front landing. Shadowy and odd figures can be seen all along the ridge that runs through The Devil's Backbone, and mysterious blue lights and the sounds of a large band of horses are common in an area where no one is present.

## Adobe Verde

The Adobe Verde is located in the town of Gruene, in the 1920's this Tex-Mex restaurant was one of the first electric cotton gins. Back in the early days of the cotton gin, a grounds keeper known to present employees as "Frank" supposedly hung himself from the rafters of the vaulted ceiling. He couldn't bear to live without his recently deceased lover.

"Frank" now roams the restaurant playing practical jokes like turning lights on and off, throwing things off counters, and bumping glasses together. Sometimes you can even hear someone with boots on running back and forth along the upstairs dining area, but when you go and look around know one is there.

# ELDORADO, TEXAS

Eldorado, the county seat of Schleicher County, is at the intersection of U.S. highways 190 and 277, forty-five miles south of San Angelo near the center of the county. The area was part of a grant made by the state of Texas to the Houston East and West Texas Railway Company in 1878, but the railroad laid no track there. In 1895 W. B. Silliman acquired half interest in one of the sections of land and formed a company with two other men to establish a new townsite. Silliman surveyed the site, named the new town Eldorado, opened a store, and attracted residents from nearby Verand by offering them free town lots if they would move to Eldorado. The post office at Verand was officially transferred to Eldorado in 1895, and by 1896 Eldorado had two general stores and 100 residents. The community's first school was established in 1897. When Schleicher County was organized in 1901, Eldorado was named county seat.

## Highway just outside of town

On this lonely stretch of highway, a man and woman were killed in a car wreck. A number of small crosses were erected in order to mark the place of their death. Sometimes passersby will see the body of a man lying by the crosses, or a woman asks for a ride back to town to call her kids. A number of good Samaritans have dropped her off at the closest convenience store, where she immediately disappears.

## North East section of town

The time of day plays no concern for the unusual sightings that occur in this area. During the daylight hours, voices of children playing and adults talking can be heard, though no one can be found to account for the sounds. At night strange orbs can be seen floating along the roadways some as large as a basketball.

In some of the homes, sounds of dishes breaking are verily clearly heard but none are ever seen to have been broken. Closets in the home have auras of foreboding, as if some one was staring at you as you passed. One homeowner shot a trespassing dog at night only to find that it vanished before his eyes at point blank range.

As children walk from one home to another, they would here additional footsteps along side. During a family get together several family members slept out in the back yard under a night-light placed in the yard, during the night they awoke to see a hat that belonging to the owner of the house rise from the table, lift about 6 feet in the air, go toward the back door. Once there the screen door opened and the hat proceeded inward after a brief pause. The screen door shut after the hat entered. All of this time there was no wind, and it was all done in silence.

## ELGIN, TEXAS

Elgin is at the intersection of U.S. Highway 290 and State Highway 95, fifteen miles north of Bastrop in north Bastrop County. In 1871 the Houston and Texas Central Railway built through the area and established a flag stop called Glasscock. The name was changed to Elgin, in honor of the railroad's land commissioner and surveyor, Robert Morris Elgin, on August 18, 1872, when the town was officially platted. Elgin was incorporated and received a post office the following year, and a Baptist Sunday school began meeting in a private home. Much of the community's early population was drawn from nearby Perryville, which the railroad had bypassed.

### Elgin Elementary school

Elgin Elementary School is located at 1005 W 2nd St, Elgin, TX. There are many current and former students who believe that the girls' restroom is haunted. Students are so certain that they advise each other not to go in alone.

## FISCHER, TEXAS

Fischer, twenty miles northwest of New Braunfels in the Hill Country of northern Comal County, developed in the 1850s as a supply center on the Devil's Backbone section of the road between San Marcos and Blanco. The site, settled by Hermann Fischer in 1853, became known as Fischer's Store when Fischer built a log trading post to serve the frontier community. Potters Creek School opened for local children in 1875, and a year later the Fischer's Store post office was established. Fischer Store School replaced Potters Creek in 1888, and after World War II Fischer became the center of a school district for northern Comal County. At the request of postal officials the community's name has changed twice: in 1894 Fischer's Store became Fischer Store, and in 1950 the name was shortened to Fischer. Sources in the 1960s reported that the Fischer family had held the local postmastership continuously since 1876. Fischer recorded a population of forty or fifty for most of the twentieth century but fell to twenty in the mid-1960s as Canyon Lake, four miles to the south, began filling. In 1967 Fischer was described just as it might have been a hundred years earlier-a country store and post office at a rural crossroads. Its population was listed as twenty from 1967 through 1990.

## Stage Stop Ranch

The Stage Stop Ranch is located at 1100 Old Mail Route Rd, Fischer Texas. A number of witnesses swear that if you go there between 12:00 to 2:00 you will see the ghost of a man hanging from a large oak tree that is found to the left of the main plaza. He was hung in the tree in the early 1800's for killing a sheriff's deputy. So outraged was the sheriff at the death of his deputy that he ordered that the corpse be left to hang until the buzzards picked him clean. You will also hear the wheels of the wagons that once past through.

# FREDERICKSBURG, TEXAS

Fredericksburg, the county seat of Gillespie County, is seventy miles west of Austin in the central part of the county. The town was one of a projected series of German settlements from the Texas coast to the land north of the Llano River, originally the ultimate destination of the German immigrants sent to Texas by the Adelsverein. In August 1845 John O. Meusebach left New Braunfels with a surveying party to select a site for a second settlement en route to the Fisher-Miller Land Grant. He eventually chose a tract of land sixty miles northwest of New Braunfels, where two streams met four miles above the Pedernales River; the streams were later named Barons Creek, in Meusebach's honor, and Town Creek. Meusebach was impressed by the abundance of water, stone, and timber and upon his return to New Braunfels arranged to buy 10,000 acres on credit. The first wagon train of 120 settlers arrived from New Braunfels on May 8, 1846, after a sixteen-day journey, accompanied by an eight-man military escort provided by the Adelsverein.

Surveyor Hermann Wilke laid out the town, which Meusebach named Fredericksburg after Prince Frederick of Prussia, an influential member of the Adelsverein. Each settler received one town lot and ten acres of farmland nearby. The town was laid out like the German villages along the Rhine, from which many of the colonists had come, with one long, wide Main Street roughly paralleling Town Creek. The earliest houses in Fredericksburg were built simply, of post oak logs stuck upright in the ground. These were soon replaced by Fachwerk houses, built of upright timbers with the spaces between filled with rocks and then plastered or whitewashed

## Chuckwagon Inn B & B

The Chuckwagon Inn, 909 East Main Street is an old stone house was built in the German tradition in 1854, and was even a dairy farm around the turn of the century. Electrical problems, window shades that roll themselves, disappearing/reappearing items and odd wet foot prints are mostly attributed to the ghost of Mrs. Mueller. The Chuckwagon Inn, another old (1854) home in Fredericksburg, also performs double duty as a haunted B&B in this scenice town. The spirits have different personalities, leading residents to believe they are dealing with at least two separate ghosts. Like many other spirits, these love to toy with the electricity, turning lights on and off throughout the old and new sections of the inn (and on one occasion, even exploding two light bulbs at once). Objects, especially articles of clothing, have been moved from place to place; one ghost (apparently the woman, known as "Mrs. Mueller") has even been known to hang stray items of clothing up for guests!

Out in the barn, people have also reported a set of wet footprints appear, apparently from nowhere, and then disappear after a few steps.

## Country Cottage Inn

Located at 249 E Main St in Fredericksburg, Texas the Country Cottage Inn has a well known reputation for spirit activities. Locked doors open themselves, ghost steps are heard on the 2nd floor, cold spots are noted and secure cabinets open themselves.

## Flagstone Sunday House

The Flagstone Sunday Guesthouse is located just a short walk to the heart of Main Street's downtown shopping and dining district. The TV turns itself on and off, shuffling sounds are heard on the 2nd floor, the closet door opens itself, lights turn on and off, and the shower comes on of its own accord.

## Admiral Nimitz Museum

The Admiral Nimitz Museum is located on the main street through this small town. The address is P O Box 777 Fredericksburg TX. This is the only institution in the continental United States dedicated exclusively to telling the story of Fleet Admiral Chester W. Nimitz and World War II in the Pacific Theater. Located on a nine-acre site, the complex includes The National Museum of the Pacific War-George Bush Gallery, the Nimitz Hotel museum, the Japanese Garden of Peace, the Pacific Combat Zone, the Plaza of the Presidents, the Surface Warfare Plaza, the Memorial Wall, the Veterans Walk of Honor and the Center for Pacific War Studies.

In addition to nearly 45,000 square feet of indoor exhibit space, the museum boasts an impressive display of Allied and Japanese aircraft, tanks, guns and other large artifacts made famous during the Pacific War campaigns.

However, there are those who swear that there are things in this museum that you cannot easily see. For example, there are some employees that have heard footsteps late at night in areas that should be empty of life (as we know it). They say you can see shadows of men walking through out the building, as if looking at the exhibits. Lights will suddenly go on/off during periods when there is no one else in the building.

# GATESVILLE, TEXAS

Gatesville, the county seat of Coryell County, is on the Leon River at the intersection of U.S. Highway 84 and State Highway 36, eighty miles north of Austin in the central part of the county. It was established on land donated by Richard G. Grant shortly after the county was organized in 1854 and took its name from nearby Fort Gates. James C. Newton became the first postmaster when the post office was established in July of that year. Gatesville was fairly isolated during the early years of its existence. Supplies had to be brought by wagon from Houston, 200 miles away. The town grew slowly in the late 1850s and little, if any, during the Civil War. Afterward, however, the town profited from the large influx of settlers moving to Texas to build new lives. In 1870 Gatesville was incorporated with a mayoral form of government; by 1880 its population had risen to 434, and it had become an important frontier supply station.

## Hackberry Unit 3B, TDCJ

Hackberry Unit 3B, TDCJ was formerly the Gatesville State School for Boys, the correctional institution for all Texas boys in need of being corrected. This facility was established in 1887. Mountain View School was established in 1962. The facility closed down by Judge William Wayne Justice in 1979.

The former Gatesville State School for Boys is now part of the Texas Department of Criminal Justice. Guards and inmates have reported seeing young boys playing marbles and chasing each other

## Mountain View Correctional Facility

This facility was once the Mountain View School affiliated with the Gatesville State School for Boys. This is now a women's prison but was once State School for boys. When you first start to work there the prisoners will tell you that there are little boys haunting the dorms. I witnessed this first hand more then once. One night while working 3rd shift one of the guards was standing at the sink area of the dorm and was looking in the mirror when she saw someone walking in the dayroom area. She went to investigate and was puzzled that where she had seen the movement there was no one there. Also during a 3rd shift watch one of the female guards was making her rounds when something ran out from one of the small cubical in front of her causing her to scream and wake up the prisoners. She quit not soon after that.

# GEORGETOWN, TEXAS

Georgetown is a city in Williamson County, in the Austin-Round Rock metro area. It is the county seat. The community is in the Central Standard time zone.

## Annie Pearl Elementary School

Everyone called her the nine o'clock ghost. A little girl was killed on the play ground of the Annie Pearl Elementary School by her own mother because she could not take care of her. Now every night if you drive by with your lights off and windows down you can see one of the swings moving back and fourth and you can hear a small sweet voice sing "ring around the rosy pockets full of poses ashes, ashes will you come and play with me please!"

# GOLIAD, TEXAS

Goliad, the county seat of Goliad County, originated as one of the oldest Spanish colonial municipalities in the state. The town is on the Southern Pacific Railroad, the San Antonio River, U.S. highways 59 and 183, and State Highway 239. It was established in October 1749, when colonizer José de Escandón recommended moving Nuestra Señora del Espíritu Santo de Zúñiga Mission and its royal protector, Nuestra Señora de Loreto de La Bahía del Espíritu Santo Presidio (Presidio La Bahía), from the Guadalupe River to a site named Santa Dorotea, on the San Antonio River. A new presidio, La Bahía, was built on a hill near the river, where sand, limestone, and timber were abundant. Around the presidio walls grew the settlement of La Bahía, and on the opposite bank stood Mission Espíritu Santo.

## Goliad State Historical Park

There have been ghostly nuns spotted in the Mission Espíritu Santo. Reports also tell of seeing an apparition of an Indian on horse back, hearing the sounds for drums and the smell of pipe smoke. There have also been reports of a phantom wolf that runs in the woods & disappears. The centerpiece of Goliad State Historical Park is the reconstructed Mission Espíritu Santo, founded in 1722 and moved to its present site 27 years later. There are believed to be more than 20 people buried around the stone church in the mission compound, which dates from 1777. Perhaps it is the spirit of one of these people who attracts the woman in a white shroud seen floating across the grounds on chilly, misty nights.

## Presidio La Bahia

Many spirits are seen here, among them a mysterious "Woman in Black". Some suggest that the spirits may be those of people buried on the grounds of the chapel, and some believe that they are the ghosts of Col. James Fannin and his troops. Mexican General Antonio Lopez de Santa Ana ordered the Colonel and his troops executed after they lost the Battle of Coleto.

This is an Old Spanish mission dating from the 1700s. It is reportedly extremely haunted, due to the many Texan revolutionaries executed there by general and President of Mexico, Antonio Lopez de Santa Anna on Palm Sunday, 1836. Among other phenomenon is a very short priest that roams the chapel yard, a cold, misty area in one corner, moans and sighs heard throughout the main yard, and a lady who is often seen praying in the chapel. More information can be found here: www.lonestarspirits.org

Historical parks under the stewardship of the Texas Parks and Wildlife Department have been meticulously preserved or restored to present an accurate and authentic picture of the state's past. So authentic are these places, it's easy to see why history can come alive in an almost literal sense for some people. But reports of figures such as the woman in black at the reconstructed Presidio La Bahía near Goliad State Park should in no way draw attention away from the sites' historical and educational value. Similar stories have been reported from many of the parks, tales that often reflect the attitudes and cultures of past generations.

## Execution Site of Colonel Fannin and his Troops

More recent history was the 1836 execution of Colonel James Fannin and his troops on orders of General Antonio Lopez de Santa Anna, an event known as the Goliad Massacre. The executions took place a short distance outside Presidio La Bahía and many say that the spirits of those executed still haunt the area. A camper in the park recently told Superintendent James Hudnall that he was awakened by men's voices and moans coming from the area of the massacre. People have also told about an unsettling experience they have had as they walked across a bridge in front of the park. They report hearing someone walking behind them, right in step. When they turn to investigate, no one is there and the footsteps stop. When they start walking again, the footsteps resume.

## HUTTO, TEXAS

Hutto, on the highway to Taylor, was named for James Emory Hutto, a pioneer of Texas. James Emory was born in Greenville, South Carolina to John Castleberry Hutto and Nancy Holliday, May 8, 1824, and was reared on a farm in his native state. James with his family moved to Madison County Alabama where later his mother died, about 1836 or 1837. James' father remarried about 1840 and when James was age 23 he moved to Texas while his father and stepmother moved to Arkansas. Up on his arrival in Texas in 1847 he engaged in farming and stock raising in Travis County. About 1855 he moved to Williamson county, settling near were Hutto has since been built, this town having been named in honor of him. For 20 years, between 1855 and 1875, he was one of the wealthy cattlemen of this section of the country. He did take time to serve in the Confederate army 3 years. He was appointed postmaster on June 27, 1877.

## Jake's Bridge

The legend is that if you go out to Jake's Bridge at night, you can see the body of a man who committed suicide on the bridge. You will also be able to hear his wife crying out for her children. Later it was added that your headlights on your car would go out!

# JUNCTION, TEXAS

Junction, the county seat of Kimble County, is on U.S. Highway 83 ninety-eight miles southeast of San Angelo. It is named for its location at the confluence of the North and South Llano rivers. Junction was founded in the spring of 1876 following the organization of the county in January of that year. It was originally named Denman after its surveyor, but became Junction City in 1877 and simply Junction in 1894. Junction City won the role of county seat from Kimbleville, an unsuccessful settlement, in late 1876, after the first county court session, probably because Kimbleville was subject to floods.

## Bridge

On the east side of town is a steel girder bridge where some say you can still hear the echoes of a long-ago car crash.

## Junction High School

Former students of the Junction High School are apparently still "Smoking in the Boys' Room" as the smell of cigarette smoke will sometimes fill the room and at least one person has heard voices from the bathroom when he knew it was empty

# LA GRANGE, TEXAS

La Grange, the county seat of Fayette County, is on the Colorado River and State Highways 71 and 159, U.S. Highway 77, and the Union Pacific Railroad in the central part of the county some sixty-three miles southeast of Austin. It is at the site where La Bahía Road crossed the Colorado River. Aylett C. Buckner settled in the vicinity about 1819, and in 1826 John Henry Moore built a twin blockhouse within what are now the city limits; he named it Moore's Fort. Area settlers sought shelter there from Indian attacks, and by 1831 a small community had developed around the fort. A town was platted in 1837, and when the Congress of the Republic of Texas established Fayette County that year, La Grange became its seat of government. The county had been named after the Marquis de Lafayette, and the county seat took its name from his chateau.

## Old La Grange High School

Some say former teacher, Rosa Mieneke, haunts the second floor of the La Grange High School. There is no question that a substantial number of people have heard footsteps and a woman's voice late at night coming from the second floor. Some have also been adamant that books fly across the room, and papers tear themselves in half.

# LLANO, TEXAS

Llano, the county seat and largest town of Llano County, is on the Llano River and State Highway 71, seventy-five miles northwest of Austin. It was founded in compliance with a February 1, 1856, state legislative act establishing Llano County. Tracts donated by John Oatman, Sr., Amariah Wilson, and the Chester B. Starks estate provided a surveyed site of 250 acres for the county seat on both sides of the Llano River near the center of the proposed county. An alternative site, on Wright's Creek, was proposed by the residents of the Bluffton-Tow Valley area. The Llano River location was chosen in an election held on June 14, 1856, under a live oak on the south bank of the river, near the present site of Roy Inks Bridge in Llano. Into the 1870s the town was little more than a frontier trading center, with a handful of log buildings housing business establishments, a post office, and a few homes.

## <u>Badu House</u>

The Badu House, located on Texas Highway 71 in Llano was originally built as a small-town bank in 1891. However, it was converted into a home for Professor Badu in 1896. The Professor apparently loved his house and the town of Llano so well that many say that he has never left.

Today, this historic old building has been restored as a country inn and restaurant. It has a marble-floored front room, quaint dining rooms, original fixtures, and antique furnishings; six rooms and one suite with baths.

One guest reported that he and his wife had stayed in room 6 and that during their stay, they experienced many strange occurrences. There was a little girl who repeatedly entered their room during the night. She was crying each time they saw her, but she never stayed long enough for them to touch her or to find why she was crying. According to the witnesses, the scariest part was that she looked dead, she was transparent. It was very unsettling, and sad.

According to one of the employees, since there has been an investigation of the ghosts, the spirits seem somewhat unhappy. According to one employee, since the ghost hunters had left, his chair has been pushed forward a couple of times, his name has been called, and guests have reported a loud banging in the hallway. The new dishwasher was greeted with a rude voice of "do you have to be so loud ".

The Manager, George Rozelle, says there have been several reports of ghostly activity in the old building and he's even had the presence of spirits validated by an organization that specializes in such things. From all reports, the ghosts are friendly[27].

---

[27] Austin Chronicle, Volume 21, No. 32, April 5, 2002.

# LOCKHART, TEXAS

Lockhart, county seat of Caldwell County, is at the intersection of U. S. Highway 183 and State Highway 142, thirty miles southeast of Austin. It was named for Byrd Lockhart, who in 1831 received the land that later became the Lockhart town site as partial payment for his surveying work for the Mexican government. During the 1830s settlement in the area was limited by the threat of Indian raids, but after the battle of Plum Creek in 1840, more settlers began to arrive. By the mid-1840s, several families had made their home near Lockhart Springs, and when Caldwell County was established in 1848, the new town of Lockhart became the county seat.

## Lockhart County Court and Jail House

The original Lockhart Court and Jail building in this small town was just a log cabin built in 1855. Just after the turn of the century it was decided the city needed a larger, more permanent, and more secure structure, so a limestone jail was built downtown. It was later bought and torn down to make way for new businesses. That's when the current building was erected nearby.

This new building looks like a red brick castle, and had nine lockups divided into cells on the top three floors. The second floor of the building was for jail administration, and the ground floor was where the County Sheriff lived. The basement was storage. When a new, again larger, jail was built this uniquely designed building was closed in the early 1970s and eventually renovated and turned into the Caldwell County Historical Museum.

Some visitors say there is a great sense of sadness that permeates the top three floors of the building. Those who claim to be sensitive to psychic events say it can be suffocating. The jail section is filled with so much pain and sadness and death, it's hard for some people to even breathe! The whole place gives off bad vibes. You can sense that a lot of people died up there, and there was a lot of suffering. It's sad and creepy at the same time.

# LUCKENBACH, TEXAS

Luckenbach was established in 1849. One of the first settlers in the area was Jacob Luckenbach (1817-1911). A group of German nobility, the Adelsverein, hoped for great riches by establishing a colony in the New World. In 1845 Jacob signed up and sailed with his family on the Johann Dethardt to Indianola in December. Luckenbach was virtually unknown until Texas humorist and writer Hondo Couch bought the 10-acre town in the 1970s, supposedly because Dallas wasn't for sale. Although Couch has passed away, Luckenbach is alive and kicking, especially during concerts and events like the Mud Dauber's Ball. Check out the dance hall, blacksmith shop and general store.

## Kung Residence

The Kung Resident is a must see house in Luckenbach. According to witnesses, there are phantom whistles, mysterious footsteps can be heard climbing the stairs and faucets turn on and off by themselves. Others tell of doors that open themselves, even when latched and more than one startled witness has seen a male apparition in a blue shirt.

# NEW BRAUNFELS, TEXAS

New Braunfels, the county seat of Comal County, is at the confluence of the Guadalupe and Comal rivers and the intersection of Interstate Highway 35 and Farm Road 725, thirty miles northeast of San Antonio and forty-five miles southwest of Austin near the southeastern border of the county. It was founded on March 21, 1845, when, under the auspices of the Adelsverein, Nicolaus Zink led a German immigrant wagon train up the Guadalupe River to the ford of the San Antonio-Nacogdoches road. They made camp at a site on Comal Creek (now Dry Comal Creek) chosen by Prince Carl of Solms-Braunfels, the first commissioner general of the Adelsverein, and promptly organized to receive later arrivals.

## Prince Solms Inn

Prince Solms Inn Bed & Breakfast has become one of Texas' most famous landmarks. This establishment has been in continuous operation since being built by German craftsmen in 1898, originally named the Comal Hotel by the Eggeling family who built and operated it for more than 50 years. The Prince Solms Inn is located at 295 East San Antonio Street, New Braunfels, Texas one block east of the Town Plaza. It is the oldest operational hotel in New Braunfels.

There are said to be a number of spirits who reside within the walls of this historic old Inn. There is a former waitress that is said to haunt the bar and the Huntsman Room is said to be haunted by a former Union soldier. However, the most interesting story is about the ghostly bride.

In the early 1900's, a young woman and her family came to the hotel to celebrate her wedding to her fiancé. On her wedding day, the young woman got dressed into her beautiful wedding dress and waited patiently for her groom to come so they could be wed in the hotel. She waited and waited, he did not arrive. Fearing that her husband to be had changed his mine, her two brothers decided to ride back along the trail that they knew the groom would have followed. They never found him so the two brothers returned to the hotel to tell their sister they could not locate him and suspected something had happened to him. The young woman told her family that she was not going to leave the hotel, but she was going to wait for him to come so they could be married.

The sympathetic owners of the hotel offered the young woman a job so that she could stay at the hotel. The young woman agreed later became the innkeeper of the hotel. Sometime in the late 1920's or early 1930's, the woman passed away due to natural causes. Most thought that this was the end of the story, however, they were wrong.

In 1935, a young gentleman came through the front doors and proceeded through the hallway of the hotel toward the staircase to the second floor. The new innkeeper, sitting in the parlor, heard the man come in and as he started to go upstairs, she asked him if she could assist him. He continued up the staircase, only saying that he was here to see someone.

The innkeeper looked up the staircase and, to her amazement, saw a young woman in a wedding dress at the top of the staircase. As the young man reached the top of the stairs, he embraced the young woman, kissed her, and then they both disappeared. At this point, the innkeeper realized that the woman at the top of the stairs was the young woman who worked there for so many years while waiting for her true love to come. Was this man her true love she was waiting for?

The innkeeper did not believe what she had seen, so she went out the front door to ask if anyone else saw anything. On the front porch, there were three gentlemen, who were guests of the hotel, talking with each other. She asked them if they saw the young man enter the hotel. One of them said, "Sure, his horse is over by the hitching post." He pointed to the side of the building and sure enough there was a horse tied to the post.

The innkeeper told the men what she saw. They did not believe her, so they went into the hotel to look for the young man and the young woman in a wedding dress. The men searched every room, every closet, in the basement, and in the attic. There was no sign of either one of them. Where did they go? Who was it? The horse that was tied to the hitching post remained at the hotel for three months. No one ever claimed it.

After this sighting, the ghost of the young woman in a wedding dress has been seen several times since 1935. She has been seen in Sophie's Suite lying in bed with her wedding dress on. Also, she has been seen upstairs walking around in the hallway. Again, in her wedding dress and smiling in happiness. She has been seen downstairs in the cellar, as recent as 1960.

## The Hotel Faust

The Hotel Faust has the dubious reputation of being the most haunted hotel in Texas. Newspaper articles about the hotel ghost, noted for drifting in the hallways of an upper floor, entering closed doors, turning water and lights on and off, etc. A young girl, a cat, the former owner, and a former bellboy have been known to show up. One guest in room 218 had the water faucet come on in the middle of the night.

It was shortly after the First World War, city leaders felt that New Braunfels deserved a world class Hotel and groundbreaking for what is now The Faust began. The hotel opened officially in 1929, just in time for the Great Depression era. Originally called The Travelers Hotel, standing adjacent to the rail lines that converged nearby, soon the hotel became the place where business leaders and traveling businessmen sealed their deals. As devastating as the Depression was, the City only saw its first real economic test when the boll weevil blight hit the area, virtually destroying the textile industry of the region[28].

The Travelers weathered the Depression and blight thanks in great part to the people who originally envisioned a need for the hotel in the first place. Renamed The Faust in 1936, managed to struggle through the hard times prior to World War II. During the war, the hotel gained yet another reputation, this time as the honeymoon capitol of Texas. GI's training at nearby military facilities flocked to the hotel with their brides before going into combat.

Beginning some time after the death of the hotel's founder in 1932, a remarkable series of seemingly unrelated events began at the Faust. Walter Sr. had resided at the hotel and he had a reputation of being something of a trickster in life. When the hotel staff noticed that the furniture on the 4th floor hall was being rearranged virtually every night, they had no qualms about placing the blame at the feet of their most famous resident. In fact, some guests have even reported seeing old Walter on the 4th floor to this day and commented on how dashing he looked in his period suite and tie. He is also blamed for resetting the old fans in the hallway to high and opening doors for guests as they approach the front door. The doors are very heavy and have never opened by themselves, even in near tornado conditions.

While the permanent guest of the 4th floor may or may not be Walther Faust Sr., there is no doubt that his portrait, now located in a hallway leading to the basement, holds some energy from his brilliant spirit. As the story goes, there was a massive thunderstorm some years back, which plunged the entire hotel into darkness. This is not unusual in Texas, where severe weather often can take out an entire city. The manager on duty at the time found her way down the stairs toward the basement and was somewhat surprised to see light radiating from an alcove adjacent to the door to the basement's power room. The light was coming from the small lamp that lit the portrait of Walter Sr. and the woman thought nothing more about it, though it was unusual for this light to have power when the rest of the hotel did not. As she turned away to go into the basement proper, she heard a distinctive snicker, much like one you might expect hearing from a practical joker who has scored a complicated trick.

Thinking someone else was in the basement, she turned again and saw the picture was still illuminated, but saw no one and thought the sound must have been the wind. There were no doors or windows from which the light might be reflected from another source, she noted.

A few moments later, she reset the circuit breakers and retraced her steps back to the lobby, stopping momentarily to note that the bulb on the hotel founder's portrait was now out. Once everything else was back to normal, she asked a maintenance worker in the hotel to replace the bulb, which she surmised

---

[28]http://www.realtraveladventures.com/FavoriteFinds/faust_s_ghost__haunted_hotel_in_t exas.htm

had to have blown out when she reset the breakers. To her astonishment, the maintenance man told her that it was useless to replace the bulb and impossible to have seen the light on that night. That electrical line, he reported, was cut at the main breaker box, had no power and had been inoperative for years. To prove his point, he returned to the alcove with the manager and tested the circuit, which was indeed cold.

Both guests and employees have reported other spirits at work in the historic old hotel. The most common report is of "cold spots" usually related in spirit phenomenon. A recent guest noted one evening that with the air conditioning off, there was a constant corner of her bedroom, near a window overlooking the front of the hotel, that was unbelievably cold, a good trick when the temperature outside was well into the 90's. One night clerk noted that on some evenings the door to the front desk area will begin to swing open and shut without anyone touching it and there is no strong draft to cause the phenomenon.

Before the existence of the microbrewery in the taproom there was a regular hotel bar. The last of the old bartenders would tell the story about a ghost who would rearrange bottles behind the bar at will. The barman said that he always placed the half empty bottles in front of the full ones each night at closing time, and without fail, he would regularly return to find the process reversed the next day.

A hotel maid reported while servicing a guest room on the 2nd floor, she walked into the hallway to see a little girl standing near her linen cart. When she attempted to talk to the youngster, the girl turned and ran, straight into and through a solid wall. The maid later found that there is a photo of the child hanging in the 3rd floor hallway. A little research showed that the wall through which the little girl ran was once a doorway into a suit of rooms, long since subdivided. The child has been nicknamed Christine, a name that kept surfacing in the maid's head after her first sighting, although no one really knows what her name might have been or why she is still in residence here.

The second floor also has a second ghostly presence; a man in what is reportedly turn-of-the-century dress, who is seen walking into the elevator. After several sightings, both regular guests and hotel employees decided they wanted to see who this man was since they had only been able to see him from the side and back in the hallway. One of the employees did have the opportunity to get a good enough look to identify him as a man from a photo on the second floor, who is pictured with his wife. Other ghost hunters have tried to beat the man down the single flight of steps to meet him face to face in the lobby, but all have failed. Though the 80-year-old elevator is slow, the elevator always arrives at the lobby without its passenger!

## Karbach Haus B & B Home

Located at 487 West San Antonio Street, the Karback Haus Bed & Breakfast is managed and owned by the descendants of Dr. Karbach - and relatives of the ghosts.

There are a number of spirits that are said to reside in this lovely old home. The mysterious sound of children playing is attributed to "Roy", the owner's son who died in an accident several years ago. Other ghosts include Katherine Karbach, the owner's mother, Martha Jo Karbach, the owner's sister, and Hulda Eiband, one of the original owners of the home. They straighten up, turn off lights, and rock on the shaded porch.

## NOACK, TEXAS

Noack is on Farm Road 112 thirty-six miles northeast of Austin in eastern Williamson County. It was established as a Wendish[29] settlement called Hochkirk when Peter Zieschang moved there in 1870. It was renamed Noack in 1902, when John Ernest Noack became postmaster. The community's Lutheran church was organized in 1891 and was still active in 1984. A school was established there in 1922, and the Noack oilfield was developed in 1933.

### <u>Lawrence Chapel</u>

The old Lawrence Chapel has been in use since it was erected and has managed to collect quite a number of stories of odd happenings. It is said that late at night corpse's candles[30] can be seen in the graveyard behind the church. Generally, after this happens, someone in the area dies. There is also the story that many years ago, a preacher dropped dead during his sermon. Now after dusk the dead preacher can be heard trying to finish his sermon.

## PAINT ROCK, TEXAS

Paint Rock, the county seat of Concho County, is in the north central part of the county at the junction of Ranch Road 380 and U.S. Highway 83, about

---

[29] The Wends were a little-known immigrant group that settled in Texas among the Germans in the mid-19th century. An ancient Slavic people also known as Lusatian Sorbs, they had resisted assimilation in Europe for over 1,000 years, preserving their own language and customs though not their political independence.

The ancestors of the Wends were West Slavs called the Milceni and Luzici who occupied an area east of the Oder River in the early middle Ages. The Wendish homeland is part of the territory known as Lusatia in East Germany. Approximately 50 miles southeast of Berlin, it is about 1,800 square miles in area and is bordered by Czechoslovakia on the south and Poland on the east. The Spree River flows through its two major towns, Bautzen and Cottbus. The Wends have managed to maintain their identity although they have been ruled at various times by Germans, Hungarians, Poles, and Bohemians. In both world wars they unsuccessfully sought recognition by the major powers as a nation-state.

[30] Corpse Candles are very mysterious lights that are often seen in churchyards or graveyards. They are sometimes also called Dead Men's Candles, Jack O'lanterns and Fetch lights. The Candles are supposed to presage death. The size of the candle will indicate the age of the victim. The candle lights may be red, blue or white. They can appear near the Earth or up in the air.

twenty-one miles northeast of Eden. The town was named for the extensive Indian pictographs about a mile away on the bluffs of the Concho River. County commissioners, selecting a site for the county seat in July 1879, chose a location just west of the junction of the Concho River and Hog Creek. The site was at one of the few good fords on the river, which carried more water at that time than it did in the 1990s. Despite an initial error that led to the construction of the first buildings on the wrong survey, which necessitated their removal to a site about a half mile to the east, Paint Rock grew steadily.

## Weldon Ostrander House

According to legend, the entire Ostrander family disappeared one evening in 1889. No explanation was ever found to explain where the family went, nor were any of them ever seen again. However, since the time of the disappearance, there have been ghostly noises heard coming from inside the old Weldon-Ostrander House, and a number of apparitions are sometimes seen in and around the house.

# PALESTINE, TEXAS

Palestine, the county seat of Anderson County, is at the intersection of U.S. highways 79 and 287, at the center of the county, some 108 miles southeast of Dallas and 150 miles north of Houston. It was the early home of Daniel Parker and was named after the Parkers' former home of Palestine, Illinois. It was also the home of John H. Reagan and Governor Thomas M. Campbell. When the Texas legislature established Anderson County in 1846, no community existed at the stipulated center of the county, so Palestine was established.

## Palestine County Courthouse

There is a legend of when a baby fell out of its mother's hands at the Palestine County Courthouse and died. At night or anytime when you are alone in the courthouse you can hear a baby crying. Some times you can hear footsteps of a baby.

## Wiffletree Inn

Located at 1001 N Sycamore St the Wiffletree Inn was built in 1911. The Inn is an excellent example of The Craftsman Era in home building. We have four guest rooms, two with private baths and two that share a hall bath (note we never rent a shared bath situation without the consent of both parties.) A vacuum putting itself up, a tirade of door banging that lasted more than 20-minutes, and wispy apparitions were reported during renovations. Recently guests have reported feeling like someone sat down in bed next to them at night.

# PEYTON COLONY, TEXAS

Peyton Colony is unique in the history of Texas Hill Country for it was founded exclusively by black freedmen after the Civil War. The founder, Peyton Roberts, and others came not from Texas but from former homes in the South. The blacks formed a settlement in a beautiful setting in eastern Blanco County. They constructed a number of homes, a church and a school, the first black school in Blanco County. The residents named the community Peyton Colony in honor of it founder, Peyton Roberts. As the years passed, the Colony declined in population although much of the land is owned by descendents of the original settlers. The school was integrated in the 1960s and, although it is now closed, it still stands, as does the Mount Horeb Baptist Church. Ruins of former structures may still be seen around the church and school.

## Settlement

There have been a number of stories about unusual occurrences at the Peyton Colony Ranch, which is located where the original settlement was constructed. On one occasion, visitors to the ranch noticed that the satellite dish was buzzing and moving as if switching to monitor another satellite. One of the visitors made a comment to the owner regarding the delights of satellite TV and was informed that the dish had been disconnected years before. When examined, it was found that while the dish had moved its orientation, it was not longer active and clearly had not been operational for sometime just as the owner had said.

Voices have been heard in and around the barn when no one has been in the area and apparitions have been seen around the house. Mysterious footsteps have been heard in various parts of the house, there have been reports of the floor shaking as if in response to earth tremors and, though it was re-wired recently, there have been a number of unexplained electrical problems. There have also been reports of the doors to some of the kitchen cupboard slowly open as if someone was looking for something inside the cupboard. Visitors have heard very clear sounds of footsteps near them, but been able to see no one. One guest had the daylights scared out of her when, while in the bathroom, she heard voices outside the window and someone pounded on the side of the house below the window. A subsequent investigation showed that no one was in the area that could have been near the window.

# PFLUGERVILLE, TEXAS

Located about fifteen miles north of the Colorado River on the eastern edge of the blackland prairies, Pflugerville was founded in 1860 when William Bohls established a general store and post office in his residence, and named the town in honor of Henry Pfluger.

Pfluger first arrived in the area in 1849, leaving his German homeland to escape the Prussian War. He first purchased 160 acres of land two miles east of

Austin from John Liese, a brother-in-law who had immigrated before him.  In 1853, Henry Pfluger exchanged the land for a larger farm about five miles east of present day Pflugerville.  There the family lived in a five-room log cabin and raised corn, wheat, rye, beans, sweet potatoes, and sugar cane.  They also raised cattle which Henry and his sons drove to market on the Chisholm Trail.

## Cinemark Tinseltown 20

Though the Cinemark Tinseltown 20 is a fairly new and modern movie theater, there are many who swear that it is haunted. Most of the reports deal with the feeling of being watched and there are a number cold spots in certain parts of the building. Others talk about soft drink cups and popcorn bags, as well as the larger tubs being knocked over as if someone had kicked them. More disturbing, however, are reports of patron's possessions such as watches and rings simply vanishing.

# REFUGIO, TEXAS

Refugio, the county seat of Refugio County, is on the north bank of the Mission River at the intersection of U.S. highways 183 and 77 and State Highway 202. The site of the present city was a favorite camping ground of the Karankawa Indians, who developed a permanent village there known to the Spanish as Paraje de los Copanes (Place of the Copanes, a Karankawan tribe). The Spanish probably knew of the settlement as early as 1749, and according to some accounts José de Escandón wanted to establish a pueblo and presidio there. In 1795 the Nuestra Señora Del Refugio Mission was moved to the site. The Refugio Mission, the last Spanish mission to be secularized after the area became part of Mexico, operated continuously until February 1830. By then, at least 100 Mexicans lived on ranchos in the immediate vicinity, and a village existed around the mission. In 1831 James Power and James Hewetson acquired the rights to the old mission building and the town that surrounded it, and that same year the villa of Refugio was officially established.

## Refugio County Court House

A prisoner named Henry died while in the detox cell of the old jail which was located in the Refugio County Court House. Since that time, after all the lights have been turned off, he will turn them back on. Doors leading from the courtroom to the old jail will open by themselves and lights will turn on and off by themselves. Henry has been known to move things around and sometimes items from the jail will end up in employees' cars.

# SAN ANGELO, TEXAS

San Angelo, the county seat of Tom Green County, is on U.S. highways 87, 67 and 277, State highways 208 and 126, Farm roads 584, 765, 1223, 388, and 853, and the Atchison, Topeka and Santa Fe Railway, 220 miles northwest of

San Antonio. The history of the frontier town began in the late 1860s across the North Concho River from Fort Concho, which had been established in 1867. As an early frontier town, San Angelo was characterized by saloons, prostitution, and gambling. Officers of nearby Fort Concho would not leave the garrison after dark so shortly after the fort was established, Bartholomew (Bart) J. DeWitt, the founder of San Angelo, bought 320 acres of land from Granville Sherwood for a dollar an acre and, over the river, established a trading post, which was later called Santa Angela. There are several stories as to how the town was named, including one in which it was named for DeWitt's sister-in-law, a nun in San Antonio. A local historian found that DeWitt named the town in memory of his wife, Carolina Angela, who died in 1866.

## Angelo State University

Angelo State University was established in 1928, grew from an enrollment of 528 and thirty-eight faculty members into a major regional university with an enrollment of 6,500.

## Housing Office, Dorsey B. Hardeman Building

At Angelo State University, the murder and memory of Leandra Morales in the Hardeman Building in 1978 continues to haunt the university[31]. In late 1978 this lovely young coed, who is still referred to as Leandra by the Housing staff, worked for the school paper. She was very pretty and had a number of admirers. According to the story, one evening as she worked late on a story, one of the staff members of the paper, it was said that he was the photographer, made unwelcome advances. When she refused his advanced, he went into a rage and stabbed her to death with a pair of scissors. Then he drug her dead body to room 200 (now the housing office) and tried to conceal the evidence of his crime.

Members of the Ram Page staff have said the Hardeman Building was indeed haunted. Winston Hall, a columnist for the paper last year, included in his research of the haunted building accounts of "footsteps in the hallway, reflections of hazy apparitions appearing behind them while on the staircase, and even 'cold spots' in the hallway." The Ram Page staff, however, is now located in the third story of the library and there have been no appearances of Leandra … yet.

I might make mention that other witnesses have said that unexplained footsteps and the sounds of their argument can still be heard late at night on the second floor. The elevator by the housing office operates independent of corporeal human influence. Some students have reported spotting the girl's apparition. There are also a number of stories of unplugged radios in the Hardeman building having a disturbing tendency to plug themselves in and start playing.

---

[31]http://www.asurampage.com/vnews/display.v/ART/2004/10/29/4181647949c59.
Unsolved Mysteries by Jessica Garcia, October 29, 2004.

## Angelo State University - Girls High Rise Dorm

On the ninth floor of the girls high rise dorm, many former students swear that there is the ghost of a college student who was killed in April 1978. While those who see her are naturally startled, almost all agree that she is a very nice ghost.


## Fort Concho Historic Site

The Fort Concho National Historic Site is located at 630 South Oaks San Angelo, TX. Fort Concho was constructed in 1867 to protect settlers and the transportation routes between a chain of forts in the heartland of Texas. Situated at the junction of the North and Middle Concho Rivers, the site selected for the fort was very strategic to the government's stabilization of the region because no less than five major trails passed nearby. Even though the fort was surrounded by miles of flat treeless prairie, it was considered to be "One of the most beautiful and best ordered posts in Texas."

Several successful Indian campaigns against the Comanches were launched from Fort Concho. In addition, the post played a pivotal role in the suppression of illegal profiteering that was being conducted by Mexican and American traders known as "Comanchero's".

One of Fort Concho's most illustrious commanders was Colonel Ranald Mackenzie. Mackenzie was such a prominent character at the fort that it is said that he still attempts exert his command influence there from beyond the grave; so naturally, one of the most haunted locations at Fort Concho is the officer's quarters also known as "Officers Row". Located across the parade ground from the enlisted barracks, this row of sturdy stone houses serve as the impetus for most if not all of the ghostly tales that are told about Fort Concho.

Colonel Ranald Mackenzie is said to haunt his old residence at the center of Officers Row. The ghost of Colonel Mackenzie has been seen by visitors and staff at the old house on more than one occasion. It is said that Colonel Mackenzie was fond of his house and its location because he could see almost everything that was going on in the fort at any given time. The house was also located in a position that afforded Colonel Mackenzie a full view of the old stone corral where his units 127 Indian captives were held over the winter of 1873.

While preparing for a winter event one December, a female staff member working in the Mackenzie house reported that she had heard the unmistakable sound of footsteps walking around the back of the room behind her. Just as the woman turned to see who was there, she was knocked up against a wall by an invisible blast of cold air. Frightened and disoriented, the women also noticed that the "unique sound of knuckles cracking" seemed to accompany the strange manifestation. Since Colonel Mackenzie was known for cracking his knuckles, there was no doubt in the woman's mind that she had come face to face with the spirit of the famous commander.

Another of the "row's" many distinguished families was that of Colonel Benjamin Grierson, regimental commander of the 10th cavalry. It is said that

Colonel Grierson's, 12 year old daughter Edith died in the upstairs bedroom of one of the houses around her twelfth birthday. Over the years, many people have encountered Edith in the houses along officer row. In most instances, Edith is often seen quietly playing jacks.

Those people who have encountered her say that the first thing they notice is that the room where the girl is playing is substantially cooler than any of the other rooms in the house. Edith will acknowledge the presence of a person when they enter the room by turning her head and smiling at them before she turns her attention back to her game of jacks, but she will rarely say anything them.

One day, a florist delivered some flowers to one of the houses along Officers Row. The lady of the house told the driver to place two bouquets of flowers in the bedrooms at the top of the stairs, one to the right and one to the left. As the delivery man ascended the stairs with a large bouquet of flowers in each hand, he noticed that the temperature seemed cooler than in the foyer of the house. Reaching the top of the stairs, the man turned and entered the first bedroom on the right nearly tripping over a small girl playing jacks on the floor just inside the doorway. The man excused himself but the girl never appeared to even acknowledge his presence. The florist placed the flowers on the bedside table as instructed. Once finished, he left the room and placed the last bouquet of floors in the bedroom across the hallway.

Before going back down stairs, the florist looked in on the little girl across the hall and noticed that she was gone. He noted with some satisfaction that the flowers he had placed on the nightstand had been moved to a table in the corner of the room. He figured that the little girl had moved the flowers because he noticed that the girl's jacks were now laying on the table next to the bed.

Just as the florist was about to leave, he happened to see a picture hanging above the fire place. To the man's surprise, the little girl in the picture was a twin of the young girl he had just saw upstairs playing jacks. Believing that the small child was the daughter of the woman staying in the house, the florist mentioned that he had met the girl in the picture only moments before and commented on how she had moved the flowers from the nightstand. To the delivery man's surprise, the woman stated that she did not have a daughter and explained that Colonel Grierson's daughter Edith had died in upstairs bedroom where he had placed the flowers. Chuckling to herself at the delivery man's apparently look of distress, the woman informed the florist that countless others have seen the ghost of Edith in the house, and that he was not the first.

The Officers Quarters is not the only location at Fort Concho where ghostly activity has been report. The fort's headquarters building is also reputed to be a hot bed for paranormal encounters.

Once during one of the Christmas tours, Conrad McClure, a staff member working in the headquarters building saw a shadowy figure in a blue soldier's uniform brush past him while he was tending to the fireplace. Intrigued by his encounter with the unidentified ghost, McClure did a little detective work and learned that Second Sergeant Cunningham was the only soldier to ever die at Fort Concho. Cunningham was a chronic alcoholic who was hospitalized due to complications from liver disease. Knowing that he was going to die, Sergeant Cunningham requested that he be moved back to his barracks so that he could spend his last days with his friends and fellow soldiers. The end for old Irishman finally came one cold Christmas Day. Sergeant Cunningham suffered no more! After reading compiling all of this information, McClure was sure that the spirit he encountered in the headquarters building could be none other than that of Sergeant Cunningham.

Several of the other staff members believe that Sergeant Cunningham does not like females to be in the headquarters building but that he always seems to be looking out for the building and it occupants.

In addition to the ghosts of Colonel Mackenzie, Sergeant Cunningham, and Edit Grierson, several other lesser known but still active spirits have taken up residence at Fort Concho. The disembodied voices of Chaplain Dunbar and that of an unidentified officer's wife have been heard talking in the post's chapel and phosphorescent lights believed to be the ghosts of several drifters murdered in one of the officers quarters in the 1890's have been observed in what is now the museum's library. No one knows why Fort Concho is so haunted. Clearly the post's ordered appearance does a good job of hiding the truth about the invisible figments that hide in its shadows. If you doubt whether ghosts exist, a visit to Fort Concho when the spirits are restless will make a believer out of you[32].

## Miss Hattie's Whore House

This bordello, known as Miss Hattie's Whore House is located at 18 E. Concho Street in San Angelo, only two doors down from Miss Hattie's café, opened for business in 1896 and operated continually until it was closed by the Texas Rangers in 1946. The building has been restored to its original glory with furnishings and is operated as a museum Texas. Several items, to include a pair of men's shoes, have been known to move about the building during the night, being found in different places than where they were left.

## Santa Rita Park

Santa Rita Park is located just to the left of Santa Rita Elementary School. It is said that a woman named Marie, who apparently used to reside in the Santa Rita area and frequently walked in the park, still hangs around the park. She died without much family. There are a number of stray dogs that tend to roam the park at night, whether they are looking for food or a place to sleep. Neighbors have noticed that their behavior is very peculiar, jumping up in the air, excitable, running to and fro, barking in a direction where no one or nothing can be seen.

---

[32]For more information go to http://www.militaryghosts.com/concho.html

Old times remember that Marie seemed to enjoy the dogs' company when she was alive and would often play with t hem and feed them tidbits. Now, it is said, she tends to sit on the bench closest to the school and anyone who stands near or sits on that bench at night is sure to feel a chill and a sense of restlessness. One will also find that looking into the creek (which runs through the park) at night takes much courage, though nothing has reportedly been seen in the water.

## Sun Set Mall

Sun Set Mall, located at 4001 Sunset Drive in San Angelo is the only enclosed regional mall within 90 miles of San Angelo. The mall contains approximately 85 stores, including anchor stores, Dillard's, JC Penney's, Sears, and Beall's, numerous specialty stories including, Bath & Body Works, Gap Stores, Old Navy and Victoria's Secret, and a number of food outlets.

The hauntings in this modern day shopping Mecca seem to center around the former location of an old Luby's Cafeteria. A number of patrons of the Mall have reported seeing small children playing inside of the space formerly occupied by Luby's. Others, who have had occasion to go inside the space report that you can hear the voices of two kids who seem to be playing inside one of the closets of the old Cafeteria.

## Regan Elementary

Located at 1600 Volney, San Angelo, TX Regan Elementary School has long had the reputation of being haunted. According to local legend, the school is haunted by the spirits of two cheerleaders who were murdered in the girls' bathroom. According to the stories, one of the girls was hung from a pipe and the other had her head cut off. The killer was never found. Female members of the night janitorial staff are usually the ones who come in contact with these unfortunate young ladies and have been known to run screaming out of the building.

# SAN PATRICIO, TEXAS

San Patricio was founded in 1829 by the impresarios James McGloin and John McMullen after they received permission from the Mexican government on August 16, 1828, to settle 200 Irish Catholic families in Texas. After recruiting settlers in New York, the impresarios hired the New Packet and Albion to transport the colonists to their new home. The first settlers arrived at El Cópano and Mesquite Landing in late October 1829 and made their way to the old mission at Refugio, where they remained for some time. They eventually chose a townsite where the Camino Real from Goliad to Laredo and the Atascosito Road from Louisiana crossed the Nueces River. It is not known just exactly when the settlers moved from Refugio to the Nueces River site; however, by November 18, 1830, the move was completed.

Local autonomy under Mexican rule was increased in 1834 when the municipality of San Patricio was established. William O'Docharty was named Alcalde, and Thomas Adams, Francisco De León, Francisco Leal, and Patrick O'Boyle were elected aldermen. It appears that the residents of San Patricio were not caught up immediately in the revolutionary spirit that prevailed over most of Mexican Texas in 1835; however, representatives from San Patricio participated in all conventions except the first.

## Old Court House

The only woman legally hanged in Texas was Josefa Chipita Rodriguez. She lived in a shack on the Aransas River where she cooked for weary travelers and let them sleep on cots on her porch. When a traveler named John Savage fell victim to an axe murder, Chipita was the prime suspect. $600 in gold was recovered from the Aransas River north of San Patricio, as well as Savage's body, in a gunny sack.

Josefa Rodriguez and her son, Juan Silvera were indicted on circumstantial evidence. After Chipita pleaded not guilty, the jury recommended mercy, but the judge ordered her executed on November 13, 1863. Chipita was kept in leg irons and chained to a wall in the courthouse until the day of her hanging. Her coffin was placed in an unmarked grave. Though her body was buried, the mysterious events began almost immediately as it was said that a moan came from the closed casket as it was being lowered into the earth. Many people claim to have seen her ghost, a woman with a rope around her neck wandering the grounds of the old Courthouse.

## SCHULENBURG, TEXAS

Schulenburg is at the intersection of Interstate 10, U.S. Highway 77, and Farm Road 1579, on the Southern Pacific Railroad, eighteen miles south of La Grange in southern Fayette County. The area was settled by German, Austrian, and Czech settlers in the mid-nineteenth century. Schulenburg was founded in 1873, when the Galveston, Harrisburg and San Antonio Railway built through the site, and was named for Louis Schulenburg, who donated land for the railroad. The community was granted a post office in 1874 and incorporated in 1875.

## Von Minden Hotel & Cozy Theater

The Von Minden Hotel & Cozy Theater was built in 1927 and is still in operation. This is the last Hotel/Theater left in Texas. The historic old hotel was built in 1927, the date appearing on a stone in front of the building. A couple named Speckels had owned the Cozy Theater and Von Minden Hotel since it was built. Mrs. Speckels (nee Von Minden) took care of the Hotel while Mr. Speckles ran the theater. She also formed Schulenburg's Girl Scout Troop, the only one in the Country with its own marching band.

The Pettits bought the place in 1977 and busily went about not changing a thing. Mr. Pettit is an attorney with his office on the second floor, next to the projection room. The Speckles retired a few blocks away where they passed away several years apart.

According to legend, in Room 23 of the hotel there once lived a Railroad worker who went to bed sick and woke up dead and they had to have a co-worker (a very small co-worker) climb through the transom to open the locked door.

In Room 37 was a returning WWII veteran who found his girl had married someone else. He was so depressed that he jumped out the window. As the old joke goes, the ground would've broken his fall, but sadly in this case his neck encountered the clothesline. This death is especially ironic as the jumper was a paratrooper who had lost his leg and was badly disfigured when his drop plane was shot down. After spending time in a Prisoner of War Camp, he returned to a family who had only been notified he was "missing in action". Upon his arrival he was given a batch of letters written by ghostly Miss Polka Dot, one of which was a "Dear John". Although she had changed her mind, he read that letter out of sequence and jumped. Dot showed up the afternoon after the sad event and it's room 37 she's asking directions for.

The on the fourth floor of the hotel is the mysterious Ms. X. A relative of the owner lives on the forth floor and has encountered Ms. X several times. His description is quite detailed. The mysterious woman, who is believed to be the fiancé of the jumper in room 37, is wearing a polka-dot dress and a broad-brimmed straw hat, with white gloves. She is about 20 years old and carrying a cardboard suitcase, Ms. X depends on the kindness of strangers for directions.

"They're always simple directions to give," said Garrett, "but after you turn to point or gesture, when you turn back around she's gone."

The Von Minden was built as a combination theater and hotel, something fairly rare in the Southwest. Just as the ghosts of the hotel make themselves known, there are also a few spirits that hang out in the theater. One day while walking through the dark theater to turn on the theater marquee, Mrs. Pettit was halfway down the aisle, feeling her way along, expecting to touch nothing more out of the ordinary than the rigid feel of a chair back, when her hand struck human flesh. Nothing quite feels like the human hand, and that's what she felt. After the initial surprise, she had the comforting feeling that the hand's owner was the late Mrs. Speckles.

## SEALY, TEXAS

It was 1879 when George Sealy, president of the Gulf, Colorado and Santa Fe Railroad, purchased land originally granted to the township of San Felipe de Austin, for the purpose of establishing both railroad lines and a depot. The town of Sealy became a main division point between Galveston and Temple. The railroad became the town's principal employer. With the arrival of the German and Czech settlers farming and ranching became part of the economy.

## Sealy High School

Sealy High School is located at 939 West St, Sealy, Texas. There are many current and former students who can attest of hearing the sounds of walking and doors opening and closing on the second floor even when there is not supposed to be anyone on that floor. The elevator is also known to operate by itself.

## Sealy High School Football Field and Track

There was a senior track star that was driving home from an out of town track meet. It was late in the evening and he was tired, so he fell asleep behind the wheel and in the ensuing wreck, he somehow cut himself. When rescue workers found him the next day, he had bled to death. It is said that if you go to the Sealy High School Football Field and Track at midnight you can see him running around the track.

## Sealy Jr. High Gym

Several years ago, there were twin cheerleaders that attended Sealy Jr. High School. Being beautiful and very popular, these young ladies were the center of social activities for the school. One of the twins was the head cheerleader and she had been dating one of the football players for some time. After a fight at school over a minor issue, she broke up with her boyfriend.

Devastated at losing his girlfriend, the guy hung himself in one of the upstairs rooms. It was the twins that discovered the body and they got into a fight as one of them accused the other of being the cause of the boy's death. The argument elevated until the two were in a killing rage at each other over the death of the boy. Finally, the one sister pushed the other (the head cheerleader) down the stairs injuring her severely.

Determined to make her pay for her heartlessness, the one sister went down the stairs, grabbed her sister by the feet and drug her back up the stairs. At each step, the injured sister's head would slam into a step. The other one always said she never wanted to kill her sister just punish her for causing the death of the player. Unfortunately, the head cheerleader died of her injuries anyway. Now it is said that if you go to the Sealy Jr. High School Gym on Halloween night you can hear the screams of the one sister and her head dragging across the floor.

# TENNYSON, TEXAS

This area was once the home of wandering bands of Indians for centuries. However, cattlemen began to use it for grazing in the late 1870s and the first permanent settlement was established in the 1880s. A post office, named for British poet Alfred Tennyson, was established in 1894 with Mrs. Sarah E. Diser as the First Postmaster. Over the years, the area has had several schools, but all are now closed. Near Mt. Margaret (height 335 feet), once locale of Indian

Activities, is now site of annual community homecoming (the Saturday before Labor Day in March) and Easter Sunrise religious services each spring.

## Mount Margaret

A stagecoach traveling through the area fell victim to Comanches. The lone survivor was a six-year-old girl named Margaret. The Comanches took her back to their village to join their tribe, but she refused all nourishment and soon died. They placed her body on a nearby "mountain" (probably just a large hill to states outside of Texas). The mountain took her name, and became known as Mount Margaret. Her ghostly sobs can still be heard as she searches for her murdered parents.

# VALLEY MILLS, TEXAS

Valley Mills is on State Highway 6 near the Bosque River eleven miles south of Clifton and twenty-four miles north of Waco in southwestern Bosque County. It was named for a flour mill established on the banks of the Bosque River in 1867 by Dr. E. P. Booth and Asbury Stegall. In 1881 the Gulf, Colorado and Santa Fe Railway laid tracks a mile south of the community. Merchants, hoping to benefit from the railroad, began moving their stores to the tracks. On February 27, 1882, a cyclone hit the new townsite, destroying a large number of buildings. Nevertheless, the remaining residents from the community's original site moved across the river and rebuilt their homes. Thus, by the end of 1882 Valley Mills had a new site which extended into McLennan County.

## Middle Bosque River

A number of witnesses have reported that while standing on he bluff that overlooked the Middle Bosque River, they felt like there was someone standing beside or near them. The presence was so strong that there was no doubt in their minds that there was some else there.

# WACO, TEXAS

Waco is in central McLennan County about seventy miles south of Dallas near the confluence of the Brazos and Bosque rivers. The city's transportation links include Interstate Highway 35, U.S. highways 84 and 77, State Highway 6, the Missouri Pacific Railroad, and the St. Louis Southwestern Railway. The city is built on the site of an ancient agricultural village of Waco Indians. About 1830 a group of Cherokee Indians moved into the area and drove the Wacos from the village. Fort Fisher, a Texas Rangers outpost and the first white settlement in the area, was established in 1837, but was abandoned after only a few months. In 1844 George Barnard began operating Torrey's Trading Post No. 2 on a small tributary of Tehuacana Creek, eight miles south of the old Waco village. A year later Neil McLennan moved onto land nearby on the South Bosque River.

## **Baylor University Library**

Elizabeth Barrett Browning has been seen in the Baylor University Library where some of her original works are kept. She has also been seen walking the halls at night holding a candle, wearing a white gown. Some residents have reported that they have seen her in the top floor window peering outside. Also, there has been some unusual activity around a statue of her sits out in front of the library. Her arms are at her sides, however, some nights the shadow that has been cast on the library behind her showed her arms held up high above her head.

## **Baylor University - Brooks Hall**

At Baylor University, the oldest college in the state of Texas, there exists a mysterious phantom on the abandoned fifth floor of Brooks Hall, the oldest dorm on campus. Violin music is heard in the dead of night and chilling sightings of a cloaked figure in top hat and cloak staring down and illuminated by an eerie candlelight have been widely reported by spooked residents. Investigations have wielded little in the way of facts but the enormous amount of eyewitness accounts and spine tingling sightings have given the legend a grand following.

One night the shattering of glass was reported as the phantom peered down and paused his playing and in a fit of apparent rage struck a window. Come morning when level heads prevailed and the storm of the previous night had passed, no damage was found. Still the unpredictable toiling of the phantom has attracted audiences in the witching hour in hopes of catching a glimpse of the mysterious floating candlelight that often hovers from room to room and then vanishes only to appear in the other wing of the building. One unsettling account recollects the viewing of a noose and dangling of a shadowy corpse after the phantom finished the evening's mournful serenade.

Still more haunting is the episode on record of the lights failing the building and an ungodly tapping and cold sensation filtering through the respective doors of the fourth floor of the building. Only one resident dared investigate the unwelcome visitors calling. It is claimed that he peered into pitch darkness to find the horrific silhouette of a cloaked figure in a top hat turn and stare him down through the darkness and calmly vanish out of sight as he glided parallel down the corridor; needless to say it was not pursued.

The university has failed to satisfy rumors of hauntings and has downplayed the events for close to half a century now. The Victorian styled villain who roams the corridors of the uninhabited floor and occasionally mingles with the living loves to make an entrance, the hoax is to elaborate for any collegiate prankster and the tradition has endured for too long. Perhaps the only explanation is that the phantom is ultimately unexplainable.

## **Cameron Park - Lindsey Hollow Road**

Two alleged horse thieves use to hang out on Lindsey Hollow Road. The bodies of the two brothers were found hanging from a tree about 100 feet from the road, killed by vigilantes in 1880. Shadowy images of the hanging brothers can still be seen in the old tree. There have also been reports of reflections of unknown persons, a spectral party taking place near the hanging tree, the sounds of screams, feeling paralyzed, & apparitions.

## Cameron Park - Witches Castle

The place that the locals call "The witches castle" is inside Cameron Park. There castle is actually a run down old shack on the road leading to the top of Cameron Park. It is scary looking and looks like a run down shack from a horror movie. When you get close to the Witches Castle, you start to smell the terrible odor of something dead. Supposedly it is the bodies of the victims of the witches who were killed inside the Castle and buried in shallow graves. You can also hear screams, gasps and banging.

## The Hiking Trail

Another spot within the confines of Cameron Park is the ruins of an old house set back in the wood off one of the hiking trail. It is said to be very creepy, even in the daylight. According to the story sent to me, some hikers were exploring the ruins out of curiosity and discovered the usual debris found in old houses, such as beer bottles and trash, etc. Just as the hikers were ready to leave the scene and continue their hike, they swear that suddenly a voice from only a short distance away began to curse them for entering the ruins. Though the voice sounded like it was very close, at no time did they see anyone.

One of the others in the group heard a young girl screaming in terror, but could not pinpoint the direction. Spooked, the hikers turned and retraced their path at a fast pace. Suddenly, they skidded to a stop as their path was blocked by what appeared to be a large pool of fresh blood. The pool of blood had not been there when they entered the ruins. Suddenly, they heard loud screams from just behind them and without waiting to examine the pool of blood the hikers took off running at top speed.

## University High School

University High School is located at 2600 Bagby Ave, in Waco. According to reports, there are a lot of strange noises heard in the gym during basketball games as if a much larger crowd is present. Then when somebody goes in the boys' restroom they can hear two boys talking to each other in there but when they search for the speakers, no one is ever found.

## Rainbow Lake/Creek

The whole Rainbow Lake area has been plagued with rumors of witchcraft, cult activity, and peeping Tom's. Some homes that back up to Rainbow Lake have reported seeing paranormal figures, hearing shrieks during the night, and cold spots in the heat of summer. Rumors of a dead body being found further upstream in the Rainbow Creek area have also turned up as well as a sighting of a ghost-like male deeper into the woods who seems to vanish when pursued. A few mysterious graves have also been found in the area, some marked with simple wooden crosses while others remain unmarked.

# CHINA SPRING, TEXAS

China Spring (China Springs) is on Farm Road 1637 twelve miles northwest of Waco in northwestern McLennan County. Settlement of the area began as early as 1860, and the community was founded in 1867. It was named for a spring in a chinaberry grove. A post office was established at China Spring in May 1873 with Charles S. Eichelberger as postmaster. By the early 1880s the community had five steam cotton gins and gristmills, three general stores, a Methodist church, and 200 residents. Cotton, corn, and wool were the principal shipments from the area.

## Copper's Crossing

Copper's Crossing has long been used by travelers as a safe place to cross the river. However, almost since the beginning, witnesses have said that when they are near the crossing, they have the feeling of being watched. The closer that they get to the river, the stronger the feeling becomes. Some have also reported that they felt a person brush against them even thought there was no one else in the area.

## Patrick Cemetery

There is a little graveyard, called Patrick Cemetery, located just outside of Waco in China Springs that has a strange reputation. Most visitors get a really creepy feeling. Cold chills are common, pictures get interesting, and even the animals act weird. And rumor has it that if you knock on a certain headstone at midnight an apparition appears screaming loudly. Also there are witnesses that swear that headstones tend to move around frequently.

**PART SIX**

**GHOSTS OF SOUTH TEXAS**

# CORPUS CHRISTI, TEXAS

Corpus Christi, a seaport at the mouth of the Nueces River on the west end of Corpus Christi Bay, is the county seat of Nueces County and the largest city on the South Texas coast. It lays at the junction of Interstate 37 and U. S. highways 77 and 181, 210 miles southwest of Houston. The city's transportation needs are also served by the Texas Mexican, Southern Pacific, and Missouri Pacific railways and Corpus Christi International Airport. In prehistoric times the area was inhabited by various tribes of the Karankawa Indian group, which migrated up and down the Coastal Bend region.

It not known who the first Europeans were to visit the area, but it seems most likely that Álvar Núñez Cabeza de Vaca and his band were the first Europeans who actually set foot on the site. The Spanish, however, largely ignored the region until the 1680s, when Frenchmen under René Robert Cavelier, Sieur de La Salle, established a colony in Texas. Spanish authorities dispatched an expedition to the area in 1689 under Alonso De León, but the Corpus Christi Bay area remained unknown and unexplored until 1747, when Joaquín de Orobio y Basterra led an expedition down the Nueces River, reaching the bay on February 26.

## Aviation Street

Aviation Street is located near the Corpus Christi Naval Base. Near a naval base, reports of paranormal activity include spectral wolves and transparent Native Americans.

## Blackbeard's on the Beach

Located at 3117 E Surfside Blvd, Corpus Christi, Blackbeard's on the Beach has long been a gathering place for the locals. In 1955, this building housed a popular bar. According to the story, one evening in the late 1950s, two men got into a fight over a very pretty redhead. Shots were fired, a man died and the redhead and her lover escaped over the causeway to the north. Despite what is printed on the menu about the history of the building, Colonel Larry Platt maintained that he demolished the original building in 1962 when he purchased the property.

He added a dining room to the bar and called his eating establishment was originally called the Spanish Kitchen and it was a success from the beginning. However, it would seem that along with a drove of customers, he also acquired a ghost.

Strange noises have long been reported in this building. Most commonly, they are the sounds of pots and pans in the kitchen at a time when no one is there. Subsequent investigation shows that nothing is ever disturbed.

Some workers have reported seeing the ghostly figure of a woman. It is believed she was once an employee, who lost a piece of jewelry in a fire. There have also been many reports of moving chairs, roving cold spots and jumping salt shakers could be caused by one of two people. The ghost could be that of the man who was killed in a fight over the redhead, or that of a man who committed suicide nearby after losing his wife. Not architecturally significant in any way, Blackbeard's is, however, culturally significant to the local populace, and especially those who believe in the paranormal. Still, it is a popular local hangout, in part because of its proximity to a popular beach.

## Ft. Lipantitlan

Near this area, a wooden picket fort called Fort Lipantitlan was constructed around 1831 by Mexican forces in anticipation of trouble with Anglo immigrants. The fort apparently was named for a camp of Lipan Apaches in the vicinity. In 1835, the small guard force that held the fort surrendered it to Texan forces without a shot being fired.

In 1842, a battalion of Texas volunteers camped in this area. In an attempt to lay claim to the territory between the Nueces River and the Rio Grande, the camp was seized by Mexican general Antonio Canales, but the Mexican forces later retreated. Around 10 years later, during the Mexican War, troops under General Zachary Taylor passed through this area on their way to the Rio Grande

This old Mexican fort was home to a living apparition known as the Lady in Green. For many years it has been rumors that the old fort site is still haunted by a spirit called the Lady in Green. Researchers believe that this spirit might be Senora Garcia, wife of Marcelino Garcia, who died when the Texicans took the fort. As Marcelino Garcia lay dying from wounds suffered when Texans captured the fort, the ghost of his wife appeared near his bed for several days in a row. Dozens witnessed the strange phenomenon, yet the woman was still alive in Mexico City. A friend's letter had informed her of her husband's plight, and somehow her spirit managed to be at his side. Even after he died, the Lady in Green continued to walk through the door and stand vigil over to his former bed. For twenty five years, the uncanny image appeared at Fort Lipantitlán, and only stopped in 1810, on the day the woman died. Now it is said that she walks again.

## Headless Horseman Hill

The ghost of a headless cowboy riding a steaming horse has been seen for over a hundred years on what is called Headless Horseman Hill. The cowboy is said to be a horse thief captured by a posse and crudely beheaded because the men could not find a suitable tree from which to hang him.

## Bill Witt Park Airplane Hangar

The Bill Witt Hangar is located in the midst of an old abandoned World War II Air Base. There have been a number of reports that those who explore this old building are followed by someone or something that they cannot see on the stairwells. Others say that the old Hangar is haunted by the spirit of a man who hung himself from the rafters. He has been seen looking out through the broken windows of the now abandoned hangar.

## USS Lexington

The USS Lexington, CV-16, is a vintage wartime aircraft carrier. Commissioned in 1943, she served the United States longer and set more records than any other carrier in the history of naval aviation. The ship was the oldest working carrier in the United States Navy when decommissioned in 1991. The Lexington, an Essex-class carrier, was originally named the USS Cabot. During World War II, the final work on it was being completed at Massachusetts' Fore River Shipyard when word was received that the original carrier named Lexington, CV-2, had been sunk in the Coral Sea. A campaign was launched to change the new carrier's name to Lexington, and the rest is history. The USS Lexington was commissioned on February 17, 1943.

After training maneuvers and a shakedown cruise, the Lexington joined the Fifth Fleet at Pearl Harbor. During World War 11, the Lexington participated in nearly every major operation in the Pacific Theater and spent a total of 21 months in combat. Her planes destroyed 372 enemy aircraft in the air and 475 more on the ground. She sank or destroyed 300,000 tons of enemy cargo and damaged an additional 600,000 tons. The ship's guns shot down 15 planes and assisted in downing five more.

The Japanese reported the Lexington sunk no less than four times! Yet, each time she returned to fight again, leading the propagandist Tokyo Rose to nickname her "The Blue Ghost." The name is a tribute to the ship and the crew and air groups that served aboard her.

After the war, the Lexington was briefly decommissioned (1947-1955). When reactivated, she operated primarily with the Seventh Fleet out of San Diego, California. Although not involved in actual combat, the Lexington kept an offshore vigil during tensions in Formosa, Laos, and Cuba. In 1962, the Lexington sailed into Pensacola, Florida, and began training operations, eventually being officially designated CVT-16, Navy Training Carrier. The USS Lexington was decommissioned on November 26, 1991.

Now permanently located at 2914 N. Shoreline Blvd, Corpus Christi, Texas, this famous fighting ship is now a museum. But it is a museum with some permanent visitors. workers have reported the sounds of chains being drug across the deck when no one was present The USS Lexington, also known as "The Blue

Ghost," is a vintage wartime aircraft carrier permanently docked in Corpus Christi. Commissioned in 1943, she has a 19-year old ghost, with piercing blue eyes, which has been seen and heard by several visitors aboard the ship. See if you can spot him on any of several cams on board.

He's polite, knowledgeable and kind. Smartly dressed in a summer white Navy uniform, he's good looking, too, with light hair, a clear complexion and piercing blue eyes that haunt like a good ghost story. Those who have seen him say he might be found in the engine room of the Lexington Museum, although none of the museum staff has seen those blue eyes for themselves. He wears no nametag, but is known solely by description.

His character so impressed a couple from Peoria, Ill. that they told tour guide David Deal about it. "The woman said, 'You know, I really did appreciate that knowledgeable young sailor down there in the engine room who gave us all that information on how the engines work,'" Deal said.

Deal, who had gone up to the hangar deck to get coffee on a quiet Friday, had been in the engine room and knew no one else was there. So he probed for more details. The couple said the seaman was 19 years old, maybe 20, and wore a white uniform. He had a slight limp to his left leg. He had memorable blue eyes. And he knew all about the engines, their horsepower and the use of steam.

Deal, who had first shipped on the USS Lexington in 1959-60, checked out what the couple had learned. "This apparition told things about the engine that I don't even know," said Deal, who made the rank of airman on the Lexington and retired in 1976 as a catapult chief.

"It's fascinating because I'm one of these hard nuts to crack on something like this," said Deal, who judged the couple to be adamant about what they said and without reason to fabricate the story. So he ran to the engine room, calling "Anybody home?" and searched for a hidden uniform. He found nothing.

## Bokenkamp

Bokenkamp is located at 5517 S. Alameda St and is affiliated with the Lutheran Social Service, Inc. This medical facility seems to have more than just its patients to be cared for. Many of the paranormal events have taken place during the night shirt where many workers have heard voices and footsteps in areas where there have been one to account for the sounds. It is said that the majority of these unusual occurrences have been in the front ICU wards and the first unit. Staff and residents alike have seen these human like shadows, heard footsteps and whispering. Many of the staff members have also complained of cold spots and the feeling of something or someone brushing up against them.

## Calallen High School

Calallen High School is located just outside of Corpus Christi in Calallen, Texas. Local rumor has long said that the school is haunted. The elevator by the Theater Arts room is said to be one of those areas favored by the spirits. At night the elevator door opens and closes by itself when no one is there to push the buttons. It's been sighted once or twice by students who are there for extracurricular activities. One of the night janitors has also seen the ghost of a young teenage girl roaming the halls after all of the students have left for the day.

## Center Theatre

The Center Theatre was opened in 1942. The story is that a married couple was having a long running argument and in a fit of rage, the husband murdered the woman as she walked out of the upstairs women's bathroom.

There is an area of seating in the upstairs area and this is the area in which the couple was seated prior to the murder. It is said that if someone goes to this area, they feel the sensation f someone standing near them. It's almost like she doesn't want you there at all. She'll try to make you move, and it gets really cold standing there. At times, if the activities of those seated in this area "bother" her during a show, she will find ways make them stop. One young man found out the truth of this legend the hard way. He was on his cell phone during a play and talking fairly loudly. Suddenly his cell phone cut off and he felt hands pushing him down the steps even though there was no one near him at the time.

## Days Inn hotel

It is said that the spirit of murdered Tejano singer Selena still wanders restlessly about the door way of the room at the Days Inn Hotel where she was shot. She has also been seen in the hospital where she sought treatment and eventually died. Though she is rarely if ever seen by witnesses, many people have reported hearing faint singing as well as the smell of roses followed by an overwhelming sense of sorrow.

## Del Mar College- Memorial Building

Room 222 of the Memorial Classroom Building at Del Mar College has long been said to be haunted. Late night custodial staff as well as campus security personnel has reported noises such as howling and laughing coming from around the room. However, when backup arrives and investigations are conducted, nothing it ever found out of place. On one specific occasion a security officer patrolling the building heard what he described as "Furniture being moved around" at 1:00 am.

## The Smith Building

The Smith Building has been under construction for some time now and some of the workers were complaining that they would hear things move and fall. At times the doors would close by themselves. One worker has said to seen a little girl in a white dress. Nobody seemed to have believed them so one man took a home video camera and went throughout the rooms on the second fall and you can see the doors close after he had passed by and three times you can see the little girl standing in the corner. Of course ha ran but went back and saw her again but this time she looked liked she was going towards him so he took of running again and you could see stuff being thrown at him. The video is real its something that if you see you will believe.

## Heritage Park Museum

There are four houses at the Heritage Park Museum that are said to be haunted. In one (Sidbury House) a child supposedly haunts the children's room by playing with the dolls and moving stuff and knocking things down. In another (The Galvan House) a ghost is said to tap unexpected people on the shoulder a on the second floor and someone once heard footsteps leading up to the attic. In another house (Now a restaurant named The Christian House Bistro there have been reports that at night a lady with a long old fashioned dress and a big hat and shoes is seen walking into the front door and disappearing. People have only seen the backside of her. Then in another house (The MacCambell House) there is a ghost named Mary, that died of pneumonia, is said to not let the tour guides in the house or to cause a great deal of noise. If tour guides do come into the house and go out onto the patio, she is known to lock them out and they have to summon help from passersby.

## Nueces River

Many years ago a woman and her baby were home alone when their house caught fire. Out and realized they both perished in the fire. It is said that she walks the river and moans in mourning for her baby.

## The Old Courthouse

It has been established that many people have been hung in the Old Courthouse building or at least sentenced to death there. The rumor is that a young boy went to the courthouse on the night of Halloween in the early 1900's. He did not believe in ghosts until this incident. He went up to the 10th floor where all the death sentences were carried out and walked over to the window to look at a rope that what looked like blood on it. As he examined the rope, some force threw him over the edge of the window. Investigators later found blood from the rope on the window seal where he tried to hold on. Unfortunately, the boy was not able to save himself and hit the cement face first.

## Wilson Tower

The Wilson Plaza Historical Development started in 1927. In 1951 Mr. Wilson built a 17-story office tower with a four-story penthouse. The penthouse was Wilson's pride and joy. The 20th floor was finished out as a game room with a private bar constructed on a grand scale of mahogany and trimmed in tufted leather and brass. The view from the penthouse was described as rivaling that of the Top of the Mark Restaurant in San Francisco. It was the scene of many "invitation only" parties attended by Corpus' elite, where Wilson negotiated many of his major business deals. Most of the talk centered on "Sam's" parties and card games. The 21st floor contained guest rooms for "out-of-town" clients. After Mr. Wilson's death in 1957, Mrs. Wilson hosted society, civic, bridge and debutante functions in the penthouse. Today the Wilson Tower is said to still be inhabited by Mrs. Wilson, overseeing what goes on in the building. Many Tenants have witnessed shadows and sounds while alone in their offices, especially in the early mornings or late nights. Elevators also have unusual happenings such as stopping on different floors that are not lighted up, with an eerie feeling of someone else catching a ride with you.

# ALICE, TEXAS

Alice Texas, the county seat of Jim Wells County is centrally located in South Texas, making it a commercial center for petroleum industry, tourism, healthcare, agribusiness and distribution to surrounding areas.

The City of Alice was named after the daughter of one of the founders of the famed King Ranch, Alice King Kleberg. The combination of a growing industry, an outstanding education system, an abundance of wildlife, and economic activity for the region makes Alice a favorite among residents and visitors alike.

## Hwy 281@FM 141

Leonora Rodriguez was hung at this site by her husband's hired hands after she was accused of adultery. To this day motorists stop to help this sad "Lady in Black" who is seen walking along the side of the road.

## Alice High School Library

It is said by many staff and students alike that there is a ghost in the Alice High School Library. The ghost is supposed to be of a man working at the school who died when the library was being built. The ghost has thrown books off of the shelves and been heard walking and talking.

## Alice High School Little Theater

There are many who say that the Alice High School Little Theater is haunted by one of the workers who died while helping build the theater. Theater students claim to hear strange noises. Some students have even sighted the ghost, mainly in the catwalk overhead, and in the upstairs costume room. And an incident happened where red and yellow feathers fell from nowhere during rehearsals. No explanation for this unusual "rain" was ever discovered.

## Old Hospital

At the old Alice Hospital there is a room on the second color where very odd things occur. There have been many nurses who have complained that the call bell in one particular room will go off even when there is no one in the room.

The problem was solved, it was believed, when the call bell was unplugged. Imagine everyone's surprise when the unplugged call bell continued to ring.

## Memorial Middle School

There are four different wings to the Memorial Middle School. If you go into the girls' bathroom in the wing closest to the cafeteria you can hear someone bouncing a basketball. It is said that the ghost of a student who died at the school is now continually bouncing the basketball.

## The Reservoir  aka - Alice Lake

A number of witnesses who have gone to the Alice Lake Reservoir Marina after the gates are locked have said that when you get out on the pier you can feel several cold spots and hear the sounds of oars in the water, though no one can be seen on the water. Others have said that they were fishing and heard the sound of someone falling into the water and then the screams of a little girl calling her mother for help. However, though many have searched, no signs of a little girl in the water can be found.

## The Old Rialto Theater on Main Street

This old Rialto Movie Theater was closed in the 1980's. A number of former employees and some regular patrons claimed to have seen shadowy figures moving silently about the upper level darkened hallways and to have experienced feelings of dread in certain areas. Night shift employees have talked about their certainty that there were being watched by someone or something from the upper levels as they went about their duties.

## Sutherlands

Sutherlands was formerly a Wal-Mart and there are many who are familiar with the stories told by Wal-Mart staffers about strange happenings in this old building. According to the story, there is said to be a ghost who roams the aisles of the store and plays practical jokes on the staff. There is also another spirit that has caused major problems in the store by making accidents happen that has caused damage to both the merchandise and equipment at the store.
The Wal-Mart associates nicknamed the practical joker "Matilde" or Matilda" because the sex is not known. On the other hand, the problem causing spirit has never been named because the associates prefer no contact with that spirit. The building that was formerly Wal-Mart[33] and now Sutherlands is built on an old homestead site of the original Collins Family who founded Alice. The Old Collins Cemetery is also immediately adjacent to the store

---

[33] Wal-Mat vacated the premises in April of 2004.

### William Adams Junior High or Middle School

Adults may laugh at the idea of puppy love, but it can be as beautiful or as deadly as adult love. At the William Adams Middle School, there was a young teenage couple who believed that they were in love. However, they had a falling out and it is believed that the boy killed his beloved. Now this permanently teenage girl is said to roam the school for her love who became her killer.

## BEEVILLE, TEXAS

Beeville, the county seat of Bee County, is on Poesta Creek at the intersection of U.S. Highway 181, State Highway 59, and the Southern Pacific Railroad, in central Bee County. The site of the community was settled by the Burke, Carroll, and Heffernan families in the 1830s though several of the settlers were killed by Indians during the early years of the settlement.

When Bee County was organized in 1858, the county seat was founded at a site on the east bank of Medio Creek seven miles east of the current site of the community. This first county seat was known as Beeville-on-the-Medio. This location proved inconvenient, and in 1859 Ann Burke Carroll, Patrick Carroll, and Patrick Burke donated land for a townsite at the current location of Beeville. The first name for the new community was Maryville, after a member of the Heffernan family who had survived the Indian massacre.

### Charco Rd. @ 181

Some really strange stories come out of this area. It is said that at Charco Road and Highway 181, if you hear a baby crying, stop your car immediately. If you drive on by, it is said that you will have a serious accident, but if you stop, the legend says that the sounds will lead you to a treasure

## BOERNE, TEXAS

Boerne, the county seat of Kendall County, is located on Cibolo Creek, Interstate Highway 10, and U.S. Highway 87 thirty miles northwest of San Antonio in the southern part of the county. In 1849 a group of German colonists from Bettina camped on the north side of Cibolo Creek, about a mile west of the site of present Boerne. They called their new community Tusculum, after Cicero's home in ancient Rome. In 1852 Gustav Theissen and John James laid out the townsite and changed the name to Boerne in honor of Ludwig Boerne, a German author and publicist. A post office was established in 1856 with August Staffell as postmaster.

### Country Spirit Restaurant & Bar

The Country Spirit Restaurant & Bar, located at 707 S. Main in Boerne, has got great food and spirits, both the drinking kind and the scaring kind. The basement is haunted by a middle-aged man named "Fred" who likes to pretend to eat food left by patrons. A young teenage boy named "David" frequents the men's bathroom and likes to flip potato chips off of plates and push wineglasses off of the bar. "Augusta" likes to lounge around on the green couch near the bathrooms. A number of staff and patrons have heard doors opening on the top floor even when it is known that there is no one on the top floor.

## Library (Dienger Building)

This native limestone structure was originally built for Joseph Dienger and has been prominent in Boerne's history for over 100 years. Originally, it was a grocery store with living quarters upstairs. Later, it was a dry goods store and after that, the Antlers Restaurant. Finally it became offices for Bill and Paige Ramsey-Palmer who restored the building. In 1991, after extensive renovation, the building, now owned by the city of Boerne was dedicated as the Boerne Public Library. It is said that the ghost of Joseph Dienger has not left the building at 210 N. Main Street that was named after him. A number of witnesses have reported seeing the lights inside the building turning on and off long after everyone had left for the day. There are also rumors of underground tunnels connecting the Dienger Building to the Ye Kendall Inn, another haunted building in town.

## Meyer B & B

The well known Meyer Bed & Breakfast is actually a complex of buildings located on Cypress Creek, just one block from Historic Downtown Comfort, Texas and within walking distance of the Guadalupe River. Since its beginnings in 1857 as a stage stop for travelers preparing to cross the Guadalupe River on the fabled Old Spanish Trail, the Meyer has invited travelers to rest, relax and enjoy life for generations. The original building was added to in 1869 when the Meyer Family Home was built nearby. The Old Homestead is now the Innkeepers Residence.

There have also been a number of apparitions seen about these historic old buildings. The apparition of a very pretty red-haired girl named Julia is reported in the cottage, and a Native American woman is seen in the Maternity House. A number of both guests and staff have heard unexplainable footsteps in the hotel.

## Ye Kendall Inn B & B

The Ye Kendall Inn, located at 128 West Blanco was established in 1859 as the stagecoach stop in the sleepy Texas hill country town of Boerne. This historic old building is a registered state and national historic landmark offering 17 guest rooms, suites and cabins — each exquisitely appointed and beautifully restored. The Inn's 22" limestone walls and breezy front and back porches provide a true Texas experience not soon forgotten.

A number of rooms, including the Marcella Booth room, are home to very active spirits. Doors occasionally open and slam shut, or doorknobs rattle unexpectedly as if someone wants into the room. There have been a number of unexplainable electrical problems and shards from a chandelier fall to the floor at an unexpected rate. The ghost of an elderly woman in period clothing has even been seen and spoken to on occasion, and is known as "Sara." An invisible entity sits on the bed in the Marcella Booth room[34].

# BROWNSVILLE, TEXAS

Founded in 1848, the city of Brownsville was named after Fort Brown Post Commander Major Jacob Brown. During the Civil War, Brownsville became the "back door to the Confederacy." With their seaports blockaded by the Union Navy, Confederates shipped their cotton through Mexico. After acquiring foreign ownership, the cotton was then shipped to European mills, free from military intervention. Both Brownsville and Matamoras grew during this period of time. The rate of growth declined following the Civil War.

As cargo traffic increased, a narrow gauge railroad was constructed to connect Brownsville with the tiny seaport now called Port Isabel. In 1904 a major railroad line connected the valley to the interior of the United States. This opened markets for winter vegetables and fruit raised in the pleasant climate of the Rio Grande Valley.

When Mexico began a series of revolutions in the early part of the century an unusually large force of soldiers, both regular Army and National Guard, swelled the population. The military presence gave the city both security and economic prosperity.

## Channel 23

KVOE TV is located at 394 N Expressway in Brownsville. It is hard to think of a modern television station have problems with ghosts but there have been a number of reports that apparitions show themselves to the janitors after hours. This has certainly made the night shift less boring.

## Community Development Building

The building that houses the Community Development Corporation of Brownsville (CDCB) is also the home of unseen entities. The Community Development Corporation is a CDFI owned by six investor banks that has been building and financing homes in the Texas border region since 1997. More than 140 homes have been constructed and financed for families earning an average of 34 percent of the area median income, so the staff is not prone to flights of fancy.

There have been a number of reports of strange organ music, shaking furniture, mysterious lights and shadows, disappearing items, ghostly footsteps and a black figure in a hood seen roaming the darkened halls after hours.

---

[34] As of this writing, Marcella Booth is alive and living in Boerne.

## Central Middle School:

Several ghosts are known to roam the grounds of the Central Middle School located at 708 Palm Boulevard. There are also rumors of poltergeist activity inside the building that has spooked more than one teacher. There is also the story that a student was run over by a school bus one afternoon and he is often seen where the buses board.

## Clearwater Elementary:

Clearwater Elementary School is located at 733 Palm Blvd. There have been a number of reports of a lady dressed in white roaming the school grounds at night. People call the ghost "Ms. Clearwater".

## Simon Rivera High School:

Located at 6955 Coffeeport Rd, there have long been reports from Simon Rivera High School of at least two ghosts roaming these halls. There is said to be the ghost of a student basketball player that died after a game of a heart attack. The night cleaning crew is said to have both heard and seen the student bounce the basketball.

There is also the story that a female student was murdered in the girls' locker room. According to the story the girl was said to have been murdered in the shower stalls of the girls' locker room. On late practices students sometimes have heard the showers go off and what looked like liquid pouring down the drain. In last stall, the toilet flushes on its own numerous times. Then at that point they will hear a blood curling scream that would make them run out in a heartbeat.

It is usually a student that is alone in the locker rooms that will heard the slamming of lockers, but even the volleyball coach said when he was painting the raider logo on the wall he heard the scream and sounds as if someone was being banged against the lockers.

## Cemetery on FM 511 and South most Rd:

There have been reports of a lady dressed in white outside the cemetery at night, by several people. No one has ever been able to see her face. Farm road 511 is a fairly well traveled road, but it has been reported, in the local newspaper and other media, that if you travel these roads late at night People have encountered what are known as "ghost cows" in this desolate stretch or road in the middle of the night. As you drive down the road you may suddenly see a cow six feet in front of you and try to avoid it... only to find out that your evasive action was unnecessary, since there was never really anything there. We have had some people get into serious accidents, causing great damage to their vehicles and person only to get out of their vehicles and find no sign of any animal of living creature in sight.

## Stanolin Road

When you are driving down Stanolin Road, at one point it starts to curve According to legend, a man was said to have been driving too fast, lost control on the curve and his car crashed. The young man was killed. To commemorate his death, his friends planed a cross at the spot where he died. Now, witnesses have said that a young man has been seen standing beside the cross. If someone stops to pick him up, he will approach your car and then vanish

## Camp Lulu

What happened at Camp Lulu Sams is the stuff horror movies are made out of. According to record, Camp Lulu was a camp for young kids that is said to be still in operation, though at one point it was closed down after one of the counselors went crazy. With the cunning shown by many of the insane, this Counselor managed to kill the other counselors and then raped and killed the girls attending the camp. Now if you go at night you can hear the crying of the dead girls. But if you are caught trespassing on this private property you might get shot by the owner of the property who, it is said, tries to preserve the souls of the young girls.

## Fort Brown

Brownsville, Texas was the location of Fort Brown, a military post both during and after the Civil War, however, the post actually predates this bloody family feud. The last battles of the Mexican American war occurred in Brownsville. One of the battles that took place during this extensive campaign was the siege of Ft. Texas[35]. The Mexican campaign to capture Fort Texas started May 3rd and ended May 9th, 1846. There were only 2 Americans killed and 7 wounded, so the hauntings are believed by many to be related to residual hauntings left over from this event. However, the hauntings could also come from those in the Mexican army that was literally slaughtered both at the fort and at the other two battle sites in the area.

The buildings that house the University are historical monuments that have seen a lot of bloody history. Sightings and sounds have been experienced in almost every building on campus. There have even been reports that some witnesses have heard bombs exploding and men screaming in pain. A witness claims to have seen some soldiers marching by the side of her car though they didn't seem to pay any attention to her. The sighting and noises that haunt this historic old post are generally heard at night past 10 PM.

---

[35] Fort Texas was later renamed Fort Brown in honor of Major Jacob Brown, who died during the siege on Fort Texas.

## Old Morgue Building

As stated earlier, many of the buildings that comprise the campus of the University of Texas at Brownsville are old, have been used for many functions and have seen a great deal of history. One building in particular, the old Morgue Building[36] is currently used as a storage building and a three room accounting office. There are reports of many strange noises in the building, which cannot be identified. There have even been reports of apparitions of a woman and small child who seem to wander aimlessly through the wide hallways of this old building.

The staff reports that books fall from shelves and chairs move in the library of their own volition. Others have heard voices and seen doors opening and closing without any human assistance. A lady dressed in black has been seen sitting on a wall in front of the Old Morgue. Electrical devices in the building will suddenly stop working or break for a while, later they will start working again. Plugs will also pull out of sockets by themselves and stored items will move themselves. These unusual events are said to be caused by the ghosts of soldiers whose bodies were stored here prior to burial. A picture was taken in May of 2001 inside the building and appears to show a hanged body dangling form the ceiling.

## Resaca Middle School

There have been a number of reports from the night cleaning crew at the Resaca Middle School that they have heard the sounds of running feet and the giggles of children coming from darkened areas of the building. Some janitors have said that when they clean the gym, often things are thrown at them, though they can never find the culprit.

## Keys Crossing

Keys Crossing is by the River. A number of witnesses passing this area have reported that some nights they have seen three ghosts kneeling on the riverbank throwing what appear to be roses into the water. According to local legend, these three figures were killed in a car wreck at the spot and now they come back to mourn other family members who also died on the spot. There are also tales of an Indian curse on anyone who would disturb this crossing site.

## Lake Brownwood

Many people like to camp at Flat Rock Park since the camping area is well maintained and it borders on Lake Brownwood. However, many visitors have experienced problems with their boats while they attempt to load or unload using the boat ramp at Flat Rock Park. People have also mentioned receiving

---

[36] It seems that the building took the name The Old Morgue Building since at one time in its history, an actual morgue operated in the building ad bodies were stored in some of the rooms.

damage to their boats like they hit a large rock, but no rock would be anywhere near the location. Several people have also drowned in the swimming area around this portion of the lake. Legend has it that a small girl drowned in the Pecan Bayou before the lake was built. Some campers as well as permanent residents of the area have mentioned hearing a little girl laugh at night, though searchers have never found a little girl. Other resident have said that they have seen a little girl run down the walk to their dock and jump into the lake.

# CARRIZO SPRINGS, TEXAS

Carrizo Springs, the county seat of Dimmit County, is on U.S. Highway 83 eight miles northwest of Asherton. The name of the town comes from the local springs, which were named by the Spanish for the cane grass that once grew around them. Carrizo Springs is the oldest town in Dimmit County; it was founded in 1865 by a group of fifteen families from Atascosa County, led by Levi English, who had visited the area earlier. A second group of settlers arrived from Goliad about two years later.

## Dimmit County Courthouse

The Dimmit County Courthouse was built in 1884 and has, naturally, seen a lot of history. The jail also occupied a portion of this historic old building and the sheriff, as the senior law enforcement official of the county spent a great deal of his time in the jail complex.

A number of years ago, there was a sheriff named Doc Murray. He was a man known for his sincere dedication to his job. A number of former members of the department have confirmed the stories of footsteps mounting the steps to the second floor of the building and the rattling of what sounds like a big key ring.

According to local legend, it is also rumored that, as Doc Murray did when he was alive, he also shows up at the jailhouse and prepares the dinner meal for the prisoners. A number of witnesses have sworn that they can smell the food cooking, dishes rattle, and hear the old Sheriff's steps leaving the cooking area and entering the cell block. Many inmates and guards have actually seen Sheriff Murray.

## Glass Ranch

The Glass Ranch has been a popular hunting location for area hunters for many years. However, a number of hunters have reported hearing the sounds of children's laughter when sitting in one particular deer stand, though no children are ever found in the area. The story is that a busload of children disappeared in the area in the 1920's, there were no ransom demands and none of the children were ever seen again. However, when the land was cleared in the 60's, the missing school bus was found buried in a clearing. The missing children were still on the bus.

## Dimmitt County Memorial Hospital

The Dimmit County Memorial Hospital is located at 704 Hospital Dr. This is not a terribly old building, but it does seem to have its share of mysteries. Nurses who work on the night shift have, many times, seen an elderly nurse, dressed in outdated clothing walking in the maternity ward as if she is checking on the newly born babies.


## Lake Espantosa

There is a very real Texas mystery associated with this Lake and Devil's River. In 1835, a group of American colonists, led by Dr. Charles Beale, were camped at Lake Espantosa, near what is now Carrizo Springs in southwest Texas. Half a mile away from the Beale group, John Dent and his pregnant wife Mollie Pertul Dent had built a crude cabin. Dent had come to trap beaver in the Devil's River area, north of the present day Del-Rio, but was also on the run from the law for the murder of a fellow trapper in Georgia.

The Dents were to prove fortunate in their choice of a site distant from the lake. A band of Comanches raided the main Beale camp and massacred most of the inhabitants. After the killing, the Indians threw the bodies of the victims and their wagons into the lake. Even at this time Espantosa Lake had acquired a reputation for strange goings-on, this incident adding to the store of ill-luck and sorrow centering on what, to this day Mexicans consider a haunted location, the name Espontosa meaning 'frightful'[37].

As Mollie was approaching the end of her pregnancy, the couple was reluctant to travel despite the danger of hostile Indians. One night in May 1835, there was a severe thunderstorm and Mollie went into labor. She appeared to be having problems with the birth so Dent decided to ride westwards for help. He arrived at a Mexican goat ranch on the Pecos Canyon, and told them desperately about his wife's condition, begging for someone to ride back with him. When the Mexican heard of the camp's location near the haunted Espontosa Lake they were at first unwilling to go, especially as it would be dark when they got there. Eventually Dent managed to persuade the ranchero and his wife to accompany him. But as the Mexicans prepared their horses to leave there was a furious crash of thunder and a bolt of lightning struck Dent from his horse killing him instantly.

After a considerable delay the goat herders mounted up and followed Dent's directions. However, darkness fell before they had got over the divide to Devil's River, thus delaying the search. Finally, at sunrise the next morning they located the Dent's isolated cabin. But what they found outside the cabin, in an open brush arbor, was Mollie Dent lying dead, alone. She had apparently died in childbirth, but there was no trace of the baby anywhere. The child was never found, but fang marks on the woman's body and numerous wolf tracks over the

---

[37] http://www.mysteriouspeople.com/Wolf_Girl.htm

area made the goat herders naturally assume that the infant had either been devoured or carried off by lobo wolves.

But this was just the beginning of the story. Ten years later, In 1845, a boy living at San Felipe Springs (Del-Rio) reportedly saw 'a creature, with long hair covering its features, that looked like a naked girl' attacking a herd of goats in the company of a pack of lobo wolves. The story was ridiculed by many, but still managed to spread back among the settlements.

Around a year after this incident, a Mexican woman at San Felipe claimed she had seen two large wolves and a naked young girl devouring a freshly killed goat. She approached close to the group, she said, before they saw her and ran off. She noticed that the girl ran initially on all-fours, but then rose up and ran on two feet, keeping close to the wolves. The woman was in no doubt about what she had seen, and the scattering of people in the Devil's River country began to keep a sharp watch for the girl.

There were similar reports by others in the region during the following year and Apache stories told of a child's footprints, sometimes accompanied by hand prints, having been found among wolf tracks in sandy places along the river. A hunt was organized to capture the 'Lobo (or Wolf) Girl of Devil's River' as she had now become known, comprising mainly Mexican vaqueros. On the third day of the hunt the girl was sighted near Espantosa Lake running with a pack of wolves.  The cowboys managed to separate the girl from her wolf companions and cornered her in a canyon, where she fought like a wildcat clawing and biting frantically to keep her freedom. They finally managed to lasso her to keep her still, but while they were tying her up she began to make frightening, unearthly sounds somewhere between the scream of a woman and the howl of a wolf. As she howled, the monster he-wolf from whom she'd become separated appeared and rushed at her captors. Fortunately one of the cowboys reacted quickly and shot it dead with a pistol, at which the wolf girl fell into a faint. Securely bound, the men were now able to examine the girl and noted that despite a body covered in hair and her wild mannerisms, her appearance was human. Her hands and arms were well muscled but not out of proportion, and she lacked the ability to speak, only making deep growling noises. She moved smoothly on all fours, but was rather awkward when made to stand up straight.

The girl was put on a horse and taken to the nearest ranch, an isolated two-roomed shack amid the desert wilderness. She was put in one of the rooms and unbound, the cowboys offering her a covering for her body and food and water, but she refused, cowering in the darkest corner. They then left her alone for the night, locking the door and posting a guard outside. The only other opening in the room was a small boarded up window.

But as night fell the cowboys heard terrifying howls coming from the wolf girl's room. The strange cries carried through the still night air, unsettling her captors and soon finding answers from among the wolf pack in the wilderness beyond the shack. Soon there were long deep howls coming from all sides as the pack drew closer to the house, and occasionally strange howling screams from the girl answering them from inside her dark room. Suddenly the large pack of wolves charged into the corrals, attacking the goats, cows and horses and bringing the cowboys outside shooting and yelling to drive them away. In all the confusion the wolf girl managed to tear the planks from the window and escape into the night. The howls soon abated and the wolves crept back into the wilderness. The next day not a trace of the girl could be found.

Though there were a few unverified reports in the following years of a young hair-covered girl being seen with a wolf pack in the area, no one ever came in close contact with her. Meanwhile gold had been discovered in California and westward travel had increased significantly. In 1852 a surveying party of frontiersmen searching for a new route to El Paso were riding down to the Rio Grande at a bend far above the mouth of Devil's River. They were almost at the water's edge when they saw at close range, sitting on a sand bar, a young woman suckling two wolf cubs. Suddenly she saw them, quickly grabbed the pups and dashed into the breaks at such a rate that it was impossible for the horsemen to follow.

The girl would have been seventeen years-old that year. After that she disappeared into the wilderness forever. It is impossible now to know what became of Mollie Dent's daughter, presuming that's who the wolf girl was. There were subsequent reports of 'human-faced' wolves in the area right up until the 1930s, and author L.D. Bertillion, wrote in 1937, 'during the past forty years I have in the western country met more than one wolf face strongly marked with human characteristics'.

However, the Wolf Girl of Devil's River does seem to live on in subtler forms. Her 'ghost' has apparently been seen in the old San Felipe Springs area beside the banks of Devil's River. In 1974, a hunter in this area claimed to have seen her again, in the form of a white apparition which vanished before his eyes.

Back in the autumn of 1835, when John and Mollie Dent had newly arrived in Texas, Mollie wrote her mother an odd letter. It said merely -
'Dear Mother,
The Devil has a river in Texas that is all his own and it is made only for those who are grown.
Yours with love
Mollie'.
Whatever happened to the Wolf Girl of Devil's River?

## COMBES, TEXAS

Combes is on Business U.S. Highway 77 and State Highway 107, bordering Harlingen in northwestern Cameron County. The site was originally the headquarters for the Combes Ranch, named for Charles B. Combes, a settler from Kentucky, who moved to the region during the early 1900s. The town developed after 1904, when the St. Louis, Brownsville and Mexico Railway built a line through the region. There is some debate as to whether the town was named for the ranch or for a Brownsville surgeon named Joe Combe.

## Orphanage Rd.

Many years ago, there was a large orphanage located on Orphanage Road. The majority of the residents were younger children. There had many stories of lack of competent care on the part of those that managed the facility. One night a fire broke out and many of the doors and windows could not be opened so that the children could escape. Now it is said that if you pass by the burned out shell of the old building late at night you can still hear the screams and cries of the little kids that died in the fire.

# DEL RIO, TEXAS

Del Rio, the county seat of Val Verde County, is on U.S. Highway 90 and the Southern Pacific Railroad near the confluence of the Rio Grande and San Felipe Creek, 154 miles west of San Antonio in the southern part of the county. The Spanish established a small presidia complex near the site of present Ciudad Acuña, the Mexican sister city of Del Rio, and some Spaniards settled on what became the United States side of the Rio Grande.

## Denim & Diamonds

Denim & Diamonds is a popular night spot located at 2400 Avenue F, Suite 23. The building is believed to be haunted by woman that is sometimes seen mingling with the patrons. Many times, ectoplasm is said to appear in photos taken inside the building.

# DONNA, TEXAS

Donna is off U.S. Highway 83 and State Spur 374, fourteen miles northeast of McAllen in southeastern Hidalgo County. It is in territory that was granted to Lino Cabazos as part of the La Blanca land grant on May 19, 1834, by the Mexican state of Tamaulipas. The Cabazos family inhabited the area for at least twenty years after taking possession of the land, and their descendants continued to live in the area into the twentieth century. The first known Anglo-American settler was John F. Webber, who, accompanied by his wife Sylvia (Hector), a former slave, settled in the area in 1839. The Webbers moved to the area in order to escape persecution for their interracial marriage.

## EL Cascabel

El Cascabel is an old bar that is out in the country, northeast of Brownsville off of Highway 83. The tavern has been abandon since 1995. This abandoned tavern is inhabited by the spirit of a man who was killed in a bar fight. Two men got into an argument one night and one of the men, while still bellied up to the bar was shot and killed. Reportedly if you look through the windows at night the dead man can be seen finishing his drink at the sagging bar.

## Silver Nugget Saloon

The Silver Nugget Saloon is located northeast of Brownsville off of Highway 83. There are many who swear that they have heard phantom music, laughter, and the sounds of dancing and see the lights turning themselves on and off long after closing time.

# EAGLE PASS, TEXAS

Eagle Pass, the county seat of Maverick County, is located on the Mexican border at the intersection of U.S. highways 277 and 57, Farm Road 1021, and the Southern Pacific Railroad in the far western part of the county. During the Mexican War a company of Texas Mounted Volunteers under the command of Capt. John A. Veatch established an observation post on the Rio Grande opposite the mouth of the Mexican Río Escondido and beside an old smuggler's trail that crossed the river at this point. The crossing, known as El Paso del Águila, was so named because of frequent flights of Mexican eagles from the wooded grove along the Escondido. Though abandoned by the military at the conclusion of hostilities, the site remained a terminus and crossing point for trappers, frontiersmen, and traders. In 1849 Fort Duncan was established two miles upstream, and its proximity caused a rudimentary settlement to spring up at the crossing below the post. In 1850 San Antonio merchant James Campbell opened a trading post there, and he was soon joined by William Leslie Cazneau and his bride, Jane Cazneau. The village, named after the crossing on the Rio Grande, changed from El Paso del Águila to Eagle Pass as the Anglo presence grew.

## Las Chimeneas Ranch

The historic Las Chimeneas Ranch is located in southwest Texas near the community of Eagle Pass. Many witnesses have reported hearing the sounds of violence such as men fighting, and screaming can still be heard here. Many of these same witnesses have also sworn that apparitions have been spotted.

## Abandoned Radar Base

Eagle Pass Army Airfield was activated in 1942 as an Army Air Force advanced single engine flying school. Eagle Pass AAF was converted to a basic flying school in 1944. During WW2, Eagle Pass AAF had two auxiliary fields: Pinto Aux #2 (35 miles NNW of Eagle Pass), of which no trace has been located, and Eagle Pass Aux #3 (9.5 miles ESE of Eagle Pass). At some point between 1957-61, the airfield had apparently been relinquished by the Air Force reused as a civilian airport, and then closed, as it was labeled "Maverick County (Closed)" on the January 1961 Edward's Plateau World Aeronautical Chart (courtesy of

Chris Kennedy). The runway length had also been reduced, as it was listed as having a 5,700' hard-surface runway.

However, though the government was finished with the base, apparently those that haunt the facility are "alive and well" so to speak. Many teens who have gone out to the abandoned base to party have reported seeing many strange apparitions and spirits that haunt the base grounds and have heard the sounds of propeller driven aircraft though the skies are empty.

## Old Texas Ballroom

The Texas Ballroom is located at 1324 Agarita Street in Eagle Pass. In the late 1950's it was said that an old man went crazy and shot himself. If you take pictures of the interior of the ballroom you will see the old man waiting for his next dance.

# EDGEWOOD, TEXAS

Edgewood, on Farm roads 859 and 1504 and U.S. Highway 80 ten miles northwest of Canton in north central Van Zandt County grew in three phases reflected in the community's three cemeteries. From 1840 to the 1870s settlers from eastern states founded a community two miles southeast of Edgewood close to the Dallas-Shreveport road and established the first cemetery. Barren Ridge, as this place was called, was the site of a post office opened in 1850. A second phase and second cemetery date roughly from 1870 to 1890; the railroad arrived, and in 1877 a county-seat war between Canton and Wills Point led to a decision to establish a new shipping point at Edgewood. District judge-elect John C. Robertson and his partner William S. Herndon gave land for a railroad depot on the Texas and Pacific Railway. A section house and a freight and passenger depot were built at the edge of a wood and named Stevenson Switch.

## Crooked Creek

Going back to 1958 there are a number of reports of a woman in white walking the road along Crooked Creek at night. Numerous drivers have kindly offered her rides and she accepts asking to be taken home. Her directions lead to this old abandoned house where she goes inside. No lights are ever seen inside the old house and if attempts re made to follow the woman, nothing is found.

# EDINBURG, TEXAS

Edinburg, the Hidalgo county seat, is on U.S. Highway 281 and State Highway 107 in the south central part of the county. It is part of the McAllen, Pharr, and Edinburg metropolitan area. Hidalgo, on the Rio Grande, was the original county seat. John Closner and William Briggs, who had land-development projects in the vicinity of Chapin, seventeen miles north of Hidalgo, made Chapin county seat. The townsite was named after Dennis B. Chapin, another of its promoters. Chapin's involvement in a homicide caused a change of name in 1911 to Edinburg, in honor of the birthplace in Scotland of John Young.

## Train Depot

The beautiful and haunted 1928 Southern Pacific Railroad Station, located at 602 West University Street is now the Edinburg Visitor Information Center.  This is one of the four Southern Pacific stations in the Valley built in Spanish Colonial Revival style in the late 1920s. The others were McAllen (now a law office), Brownsville (the Historic Museum on Elizabeth St.), and Harlingen (razed).

According to the story, Aida R., President of the Chamber in this small town is actually somewhat involved in one of the hauntings in this historic old building. It is her touch activated music box that periodically plays for no reason.

One of the spirits could well be that of a dead conductor punching passenger's one-way tickets on a phantom hell-bound train. This ghostly conductor has been sighted moving about the Depot and has been seen to set off the music box which sits inside the depot.

There have also been a number of sightings of apparitions! Witnesses have talked of figures walking quickly and silently past the reception desk. There is a black man in what was the segregated side of the depot; however, searchers are never able to find him.

A number of witnesses have also talked about hearing indistinct and muffled voices. A few have said that they heard voices, but the ones that they heard were sometimes clear and interrogative. And then there was the note!

Now in police hands, it demanded help in finding the spirit's body. The spirit claims to have been killed by two black-hearted coworkers who killed him after he overheard their plans to hijack a train. The note also mentioned a deadline, which is unusual since ghosts can afford to be extremely patient (eternity and all that).

## House at Shunior & 18th St.

In Edinburg, there is a house that is located at the corner of Shunior and 18th streets. There have long been rumors that this house is haunted, though no one will give specifics about the events. Supporting the theory of the hauntings is the fact that this house has always been there for rent, and people that move in wont last no more than 3 months, due to what are described as extremely horrible, terrifying noises heard at night.

## Austin Elementary

Located at 1023 E Kuhn St, Austin Elementary School has long had the reputation of being haunted. A number of witnesses have reported seeing strange things around the school. It is located just 1/4 of a mile from Hillcrest cemetery and some students claim that at night the dead rise from the cemetery and come to the school. It is said that late at night you can see figures walking on the school grounds.

## Museum of South Texas History

The Museum of South Texas History located at 121 E. McIntyre was formally the old Edinburg courthouse and jail. In the original part of the building you get an eerie feeling as you walk up the stairs to the tower of the old building. The tower was the hanging room, were they would hang the convicted prisoners that were sentenced to death in the courtroom below. It is officially recorded that only one man was executed in the tower, however, some people claim that more than one was executed. There is no question that a visitor can feel a cold spot in the tower. Some claim that the rope that is still hanging there swings back and forth as if a body dangled at the end. Shadows of a man hanging have been seen by some and many people who have passed by the building at night claim to hear voices, sounds, and wails coming from the original part of the building where the cells were located and the tower stands.

## South Middle School

South Middle School is located at 601 W Freddy Gonzalez. It is reported that a couple of years ago a student fell from the west side staircase and died of injuries received in the fall. Now it is said that around midnight you can see a white figure walking around the staircase, though a search will reveal that there is no one in the building.

## University of Texas Pan American - Troxel Residence Hall

There is a legend that a girl attending the University of Texas Pan American and living in Troxel Resident Hall got pregnant by a guy who took her as a one-night stand but she thought he really liked her. When she found out that she was pregnant she was afraid to tell her parents so she attempted to give herself an abortion in her dorm room. She found that she was afraid to do the abortion so she took the easy way out and committed suicide. Now some students living at Troxel say that at night sometimes they hear knocking on a certain door, but when the door is opened, there is no one there.

# GEORGE WEST, TEXAS

George West, the county seat of Live Oak County, is at the intersection of U.S. highways 281 and 59, sixty-three miles northwest of Corpus Christi, in the approximate geographic center of the county. It was named for George Washington West, who established his ranch in Live Oak County in the early 1900s. In 1912 he donated his name, a townsite, $100,000, and thirteen miles of railroad right-of-way through his ranch in order to establish a town on a railroad. The San Antonio, Uvalde and Gulf Railroad laid the tracks in 1913. George West was recorded in the county clerk's office of Live Oak County on September 22,

1914. In 1856, when Live Oak County was established the county seat was Oakville. George West became county seat in 1919. The town's first public school was opened in 1912 and enlarged in 1921. The first church service was held in an office building in 1914; in 1979 Baptist, Methodist, and Episcopal congregations were thriving in the town.

## Live Oak County Courthouse

People have reported hearing the sounds of children playing and laughing inside the Live Oak County Courthouse, although there never any children found to account for the sounds. It is also fairly well established that there were never any children harmed or killed within the courthouse. There is also a picture in the District Courtroom of an ex District court justice who's eyes will follow you all over the courtroom. It has also been said that if you walk on the south hall on the second floor you will hear footsteps following you. The City founder George Washington West has been seen in the same hallway.

# GONZALES, TEXAS

Gonzales was established by Empresario Green DeWitt in August, 1825, near the junction of the San Marcos and Guadalupe Rivers and was made the capital of his colony of settlers. It was the first Anglo-American settlement west of the Colorado River and was named in honor of Don Rafael Gonzales, provisional governor of Texas and Coahuila, Mexico. Surveyed by both James Kerr and Byrd Lockhart the city today remains as it was originally laid out.

In July of 1826, the settlement was attacked by Indians, one man was killed and the cabins plundered. In 1831 the Mexican government gave the settlers a small brass or bronze cannon for protection. During the years unrest developed among colonists because of increasing restrictions and controls. As a frontier settlement, Gonzales was destined to play an important role in the resulting Texas Revolution.

## Courthouse

Since Albert Howard cursed the Courthouse clock prior to his hanging in 1921, the clock has never worked right. One legend holds that Albert Howard was sentenced to be hanged in 1921. Howard claimed to be innocent of murder and strongly protested his conviction. As his day drew near, he kept track of the remaining hours by watching the courthouse clock, which had faces on four sides. He vowed his innocence would be proved, evidenced by the fact that after his hanging the four sides of the clock would never agree.

He was right. After the hanging, the four sides of the clock failed to agree. In following years the clock was repaired, but lightning struck the courthouse tower -- not once but twice -- damaging the clock both times. Today, after the extensive remodeling, the clock works, but locals wonder when Howard will return to prove his innocence. During thunderstorms many stay clear of the courthouse.

## St. James Inn

The St. James Inn, completed in 1914, was designed by noted San Antonio architect James Phelps and executed by craftsmen from San Antonio and Austin. It was the home of Walter Kokernot, the son of David Levi Kokernot, cattle baron, personal confidante to General Sam Houston and unsung Texas hero. Every detail of the transitional period mansion has been carefully planned and carried out, from the living room mantel to the coffered ceilings in the reception hall and living room. It has been restored by the current owners, Architect J. Rew Covert and his wife Ann.

However, it would also seem that in addition to the splendor of another age, this historic old building also has its share of ghosts. Footsteps heard upstairs are attributed to Walter Kokernot. Doors have also been known to slam when no one has been near them and there has been no breeze to cause them to shut.

# HARGILL, TEXAS

Hargill is on Farm roads 490 and 493 twenty-four miles northeast of McAllen in eastern Hidalgo County. It was developed and named by W. A. Harding and Lamar Gill during the early 1900s. A post office was in operation in Hargill in 1924, and in 1926 a railroad station was established there on the St. Louis, Brownsville and Mexico Railway. By 1930 Hargill had ten stores, a school, three churches, and an estimated population of 400. In 1947 it had a population of 450 and nine stores. In 1963 the community had three churches, one school, multiple dwellings, and a population of 100. The population had increased to 1,349 by 1990.

## Hargill Elementary School

At Hargill Elementary School in the girls PE bathroom, witnesses have maintained that the student lockers are always opening and closing by themselves; the water comes on by itself; and the bathroom doors lock themselves. There are many that think that the ghost is that of a young girl, since some have claimed to hear a girl's soft laughter after one of these pranks.

# HARLINGEN, TEXAS

Harlingen was named after a Dutch town with a very good system of canals. At the time of its founding (1910), founder Lon C. Hill considered commerce to be a new town's lifeblood. Tourism per se was unknown except for the Holyland and Mecca. Although today the highways have replaced the planned canal system, the beautiful Arroyo Colorado is still a town attraction, if only for the migratory birds (the first Winter Texans). We hope the city will keep the old Iron Bridge over the Arroyo.

### Dishman Elementary

Dishman Elementary School, located at 309 Madeley has a long reputation of strange occurrences. Teachers have reported that fifty years ago a child was beaten to death by another student in the old girls' bathroom. Now it is said, if you stay alone in the bathroom you can hear soft cries coming from the last stall where the young girl died.

### Harlingen Insane Asylum

The Harlingen Insane Asylum was one of several opened in the 1950s. Supposedly it is closed now. Witnesses report that if you go there at night you can hear people screaming and see people walking around inside the deserted facility. Many people had died there so maybe it's their ghosts walking around. Disembodied screams have been heard in this abandoned building.

### Matz Street

There is said to be a young girl that walks up and down Matz Street after midnight. According to witnesses, she is sobbing and holding her face, but refuses to answer anyone that she might met that inquires if she needs help. If someone should approach the young girl, she will fade away.

### Shirley Street

Some have said that they have seen a little girl that is said to haunt Shirley Street and the houses nearby. Locals maintain that the little girl haunts Shirley Street because her family lived there and due to an unfortunate series of events, they died there as well. Others have said that they have seen a white lady in back of the lake.

### Memorial Middle School

Memorial Middle School is located at 300 N 13th St. Locals have long said that this school is haunted by two little girls who had died there under very mysteriously circumstances. Teachers and janitors have reportedly seen the little girl ghosts and have heard them crying.

## HELOTES, TEXAS

Helotes is on State Highway 16 some sixteen miles northwest of downtown San Antonio in northwestern Bexar County. It was first settled around 1856 by Mexicans who intermarried with the Apache Indians camped in the vicinity. A man named Chaca was supposed to have been the first person to build a house and cultivate a cornfield at the site and may have been responsible for the name, which in Spanish means "green roasting ear of corn." Another tradition claims that the name derived from the problems Anglo settlers had with Indians stealing their ripening corn. Yet another story has it that San Antonio vegetable-sellers could always rely on the town for corn, even in periods of drought.

## Grey Moss Inn

The Grey Moss Inn located at 19010 Scenic Loop Road, gained fame for its combination of Southern hospitality and fine food, thanks to Mary Howell, who founded the Inn in 1929. The Inn has never been closed and is the oldest continuously operating restaurant in Central Texas.

This restaurant is supposedly haunted by 3 spirits; that of Mary Howell who it is said cannot bear to leave beloved home, an Indian maiden and an unknown man.

## Stinson Middle School

It's said that at Stinson Middle School, even during class that books will be taken away from students, lights will go out, and sometimes terrible screams are heard echoing through the building.

# HIDALGO, TEXAS

Hidalgo is on the Rio Grande at the junction of State Highway 336 and U.S. Highway 281, five miles south of McAllen in southern Hidalgo County. The first settlers were members of the José de Escandón colony, who settled the area in 1749. At the time the community was known variously as La Habitación, as Rancho San Luis, and as San Luisito. In 1852 John Young, a native Scotsman, settled in the area and renamed the town Edinburgh.

## Hidalgo High School

One of the buildings of the Hidalgo High School Complex, located at 910 Pirate Drive, is called the "G Wing". This building is considered to be extremely haunted. It is said by teachers that after school hours books are thrown off of the shelves. It is also said that teachers and janitors have seen the ghost of a janitor who passed away a couple of years ago walking in the halls of this building very early in the morning.

## Shary Mansion

John H. Shary, the "father of the Texas citrus industry," built his mansion in 1917 to prove that he was committed to the area and planned to spend his life there. He chose the site carefully, next to a large ebony grove on the east and a large depression on the south where he built a three-acre lake for watering the lawn and fire protection. He added a large bathhouse and it became a popular place for community swimming parties.

The Shary Mansion has been the site of many events important to the Rio Grande Valley. President Dwight D. Eisenhower, war correspondent Ernie Pyle, and author Dale Carnegie, among other distinguished guests, have stayed at the estate. In 1937, Shary's daughter, Marialice, married Allan Shivers in the mansion. Shivers served as governor of Texas from 1949 to 1957. After the death of Shary in 1945 and his wife in 1959, the Shivers continued to care for the home spending holidays there. Now, the home has been donated to The University of Texas-Pan American Foundation by the four children of Marialice and Allan Shivers.

However, Mr. Shary, who is buried across the street of what used to be his home, may not be totally happy with this donation. It is said that he has been seen walking across the street at night, from his burial place to his home. He is also said to have been seen by some sitting on a rocking chair on his front porch.

# KERRVILLE, TEXAS

Kerrville, the county seat of Kerr County, is sixty-two miles northwest of San Antonio on Interstate Highway 10, at the junction of Texas Highways 16 and 27. The official elevation is 1,645 feet above sea level, though many of the residential districts in the hilly township are higher. Geography has always been the dominant quality of the Kerrville area-from prehistoric times, with archeological evidence suggesting human habitation as early as 10,000 years ago, to the present, when the town has achieved a national and international reputation for its karst landscapes, scenic roadways, river and streams, lakes, caves, biological diversity, ranches, architecture, and popular culture. The original settlement, named for James Kerr and situated on a bluff north of the Guadalupe River in the eastern half of the county, grew from a successful shingle makers' camp into a mercantile and shipment center for the middle and upper Hill Country, and eventually into a medical, recreational, professional, cultural, and, to some extent, educational hub for parts of a five-to-seven county area.

## Kerrville's Court Yard

Most of the locals are certain that a young woman was killed by her boyfriend in a fit of jealousy in the late 1800's in the Kerrville Court Yard. According to the story, after killing the girl, the boy friend then hung himself. A number of people have claimed to have seen her and her boyfriend fighting around midnight. Then as the witnesses watch, the man kills her then later. A few moments later, those who have not fled in terror will see a body hanging from a nearby tree.

Most of those who watched this recreation will leave feeling sad and many have reported that they started to cry for no reason. At this point, it is reported that they feel someone breathing on their neck, even though there is no one around. At this point, some have said that their car began to lock and unlock and the lights flickered on and off in the court house. Others have reported seeing a young woman fleeing from a man run by the car and then heard heavy pounding on the roof of the car.

## <u>Schreiner University - Delaney Hall</u>

Schreiner University, located at 2100 Memorial Boulevard, was founded in that year when a Hill Country rancher, merchant and former Texas Ranger, Captain Charles Schreiner , asked the Presbyterian Church to help him put bricks, mortar, and people around a dream he had nurtured for many years. He donated land along the Guadalupe River and together they established "facilities for high grade instruction and military training to boys and young men as preparation for college and university work." Not a Presbyterian himself, it is said that Captain Schreiner chose to work with the Presbyterians because their charter most closely resembled the constitution of the United States.

Most people living in Kerrville already know that Delaney Hall on the campus of Schreiner University is said to be haunted by 8 spirits. Rumor has it this school suffered several freak accidents in the 1950's and 1960's. These mysterious deaths include: One kid who killed himself and another who suffered a fall down the steps of Delaney hall in which he died instantly from a broken neck. Recently the students of Delaney hall tried to reach a spirit using a Ouija board. This is how the students learned of the other 6 spirits as one of the spirits told of the news. Many strange occurrences have gone on in Delaney Hall such as apparitions of kids being seen roaming the halls late at night. Once when the building was empty the security on the campus of Schreiner witnessed a light being turned on and off inside the building. When the Kerrville police department arrived nobody was in the building. Delaney Hall is also full of cold spots. Students are also awakened by their televisions and radios being turned on and off by themselves.

## <u>Tivy High School</u>

Tivy High School is located at 3250 Loop 534. It was named after Captain Joseph Tivy, a former Texas Ranger, trustee of the Kerrville School Association as well as Mayor of Kerrville. Many students as well as faculty members that have had occasion to be inside the building alone report that they have very strong feelings that they are not alone. Some have reported seeing apparitions moving inside the hallways of the school.

## <u>Y.O. Ranch Hotel</u>

The Y.O. Ranch Hotel is a rather historic lodging located on the Y.O Ranch. A number of guests, as well as staff, have reported seeing apparitions of cowboys walking around the courtyard after 3am in the morning near the swimming pool. If anyone approaches these figures, then they simply vanish.

## <u>Y.O. Ranch Hotel -The Sam Houston Cafe</u>

This eatery has been the scene of a number of unusual encounters. According to some former employees, there is a phantom patron that has been known to ask to use the bathroom. The entity appears real so the employee in question will direct the individual to the restroom. However, when the patron does not come back, the restroom is checked and there is no one there.

# KINGSVILLE, TEXAS

Kingsville was born on July 4, 1904, when the first regular passenger train of the St. Louis, Brownsville and Mexico Railroad arrived. The much celebrated event was the culmination of a great deal of work and planning over a number of years. Kingsville's roots go much deeper than the railroad, although the city marks its birthday from that event. In 1853, Captain Richard King purchased land that was once part of the Rincon de Santa Gertrudis Spanish land grant on the Santa Gertrudis Creek. When King died, his widow, Henrietta, continued to build a ranch that now extends over 825,000 acres.

The headquarters of the ranch are located a half mile west of the city limits on State Highway 141. One of the King's children, Alice, married Robert J. Kleberg, a lawyer and a man of great vision. As he worked to build the ranch, he and Mrs. King dreamed of a city near the ranch with a railroad that would expand the agricultural potential of the area. Kingsville started as a tent city as workers put down tracks for the trains. Within a year, it was a small city with businesses and homes.

## Jones Auditorium

The Edward Newton Jones Auditorium is located on the Kingsville Campus of Texas A & M University and has long been viewed as haunted. During construction it is said that a worker fell to his death from high up in the rafters. Since that time it is believed that he haunts the scene of his death.

Many witnesses have seen lights going on and off, encountered doors locking or unlocking themselves, and found wayward costumes that have been pulled form their hangers and thrown to the floor. Most people blame the worker that died in the fall.

## Texas A&M University – Lewis Hall

Lewis Hall is supposed to be a 24 hours dorm, inhabited by mature students. However, it is said to actually be party central at this University. It is also said to be haunted by the ghost of a female student who, in a fit of depression committed suicide. Many students reports encountering cold spots, having feelings of being watched and seeing apparitions. Turner dorms are haunted by students who committed suicide. Cold spots and feelings of being watched are experienced in each one Apparitions have been seen by numerous people.

## Chela's Market

I do not have an address for Chela's Market, but there have been many reports of the sounds of loud thumping coming form inside the closed stores as well as lights flickering on and off at night and a number of people swear that they have seen figures about the store through the windows

## Texas A&M University - The Bell

Donated to Texas A&M University and dedicated on October 6, 1984 by Martha and Ford D. Albritton, the Albritton Tower is 138 feet tall and contains Westminster chimes which ring every quarter hour. There are 49 carillon bells, the largest one weights more than six thousand pounds, can be programmed to play music such as the "Spirit of Aggieland". A student is said to have hung himself in the Tower and now at midnight it is said that you can see his shadow on all 4 corners of the Bell.

## Texas A&M University - Bishop Hall

Bishop Hall is one of the dorms at this historic University. It is said that at night you can hear a girl laughing in the halls though a search will not reveal the presence of anyone that could account for the sounds. Some students get feelings of coldness in some places and some female residents have even felt the presence of a person in their room. Sometimes girls report that they can feel somebody playing with their hair along with the sound of somebody breathing near them.

At times dormitory doors that are locked have unlocked on their own and swung open. Other girls have even heard the sounds of chairs being drug across the floor from inside dorm rooms that are not being occupied. Showers have been said to turn on and off on their own when there is nobody else in the dorm bathrooms. Most of these experiences have happened on the third and Second floor. Some say it is the spirit of a young girl that went crazy by playing the Ouija board and hung herself.

## Texas A&M University - Turner Hall

Turner Hall is said to be haunted by male student who committed suicide. In the second floor in restroom on the north side, students have reported that late at night you can see, out of the corner of your eye, a passing black shadow flowing from the last toilet near the window to the east exit. You can also see a passing shadow on the window curtain.

# LA FERIA, TEXAS

La Feria is at the intersection of U.S. Highway 83 and Farm Road 506, twenty-four miles northwest of Brownsville in western Cameron County. The area was first settled when the land was assigned by Spain in 1777 to Rosa María Hinojosa de Ballí as part of the La Feria land grant. The Ballí family established several farms with headquarters on the La Feria grant. The family maintained control of the land well into the mid-1800s, and the community that grew up on the grant remained a ranching center into the twentieth century. In 1909 G. J. Schoenberg, a local land developer, developed the town of La Feria. That year the La Feria post office was opened. A railroad stop named Bixby was established a mile from the town when the St. Louis, Brownsville and Mexico Railway was built through the area in 1911. In July 1912 the founding fathers of La Feria stole the Bixby depot and hauled it to the new townsite.

## C.E. Vail Gym

The C.E. Vail Gym is gone now, demolished to make way for progress, or perhaps to try and remove a haunting. During the demolition, it was found that the gym had been inadvertently built over a small cemetery. The school associated with the old gym used to be a high school, but was converted to an elementary school.

In 1978 there was a suicide by a young girl who hung herself in the gym. For many years students and faculty workers have claimed to have seen her. A Custodian was once cleaning the gym at 5:30 and claimed to have seen her walking with a rope in her hand. Also students have reported to teachers that the young girl had chased them out of the gym.

# LAREDO, TEXAS

San Agustin de Laredo, a colonial city of New Spain founded in 1755, was named for a town in Santander, located on the north coast of Spain. Nuevo Santander, one of the last northern provinces of New Spain, was established by the Spaniard José de Escandón as part of a program to colonize northern Mexico. Appointed governor, Escandón was responsible for the colonization along the Rio Grande, and a chain of six settlements were established, with Camargo being the earliest in 1749. The other outposts included Reynosa (1749), Dolores (1750), Revilla (1750), and Mier (1752). Since no missions or presidios were associated with its founding, Laredo is considered the oldest independent settlement in Texas and is the only remaining Spanish colonial settlement on the north bank of the lower Rio Grande. Laredo was founded on the north bank of the Rio Grande on May 15, 1755, when Captain Tomás Sánchez, with three families, was granted permission to settle 15 leagues of land near an Indian ford on the Rio Grande. Operated as a family rancho, the Sánchez estate ran cattle, sheep, goats, horses, mules and oxen. In 1767, the city was laid out, and in the years to follow, ranching became the sustenance of the colony.

## Bracht-Fisher House

The 120+ year-old Bracht-Fisher House has a long and mysterious past. No one seems to understand what could have caused all of the strange events that are said to take place inside this building. Witnesses have reported an odd fog that can quickly fill a room as well as ghost steps, self-operating porch lights and kitchen doors that open and close of their own accord. Perhaps Leopold Bracht is responsible for the hauntings.

## Laredo ISD

The Azios Building, which houses the Laredo ISD, is home to a spectre that plays with lights and door, and likes to startle the ladies by showing up unexpectedly in unusual places!

## The Old Plaza Hotel

Now the Laredo National Bank Plaza Building, the Plaza Hotel is one of the oldest hotels in Laredo. A whole article was done about 10 years ago regarding the history of the building as well as the hauntings in a circular called "LareDos." The publication is still in print today. Employees who worked in the building during the night shift would hear sounds of someone moving about in the restroom. They would go in (thinking it was the security guard on duty) to investigate and find no one there. Others reported heard the sounds of people talking coming from empty rooms and apparitions have been seen in some areas.

## Alma Pierce Elementary

According to the story, inside the Alma Pierce Elementary School there's a rest room that has been closed off for several years. Students say that this room is haunted. One Halloween an event took place that involved three girls by the name of Ashley, Maria, and Tiffany. Ashley and Tiffany thought it would be good fun to lock Maria in the restroom. Unfortunately, in the excitement of the Halloween events the two girls forgot about their friend until Maria's mom called the two girls asking if they had seen Maria. They told Maria's mom that they were joking around and locked her in the restroom and that they had simply forgotten about her. Maria's mother sent the police to the school at around 10:00 pm to rescue her daughter. When the officers looked in the restroom they only found her shoes and clothing. Maria's body was not there, only a pool of blood.

## Laredo Children's Museum

The Laredo Children's Museum is located at P-56 Fort McIntosh St., Laredo, TX. This museum, which occupies two restored buildings from old Fort McIntosh, hosts permanent and changing exhibits designed especially for kids. Among the many "play" areas are a grocery store, construction area, hospital area, computer lab, sand/water table, momentum machine, and science exhibits. Most exhibits offer age-appropriate hands-on activities and role play.

The first floor of the building used to be a morgue before a newer building was built and the old one was torn down. Sometimes you can see shadows moving, hear disembodied voices and experience cold spots on this floor.

## Clark Middle School

In the 7th grade hall, Room 28, of the Clark Middle School, janitors have reported hearing voices at night. There have also been reports of hearing children laughing and playing in the room, which always empty when the janitors investigate. In some cases the computers have turned on and off and lights have flickered.

## Cigarroa Middle School

It is said that in the section of the Cigarroa Middle School known as the sixth grade hall, you can hear the bouncing of a ball which is being chased by a young boy. Janitors say that at this exact time the clocks posted at every hall start to spin like crazy and they have never been able to set them on time.

## Circle K McPherson Rd.

Employees of the Circle K on McPherson Road have seen the apparition of a little girl wearing a sundress walking thought the isles carrying a carton of milk in her left hand and a package of candy in her right hand. When she is approached, she vanishes.

## Civic Center

A man had an accident in the area of the Civic Center where the dressing rooms are located. It is said that the ropes holding some of the weights that make the curtains move, snapped and the weights fell down on his head killing him. It is now said by the janitors that you can hear him walking at night and that he even pinches you! If you go up the second floor were the dressing rooms are, stage left, you can still see the cracks on the wall and floor left by the weights!

## Laredo Community College

The site of the Laredo Community College is actually an old fort. A lot of the old buildings are still in existence and either used as classrooms or offices. If you check the campus maps there used to be a cemetery that went with it, which is where people claim to have seen apparitions.

## Fire Station #2

Beneath Fire Station #2 there is believed to be an old grave site that dates from a time long before the station was built. The firemen say that this station is haunted by a firefighter by the name of Lupito. Firefighters feel their legs being pulled off the bed while they try to sleep; the furniture periodically shakes and moves and there have also been reports of actual levitation.

## Hamilton Hotel

The historic Hamilton Hotel, located at 1401 Farragut Street is a 1920s Spanish Colonial hotel that had slipped far beyond its days of grandeur by the end of the 20th century. By then, It was and eyesore and marred the Laredo skyline, sitting partially condemned and completely neglected. Initially the city planned to demolish the building, freeing valuable land for more practical projects. Mayor Elizabeth Flores, however, recognized the still-present elegance of this Laredo landmark and sensed the potential hidden in its walls. Flores initiated a unique public/private partnership to resurrect the Hamilton Hotel as a home for Laredo's low-income elderly, more than two-thirds of whom live in poverty. Now many of the residents and staff report hearing the voices of children running and playing though there are seldom any children on the premises.

According to legend, there was also number of murders that took place inside this building, including a priest that was pushed out of a window to his death a few decades ago. Now the hotel has furniture that moves itself, lights that go on and off on their own, and an elevator that functions on its own. There may have been more murders than just the priest, but we don't have anything more solid than that at the moment.

## Health Department

The building that houses the City Health Department located at 2600 Cedar Ave has long been said to be haunted. Many current and former employees talk about seeing apparitions of people, figures more than actually people, who walk around once the offices are closed. Lights flicker on and off, and the janitors often walk into cold spots which leave them with eerie feelings and to make matters even more strange, they often find that their cleaning supplies move without anyone being around.

## H.E.B. Guadalupe

Many witnesses have reported seeing the apparition of a man literally dragging himself from section to section trying to find a way to get out of the H.E.B. Guadalupe store.

## J.P. OSCAR MARTINEZ'S OFFICE

The office of Justice of the Peace Oscar Martinez was formerly the old Department of Public Safety office. Several employees have witnessed a deceased DPS officer wandering around the building at all times. He turns lights, computers, and other electrical devices on/off; he slams doors shut; shuffles papers/files around. Several witnesses have said that you can actually see the door knob turning (like someone on the other side trying to open the door) but there is no one in the other room; strange sensation of being watched and cold chills.

## La Posada Hotel

The La Posada Hotel is located at 1000 Zaragoza, Laredo, Texas. This hotel is set beside the Rio Grande River and just beside of St. Augustan Church. The building used to be a convent many years ago and many guests and staff members have seen a nun roaming around the hotel as well as a spirit that takes the form of employees and looks just like them but will not talk.

There have been a number of other odd occurrences such as other sightings, cold spots, someone calling out your name, objects moving and falling with no explanation. You can also clearly hear footsteps and running in the St. Augustan Ball Room when there is no one there.

## Lake Casa Blanca Ballroom

There is a story associated with the Ballroom that still has people mystified. It seems that one night after a dance at the Lake Casa Blanca Ballroom a young man by the name of Mario gave a young woman with whom he had been dancing and who was wearing a very distinctive necklace, a ride to her house. When she got out of his car, Mario discovered that she left her necklace lying on the seat of the car. Mario looked around, but discovered that the young lady had disappeared. He assumed that she had already entered her home.

Mario got out of the car and rang the doorbell to her house. A man answered and Mario explained that had given a very pretty young lady a ride home and that she had left her necklace in his car. The man sadly explained while the necklace was his daughter's necklace, it could not be returned to her as she had been dead for over 5 years because she had drowned at the lake.

## Laredo Mall

According to many locals, the Laredo Mall is also the scene of some very unusual events. Night custodians have said that around 10:30 in the evening, long after the mall has closed for the day, they see a little girl walking around the mall. She always has a doll clutched tightly in her right hand and they hear her crying for her mother. She is also described as wearing clothing such as was worn in the 1940s or 1950s. If she is approached, she will vanish.

## Main Boy's Club

Through out the years there have been reports of sounds coming from all over the Main Boys' Club building when rooms are empty or after hours. In the gym people have heard laughter and basketballs bouncing as if a game is underway. However, when they investigate the sounds, witnesses have reported that the gym is empty. Others have reported sounds coming from the swimming pool area. People have very clearly heard the water splashing and the diving board being used. As with the gym, when the sounds are investigated, the pool area is always found to be empty. There is a story that some years ago a child drowned in the pool which might explain the cause of the sounds in the pool area, but what happened in the gym?

## Martin High School

It is said that Martin High School is haunted, though most seem to feel that these stories have been told only because there was a cemetery where the school was built. A number of area residents believe that the hauntings take place because those charged with moving the cemetery only took the head stones and not the bodies! At night you can here the sound of wielding, or see shadows moving about in the school gym.

## Memorial Middle School

A number of students have reported that they have seen a priest on the top floor of the Memorial Middle School. A number of area residents say that Memorial was once a Catholic all boys school and that the priest seen wandering the building once lived on the top floor. No one seems to know the details, but it is also reported that this priest died in the building and now continues to walk the hallways.

## Mercy Regional Diagnostic Center

The building that houses the Mercy Regional Diagnostic Center used to be an old apartment building that is located just south of St. Agustin High School in the old heights area. A number of witnesses claim to have seen demonic looking figure that has glaring eyes and a wide grin from ear to ear with a reptilian like tongue hanging down to his chest.

## Nixon High School

During the 1970's, a girl on the Nixon High School dance team was killed by her jealous boyfriend. She was supposedly decapitated and her head was never found. Witnesses have claimed to see her spirit roaming about the school with no head. It is said that if you are by the school gym at night, you can hear the spurs she wore on her boots chiming in the dark.

## Old Mercy Hospital

The original Mercy Hospital was closed long ago, but not before it had developed a solid reputation as being haunted. Visitors report seeing figures wearing old style nurse's uniforms moving about the halls and there have been many reports that it is possible to hear voices of people talking in the old morgue area.

## The Old Police Station

Almost every time someone goes in this old building they report hearing footsteps and they hear voices whispering behind their back. In some areas of the building, visitors can feel a cold breeze and others have reported seeing what looks like a cat minus its head. A number of the locals report that after the police station was closed, that a satanic cult used to practice its rituals in the basement.

## The Texas Rural Legal Aid building

The Texas Rural Legal Aid building is about a block south of the Magnet School and it is rumored to have once been inhabited by monks. Workers have stated that they have seen a dark shadow walking around from room to room and stopping at one of the desks and pausing for along while. Witnesses report that in the area where the shadowy figures pauses there used to be a bell which one of the monks would ring in order to announce things.

At one point the staff left a tape recorder on overnight on a staircase to see if they could record strange noises and they recorded footsteps going up and down, an abrupt stop and someone screaming just before what sounded like someone kicking the tape recorder down the stairs. Interestingly enough, the tape recorder was found to have been kicked down the stairs the next morning.

## United High School

United High School has been haunted for years. Some say they would see a dirty little girl under the portable building playing or looking for some thing in the dirt. If someone tries to speak to her, she darts away and disappears. Others say that the school is haunted by an Indian. Janitors have experienced this haunting at night.

One night a janitor was cleaning one of the portables, picked up the trash, put it in a bag and fixed the desks, turned off the lights and locked the door. As he was walking away he looked back and saw that the lights were on. He opened the door and the trash that he had neatly bagged had been thrown on the floor and desks were messed up again.

## United Middle School

There is a section of the United Middle School that is said to be closed off because it is said that a girl was killed after a basketball game. She had been playing with one of the basketballs and it got away from her and went rolling down the stairs. She ran after the ball and the few people still remaining in the gym heard her scream. When they reached her, she was dead. It was never conclusively determined how she died.

Now it is said that if you enter the gym after a game, you can hear her bouncing the ball and she her shadow moving about the court.

## V.M.T. Magnet School

Students at the V.M.T. Magnet School have reported hearing footsteps on the second floor long after every one has left that floor. There have also been a number of reports of a foul odor that travels around the building and also that there are several cold spots.

## Zacate Creek

There have been many reports of a lady covered in mud wearing a white dress seen walking through Zacate Creek in La Azteca area. There is also usually a foul odor in this area; people say it is the sewage that smells, but others say it's the smell of a ghost.

# LOCKHART, TEXAS

Lockhart, county seat of Caldwell County, is at the intersection of U. S. Highway 183 and State Highway 142, thirty miles southeast of Austin. It was named for Byrd Lockhart, who in 1831 received the land that later became the Lockhart townsite as partial payment for his surveying work for the Mexican government. During the 1830s settlement in the area was limited by the threat of Indian raids, but after the battle of Plum Creek in 1840, more settlers began to arrive. By the mid-1840s, several families had made their home near Lockhart Springs, and when Caldwell County was established in 1848, the new town of Lockhart became the county seat. The Plum Creek post office, which had served the area since the previous year, was transferred to Lockhart.

## Old Jailhouse/Museum/Courthouse

Built in 1894 of Muldoon limestone and Pecos red sandstone at a cost of $64,000, the Caldwell County Courthouse, also incorporated the county jail. Although originally equipped with electricity, it had no indoor plumbing. Later, broom closets were converted into restrooms, and it is said when the first water bill was received, the county judge was so shocked at the charges he padlocked the restrooms.

According to some of the prisoners, the old sheriff and his wife have opted to hang around as they have been spotted roaming the corridors.

# MISSION, TEXAS

The settlement of Mission is directly tied to what once was the La Lomita community, some 5 miles south. The French Oblates of Mary Immaculate developed a chapel on this portion of land which had dated back to a Spanish land grant. Up until 1904, the railroad had only advanced 5 miles from La Lomita to a railhead town known as "Mamie." The railroad was enticed (by a new depot and 20 acres of land) to extend the remaining distance to what became Mission.

In 1907 when the railroad arrived Mission developed from an influx of new arrivals and the moving of the operations of the Oblate fathers. John J. Conway and J. W. Holt purchased the La Lomita Ranch from the religious order and with other acquired properties they parceled the land into small tracts for resale. The naming of the post office in 1908 accounts for the name change.

Since another Lomita, Texas had been granted a post office under that name, the name Mission was submitted to and accepted by postal authorities.

### Mission High School Football Stadium

In the excitement of one of the Mission High School football games, a female student fell from the Mission High School Football Stadium bleachers, hit her head and died. Now it is said that at dusk, the ghostly student can be seen in the stands still rooting for her team to win.

### City Cemetery

The Mission City Cemetery is said to be haunted by strange looking creatures. It is said late nights there are small troll-like creatures that have chased or frightened people off.

### La Lomita Mission

The old La Lomita Mission has just recently been open to the public. In the mission's heyday, priests were rumored to be having intercourse with the nuns at a nearby Convent and burying the resulting children's bodies on the grounds. One night some illegal emigrants, who were aware of what was going on, went in and killed two of the priests while searching for valuables that they could steal and sell. The third priest went to get help, but died while searching for assistance. The Church opted not to re-staff the mission, so it became an asylum for the mentally challenged. Many of the people working there reported seeing figures in robes walking around the grounds at night. The asylum shut down recently, but the grounds are still open to tourists during the day.

### Mission Junior High School

In the east stairwell of the Science Building at Mission Junior High School (formerly Mission High School) at night, you can just make out the shadow of a man walking up and down the stairs. According to local legend, a teacher fell down the stairs when he was leaving one night after school and died. During the daytime, that side of the building is colder than the other and lights and electronic devices have trouble.

## MCALLEN, TEXAS

McAllen is on U.S. Highway 83 about sixteen miles west of Weslaco and thirty-five miles west of Harlingen in southern Hidalgo County. It is situated on land that was part of porciones 63 and 64, granted respectively by Spain to Antonio Gutiérrez and Juan Antonio Villareal in 1767. Gutiérrez and his heirs inhabited the land at least up to 1883, and Villareal's heirs lived on his land for at least fifty years prior to 1852. The Santa Anita Ranch was established around 1797 by José Manuel Gómez, who received the land grant from Spain in 1800. He raised cattle, sheep, goats, and horses on his ranch and helped to continue colonizing the area. His great-granddaughter Salomé Ballí, who inherited the land in the early 1800s, married John Young, a Brownsville businessman, about 1848. They proceeded to acquire land in the surrounding area, and in 1852 Young applied for porciones 64 and 65 in southern Hidalgo County. Young died in 1859, leaving his holdings to his widow and son, John J. Young, with John McAllen, Young's assistant, as manager. McAllen married Salomé Ballí de Young in 1861, and in 1862 they had a son, James Ballí McAllen. They continued adding land to the ranch, which was renamed the McAllen Ranch. The site of present-day McAllen was within the ranch's boundaries.

## Old McAllen High School

There are many of us who have fond memories of out high school days. However, I question whether high school is where I would choose to spend eternity. Be that as it may, there are many who swear that students killed during WWII have returned to haunt their Alma Mater at the McAllen High School.

## Toys R Us

It is certainly interesting that almost every Toys R Us store that I have investigated seems to be haunted. In this location, several years ago a young boy was climbing the ladder to get to the loft. When he got to the very top he fell and was killed instantly by having his neck broken. Every once in a while during the night the cleaning crew hears the sounds of a young boy laughing and running around in the loft. Lights sometimes turn off and on and certain locked doors will open even though they have not been unlocked.

# MONTE ALTO, TEXAS

Monte Alto is an unincorporated community in Hidalgo County, some 23 miles from McAllen.

## La Bodega

There are many strange stories about La Bodega. It is said this place has claimed the life of many. There are many stories of people dying from accidents, or shootings. There have also been many sightings and unusual stories about noises when there is no one present but the people who cleanup.

Witnesses have sworn that they are always hearing noises that sound like the place filled with people that the workers cannot see. Workers have reported hearing laughter from rooms that are not in use. People claim to feel unexplained chills and see shadows that move.

# PARIS, TEXAS

Paris, previously known as Pinhook, is the county seat of Lamar County. It is on U.S. highways 271 and 82 in the central part of the county in the upland separating the tributaries of the Red and Sulphur rivers. The first recorded settlement in the vicinity was in 1826, and settlements were known to be in the area as early as 1824. The town was founded by merchant George W. Wright, who donated fifty acres of land in February 1844, when the community was also designated the county seat by the voters. It was incorporated by the Congress of the Republic of Texas on February 3, 1845. The community, originally known as Pinhook, was named for Paris, France, by one of Wright's employees, Thomas Poteet. Paris was on the Central National Road of the Republic of Texas, which ran from San Antonio north through Paris to cross the Red River. By the eve of the Civil War, when it had 700 residents, Paris had become a cattle and farming center. Lamar was one of the few Texas counties that voted against secession, though many of its inhabitants later served in the Confederacy. In 1877 and 1916, major fires forced the city to rebuild.

## Gated House off of FM 195

There is a large gated estate located along FM 195. The house is abandoned, but like most old houses it has gained a reputation as being haunted. A number of visitors have reported seeing a small boy crying in the corner of one of the old bedrooms. Others say that the house exudes a sense of evil, as it sits brooding on its tree covered grounds.

Some who have had he nerve to look in the windows have reported seeing empty wheelchairs slowing rolling across some of the rooms. Entering the house seems to be dangerous, as there are a number of missing floor boards.

## Old Plantation home in Slate Shoals

Most people get a bad feeling just looking at this house because of the sensation that someone inside the house is staring back at you. Witnesses have reported seeing a woman looking out of the attic windows and some who have approached the house have heard strange noises. It has also been reported that some who have looked in the windows have reported seeing a wheelchair move across the room.

If you go onto the back porch look down into the well located at the corner of the kitchen in the front of the house, you can see a reflection of someone other than yourself. Locals say that this reflection may be that of the son of the slave master. Out back of the main house there are eleven cabins, on one side there are six and on the other there are five. Some who have explored these old buildings have reported that if you go to the middle cabin, known as cabin number five, on the side with only five cabins you may hear screams. Cabin number five is where it is believed that some of the slave girls were raped and killed by the slave master's son.

# PEARSALL, TEXAS

Pearsall, the county seat of Frio County, is on Interstate Highway 35 and the Missouri Pacific Railroad fifty-five miles southwest of San Antonio in the central part of the county. In the 1870s wagon trains stopped at a well on a large sheep ranch when they traveled the road from Frio Town to Pleasanton; this well was known as Waggoner's (Wagner's) Well. On February 6, 1882, the International-Great Northern Railroad gained control of 2,000 acres of land around the well. An affiliate, the New York and Texas Land Company, allowed them to circumvent Texas laws limiting railroad ownership of land, and, on February 15, 1882, they platted the townsite of Pearsall, named after the vice president of the railroad, Thomas W. Pearsall, east of the newly laid railroad tracks opposite Waggoner's Well.

## Junior High School

It is said that while constructing the Junior High School several years back a construction worker was killed in a fall. Now, witnesses reported that when all of the lights are out at the school, the dead worker is heard roaming the sixth grade hall, opening and closing classroom doors as if desperately searching for something.

# PHARR, TEXAS

Originally a Spanish land grant made in 1767, heirs broke the grant into smaller tracts in the late 1800s. John Connely Kelley and Henry N. Pharr arrived about 1909 and bought 16,000 acres of land. Pharr, a Louisiana sugarcane grower founded the Louisiana and Rio Grande Canal Company to construct an irrigation system for a sugar plantation. Kelley formed the Pharr Townsite Company, naming the new town after his partner. Pharr became a stop on the St. Louis, Brownsville and Mexico Railway around 1911. Four thousand acres had already been sold to settlers and the town had a depot, hotel and bank. The Rio Grande valley sugarcane industry went bust - dashing Pharr's hopes. Kelley assumed control of the existing irrigation system and supplied water to vegetable and cotton farmers. In 1915 the population was a mere 600.

## Whalen Road

There's a dirt road that leads to a corn field and around the corn field there used to be a ranch that had two barns and a small house. Most believe that the family that lived on this small ranch died in the burning of Pharr in 1963, over 40 years ago. They say to this day you can hear the family talking and running through the trees screaming for help. Witnesses have also reported that they throw rocks and sticks at the people that walk and drive by. Others have reported seeing a figure, thought to be the father of this cursed family, who walks the fields carrying an axe as he searches for his cattle.

# PORT ARANSAS, TEXAS

The little fishing village known as "Sand Point" in 1833 was inhabited by the Karankawa Indians. The Karankawas were the first settlers of the "Wild Horse Island", later known "Mustang Island." Many explorers have also passed through the island, including Alonzo Alverez de Pineda, Nunez Cabesa de Vaca and their shipmates. Pirates also frequented the island. In 1834 the remains of a pirates' camp were found on St. Joseph's Island with large iron rings implanted in the sand.

According to local legend, somewhere on Mustang Island there is said to be a Spanish dagger with a silver spike driven through the hilt. This marks the spot where Lafitte buried a chest of gold and jewels. The first recorded permanent settler in what is now Port Aransas was an Englishman from Lancaster, Robert Ainsworth Mercer, in 1853. He built a ranch house, imported cattle and sheep herds, and sent for his wife and three youngest children to join him.

## Beulah's Tarpon Inn Restaurant

The old hotel that is now the Beulah's Tarpon Inn was built in 1886. The rooms are all small and cramped, nor has any restoration been done. Guests staying on the top floor have reported hearing footsteps above them as if there was another floor of rooms. Others have also reported hearing voices coming form their bathrooms and several of the rooms have boasted cold spots. Some visitors have reported hearing the sounds of pots and pans clattering when no one was there. Some have seen an apparition of a woman, and there have routinely been mysterious wet footprints appear seen on the floor.

# PORT ISABEL, TEXAS

Port Isabel is on the point where Texas Highway 100 meets the Laguna Madre in southeastern Cameron County, sixteen miles northeast of Brownsville. It is connected to South Padre Island by the two-mile-long Queen Isabella Causeway (Park Road 100). The first settlement in the area, Brazos Santiago, was on nearby Brazos Island. In 1788 water sellers traveled to the area to obtain water. The site was also used as a summer resort by 1800. Jean Laffite is said to have had a fifteen-foot well dug near the site of present Laguna Vista, five miles northwest of Port Isabel. Official claim to the land was not made until 1828, when it was granted to Rafael García as part of the Potrero ("Pasture") de Santa Isabel. During the 1830s a small community developed at the site, known as El Frontón de Santa Isabel. Later that name was changed to Punta de Santa Isabel, that is, Point Isabel. A post office was established in the community under the name Point Isabel in June 1845.

## Padre Island

Padre Island is a paradise with mils of sandy beaches and more history than most places. It also seems to have a few ghosts. A number of witnesses have reported seeing apparitions of long-dead pirates that once roamed this island. A number of the ghosts also appear to be Spanish as it is known that hundreds of

Spanish sailors died in the waters around this island during the sinking of a Spanish treasure fleet in the 1600s.

# RIO GRANDE CITY, TEXAS

Rio Grande City, the county seat of Starr County and one of the oldest settlements in South Texas, is on the Rio Grande 100 miles from both Brownsville and Laredo in the extreme south central part of the county. It is an international port of entry connected by bridge to Camargo, Tamaulipas. The site was part of the Carnestolendas Ranch, established in 1762 by José Antonio de la Garza Falcón in the Spanish colony of José de Escandón. The ranch later belonged to Henry Clay Davis, an adventurous Kentuckian who survived the Mier expedition and formed the present town from Davis Landing or Rancho Davis in 1847 after marrying María Hilaria de la Garza, the granddaughter of Francisco de la Garza Martínez. Davis had acquired the land upon Garza Falcón's death. He designed the port with broad straight streets, on the model of the capital city, Austin. The establishment of Fort Ringgold in 1848, immediately adjacent to the town, assured its growth and permanence. The town received a post office in 1849; in 1895 the name of the post office changed from Rio Grande City to Riogrande, the name under which it now operates.

## City Hall

The original City Hall of this small town was formerly a commercial building. After the death of the original owner, it was rented to various tenants before becoming the site of the City Hall. A number of city employees have reported that the original owner has been seen inside the building. Others have reported hearing a baby crying in the back rooms, but no explanation for these unusual sounds has ever been found.

## Fort Ringgold

Fort Ringgold, the southernmost installation of the western tier of forts constructed at the end of the Mexican War, stood guard for nearly a century over the Rio Grande and Rio Grande City. On October 26, 1848, Brevet, Maj. Joseph H. LaMotte led two companies of the First United States Infantry to Davis Landing, near the newly established Rio Grande City in Starr County. The army leased thirty-three acres from Henry Clay Davis, the town founder, whose heirs sold 350 acres to the government for $20,000 in 1878. Known initially as the Post at Davis Landing, the fort bore the names Camp Ringgold and Ringgold Barracks before being named Fort Ringgold in the year of the purchase. The name was in honor of Brevet. Maj. Samuel Ringgold, the first United States Army officer to die from wounds received in the battle of Palo Alto (May 8, 1846); he died on May 11. The military chose the site to protect the area from Indian and Mexican attacks.

As with many frontier posts, even though the military has left, there remains a lots of poltergeist activity and there has been a large number of apparitions seen moving about the post by unsuspecting visitors. Some of these figures look so real that visitors believe that they are re-enactors.

## La Borde House

The La Borde House is a well known hotel and restaurant located at 601 E. Main Street. It was originally built in 1899 as a home and border store by a French merchant-riverboat trader. This historic old home was converted to a hotel that was operated by family until the 1930s. The architecture was designed by Parisian architects and combines European, Creole and Texas border styles with shady verandahs, courtyard patio.

The setting is so pleasant that many visitors say they do not wish to leave which is also the feeling of many of the spirits that haunt this historic old Inn. Witnesses have reported doors that open and close without human hands as well as lights that turn on and off. Cold breezes are felt, and disembodied giggles are heard. Some witnesses have also reported seeing strange shadows that move even as they watch.

# RIO HONDO, TEXAS

Situated on the eastern bank of the Arroya Colorado; land promoters divided lots for the town in 1910 and sponsored a contest to name the townsite. Rio Hondo was selected, which means "Deep River"; incorporated in 1927. The city is part of very fertile farmland in the Rio Grande Valley with cotton and grain being the principal crops. Mid Valley temperatures lure many winter visitors.

One of two lift-span bridges in Texas is in Rio Hondo. Built in 1953, bridge allows barge and boat traffic to make their way to port at Harlingen. Visitors often seek sodas and other fountain drinks from an old-time soda fountain in vintage downtown drug store.

## Rio Hondo High School

When the Rio Hondo High School was being constructed, a workman was accidentally electrocuted and died. Now the janitors that are cleaning late at night claim to see a shadow of a man in the sophomore hall chemistry department. This is the same location where the workman accidentally died. Teachers who stay at night to grade paper also claim to hear unusual sounds and steps in the halls

# ROMA, TEXAS

Roma-Los Saenz is a port of entry on U.S. Highway 83 and the Rio Grande, directly across from Ciudad Miguel Alemán, Tamaulipas, Mexico, in southwestern Starr County. Roma and Los Saenz are actually two adjoining settlements that have incorporated jointly; Spanish is the primary language. Corrales de Saenz was founded in the mid-1760s by local ranchers Miguel, Gerónimo, and Juan Ángel Saenz, followers of José de Escandón from the Spanish colonial city of Mier, and it is possible that what came to be known as Roma-Los Saenz and Ciudad Miguel Alemán were originally part of the same city, San Pedro de Roma, Tamaulipas. The area was known as Buena Vista and then Garcia Ranch. In 1848, when it became a part of the United States, the name was changed to Roma, suggested by the Oblates of Mary Immaculate, who founded a mission there in the mid-1850s.

## Burger King

This Burger King modern fast food restaurant is built next to an old cemetery. Many patrons have reported seeing and hearing the ghosts of children laughing and playing in the restaurant's play yard.

## La Minita Creek

In the early 1950's during a severe thunderstorm a vehicle traveling across "La Minita Creek" on old Hwy 83-seven miles north of Roma, struck the concrete guardrail. The vehicle, with its three occupants, flipped over the railing and plunged into the swollen creek. The driver of the vehicle, fighting the raging water, managed to extract his unconscious wife from the vehicle. However, upon his return to the vehicle, he was unable to rescue their eight-year-old daughter. The little girl's body was never recovered.

Since then, some locals in the area have reported sightings of a little girl wandering the fields and woods adjacent to the creek. Numerous sightings of this "Lost Little Girl" have been reported in the area where the creek meets the Rio Grande River. Illegal aliens crossing the river have reported seeing a little girl running along the bank of the river. Dove hunters and campers have also reported seeing a little girl running through the woods, accompanied by sounds of a crying child.

## Roma's Historical Plaza

In the 1940's, a young girl who was about to receive her First Communion fell, was playing with some friends in Roma's Historical Plaza, fell and hit her head on a rock. She died instantly. Now, legend has it that she haunts the community's historical plaza. Citizens of this small town have claimed to see her walking through this area in her beautiful, white dress. At other times, they have complained of hearing loud noises in the middle of night when no one else is in sight.

## Deep Creek Cemetery

About a half a mile down the dirt road there is a place called Whispering Bridge where, it is said, some kids fell off on this 30 foot drop. If you stand quietly at the edge of the drop off, according to legend you can hear unexplained whispering around you and then the cries of the children as they fall!!!

# SAN BENITO, TEXAS

San Benito is on U.S. Highway 77/83 five miles south of Harlingen and twenty miles north of Brownsville in Cameron County, at the approximate center of the county. The town is on the Concepción de Carricitos grant, awarded to Bartolomé and Eugenio Fernández in 1789. The portion of the grant on which San Benito is built was obtained in the mid nineteenth century by Judge Stephen Powers in return for legal services to the Fernández heirs. In 1904 Col. Sam Robertson went into partnership with James Landrum and Benjamin Hicks, Powers's sons-in-law and administrators of his estate, to form what later became the San Benito Land and Water Company. In January 1907 the company subdivided town lots and began sales. Initially the town was called Bessie, in honor of the daughter of Benjamin Franklin Yoakum, financial backer of the St. Louis, Brownsville and Mexico Railway, which served the community. The name San Benito was concocted by Rafael Moreno, an employee of Hicks. Moreno combined the given names of Robertson (Sam or "San") and Hicks (Benny), whom he called "Don Benito." A post office was established in 1907 under the name San Benito.

## Old San Benito High School

There are said to be many spirits that haunt the old San Benito High School that once served the students of this small community. It is said that in the old high school you can hear the screams and crying of children and a little girl has been seen wandering the halls of the abandon school. Local history reports that this school was used as a hospital during World War II for injured soldiers. There is also the story of a basketball player that was killed in an accident at the middle school. He has been seen and heard bouncing a basketball at the high school.

# SAN JUAN, TEXAS

San Juan is on Farm Road 1426 and State Highway Spur 374, about six miles northeast of McAllen in south central Hidalgo County. The townsite is on land that was part of two Spanish grants made in 1767 to Narciso Cabazos and to José María Ballí. The grantees and their heirs occupied the land well into the 1850s, most likely working as subsistence farmers and cattle and sheep ranchers. San Juan was organized in 1909 by John Closner and was reportedly named for him. The town was incorporated on December 29, 1917, and in 1918 a school building was built there; previously classes had been held in the homes of local residents.

## High School

The San Juan High School is said to be haunted by a ghost named Fred. He was a custodian there and one day when he was fixing the lights on the roof, he fell off of the ladder, hit his head on some chairs that where nearby and died instantly. Now the school officials have set a red chair in front of the auditorium where he died, and every time they have a play they must dedicate the show to him or else he will destroy the show.

## Austin Middle School

There is a ghost of a basketball player haunting the gym at the Austin Middle School. Around 6 p.m. you can see the lights turn on by themselves and hear a basketball bounce on the floor, the sounds of someone dribbling accompanied by the sounds of foot steps. 30 min. later the lights go off and all noises stop. There are restrooms next to the gym that are closed because of a girl who committed suicide in one of them. Many students before reported seeing a girl in a white gown staring at them from the mirror, while they are looking at themselves in the mirrors or washing their hands.

## Garza Pena Elementary School

In the girls restroom at the Garza Pena Elementary School they have heard footsteps. While you are doing the restroom you could hear someone turn on the sink and wash their hands, then paper towels are thrown on the floor. When you get out you feel someone behind you. Then when you turn around there is water on the floor.

## Old Doedyns Elementary

Back when the Doedyns Elementary School was open, everyone would say that a little girl once went in the restroom right outside the cafeteria and came out with scratches all over her wrists. Her arms and clothing was covered with blood. She claimed that she did not see anyone nor feel anything so nobody knows what really happened. However, there have long been legends of an invisible entity that attacks girls at this school.

## The old PSJA Auditorium

It has been said that in the old PSJA auditorium years ago a janitor or tech was putting up a light in the top of the auditorium and he fell and died. Till this day if you look up that particular light has never been placed. The story is if you happen to do a production there, you have to put his name in the program because if not he will do something to ruin the show. He has been known to either drop the set, or do something else horrid.

## San Juan Motel

This San Juan Motel is no longer open for business. The number of stories of unusual happenings may have help lead to he closing, but no one knows for sure. It is said that a prostitute that used this motel as her headquarters, so to speak, was raped and murder there. Now when you pass by, either walking or with your car you could hear her screaming and crying for help. It is also said that if you go there at night and look up toward the second floor, she will wave and call you trying to entice you to come sample her wares.

# SAN MARCOS, TEXAS

San Marcos, the county seat of Hays County, is on Interstate Highway 35 twenty-five miles south of Austin in the southeastern part of the county. It was the site of several Spanish attempts at colonization before it became the center of Anglo-American settlement in the area. The first such attempt, in 1755, saw the short-lived establishment of the San Xavier missions and the presidio of San Francisco Xavier. These were relocated less than a year later, and the headwaters of the San Marcos River remained unsettled for another half century. In 1808 the Spanish governor of Texas, Manuel Antonio Cordero y Bustamante, sponsored the civil settlement of San Marcos de Neve near the same site, but floods and Indian raids prompted its abandonment in 1812. In November 1846 Thomas G. McGehee became the first Anglo-American to settle in the vicinity of the San Marcos Springs, but William W. Moon has been identified as the original resident of the site that became San Marcos proper. Moon was soon joined by other former members of John C. Hays's company of Texas Rangers and by Gen. Edward Burleson. Caton Erhard opened the first store and post office by 1847, and the First Methodist Church began soon after.

## Millie Seaton House of Dolls

The Millie Seaton House of Dolls Collection features more than 5,000 dolls from all over the world, showcased in a grand historic three-story home located at 1104 W. Hopkins Street. There have been a number of reports that the former owner of the historic home has been seen in this museum.

## San Marcos Bridge

The San Marcos Bridge, located 47 miles NE of San Antonio on I-35, is also called the Thompson Island Bridge. It is said to be haunted by the ghost of a long dead Confederate soldier that died at his post while guarding it during the American Civil War. Witnesses have reported that he appears dressed in his grey and yellow uniform with a cap, and a cape. He appears to be armed with a Kentucky Long Tom rifle. Although sightings are very remote, it is reported that the dead soldier's ghost is more active before, and during wartime.

## Belvin St. - The Pike House

There is a huge four story building now known as the Pike House that was built in the 1950s as an insane asylum. When the asylum went out of business, the building was converted to be used as a hospital. It sits empty now as it is said to be haunted. Witnesses have claimed to have seen ghosts roaming in the halls of the old hospital and some claim that there are secret passage ways that lead to hidden operating and emergency rooms.

Years later, the Pike Fraternity, bought the property, and made it the pledge house. During one of the pledge processes, some of the pledges were killed by person or persons unknown. The brothers had the pledges write down what happened in their pledge books and then nailed them to the walls. If you go in there, you can see the pledge books still affixed to the peeling walls, as well as some Polaroid pictures, blood on the walls and other gruesome reminders of a pledge night gone badly.

## Job Corps Building

The Job Corp Building used to be part of a closed U.S. Air Force Base. The graveyard shift that works in this old building has lots of stories of ghostly apparitions and mysterious footsteps being heard moving about the building. Years before it was the Job Corps Building, there was a lady murdered inside the building. Most believe that it is her spirit that is the Lady in white that has been seen by a lot of the residents. Lots of ghosts have been seen by the kids in the barracks as well as by the house aides.

## Old Main

The building called "Old Main" has two reputed ghosts, one a blatant fake, but the other seemingly real. The fake story is that the ghost of LBJ roams the halls. The other story stems from a time before the building was renovated. Before renovation (as it can be seen in the movie D.O.A. with Meg Ryan) the three-story building was open from the roof to the ground. Legend has it that a young student fell (jumped or was pushed) from the third floor and died on impact. Today, custodial staff has reported seeing the girl, still dressed as she was then, clutching her books, running through the halls trying to get to class.

## Southwest Texas State University - Theater building

A ghost referred to as "Ramsey" haunts the Theater Building at Southwest Texas State University. He supposedly hung himself inside the building. Random unusual events, such as lights turning off by themselves have been reported. It has also been said that since the building is round and surrounded by water, that it attracts ghosts.

# SAN PERLITA, TEXAS

The San Perlita area was a part of a Spanish land grant that the King Ranch acquired after proving in court that the terms of the grant hadn't been met. The land became part of the state and the King Ranch obtained it shortly thereafter. Henrietta King sold the land to developers and the town was laid out in 1926. Charles Johnson and H.G. Hecht were the town planners while Johnson's wife, Pyrle planned the landscaping. Pyrle became the namesake of the town that is the self-proclaimed "Pearl of the Valley". The post office was established in 1929 and the railroad arrived a year later. In 1933 there were eighteen businesses operating in town, but by 1939 there were less than half that number.

## Devil's Lagoon

In the late 1800's early 1900's a horse drawn carriage is said to have accidentally driven into Devil's Lagoon and everyone riding in the carriage was killed. Now on certain nights around midnight, it is said that the carriage will come out of the lagoon drive around it and then return to its watery grave.

# SANTA MARIA, TEXAS

Santa Maria is at the junction of U.S. Highway 281 and Farm Road 2556, twelve miles southwest of Harlingen in southwestern Cameron County. The area was first settled in the mid-1750s by José de Escandón colonists. The land was granted by Spain to Rosa María Hinojosa de Ballíqv in 1777. A chapel was established at the site by the Oblate Fathers in 1824, and a post office opened there in 1878. By 1880 Santa Maria included the post office, two schools, a daily stage, a military post, and a customhouse. Cotton was shipped down the Rio Grande from a wharf 1½ miles south of the community. Mark Ragowski was the first postmaster and Mark Trevine the first peace officer. By 1884 the population was estimated at 500, but in 1896 Santa Maria reported a population of 100, the post office, and three stores.

## Iglesia Antigua

Witnesses have reported that inside the old Iglesia Antigua Church you can hear noises as if a congregation is sitting in the pews, even when the church his empty. It is known that the old building has a lot of secrets, such as the existence of a tunnel that begins somewhere inside the church. Others say that the church was built on a very old cemetery.

# SANTA ROSA, TEXAS

Santa Rosa is at the intersection of Farm Road 506 and State Highway 107, six miles north of La Feria in Cameron County. It takes its name from the old Santa Rosa Ranch that Charles Stillman operated there in the 1860s. A post office operated in the area from 1859 until 1861, presumably due to use of the ranch during the Civil War as a way station for cotton export. The community began to develop in 1913, when William H. Foster settled there and wrote to friends in the north who followed him. Another post office was established in 1927. The first store in Santa Rosa was a grocery and market run by a Mrs. McAllister in the front of her home. Soon after, three more stores opened. The La Feria Water District's irrigation system supplied water to area farmers. A small frame building served as a school house, and the first Methodist church services were conducted under a mesquite tree. In the early 1920s a brick school building was constructed. It was still in use in 1990.

## La Llorona

Long ago a restless spirit haunted this town. She was called "La Llorona" or weeping woman. She would walk down the streets of one of the villages called "EL Rincon Del Diablo" or the Den of the Devil. She would weep for her children that had drowned in a canal not far from the village. The town had to perform a huge exorcism to put the restless spirit to rest. Nothing has happened in the village since then, but some say if you walk up the canal at midnight you can still hear her wails.

# SEGUIN, TEXAS

Seguin, the county seat of Guadalupe County, is on Interstate Highway 10 and the Guadalupe River, thirty-five miles northeast of San Antonio in the central part of the county. The land is suited for agriculture and ranching and is rich in oil and minerals. The Guadalupe River, the San Marcos River, and two major creeks, Cibolo and Geronimo, flow through the region. Archeological finds in the vicinity include the remains of mammoths east of Seguin and numerous Indian campsites along the Guadalupe River and various creeks in Guadalupe County. The first recorded evidence of exploration in the Seguin region was in 1718, when Martín de Alarcón, governor of the province of Texas, founded San Antonio de Béxar Presidio and San Antonio de Valero Mission in San Antonio and conducted several explorations north and east of San Antonio. Eventually Spanish, Mexican, and Anglo settlements were founded in the area that would become Seguin, where Tonkawa Indians had lived, and by 1833 there were forty land titles in the region.

## The Sebastopol/Joshua Young House

The Sebastopol House, located in Seguin, Guadalupe County, is an 1856 Greek Revival-style house sitting on 2.2 acres of its original 4-acre site. Sebastopol House was probably named for the Russian naval base during the Crimean War, is an unusual split-level, T-shaped residence made of limecrete (a form of concrete), and detailed with Greek Revival-style. Built by Col. Joshua

W. Young between 1854 and 1856, it is architecturally and technologically significant as one of the best surviving examples of early concrete construction in the southwest[38].

Witnesses say that they have seen the apparitions of a lady dressed all in white as well as a young boy in short hair wandering the property.

## Texas Lutheran University

There are two places that are haunted here. One is the Wupperman Theatre building which is said to be haunted by a little girl in a blue dress who wants to play hide and seek. Also the stage lights flicker on and off for no reason and the trap door has been said to open on its own.

The other place is a dorm room in the Trinity Building which is completely locked up, and no one is allowed to live there. Some say you can see the lights go on and off and the blinds fluttering.

# UVALDE, TEXAS

Uvalde is on U.S. highways 90 and 83, State highways 55, 117, and 140, and the Southern Pacific Railroad, eighty-three miles west of San Antonio and seventy miles east of Del Rio in south central Uvalde County. It was founded by Reading W. Black, who settled there in 1853. Black and Nathan L. Stratton operated a ranch on the road between San Antonio and Fort Duncan. By 1854 Black had opened a store, two rock quarries, and a lime kiln; he also prepared a garden and an orchard, repaired nearby roads, and built a permanent home. Black hired Wilhelm C. A. Thielepape as surveyor in May 1855 to lay out a town which he called Encina. The town plan had four central plazas which still existed in 1989. Seminole, Tonkawa, and Lipan-Apache Indian raids and temporary withdrawal of troops from nearby Fort Inge discouraged settlement during the first year. The return of troops to Fort Inge and the community's proximity to the road connecting San Antonio with the western United States eventually encouraged growth. In 1856 when the county was organized, the town was renamed Uvalde for Spanish governor Juan de Ugalde and was chosen as county seat.

## Fort Clark

Fort Clark was originally a Texas Cavalry post built in 1852 on the banks of spring-fed Las Moras Creek. Fort Clark Springs served as a cavalry fort that operated for almost a hundred years (1852-1946), and later serving as a German POW Camp during World War II, now operates as a resort and retirement community, with museums displaying antiquated items from the original fort, and one of the largest swimming pools in Texas, which just happens to be spring fed.

---

[38] http://www.texasoutside.com/seguin/imagemapframes/sebastopolhouse.htm

The former officers' quarters from when Fort Clark was a POW Camp are now private residences. Some residents have reported the smell of bacon cooking at 4 am (just about right for a soldier's breakfast), poltergeist activity as well as the sound of heavy boots walking across the floor.

## Flores Elementary School

It is reported that every night on the six grade side of the Flores Elementary School building, witnesses have seen an old lady wondering outside the building wearing a 40's style white dress. The janitors that work at the school have reported that when they work late they also see her. Everyone agrees that if you call out to her she will look directly at you and then turns around and disappears.

# VICTORIA, TEXAS

Victoria, centrally located in Victoria County at the convergence of U.S. highways 59, 77, and 87, is the county seat, the largest city in the central coastal region, and the commercial focus of the surrounding counties. It is also one of the state's old, historic cities. The town was named Guadalupe Victoria for the first president of the republic of Mexico and established in 1824 by Martín De León on the Guadalupe River at a site known earlier as Cypress Grove. Guadalupe Victoria was platted by José M. J. Carbajal and developed an early importance as a stop on the La Bahía Road, as a stock-raising center, and as a shipping point for the port of Linnville. By 1834 about 300 people were living in the municipality, which was governed by a Council of Ten Friends from 1824 to 1828 and by four alcaldes from 1828 to 1836; the four were Martin and Silvestre De León, Plácido Benavides (elected twice), and John J. Linn. Though primarily a Mexican settlement, Guadalupe Victoria contributed volunteers, supplies, and arms to the Texas cause against Antonio López de Santa Anna. Its superior defensive position on the banks of the Guadalupe induced Sam Houston to order James W. Fannin to retreat there from Goliad in 1836. After Fannin was defeated at the battle of Coleto, however, Guadalupe Victoria was occupied by the Mexican army under José de Urrea until the Texas victory at San Jacinto. Soon thereafter, the Mexican residents were ostracized; they fled, and their town, resettled by Anglos, became known as Victoria. Victoria was incorporated under the Republic of Texas in 1839.

## Cinema 4, Salem 6, Playhouse 4

At Cinema 4 there is a ghost woman that watches the workers clean. Workers have reported that she is very playful and likes to call your name. While looking down from the balconies, they have seen a little boy run up to the concession stand, but when they go to the concession stand, no one it there. At all the theatres everyone has seen trash cans roll up ramps and experienced cold spots through out the buildings. The ghost only seems to mess with you if there is nothing "fun" going on.

## Tanglewood Townhouses

Some witnesses have reported seeing things in the Tanglewood Townhouse buildings moving all by themselves, lights going on and off, and other things flying through the air. Many residents have experienced unexplained temperature drops and chills once in a while inside these townhouses.

## Victoria County Courthouse

Many construction workers have claimed to have seen moving flashes of light out of the corner of their eye while on the job at the Victoria County Courthouse. Some of the same construction workers and many courthouse employees have claimed to see "floating balls of light" (-orbs) and an apparition that appears periodically on the second floor in the SE corner of the building.

# WESLACO, TEXAS

Weslaco, about fifteen miles west of Harlingen in south central Hidalgo County, is on U.S. Highway 83 and Farm Road 88. The site was part of the Llano Grande grant to Juan José Ynojosa de Ballí (1790). Upon Ynojosa's death the grant was divided among his children, and Manuela and María received the land on which Weslaco is situated. The Ballí family ranched and maintained ownership until 1852. In 1904 the Hidalgo and San Miguel extension of the St. Louis, Brownsville and Mexico Railway reached the site, promoted by Uriah Lott, Lon C. Hill, Jr. and others interested in developing the area through farming as opposed to traditional Hispanic ranching. The American Rio Grande Land and Irrigation Company of neighboring Mercedes, which had interest in the railroad purchased a major portion of the Llano Grande grant and platted the West Tract in 1913. In an effort to control raids from Mexico, the United States government stationed troops along the Rio Grande in 1916 and established a camp at the Llano Grande railroad depot, located between Mercedes and the site of Weslaco. The guardsmen erected a watchtower at Progreso.

## Weslaco High School

It is said that several years back, a classroom of students witnessed the sudden death of their teacher in the I wing of the Weslaco High School. Today his voice can be heard every Friday during lunch in the quiet classroom. He seems to be teaching an invisible class. Some students claim to have even seen words appearing on the board with no one in sight.

## Weslaco High School - J Wing

In the J wing of this same High School, it is said that a janitor died on the job several years ago and now is has been reported that you can see him in the halls cleaning and singing just as he always did when he was alive.

## Central Middle School

The Central Middle School is an old annex building that was used as a classroom for many years. It is said that a teacher went crazy and killed all of her students. People now say that you can hear students screaming and crying. The annex building still exists but is not being used.

# WIMBERLY, TEXAS

Established in 1848, the picturesque village if Wimberly, Texas today is a resort and retirement area on R.M. 12 in beautifully Central Texas Hill Country north of San Marcos. Visitors are entranced by cool, shady pools beneath towering cypress trees, frothy cascades on Blanco River, and sparkling Cypress Creek, green meadows and majestic hills; abundant white-tailed deer, Recreational communities, vacation resorts and youth camps dot the area. Climbing, hiking, fishing, swimming, boating, golf, tennis, arts and crafts, and camping are popular activities. Many artists and authors make their homes here.

## Jacob's Well

This could just as well be listed under the "Devil's Backbone" as Wimberly is at one end of the backbone. Jacob's Well is actually a huge hole in the rock, with a natural spring forming a convenient swimming hole. It has many caverns and cave-ins are common. Of the 9 divers/spelunkers who have tried to enter the third cavern, only one has come out alive. The other bodies have never been recovered. This area also has its own ghost light.

# SAN ANTONIO, TEXAS

San Antonio is world-famous as the home of the Mission San Antonio de Valero (otherwise known as "The Alamo"). If you are planning to travel in the state of Texas, do yourself a favor and plan to spend several days in this beautiful city (I highly recommend an after-dark tour of the river on the riverboats).

## Aggie Park Facility

The Aggie Park Facility has experienced a number of unexplainable electrical problems, cold spots, as well as items that move by themselves. A number of witnesses have reported seeing strange shadows and hearing unusual noises.

## The Alamo

The Alamo is located in downtown San Antonio. Not surprisingly, the spirits of those involved in that famous battle have opted to stick around, but they are not the only ones. The original incarnation of the Alamo was the Mission San Antonio de Valero, and when Santa Ana ordered it destroyed, the deceased monks supposedly reached through the walls and threatened the troops assigned to its destruction. To this day there are reports of strange creatures and apparitions dancing or walking along its outer wall. The plaza in front of it is reportedly haunted as well.

There are said to be two major reasons for all of the activity in the downtown area of San Antonio. One is because of the burial ground that was used between 1724 and 1793 that takes up most of what is Alamo Plaza today. There are probably about a thousand people that were buried in this area. 954 are recorded in Spanish records from the time.

Two, is because of the actual battle, where people died a violent death or before their time. When Santa Anna left SA to go to San Jacinto with about 1500 troops, he left about 1,000 men in SA to keep control of the area for him under the command of General Andrade. Because the bodies of the Texas defenders were burned in two or three locations around the Alamo grounds, General Andrade moved his troops about a mile or two out of SA and set up camp. When Santa Anna was captured at San Jacinto, it was reported that he got off a couple of messengers. He ordered Andrade to move his troops south of the Rio Grande, but before he was to leave SA he was to go into the Alamo and totally destroy the Alamo chapel. Santa Ann hated the Alamo for a couple of reasons. One, he lost about 1,600 troops taking the place in 1836 and two, his brother-in-law, General Cos had been run off with the 1,100 troops he had there in late 1835 by about 300 Texas Rebels.

General Andrade started to organize his troops for the march to the Rio Grande and he ordered Colonel Sanchez to go to the Alamo and destroy it. It was reported that the Colonel returned to camp rather quickly with a story about six Diablos or ghostly looking devils coming out of the front doors of the Alamo and waving flaming sabers over their heads and yelling, "Do not touch the Alamo, do not touch these walls".

General Andrade thought that this story was ridiculous and he got a group of men to go with him to destroy the Alamo. When he got there, he also saw the same six ghosts. The General also looked over at the long barracks and saw the image of a person that is larger than life and has their hands up in the air with balls of fire in their hands. This is one of the images that is depicted on the Cenotaph (the Alamo defenders monument that is located in Alamo Plaza). It is the image of the spirit of sublime heroic sacrifice and it is given credit with saving the Alamo from physical destruction. The story goes that when the ethereal energy was released from the flames of the fires that burned the bodies of the Alamo defenders, this spirit used that energy to manifest itself, make itself visible, to scare away intruders of the Alamo grounds.

The report of the six ghosts and the spirit of sublime heroic sacrifice are widely known as the first reported ghost sightings at the Alamo. But there were also reports that two women were walking across the Mission grounds back in the 1700's, right about where the Plaza is today and they were struck by lightning. One died and the other survived. There are reports today, by people that work in the plaza on a daily basis that they have seen a ghostly woman walking across the plaza. It just might be the person killed by lightning. Just talk to some of the people that sell snow cones in the plaza.

## Alamo Street Restaurant & Theater

The Alamo Street Restaurant & Theater is an old church building that is said to be haunted by the ghost of "Miss Margaret", who is said to show up in the choir loft in Victorian dress. She is believed to be Margaret Gething, an actress who lived just a few blocks away.  A former Methodist church built in 1912, the restaurant-theatre is located at 1150 South Alamo Street (the blue trolley passes right by). The old building is known to have at least four resident spirits. Most often seen and heard are "Miss Margaret," the white clad ghost of a former actress who lived in the neighborhood and seems to enjoy the theatrical productions there, and "Little Eddie," a mischievous youngster who was once crippled but whose ghost is active. He frequently pulls childish pranks around the kitchen and dining room. The owner, Marcia Larsen, will be delighted to discuss her resident spirits with you.

## Alamo Quarry Theater

The Alamo Quarry Theater was said to be built over an old cement factory and rumor has it that there are bodies buried in the foundation. Witnesses that work there have seen a child in the projection room and have felt various cold spots on the second floor on both sides of the theaters. And at night it is said that the auditorium's inside light would dim slowly down then flare brightly and then repeat the process until everyone leaves the auditorium.

## The Alamodome

Before the Alamodome was built, the surrounding area was considered a very bad neighborhood. Legend has it that shortly before the razing of the original buildings that a young lady was raped and killed. She has been seen walking around the parking lot, as if lost. Years passed and the neighborhood was demolished and the dome was built. While constructing the dome, a worker walking on a high beam made a wrong step and fell to his death. He is seen walking the long halls of the dome. Last but not least, a famous daredevil died while performing a stunt at the Alamodome. It is reported that if go into the Alamodome after hours that you are sure to hear footsteps, screams, mumbling, moans and see shadows walking along going about their business.

## **Bexar - Caribbean Apartments**

The Caribbean Apartments are now known as the Willow Run apartments. These apartments have been in business for over 60 years. Before they were turned into apartments, it was a Motel. The doors were painted in light yellow and blue pastels. Existing in what used to be the outskirts of town and just outside of Castle Hills, the old motel would meet the needs of many customers of all races and origins.

It was during this time that a rape and murder occurred in the North end of the complex. Every now and then in the middle of the night a woman's cry can be heard in the rear hallways. In one of the apartment units, a suicide occurred where a single mother overdosed on pain medication leaving her two year old to fend for herself. The child eventually died of starvation. The mother's body was found on the bed. The child's body was found on the floor next to the bed. It is unknown whether the overdose was accidental or intentional.

When this particular apartment is empty the occupants of the downstairs apartment can hear the pitter patter of little feet walking up and down the upstairs unit. On occasion, a woman can be heard crying. Loud thumps can also be heard. Lights turn on and off by themselves and the toilet will flush on its own. An occupant of the downstairs apartment noted that her young daughter told her "she was playing with a little girl". Believing that the child had an imaginary playmate, the mother discounted her little daughter's claims. Until one evening while the mother was sitting in the living room watching TV and her little girl was playing in the hallway with a small toy, she saw her daughter toss the small toy across the hallway into the front bedroom. The door had been left open. Then she heard her daughter talk to this imaginary friend to "give it back". To the mother's surprise, something or someone tossed the small toy back to her daughter. The mother kept watching and realized that there really was "someone or something" there.

On another occasion while sleeping, she felt the touch of little fingers playing with her toes or gently tugging at her blankets. The apartment where the "suicide" took place is constantly vacant. Tenants seem to come and go and never stay longer than three years. And when the apartment is occupied, the "occurrences" diminish and or are none existent until the apartment is vacant again.

## **Bexar - Kindred Elementary**

It is said that a plane crashed in the field near the Kindred Elementary School and a number of people died in the crash. Many believe that it is the spirits of those killed in the crash that haunt the school. Students have reported that when they enter the restrooms the sinks will turn on. Some have said that they could hear voices while they walk on the field where the crash occurred.

## Bexar - Spanish Main Apartments on Rittiman Rd.

No one is sure what caused the hauntings at the Spanish Main Apartments. However, there have been a number of accounts of guests and residents sitting at the bottom of the stairs seeing out of the corner of their eyes a little boy standing at the top of the stairs. Subsequent searches have failed to find the little boy.

## Bexar County Medical Health Building

The county employees working in the County Medical health Building find it somewhat disconcerting when they encounter toilets that flush themselves, doors that open with no one near them, and see items move without human assistance. A number of witnesses have reported that in the late evening, the warehouse emits loud band music though later investigations always show the building to be empty.

## Botanical Gardens

The Botanical Gardens is located at 555 Funston Place. Prior to 1877, the eastern end of Mahncke Park was a limestone quarry. Details of the rock quarry operations are not known. In 1877, J. B. LaCoste and Associates contracted with the City of San Antonio to construct a water works system. LaCoste and Associates sold the water company to G. W. Brackenridge in 1883. Brackenridge became convinced in 1888, that there was danger of complete failure of the San Antonio River as a water supply in the event of a long period of drought. By 1890, city residents became alarmed at the possibility that the river and the open reservoir would become contaminated. As a result, wells supplying pure artesian water began to be used to the exclusion of the surface water supply system, so the reservoir was abandoned. In 1899, Brackenridge deeded the water works land and properties to the City.

Mrs. R. R. Witt and Mrs. Joseph Murphy conceived the idea of a Botanical Garden in San Antonio in the 1940's. Together with their friends and associates, they organized the San Antonio Garden Center. Their first major effort was the development and presentation of a master plan for a public botanical garden in the late 1960's. The recommended garden site became the former Brackenridge waterworks land which was being held by the city.

It has been reported that the San Antonio Botanical Gardens has its own headless horseman. Research has failed to turn up a reason for this spectre or its possible identity

## Brooks House

The historic Brooks House is haunted by unexplained pipe smoke and ghostly footsteps. There is also the tall apparition of a man with a mustache who shows up in the upstairs bedroom.

## Bullis House Inn/International Hostel

The Bullis House, 621 Pierce Street, was built between 1906 - 1909 by noted architect Harvey Page for General John Lapham Bullis and his family. General Bullis, a New York native, came to Texas in 1865 after four years of service in the Union Army during the American Civil War. He became famous, however, while fighting hostile Indians on the Texas frontier from 1867 - 1882 and was instrumental in the capture of Apache Chief Geronimo. There is a legend that the Indian chief's spirit roams within the mansion which may account for the apparition of the Indian Brave many have reported seeing inside the house.

In later years General Bullis saw service in Cuba and the Philippines, and later retired to his beloved San Antonio. In 1983, the Bullis House was purchased by the Cross family for use as a Bed & Breakfast Inn.  In addition to the Indian brave wandering about the house, guests have reported hearing male voices arguing loudly.

## Brackenridge Villa Mansion

Now called the Brackenridge House Bed & Breakfast Inn, located at 230 Madison, this historic old home, built in the 1840's, is said to also have activity. Strange shadows moving about the rooms have been spotted through its windows from its windows.

## Brooks Air Force Base

Brooks Air Force Base (AFB) takes its name from Sidney Johnson Brooks, Jr., the first flying cadet to lose his life in San Antonio during training prior to participation in World War I. The twenty-two year old San Antonian was a part-time reporter for the San Antonio Light newspaper before volunteering for U.S. Army service. After completing officer training school at Camp Funston, Texas, Brooks entered the Army Signal Corps Air Service and began flight training at Kelly Field, San Antonio, Texas. Brooks had finished almost all requirements for earning his pilot's wings when he embarked on his first solo flight on November 13, 1917. On approaching Kelly Field for landing, Brooks appeared to lose consciousness, according to observers, and plummeted to his death. Later reports indicated that he may have suffered severe secondary effects from an influenza vaccination he received that morning. Brooks was posthumously awarded his pilot's wings and Army Signal Corps Commission.

On February 4, 1918, a new flying field in south San Antonio was dedicated as Brooks Field in honor of Cadet Sidney Johnson Brooks, Jr. Brooks Field later became Brooks AFB, and is today known as Brooks City-Base. In 1993, Cadet Sidney Brooks Jr.'s remains were moved from their resting place at the San Antonio Masonic Cemetery to a special memorial park near Hangar 9 at Brooks AFB. Known as the Sidney Brooks Memorial, the park commemorates the pioneers of aviation who gave their lives for their country.

When fog rolls onto the base at night, it is known that there is a mysterious young lady that walks around the silent buildings. It is said that she is always seen with a large pack strapped on her back. Cops on the base have said that when they fall asleep on duty she will tap them on the shoulder to wake them up.

## Cadillac Bar

The Cadillac Bar has a well known reputation as a San Antonio watering hole, but few seem to know that it also has a reputation as a haunted building. The ghost of an old owner is seen in the storage basement of the building and there is another ghost named "Beatrice", who was a former employee. She is a "negative spirit" because she was very unhappy and not pretty when she was alive. She turns on sinks and throws kitchen utensils. Many employees have seen both ghosts. The alarm goes off, dishes fly off of the shelves, faucets come on, a male apparition has been seen on the back steps and a homely female apparition is seen in or near the party room.

## Cafe Camille

This well known café also has trouble with the unseen. Many visitors to Café Camille, as well as staff, have reported doors that open and close as well as items that are picked up off the wall then moved and dropped. Most of those who have experienced these unusual events attribute the activity to the deceased wife of the former owner.

## Camberly Gunter Hotel

The Camberly Gunter Hotel located near the Alamo. It has long said to be haunted by the ghost of a prostitute who was murdered there by one of her tricks in the early 1960's. The room in which she was murdered, said to be room 636, was found covered in blood but no body was ever found. A picture of her hangs in the Lobby Bar.

The man who murdered her was said to have then checked in to the Menger Hotel in San Antonio three blocks away where he also disappeared without a trace.

## Chinese Graveyard

If you want to find the Chinese Graveyard, then go down Zazamora after you pass Loop 410 and keep going. The road will make a slight turn to the right and on the right (it is hard to see so go slow) there will be a big white cross. Pull in and turn the car off along with all lights (its better with the windows down.) Quickly flash your lights five times and look and listen for talking and white apparitions around the very small graveyard

## Central Texas Parole Violator Building

The Central Texas Parole Violator Building has a very dark reputation. The spirit of murdered prisoner Hugo Saenz has been seen roaming the halls of this old prison building.

## Chabot-Reed House

In 1876, German cotton and wool merchant, George Stooks Chabot built his Victorian home, located at 403 Madison, using German cut limestone, alongside other wealthy German merchants in the heart of what is known today as the King William Historic District. In 1985, Sister Schodts Reed and Peter N. Reed bought the structure and masterfully and authentically restored the whole...the gardens, the fountains, the main house, the patio, the carriage house. The building is now known as the Chabot-Reed House.

Witnesses have reported hearing old honky-tonk music and muffled conversations coming from the grounds and eerie presences have been reported moving about this old home.

## Comanche Look-out Hill

This was what could be called an early warning post used to warn residents of approaching Indian attacks. Comanche Look-out Hill is now said to be haunted by soldiers who were stationed there. Reports also indicate that Native American spirits can be seen in the area as well.

## Crockett Hotel

The Historic Crockett Hotel is located at 320 Bonham on a site that was once part of the battlefield at the Battle of the Alamo. Now witnesses have reported seeing moving curtains and seeing an unexplained apparition in the executive offices. No one is certain who the spirit(s) might be.

## Douglass Elementary School

Some say that Douglass Elementary School was built on an Indian burial ground. Others say that the hauntings are caused by the fact that a janitor died in the auditorium. Whatever the reason might be, there are a number of witnesses that have reported that the doors to the auditorium would slam shut by themselves and the piano would start playing. Witnesses have also reported hearing people walking and talking when they would spend the night there. However, every time they checked there was no one there.

## Edison High School

It's been said that teachers and janitors at the Edison High School have seen ghostly children in their classrooms late at night. Some even say that at night if you listen closely you can hear the sounds of laughing children in the hallways.

## Emily Morgan Hotel

Located near the Alamo, the Emily Morgan Hotel has gained quite a reputation as a haunted hotel. Most of the activity can be found on the 9th 12th floor, 7th floor and in the basement. Guests have reported apparitions and electrical equipment going haywire.  It is known that at one time, the building used to be a medical facility.

A number of witnesses have reported that Floor nine is a very active floor. It is said that the building housed wounded soldiers during the battle of the Alamo, so this may account for some of the activity. According to one story that I have told about some guests who stayed on this floor, through there were only a few guests on the floor, doors opened and closed all night long. The toilet seat slammed itself up and down about ten times while the bathroom was empty and a bottle of wine slid off of the counter by itself as did the coffee pot the next morning.

## Express-News

The Express-News building is located on Ave E. While the name of this ghost is not known, a medium is said to have identified him as an Irish immigrant who worked in a carriage house that stood nearby before the current structure was erected. Those who have experienced this spirit have deemed him to be benign.

## Fort Clark

Ghostly footsteps at the end of Officer's Row at Fort Clark are attributed to the ghosts of a black cook and her cat. Legend has it that the cook was killed by a colonel.  Ollabelle Dahlstrom is a spirit that enjoys touching people. Some witnesses have a strange voice and seen the beds shake in buildings 8 & 9. Many people have claimed to smell food cooking in bldg 10 when no one is in the kitchen, and several other have claimed to have seen a wispy female apparition. An unknown spirit in building 11 calls out people's names.

## Fort Sam Houston

There are several officers quarters on Fort Sam Houston that are said to be haunted. At one you can at times hear the sound of a piano playing. There is another house where there is of a child who will move items around the house. There is an older, large wooden quarters, where those that live in the house hear footsteps.

"Harvey" is a ghost that is said to hang out in Service Club #2 and at one of the pools.  Ghost footsteps, the sensation of someone lying in bed next to you, and self-flushing toilets are reported in Quarters #1. Pershing House[39] also has self-flushing toilets as well as a self-ringing doorbell, lights with minds of their own, and footsteps. In the old hotel building, there are cold spots, and items get thrown out of the closets.  The old hospital building has lights that come on by themselves, and windows open and shut.

---

[39] Fort Bliss also has a haunted Pershing House.

## Old Brooks Army Medical Center.

Brooks Army Medical Center is known to be extremely haunted. Sounds of people talking can be heard inside and outside of this building even though there is no one around. Around toward the ambulance area you get a strong sense of fear. There is also a light that remains on even though there is no electricity in the building.

## Gatlin Gasthaus

Trembling flowers and haywire lights seem to be the norm in the Gatlin Gasthouse. During one Christmas celebration the locked front door blew open and the gust of wind that accompanied it blew out all of the lit candles and knocked over the antique crystal candleholders, but remarkably, nothing was broken.

## Harlandale High School

The story goes that a teacher at Harlandale High School hung himself when he couldn't be with one of his students (with whom he'd fallen in love). Now there are cold spots and shadows that resemble ropes seen, and a number of witnesses have reported hearing disembodied voices in the room where the teacher died.

## Hertzberg Circus Museum

Hertzberg Circus Collection and Museum comprises an extensive collection of circus memorabilia. And is a department of the San Antonio Public Library. This collection was established by Harry Hertzberg (1884-1940), a prominent San Antonio lawyer, civic leader, and state senator and is one of only a handful of circus collections. It is the oldest public circus collection in the United States and one of the largest in existence. Hertzberg was an avid circus fan who accumulated American circus and related popular-culture memorabilia; he was also a prolific collector of rare books. He bequeathed both of his collections to the San Antonio Public Library, where he had served as member of the board of trustees.

Located at 210 West Market Street, the museum is just a few short blocks from the Menger Hotel. It's situated in the former city library building which was built on the site of the old John McMullen house that was built in 1837. McMullen, a successful merchant, was murdered in the house in 1853 when a thief robbed and bound him and then slit his throat. Cold spots and dark, shadowy forms have been noted, and books in the library stacks on the upper floors have been known to rearrange themselves. Whether the hauntings come from McMullen or some long-departed circus great is anybody's guess!

## Highlands High School

Students at Highlands High School have reported that the doors slam shut in bad weather, the lights keep shutting off in meetings and a number of witnesses have heard what sounds like kicking and screaming in between the walls of room #111.

## Hot Wells Motel

The Hot Wells Motel is built on the site of an old Burnt down hotel. Rumor has it that Hot Wells was known for its luxury spas and the numerous fires that took place in Rm. 13. The Fowl Smell of the dead still lingers there even though it has been burned down for over 40 yrs.

## Hope Farm

This old house at Hope Farm is the site of self-opening doors, ghost steps, rattling windows, disappearing objects, and freshly-made beds that get disturbed.

## Inn on the River

The Inn on the River, 129 Woodward Place, was built in 1916, but has been remodeled to meet today's standards of comfort. However, guests have reported encountering cold spots and shaking lamps that are attributed to an unknown female ghost. Rooms 11, 13 and the dining room are the most active.

## Institute of Texas Cultures

The Institute of Texas Cultures located at 801 South Bowie Street, is part of the University of Texas at San Antonio and explores the contributions of 28 different ethnic groups toward the settlement of the state. It also serves as a home for several spirits.

Witnesses have reported smelling unexplained pipe smoke. Books have been found that have been rearranged and a rear doors of an 1898 glass hearse have been seen to open and close with no one near it. It has been suspected that perhaps it's not the building but the artifacts that it contains that causes the hauntings.

## Jesse's Bar & Restaurant

An apparition with a handle-bar mustache has been seen climbing the back stairs at Jesse's Bar and Restaurant. Another apparition - a female with stringy blond hair and an overbite - has been seen on the top of the stairs and looking out the window.

## John F. Kennedy High School

Gus Langley was a teacher at John F. Kennedy High School that died in the building. He gets blamed for cold spots, footsteps, moving items and banging lockers that students and staff have encountered inside this building.

## John J. Wood Federal Building

The John J. Wood Federal Building was named for a judge that was assassinated in El Paso, Texas has been the subject of stories almost since it was constructed. Many workers have reported hearing strange voices in the elevators and hammering sounds coming from the roof. However, building security has been unable to find any explanation. Also still a mystery are self-opening doors, lights that turn on and off, and an apparition that has been encountered in one of the courtrooms.

## La Villita

La Villita also known as the Little Church of La Villita is located at 508 Villita Street in La Villita. In 1879, German Methodists built this Gothic Revival-style stone church. The Episcopal diocese of West Texas bought the church in 1895 and the City of San Antonio acquired the church in 1945.

According to witnesses, objects move of their own accord, and a female apparition are reported in Chamade Jewelry Store. A female apparition in white frequents the River Art Gallery. Shadows, moving items and a 19th century female apparition are experienced in the Starving Artists Gallery. A little girl's spirit is reported in La Villita House.

## The Linden House

The Linden House Bed & Breakfast has been a popular stop for many visitors. Along with a certain ambiance, there are also ghostly footsteps, electrical disturbances, several doors that open and close without human assistance, and objects that move on their own.

## Long Acres

A female spirit named Elsie may be the one causing items to disappear at Long Acres.

## McKnay Museum

This well known museum, the McKnay Museum, used to be the residence of the McKnay family. Widow McKnay was an art collector who turned her home into a museum. The West Wing of this museum was beginning construction when old lady McKnay passed away. It is said that "Old Lady McKnay" has been seen walking the halls and passing through walls when "floating" from one building to another. She's only seen at night, mostly by security and museum personnel. She never speaks, but if you're lucky enough, she might appear to 'look' in your direction. Also a female's voice "humming" an unrecognizable tune can be heard coming from the downstairs area of the West Wing library.

## Menger Hotel

Built in 1859, this beautiful hotel has been witness to births, deaths, murders, suicides and all sorts of historic events as well in its 140 years of existence. The rich and famous have signed the guest registers and walked its corridors. Most left, but a few stayed on in the form of spirits. Many say that the Menger Hotel is haunted by the ghost of a chambermaid who was murdered by her husband, a group called the "Ruff Riders" and Mr. Richard King of King Ranch fame. He reportedly haunts the "King Ranch Room" where he passed away.

There have been a number of encounters with Sally White, a former chambermaid, shot by her jealous husband in 1876, who still comes back to the third-floor section to tend the rooms she once cleaned. She's been seen wearing her bandana over her head and a long white apron, by guests and employees alike. You can see an entry in a ledger in a lobby showcase attesting to the fact that the hotel paid for both Sally's coffin and grave, so she must have been a popular employee.

A former maitre de is frequently seen "after hours" in the Colonial Dining Room, making sure his unseen guests are satisfied. The famous Menger Bar has been host to numerous specters, including uniformed military men who are said to have served with Teddy Roosevelt's Rough Riders. The Rough Riders often gathered at this historic old bar May 1898. They say that Capt. Richard King sometimes comes back to the King Ranch suite, where he died in 1885. The funeral of the famous cattle baron and founder of the King Ranch was in the Victorian lobby of the hotel. Even the dashing Teddy Roosevelt is said to spend part of his time wandering the hallways as well as an unknown lady in blue.

## Milam Square

Known to be the site of an 18th century cemetery, Milam Square has played host to the ghosts of Natives and Spanish settlers alike. This lovely park area is surrounded by Commerce, San Saba, Houston and Santa Rosa streets. Once a Protestant cemetery, most of the bodies were removed to another burial ground around 1890. However, Ben Milam, an early Texas hero, lies buried there today. The park is said to be haunted by ghosts, whom were victims of violent deaths. Any person who has "evil thoughts' may expect to see these "Devils of Milam Square,"

## Mission San Jose

Soon after the building of the Alamo, a second mission was founded in 1720 about five miles downstream. Named San Jose, this new mission was established by Fray Antonio Margil de Jesus, who had previously left a failed mission in East Texas. A model among the Texas missions, San Jose gained a reputation as a major social and cultural center. Among the San Antonio missions, it also provided the strongest garrison against raids from Indians. However, there are many who say that it also became the home of a headless monk that has been seen in the courtyard at night. A huge, black, "devil" dog has been seen in the area.

## Mission San Francisco

**Figure 18: Formerly Mission San Francisco.**

Mission San Francisco de la Espada, like its sister missions San Jose, San Juan, and Concepcion, had its beginnings in East Texas. Originally named San Francisco de los Tejas, Espada was renamed and relocated to San Antonio in 1731. It is the southernmost of the chain of missions located on the San Antonio River. Mission Espada features a very attractive chapel, along with an unusual door and stone entrance archway. This mission also has its resident ghosts. Visitors have seen a huge black dog or wolf, with a chain dangling from its neck, prowling the area and the spirit of an Indian in full ceremonial dress has been seen at the altar.

## Mission San Juan

First established in East Texas, Mission San Juan Capistrano made its permanent home on the banks of the San Antonio River in 1731. Within a short time, the mission became a regional supplier of agricultural and other products including iron, wood, cloth, and leather goods produced by the Indians in its workshops. A few miles southeast of the mission was Rancho Pataguilla, which in 1762 reported 3,500 sheep and nearly as many cattle. Like Mission San Francisco, visitors have reported seeing a number of apparitions in the main chapel to include an Indian in full ceremonial dress.

## North Star Mall

North Star Mall is bustling by day, but by night, something else seems to wanders its corridors. A number of workers report seeing strange shadows, hearing footsteps when there is no one else around as well as hearing their names called when they are alone.

## Jose Antonio Navarro House

At 228 South Laredo Street, the Navarro House is maintained by the Texas Parks Department and is open to the public. It was the home of Texas patriot Jose Antonio Navarro, a signer of the Texas Declaration of Independence. He built it around 1832 as a two-room house with a detached kitchen. It has long been considered haunted -- cold spots have been felt, a rocking chair rocks when there is no wind or drafts, and faces have been seen peeping out of the upper dormer windows by state employees working on the restoration. Other apparitions include a Confederate soldier, a child, a prostitute, and a bartender.

The adjacent corner law office building was the scene of a fire in which a child supposedly perished, and its little ghostly presence has been reported.

## Old Nacogdoches Rd - Comanche Park Tower

Many ghosts have been seen on the grounds of Comanche Park, also known as the Comanche Look-Out Hill. There have been sightings of old soldiers who were said to have been stationed there. And many people have also reported having seen the forms of Indians there. Another place that ties in with this area is Old Nacogdoches Road. Many people, usually driving down this road during the night hours, have claimed to see Indians, and soldiers walking along side the road. There is also a creek that intersects the road that has been said to be the host for many Indian apparition sightings.

## Old Stone Ridge Rd

If you drive down this street at night with your lights off en route to the old children's cemetery, strange things happen. Sometimes the car locks will lock and unlock rapidly. Supposedly, the Donkey Lady is responsible for the hauntings. Killed and badly mangled in an auto wreck when some friends of hers were driving down the road one night with no lights on, she haunts the woods around the area and protects the souls of the small children buried in the cemetery.

## Oge House

Located at 209 Washington Street, the basement and first floor of this house were built as early as 1857 by attorney Newton Mitchell. Louis Ogé bought the house in 1881, after serving as a Texas Ranger under Bigfoot Wallace and making a fortune as a rancher. He had architect Alfred Giles enlarge the house to its present appearance.

Named after its most colorful owner, this antebellum plantation cottage has had lights turn on and off, and one spirit protested the spices selected by the cook. Every time she went to add them, they were blown all over the kitchen.

## Old Menger Soap Factory

Menger Soap Works is located at 500 North Santa Rosa at Martin. German immigrant Johann Menger came to San Antonio in 1847 and started a soap factory in 1850. Menger built this early limestone industrial building in 1873 by San Pedro Creek. It operated until the early part of the 20th century. Today there are many who report have heard ghostly steps and seen apparitions. A number of cold spots are reported inside this 150+ year-old soap factory.

## Old Salinas Homestead

A pair of phantoms is reported at the Salinas Homestead here - male and female.

## Old Spanish Tower

San Antonio's very own set of ghost lights that can be seen playing around the Old Spanish Tower!

## Our Lady of the Lake University

Our Lady of the Lake University is said to carry ageless stories of past inhabitants who still walk the halls and campus grounds. Some of the more famous ones include a former janitor who now haunts the basement of the library, the ghosts of the dorms, ghostly nuns that are seen hurrying about on some ghostly business, and a famous headless apparition who walks the halls of what is now the elementary school across the street[40], but was once a dorm for the university

## Plaza Marriott

The Plaza Marriott hotel property includes 4 buildings on the Historic Register. The ghost that is called the Lady is believed to be the widow of the owner of one of these buildings. She hung herself and her cat in what is now the exercise facility (was her home, specifically the "front room" or "living room"). Now she can be seen on the upper levels of the main hotel building usually in a long white dress or nightdress, and holding her cat, stroking its head. She has been seen in the employee corridors in the basement, and standing among the trees in the garden. Lights come on and off occasionally with no warning and no reason, and drawers at the front desk have a tendency of opening by themselves.

## Providence High School

Providence High School was originally a religious school. In the 1950's there was a nun who loved the school so much that when she passed away her sisters decided that since she loved the school she should be buried on the school grounds. Years later Providence decided to build a gym over the spot where the nun was buried forgetting she was there. Today if you walk in the gym and step in a certain area it is hollow. Also a night the nun is seen walking the halls by the many freshmen that attend the lock in. Even after death the nun continues to watch over her beloved school.

## Reed Candle Factory

The Reed Candle Factory has been making religious candles for a long time. There are many long time employees who swear that the company is still being by founder, Peter Reed.

---

[40] See St. Martin Hall below.

## Rivercenter Mall

Rivercenter Mall was built on land that was part of the Alamo Battlefield. There are many locals who believe that at the head of the river near where the photo center is now was one of the pyres that burned the remains of Alamo defenders. A number of mall employees have reported seeing strange shadows in the area.

## The Riverwalk Inn

Located at 329 Old Guilbeau St., the Riverwalk Inn is a unique hostelry. The Inn is composed of five, two-story log homes, relocated from Tennessee have been combined to form the two buildings of the Riverwalk Inn. The log homes were built from cottonwood trees which mean "Alamo" in Spanish and date circa 1842 (six years after the Battle of the Alamo). The homes were brought to San Antonio log by log and reconstructed to their original authenticity.

It is the Riverwalk Inn's mission to have guests relive the history of the old San Antonio, through the lifestyle of such Texas heroes as Davy Crockett and James Bowie who fought for Texas independence at the Battle of the Alamo. The Riverwalk Inn, decorated in period antiques creates an ambience of "country elegance." However, it is possible that the Riverwalk Inn succeeded in bridging time and has become a home for some of the very spirits that they seek to honor. Many guests have reported that the TV in the common room comes on, doors close by themselves, and ghostly footsteps are heard heading up the stairs.

## Royal Swan Guest House

The Royal Swan Guest House at 236 Madison is a lovely Victorian that was built in 1892 in what later was to be designated the King William historic District. It has a gabled roof, verandas, front and back porches, fireplaces, crystal chandeliers, exquisite stained glass, and hand-carved woodwork. It also has one or more ghosts. The apparition of a Hispanic woman has shown up from time to time, and guests have reported something violently shaking their beds, and the feeling that someone just sat down next to them on the bed.

## Santa Rosa Hospital

Many people do not like to work the night shift at Santa Rosa Hospital because they have either seen or heard about a headless nun who glides around the corridors. Many people have admitted to seeing the nun.

## Santikos Century Plaza 8

It is said that at night when you are there alone at the Santikos Century Plaza 8 that you can hear what sounds like chains dragging on the ground of the theater and then you hear banging on the ceiling.

## St. Anthony Hotel

This 1909 San Antonio Hotel was a very elegant hotel probably visited in the early days by very wealthy people; everything seems very old and antique. The St. Anthony Hotel is said to be haunted by a Hispanic employee named Anita, an elderly lady in a women's bathroom, a sad young woman who is in the roof ballroom, and a ghostly couple who frequently come back to a certain hotel room to re-live their honeymoon. There have been reports of many more ghosts being there, but many are unknown. Reports of being followed, people seeing shadowy outlines, doors opening and closing by themselves, & apparitions of 2 different women have been reported by many witnesses.

One guest, in San Antonio for a convention, reported being given a huge room off by itself. The room was so isolated, that this guest rarely saw anyone else. The room was laid out like a suite, with a large bedroom and a large living room. The living room gave the guest a strange feeling and the door lock between the two rooms didn't work well, so he actually pushed furniture up against the door.

Later the guest reported that he was woken up during the night by lots of voices, like a large group returning from a night out, outside the door to the hallway, and also hotel room doors slamming like people returning to their rooms. However, every time he would get up and open his door to investigate, there wasn't a soul out there in the hallway and it was silent. The room had an eerie feeling, like something was there.

One night the guest was asleep on his back and was startled awake by a woman's face looking down into his. Later he remembered distinctly it was a woman's face, an older woman, with sort of a green glow, and he had the feeling she was looking at his out of curiosity. She went away when he jumped up. When he checked out he told the staff that he had experienced a lot of unusual stuff and they told him that a lot of people believe the hotel is haunted and that they have had a lot of experiences like voices in the halls, doors slamming, and knocking on doors.

## St. Martin Hall

St. Martin's Hall is the Elementary School across from Our Lady of the Lake University. It is said that when it use to be a boarding school there was a girl that was killed in the restroom. Unusual things have happened since that time such as lights being found on after they were turned off and things that have gone missing.

## San Antonio Academy

Established in 1886, San Antonio Academy, located at 117 E. French Place, is a non-profit, non-denominational, tax-exempt school for boys in pre-kindergarten through grade eight. The Academy is one of only 16 all-boys independent elementary schools in the nation, and the only one of its kind in

Texas! A ghost that has been seen in the upstairs of the Stribling Building is attributed to Professor Jim Roe.

## San Antonio College

San Antonio College, located at 1300 San Pedro Avenue is a public community college which provides for and supports the educational and lifelong learning needs of a multicultural community. Ghost voices and strange lights are reported in McAllister Auditorium.

## San Pedro Playhouse

Built in 1929, for the San Antonio Little Theatre that was founded in 1927, the San Pedro Playhouse is the nation's oldest city-built playhouse. Later named San Pedro Playhouse, it has been providing professional-quality live theater to San Antonio audiences for over 80 seasons, making it the oldest arts organization in the city. The ghost of a plump, balding elderly gentleman has been reported frequently moving about the building.

## Sartor House

The distinctive Sartor House, 217 King William Street, was designed San Antonio architect Alfred Giles for German native Alexander Sartor in 1881. Sartor had a prosperous jewelry business in San Antonio. Today, besides a distinctive style, this historic old home also has a ghost that has been described as a "friendly presence". The Sartor ghost is most often reported in the parlor and hallway.

## Schilo's Delicatessen

Schilo's Delicatessen, 424 E Commerce St, occupies a building that was built in 1917. The open large room and the worn wooden booths make it clear that you have entered another time. Schilo's serves great food with a dose of ghost. Lights turn on and off, the female staff gets pinched, strange shadows are reported, and objects move by themselves.

## Spanish Governor's Palace

In 1716 King Philip V of Spain sent soldiers to San Antonio to keep France from seizing the area. The troops arrived in 1718 and constructed a mission and a fort. After 1822 the Spanish Governor's Palace served as a tailor's shop, a barroom, a restaurant and a schoolhouse. In 1931, the City of San Antonio purchased and restored the Palace. Located at 105 Plaza de Armas (at Commerce Street), the "Palace," built in 1749, has seen much San Antonio history pass through its portals. There's the story of the murdered housemaid who, after being robbed by bandits, was bound, gagged and tossed into the well back of the house. Her moans and cries still have been heard coming from the old well in the patio, and caretakers say lights go on and off at times in the house.

There are cold spots as well. One custodian said, "When I close up at night and turn off the lights, I never look behind me."

## Spanish Ranch House

The Spanish Ranch House is located in the Mission District. Witnesses have reported hearing ghostly footsteps and seeing misty apparitions. A number of odd noises and cold spots are also reported here.

## St. Mary's University

A Marianist brother was practicing on some acrobatic rings that were in the current administration building at St. Mary's University. His hands slipped and he fell, breaking his neck. Now, when the sun begins to set behind the building, you can see a figure working out in the attic, and you can hear his footsteps.

## Stinson Field Graveyard

It is said that the Stinson Field Graveyard next to Stinson Municipal Airport (formerly Stinson Field) is haunted by blue lights over certain graves at night, which are in fact visible from the road when you're driving by. One of the old hangars at the Airport itself is also haunted, presumably by a man who was killed while starting his plane, though it's a condemned hangar used for long term storage only. Both of these, interestingly enough, are on the way to the Ghost Tracks of Shane and Villamin roads.

## Stinson Municipal Airport

Supposedly a man who was killed while starting his plane haunts this condemned hangar at Stinson Municipal Airport.

## Terrell Castle Inn

The Terrell Castle Inn is said to be haunted by the original lady of the house and some children. The lady has been sensed in the library, and the children play on the stairs. Footsteps that sound like a woman in high-heeled shoes have been heard on the stairs.

Guests reported the sound of a toilet seat slamming every 30 minutes or so, only to find out that the toilet seat was fine. The same guests changed rooms and ended up with a ceiling fan that spun wildly then stopped (the switch was "off"), and a TV set that jumped off the table and landed upside down on the floor. Housekeeping staff report seeing the shadow of someone pass by when no one is there.

## The Tracks

The legend has it that a busload of kids were killed when their bus stalled on the tracks and was hit by a train, and now if you stop on the tracks and put your car in neutral, your car will roll over the tracks. The legend also states that if you powder your car you'll see the kids' fingerprints in the powder and that the streets in the neighborhood are named after these kids.  There is no record of any bus being hit by a train here, the streets in the neighborhood are named after the developer's kids (who are alive and well), if you don't wash your car down thoroughly first you'll see your own prints in the powder (and those of any kid who has touched your car recently), and it can appear that you are rolling uphill when you are actually rolling downhill.  This is a very popular legend that has been made famous in recent years by the press.  The local police department is tired of dealing with the traffic problem caused by people testing the tracks (and the drugs and alcohol that seem to find their way there), and the local residents are tired of the traffic congestion caused by people stopping on these tracks.  Do not ask us for the location, we no longer disclose it out of respect for the people of San Antonio who have to live there.  Urban legends are fine and there may be many others listed on our site, but this one has gone too far.  We regret that this seems harsh, but if the number of questions we receive each week about these tracks is indicative of the number of people visiting them, I'm glad I don't live there.

## Trinity University

Trinity University is located at One Trinity Place in San Antonio. The Chapman Graduate Center and the Holt Center are known for things that are unexplained. At the Graduate Center on the bottom floor you walk-by and you feel a feeling that you need to get out of there fast. Many housekeeping and Officers feel the same feeling. At the Holt center, some members of the housekeeping will not enter there alone or at night. Police officers have felt that same feeling, to include supervisors.

## Ursuline Academy

Seven Ursuline Sisters from New Orleans and Galveston, headed by Sister St. Marie Trouard, arrived in San Antonio on September 14, 1851, to start a girls' school at Bishop Jean M. Odin's request. On November 3 Ursuline Academy opened classes. It was then the second oldest, and is now the oldest, girls' school in Texas. The original convent, built in 1851 on the San Antonio River at Augusta Street, is believed to be the oldest surviving example of pisé de terre work in Texas and is attributed to architect Jules Poinsard. The first native of San Antonio to become a professed member of the Ursuline community was Sister Magdalen de la Garza, descendant of original Canary Islanders who settled in San Antonio and daughter of José Antonio de la Garza. Sister Magdalen became an early director of the school. According to a nineteenth-century history, by 1887 Ursuline Academy drew students "from all parts of western Texas and Mexico" to its "accommodations for seventy to eighty boarders . . . with the unqualified endorsement of the parents and guardians," who found "the facilities, equipment, site, buildings and instruction first class."

Apparitions of a priest and a nun have been sighted, and some unfortunate folks have been shoved. The buildings are now part of the Southwest Craft Center.

## University of the Incarnate Word - Dubuis Hall

There is a former nun is said to haunt Dubuis Hall and at night many students have reporting uneasy feelings and the sensation of being watched. Some have claimed to catch a glimpse of a nun wearing the traditional habit of the order flitting about the hallways of this old building. Another girl claimed that she awoke one morning to find her stuffed animals had been totally rearranged in neat order during the night.

## University of the Incarnate Word - Main Administration Building

The Main Administration Building was built in 1922. Many say that it has cold spots and reports of a student's radio dial (non-digital) begin scanning through stations on its own. This same admin building's top (4th) floor was once used as a quarantine ward for victims of tuberculosis and has seen its share of deaths, which might account for the activity. Additionally, on the 3rd floor of the Admin building, a 5-year-old boy chasing a bouncing ball has been spotted regularly.

## Victoria's Black Swan Inn

Nestled in the heart of San Antonio along the Salado Creek, at 1006 Holebrook, between Eisenhauer and Rittiman Road, Victoria's Black Swan Inn sits on 35 acres of lush grounds, covered in 100-year-old oak and pecan trees, lavish gardens and lawns. Built in 1867 on the site of the 1842 Battle of Salado, Victoria's Black Swan Inn has been a home to some of the most prestigious people in San Antonio's history. It has also hosted writers such as Erle Stanley Gardner, and some of Texas' most famous musicians and artisans.

Archeological evidence has pointed to Native American occupation of this site, which later hosted the battle of Salado Creek. The Inn now functions as a restaurant and special events venue. When proprietor Jo Ann Rivera first purchased the property she was awakened nightly by the apparition of a man standing at the foot of her bed. Since that time, there have been plenty of unexplained phenomena, including lights turning on and off, music coming from the walls, and doors locking and unlocking on their own accord. This property was also investigated by the TV show "Sightings," which determined the property chock-full of spooks. Apparently the South Wing is the only area of the historic house where the presence feels ominous, though -- a man who was working underneath the house once complained of children taunting him and poking him with sticks.

## Villa Main Railroad Tracks

It is said that the Villa Main Railroad Tracks are haunted by the children killed in a 1930's fatal school bus accident. The bus reportedly stalled on the tracks and was consequently hit by a train, killing all in the bus. It is said that if you pull your car onto those tracks, the children will push your car over the tracks to safety. Baby powder placed the bumper of the endangered car is said to show the handprints of the small children.

## Weinert House B and B

The piano and drums at the Weinert House Bed & Breakfast are said to play by themselves, lights turn on and off, doors open and close, items move on their own, and a female apparition identified as Clara Maria Bading Weinert has been spotted.

## Westin Hotel on Market St.

The apparition of a cobbler at his booth has been seen in one room on the fourth floor of the Westin Hotel on Market Street.

## Witte Museum

Poltergeist activity and apparitions have been reported at the Witte Museum. Many think that the ghost is that of museum founder Ellen Schultz.

## Wolfson Manor

At the Wolfson Manor on Broadway, slamming doors, ghostly footsteps and a floating China cabinet are among the poltergeist activity experienced in this old home. Whenever anyone removes Mr. Wolfson's collection of portraits, they are quickly replaced by ghostly hands.

## Yturri-Edmunds Home

At the Yturri-Edmunds Home, cold spots and fleeting glimpses in the peripheral vision have been attributed to Miss Ernestine, a former resident.

# COTULLA, TEXAS

Cotulla, the county seat of La Salle County, is twenty-seven miles north of Encinal on U.S. Interstate Highway 35 in the northwestern part of the county. The town was named for Joseph Cotulla, a Polish immigrant. After learning that the International-Great Northern Railroad intended to extend its tracks into La Salle County in the early 1880s, Joseph Cotulla worked to build a town on the present site of Cotulla. In 1881 he provided 120 acres of land to induce the railroad to build into the county, and by 1882 a railroad depot had been built and lots in the new town had begun to be sold. By 1883 the town had been granted a post office, and several new buildings had been constructed, including a general store, a hotel, and a jail. In a special county election held that year Cotulla was designated the county seat, and the town began a period of rapid growth. By 1890 it had a population of 1,000, three general stores, two weekly newspapers, two churches, a saloon, a bank, a corn mill, and a cotton gin.

## Frank Newman Middle School

At Frank Newman Middle School, it is said that a coach died of a heart attack in the back office, near the girls' dressing room. Now more than 40 years later the lights turn off and you can feel something or someone going into the bathroom with you.

# LULING, TEXAS

Luling is an incorporated community at the intersection of U.S. highways 90 and 183 and State Highway 80, fifteen miles south of Lockhart in southern Caldwell County. Early settlement of the area began in the 1840s and was concentrated along Plum Creek. The Plum Creek post office opened in 1848. In 1874 the Galveston, Harrisburg and San Antonio line laid track from Columbus to a terminus three miles west of Plum Creek. This terminus became the city of Luling, drawing much of its early population from the Plum Creek area and from the Atlanta community. Sources vary on how Luling came by its name: one said that it was named for a Chinese worker; a second, that it was named for a Judge Luling; and a third, that Luling was the maiden name of the wife of the man who built the railroad. The Luling post office opened in 1874, and the community grew rapidly.

## The Banks of San Marcos River

An invisible "thing" haunts the marsh and surrounding woods along the Banks of the San Marcos River. Hunters and fisherman have had numerous terrifying encounters with this entity. It is not visible to the human eye, but makes its presence known by weird sounds and the disturbance or "pressing down" of nearby foliage. Ghost? Elemental? No one really knows what this frightening creature is that haunts the desolate swamp and nearby woods on the San Marcos.

## Edgar B. Davis Hospital

The ghost of Edgar B. Davis, the man who created the Edgar B. Davis Hospital continues to wander about his creation. The nurses and doctors have received reports about doors opening and closing and medicine being knocked on the ground when only one person is in the room

# MARION, TEXAS

Marion is on Farm Road 78 eleven miles west of Seguin in western Guadalupe County. It was named in honor of Marion Dove, whose grandfather, Joshua W. Young, owned a plantation that the Galveston, Harrisburg and San Antonio Railway passed through in 1877. Before the townsite was laid out, the area was a camp for railroad workers. Town lots were auctioned off in June 1877, and German settlers moved to the area from a settlement on Santa Clara Creek. By the mid-1880s Marion had steam, grist, and saw mills, two cotton gins, four general stores, a church, a district school, and 250 residents. The town was incorporated by 1941, when it had 373 residents and twenty businesses. In 1988 its population was estimated at 835, and the number of businesses had risen to twenty-eight. In 1990 the population of Marion was 984.

## Good Shepherd Clinic

The Good Shepherd Clinic is located in what used to be the old Jefferson Hospital. The clinic does not occupy the entire complex, so the ambulance crews use one section of the old hospital as living quarters. The staff work out room used to be the hospital nursery and the sounds of babies crying are heard here. There is also one room in the living quarters area that the drivers will not go into. Some have said that they have seen shadows in that room that are not caused by anything in the living area. Others have said that they have seen figures moving throughout the building, long after the clinic has closed late at night.

# SKIDMORE, TEXAS

Skidmore is on State Highway 181 and a Southern Pacific line in the central southern half of Bee County. Samuel Cyle Skidmore, a Virginia native and cousin of Gen. Thomas J. (Stonewall) Jackson, moved to Texas in 1857 and eventually settled on Aransas Creek. In 1860 a post office named River Side, for its location by the stream, opened there briefly. Then from later in 1860 to 1866 a post office called Lattington, after its first postmaster P. Lattington, operated at the site. The town of Skidmore was founded when Samuel's son Frank O. Skidmore, real estate dealer and cattleman, donated the townsite, right-of-way, and alternate blocks of land to the San Antonio and Aransas Pass Railway in 1886. The next year a post office called Skidmore opened there.

## Billmore House

People claimed to have seen a small child haunting the attic of the Billmore House and the owners also claimed to have heard crying and laughing through the walls at night. They also say that they hear dripping (they think it is blood) from the spot under the ceiling fan. The owners and townspeople say there is a ghost still haunting the house because there was a child killed by his father up in the basement, hung by a ceiling fan.

# ZAPATA, TEXAS

Zapata, the county seat of Zapata County, is on U.S. Highway 83 and the shores of International Falcon Reservoir, fifty miles south of Laredo. The first European settlers in the area were residents of Revilla (now Ciudad Guerrero), Mexico. Organized settlement of the area began about 1750, when the viceroy of New Spain commissioned Col. José de Escandón to explore and colonize the vast northern frontier along the Rio Grande. One of the inducements for colonists was the promise of large land grants from the Spanish government on both banks of the Rio Grande. After the requirements for validation of the grants were met, the final adjudication of the lands occurred in 1767. Soon thereafter, the settlers began to move across the river, and a town was begun on the north bank of the Rio Grande. The first name of the village was Habitación. Later the name was changed to Carrizo, after a local Indian group that lived in huts made of cane. In 1858 the name was changed to Bellville, in honor of Governor Peter Hansborough Bell, who signed the bill officially marking off the new Zapata County from Webb and Starr counties. In 1898 the name of the town was permanently changed to Zapata, in honor of Col. Antonio Zapata, a local rancher and respected military man who became one of the leaders of the federalist movement to found the Republic of the Rio Grande, which began in 1839. The first headquarters of this movement were in Zapata County. Two military posts, Camp Drum and Camp Harney, were located at Zapata in the early 1850s to combat border disturbances and Indian attacks.

## Old Zapata Middle School

At the Old Zapata Middle School gym (which is now Zapata Central), there is a ghostly resident of a small boy that died there. Footsteps are heard in the bleachers when no one is up and walking on them.

**PART SEVEN**

**GHOSTS OF NORTH EAST TEXAS**

## DALLAS, TEXAS

Dallas is on the Trinity River in the center of Dallas County in North Central Texas. It is crossed by Interstate highways 20, 30, 35, and 45. The city was founded by John Neely Bryan, who settled on the east bank of the Trinity near a natural ford in November 1841. Bryan had picked the best spot for a trading post to serve the population migrating into the region. The ford, at the intersection of two major Indian traces, provided the only good crossing point for miles. Two highways proposed by the Republic of Texas soon converged nearby. Unknown to Bryan, however, he had settled on land granted by the republic to the Texan Land and Emigration Company of St. Louis, headed by William S. Peters. Bryan eventually legalized his claim, and the extensive promotional efforts of the Peters colony attracted settlers to the region. In 1844 J. P. Dumas surveyed and laid out a townsite comprising a half mile square of blocks and streets.

The origin of the name Dallas is unknown. Candidates include George Mifflin Dallas, vice president of the United States, 1845-49; his brother, Commodore Alexander J. Dallas, United States Navy; and Joseph Dallas, who settled near the new town in 1843. When Dallas County was formed in 1846, Dallas was designated as the temporary county seat; in 1850 voters selected it as the permanent county seat over Hord's Ridge (Oak Cliff) and Cedar Springs, both of which eventually came within its corporate limits. The Texas legislature granted Dallas a town charter on February 2, 1856. Dr. Samuel Pryor, elected the first mayor, headed a town government consisting of six aldermen, a treasurer-recorder, and a constable.

### Flagpole Hill

There is a narrow horseshoe shaped road with lots of trees; and a few obscured houses in between that lead to Flag Pole Hill. Once you start down this narrow road, you must continue. No place to turn around. Mysterious events such as rocks flying from impossible angles towards cars; sudden unforeseen vehicular body damage, etc, have occurred. The local police department will verify this as far back as 1976.

### The Grand Crystal Palace

Anyone proceeding along the Stemmons Freeway from DWF airport to downtown Dallas, Texas, will turn in curiosity at the sight of a large, greenhouse-structure, enclosing 1.6 million square feet of space. This is Infomart, a high tech facility, set impressively along the side of the road in 1984.

It is also a flattering imitation, on a grander scale, of the Crystal Palace. Few modern buildings have so dazzled the popular imagination as did the original structure. Erected in Hyde Park, London, the Crystal Palace, a large glass-and-iron shed, was the setting for the Great International Exhibition of 1851, the mother of all world's fairs.

No building was ever so appropriately, yet lyrically named. Seeming to contain natural light, and so to obliterate the distinction between indoors and outdoors, the Crystal Palace defied the traditional regularities of stone-and-mortar structures of a monumental sort. It neither excluded nor constrained. It was light in appearance and spacious in sweep as no structure before it. It awed by its size and its seeming fragility. The Crystal Palace was an engineering feat, if not an architectural triumph, and suited the growing modern taste for open, unfettered interior space in which large numbers of people could stroll, look, and be part of what has been called the "spectacle society." It antedated the shopping mall, the civic center, the sports arena, even the contemporary mega-museum.

Today, the grand glass-covered arches found in the Dallas Infomart stand in unembarrassed deference to that once remarkable structure that still holds, as it did its 100,000 exhibits, the popular imagination.

This Swiss Ave. monument to history is also the home of several ghosts. There is a painting of young girl hanging in the building that is said to be haunted by "good" spirit. Rumor also has it that several workers were killed during the construction and now haunt the building, and a man in a dark suit haunts the theater audience seating area which is now a fashionable nightclub.

## LBJ House

The structure known as the LBJ House is believed by some to be haunted. Most say that it was the scene of a gruesome murder. The alleged crime was a family murder suicide. It is clearly marked no trespassing and gets regular visits by Dallas PD due to vagrants and some small interior fires. Inside the LBJ House some folks have been camping inside and the human stench is just overpowering. The interior rooms and hallways have no windows and no light gets in. A wife and child were supposedly killed here and now you can see blood on the walls and feel cold spots. The property has been abandoned for several decades and no one will buy the lot.

LBJ house was located at 7300 Valley View near LBJ Freeway. It was the former office of Lamberts Landscape Company but somehow it got the reputation as a murder suicide haunted house etc on paranormal websites

Actually the owners got in a bind with the city over pollution in White Rock Creek and sold it to some lawyers in CA who more or less abandoned it, now it's burned down

## Lizard Lounge

Lizard Lounge is located at 2424 Swiss Ave. Not only does Lizard Lounge routinely feature some of the best DJs in the country but most patrons agree that it's just about the sexiest club in town. The building was once a theater and many patrons have reported that a "man in black" haunts the old audience seating area, and on more than one occasion, unknown spirits have wreaked havoc in the area that once contained the dressing rooms when it was a theater.

## Majestic Theater

On April 11, 1921, the Majestic Theater, located at 1925 Elm Street, opened its doors to the theater going public. The theater once belonged to the Hoblitzelle Foundation and they turned it over to the city of Dallas in January of 1976. Dallas Summer Musicals Management Group currently operates the theater. However, it has become very apparent that there are others who roam the theater that cannot be seen.

Phone lines light up when no one is there, backdrops move of their own accord, and strange smells have been experienced. The phenomenon has been attributed to a benefactor named Karl Hoblitzelle.

## Millermore Mansion

The Millermore Mansion is a two story Greek revival home completed in 1861, is currently the center piece of Old City Park Museum. Over the last 30 years there have been continual stories of a haunting in the house. Many unrelated individuals (museum guests, volunteers, and staff) have sensed the presence of a female spirit in the house. The activity seems to center around the former nursery and master bedroom on the second floor. Consistent stories are told of a ghostly female presence in the second floor area around the former nursery. Visitors, docents, and staff have all felt the presence over the last 25 years.

The Millermore Mansion is located in Old City Park. The park was established in 1876, so in 1976 it became a grand scene of celebration, and truly there was a lot to celebrate—the nation was 200 years old, and the park was 100 years old. But, there was even more to cheer—the work of the Dallas Heritage Society. This organization turned a plain park into a walking museum.

It all started in 1966 when the Dallas Heritage Society raised $30,000 to save Millermore, the mansion built by Dallas pioneer William Brown Miller. Mr. Miller brought his family and his slaves to Dallas in the 1850s. He acquired land on what is Bonnie View Road, and with slave labor built his grand mansion, which he called Millermore. Some person of the Miller family lived in the house until 1966, when the last Miller girl died. In typical southern tradition, the house was crumbling around this maiden lady who was determined to stay in the old homestead until it collapsed. Well, it almost did. After her death, it looked like the bulldozer was going to take over. The Dallas Heritage Society an organization of interested Dallas citizens got the money together to save the building. It was dismantled, and the boards were carefully numbered, so it could be put back together again. The house was rebuilt in the Old City Park, and this majestic mansion became the nucleus of a whole bunch of structures that were going to be restored and moved into the park.

It has long been believed that the ghost of old Mrs. Miller came with the house it is true that many people have claimed to see her in the window as they drive by in the evening. Others say that she haunted the second floor nursery. For years, a female presence has been felt on the second floor of this historic home, near the nursery.

## Oak Cliff – Combs Creek Street

In the 1830s and 40s, occasional settlers set up temporary stockades and houses on the west side of the Trinity River before Dallas was founded. The first permanent settlement was established in 1845 by William H. Hord, and was called Hord's Ridge. In 1887 T.L. Marsalis bought 2000 acres and began a development of houses he called Oak Cliff. People liked the name so much, they changed the name of the town to Oak Cliff and by 1900, Oak Cliff had a population of 3,630 people.

There is the story that a little girl was out riding her bicycle on Combs Creek Street near the railroad tracks and was hit by a train. Now her spirit is seen riding her bicycle toward the railroad crossing where she died.

## Oak Cliff - Wilbur Street Play Ground

They say in the 1920s that a little girl got permission from her parents, to go play in the playground of Wilbur St. around a creek. A drunk driver was out of control and hit the girl, which was happily playing on the swing. People now say that if you look closely at the swings you will see the happy little girl swinging.

## Preston Rd.

A large group of spirits dressed in early 20th century clothing has been spotted moving north in the area between Beltline and Spring Valley.

## Snuffers Restaurant

Snuffer's Restaurant and Bar first opened its Greenville Avenue location in 1978 with 15 tables and a service bar. It didn't take long for word to spread that this was the place to meet for burgers and cheddar fries. It also didn't take long before more space was needed. Over the years that followed, Snuffer's grew and expanded, adding outdoor patios and more indoor seating to accommodate more people. Throughout this growth, Snuffer's has always kept true to the original menu and same great service.

However, it was remodeled and this apparently unset the spirit as this unidentified spirit showed up after the building was remodeled. There have been a number of reports of an apparition seen moving about the building at night.

## Sons of Hermann Hall

The Sons of Hermann Hall in Dallas has a long and colorful history.  The two Texas Sons of Hermann lodges in the hall today are Dallas #22 and Columbia #60. Dallas Lodge #22 was chartered in 1890 as Uhland lodge #22. Columbia Lodge was chartered in 1893. In 1910 the then four Dallas lodges (out of necessity and, more importantly, unity) pooled their resources and built the hall at 3414 Elm. The grand opening was held in April of 1911.  The Dallas Sons of Hermann Hall is a Texas Historic Landmark.

Witnesses have reported hearing doors slam, seeing paintings fall off of walls, and hearing the sounds of voices and children's laughter echo when no one is there. Others have seen a male and female pair of apparitions.

## Throckmorton @ Maple Ave.

Thought to be the site of a long-gone crematorium and funeral parlor (and intermittently various bars and clubs), voices have been heard when no one was around, videos would fly off shelves in the DJ booth, and a female apparition has been seen on the dance floor. The bar on an adjacent lot has a constant repulsive smell that no one can explain.

## University of North Texas

University of North Texas' Bruce Hall is said to be haunted by "Wanda", a resident who killed herself. Some suggest that Kerr and Maple Halls may also be haunted as well.

## White Rock Lake

The Lady of White Rock Lake is something of a Vanishing Hitchhiker, reportedly visiting amorous couples parked in the area.  The Lady of the Lake - or White Lady has been seen here and on the road by the lake - dressed in a 1920's evening gown and soaking wet - she asks drivers for a ride to a house on Gaston Ave where she disappears leaving nothing but a wet stain on the seat. The story is that she was the daughter of a wealthy family in the 1920's. She was on her way home from a ball when her car wrecked in the lake - she drowned, but the others lived. Now she tried to get home.

## DeGolyer Estate

The DeGolyer House is just one of the many things to see and do at the arboretum. You can visit the gift shop which is located in the DeGolyer House.

While checking out the gift shop, don't forget to tour this historical home. Built in 1939-40, this 21,000-square-foot home was one of the first in Dallas to be built with central air conditioning. You will see several interesting architectural features in this Spanish Colonial Revival home. It has seven chimneys and no two are the same. Also, there is a fireplace carved in the form of ammonite fossils. You will want to pay close attention to the details so you don't miss a thing. The 4.5 acres that surround the home include hundreds of annuals and perennials, a magnolia allee, a rose garden and a wisteria arbor. The estate also is home to several ghosts who seem to spend their time wandering the halls of this historic old home.

## Gus Thomasson/ Ferguson

On the corner of Ferguson Rd. and Gus Thomasson, is an Eckerd Drugs that is haunted by a man name Wayne. It is said that this man was a late night loader, and un-loader of delivery trucks as well as a shelf stocker. He was a good, honest, family man until one day at 6:00 am going home after finishing his shift three men assaulted him for his money. These men had been attacking people that worked the late shift for some time and had been quite successful in escaping. Unlike most of their victims, however, Wayne tried to defend himself, not knowing one of the three men had a gun. Wayne was shot three times in the heart and three times in the head.

Now visitors and staff have reported that in the upstairs part of the building, where Eckerd Drugs keeps its boxed products, they have seen a shadowy figure that seems to vanish if challenged. Some employees have reported seeing and hearing boxes fall to the floor for no reason. The radio in that area will change channels by itself as well as turn itself on and off. Cold areas are felt, and footsteps are heard going up and down the stairs.

## Hospital

There is an old abandoned hospital located across from Texas Scottish Rite Hospital for Children. Visitors have reported hearing voices and some have seen the apparition of a little girl standing besides one of the trees. If approached she will say "you're too late to help." Then she will scream and vanish. Locals say that the little girl fell out of that particular tree and died.

## Jerry's Super Market

Jerry's Super Market is located at the corner of Jefferson and Llewelyn. While by day the market is filled with patrons, at night the building takes on a different personality. According to reports, when the managers have closed and locked the exits for the day, they will heard what sounds like conversation and movement in the areas where they store merchandise waiting to be shelved. Naturally, store employees will investigate, but no one is ever found that could account for the unusual sounds.

## Lake Highlands High School

Supposedly sometime in the early 1970s, a girl named Elizabeth jumped out of one of the second story windows of Lake Highlands High School off of Church Rd. and White Rock Trail (near Flag Pole Hill) and killed herself. Most sightings or strange occurrences have taken place in the auditorium; however the technical theatre teacher claims he can sense her presence throughout the school. Tools have been found missing from the locked tool room, trashcans and other large objects have been thrown across room, doors (w/ hydraulics to keep from loud slamming) have slammed shut, and random cold spots are felt throughout the building. Some kids from Lake Highlands High School made a movie about it, called Ghost light.

## Hotel Lawrence

The Hotel Lawrence was opened in October 1925 as a high class hotel. Over its history, there have been a number of events that have taken place within its walls that have left very real impressions. A number of guests as well as staff have reported hearing crying and seeing unusual shadows on the 10th floor. According to the story, a woman jumped, was pushed or fell from Presidential Suite back in the 1940's. Now, staff members have reported hearing voices and footsteps as well as encountering many cold spots in that room during times it is empty. Both patrons and desk staff have reported hearing high heeled footsteps pacing back and forth across the lobby between midnight and 6am.

At one time during the 1920's there was an illegal casino located on the second floor of the hotel. Now the area that used to be the casino is haunted by a well dressed, very polite spirit. No one seems to know his identity, but he has been seen a number of times by both staff and guests.

## Pleasant Grove Christian Church

There are many who say that the Pleasant Grove Christian Church located at 1324 Pleasant Dr, is haunted. A number of witnesses have reported seeing children run by them and simply vanish. Others have reported hearing banging and howling noises from various parts of the grounds. One witness took several photos in an empty hallway with a digital camera at this site and obtained pictures of floating orbs, as well as a child's face and what looked like an adult sized hand holding an axe. The children spirits are not too intense but the adult spirit seems very angry and seems to want to be left alone. Many speculate that the bad tempered adult may have murdered the child whose face was seen in the photo.

## Rylie Academy

Rylie was once an independent community that was incorporated into Dallas in 1965. Rylie was at the intersection of Loop 635 and Rylie Road, between State highways 175 and 20 on the Southern Pacific line eleven miles southeast of Dallas in southeastern Dallas County. It was on the original land grant of J. R. Rylie, who as early as 1855 had settled in the area. The Rylie Academy is located at 10327 Rylie Rd. This building began life as the Rylie High school /Junior High School before becoming the Rylie Academy. Rylie Academy is a Charter School with grades 1-12.

Both students and teachers have reported hearing strange sounds and seeing lights turn on and off with no explanation. There have also been reports of apparitions being seen moving about the building after hours.

## Turtle Creek Center

The Turtle Creek Center is a 14 story modern building located at 2911 Turtle Creek Blvd. Turtle Creek is an exclusive Dallas area and this handsomely designed building boasts of prestige. With window views of The Mansion Hotel's lush grounds, flower and tree lined parks and abundant greenery winding around a beautiful creek; this is an area that should exude peace.

However, the history of this area is something less than peaceful. A successful businessman worked at this building through the 1980's. His name was Harold and on the 13th of September 1989, he died from unexplained reasons in his office at approximately 9 p.m. His spirit has been seen in the fire exit/stairways by a few occupants working in the building. They have reportedly seen a man walking between the 13th and 14th floors with blood falling from his eyes and a look of shear death on his face. When they follow him into the hallway he disappears without a trace.

# FORT WORTH, TEXAS

Fort Worth is on Interstate highways 35W, 20, and 30 and the Clear Fork of the Trinity River in central Tarrant County. In January 1849 United States Army General William Jenkins Worth, hero of the Mexican War, proposed a line of ten forts to mark the western Texas frontier from Eagle Pass to the confluence of the West Fork and Clear Fork of the Trinity River. Upon the death of Worth, Gen. William S. Harney assumed the command and ordered Maj. Ripley S. Arnold to find a new fort site near the West Fork and Clear Fork.

This site was suggested by Middleton Tate Johnson, who once commanded a detachment of Texas Rangers and founded Johnson Station, just southeast of what is now Fort Worth. On June 6, 1849, Arnold established a camp on the bank of the Trinity River and named the post Camp Worth in honor of General Worth. In August 1849 Arnold moved the camp to the north-facing bluff which overlooked the mouth of the Clear Fork. The United States War Department officially named the post Fort Worth on November 14, 1849.

## Armstrong House

The ghost of Gussie Armstrong has been experienced in the Armstrong House.

## Barbers Bookstore

The old Barbers Bookstore was located at 215 W. 8$^{th}$. The building was built about 1910 and remodeled in 1935 with an Art Deco façade. Over the years, the building has housed a cafe, a hotel, and most notably, Barber's Bookstore. The bookstore closed in late 1997 and its contents were liquidated in the fall of 1998. Greene's Antiques now occupies the ground floor retail space.

Over the years, many patrons of the various businesses that have called this location home have reported hearing the very clear sounds of footsteps when there has been no one else around to make them. Other mysterious sounds have included, the sounds of pages being turned, and a number of patrons have reported seeing strange shadows on staircase. On more than one occasion apparitions have also been reported.

## Castleberry High School

Castleberry High School is located at 215 Churchill Rd, in the River Oaks section of Fort Worth. Many students say that the building was built on an old Indian burial ground. According to the rumor, if you go up the flight of steps that leads to the roof, you will hear low pitched voices carrying on an intense conversation when no one else is around.

## Del Frisco's Double Eagle Steakhouse

Del Frisco's Double Eagle Steakhouse is located at 812 Main St. In the 1800's, this area of Ft. Worth was known as "Hell's Half Acre" because of its numerous saloons, brothels and gambling halls. This particular building used to be a bath house in the late 1800s where a man was shot in the head after an altercation. Now there are many who maintain that the spirit of this murdered man roams the banquet halls and the upstairs bar.

## Fast Freddy's Pool Hall

The well known Fast Freddy's Pool Hall is located at 5707 Crowley Road. A number of patrons as well as staff members have heard strange noises after hours. These noises have been attributed to the spirit of Utley J. Puckett, a patron and pool player who went to that big pool hall in the sky.

## Fort Worth Books and Video

The building that did house Fort Worth Books and Videos is located at 400 Main St. The building is now partially occupied by Pangburns Chocolate Shoppe, and maybe Jamba Juice. There has long been an unknown presence reported by several customers that seems to move about the building. Among the activities reports have been mysterious footsteps and strange lights.

## Glen D. Reeves Fine Arts Center

A spirit, believed to be that of "Glen" supposedly haunts one of the fly rails in the Glen D. Reeves Fine Arts Center performance hall, and has been known to play with the lights.

## Jett Building

The Jett Building, located in Sundance Square at 400 Main was built in 1902.The most notable feature of this Sundance Square building is the Chisholm Trail Mural painted by Richard Haas on its south side. The mural attracts many tourists into Downtown Fort Worth. The Jett Building was once home of the Northern Texas Traction Co. which operated the Interurban Railway with service to Dallas and Cleburne.  Although the building's architect is unknown, it appears that the structure was modeled after Frank Lloyd Wright's Larkin Building.

The building is in danger of demolition due to the construction of a central plaza along Main Street. Jamba Juice has leased the first floor. Radio Station 95.9 FM "The Ranch" KFWR operates a street-side radio studio. Windows in the studios open out to 3rd Street and a new balcony/covered porch has been constructed on the west side of the building.  Many employees have reported hearing mysterious footsteps on the upper floors and have seen unknown figures moving about the building after close of business.

## Log Cabin Village

Log Cabin Village located at 2100 Log Cabin Village Lane is a living history museum devoted to the preservation of Texas heritage. The Village was originally a project of Pioneer Texas Heritage Committee and members of the Tarrant County Historical Society. Six log houses, dating back to the mid 1800s, were selected from the North Texas region, moved to the present site, and restored in the 1950s. The Village was then donated to the City of Fort Worth, and it opened to the public in 1966. The Foster Cabin, an impressive 1850s log house, was added in 1974.

Each of the log houses, furnished with authentic artifacts, provides a vivid look at life in the nineteenth century North Texas frontier.  However, one unintended consequence of the striving for authenticity is that it would appear that the Committee also transported several spirits to this site along with the cabins and artifacts.  Over-powering presences in an upstairs bedroom, the smell of lilacs, and a female apparition have been reported in the Foster Cabin.

## Mistletoe Heights Home

The Mistletoe Heights section of Fort Worth sits on the bluffs overlooking the Trinity River. The homes in this historic neighborhood are stately built on wide tree lined streets with sidewalks and fancy lights. The houses range from small cottages to large mansions. Many have basements and some have servant's quarters in the rear.

One of these stately homes also has a ghost. There have been a number of repots of a singing female spirit in an ivory blouse that serenades all who will listen.

## Peters Bros. Hats

The Peters Brothers business at 909 Houston was started in 1911 by Greek immigrants Jim and Tom Peters. At that time, they were shining shoes in Waco, Texas. In 1917, the brothers moved to Fort Worth and set up a shoe shining business near their current location. In addition to work on shoes, the brothers started doing hat renovations. In 1921, they started making hats and the business grew from there. Peters Brothers moved into their current building in 1933. This is a very typical commercial building constructed from this time period in Fort Worth's history. The two story building features rectangular window bays on the second floor above the storefronts with a decorative brick parapet. Two large neon signs have been placed on the building. The Branding Iron Grill occupies the other half of the ground floor.

There are many who maintain that there is no doubt that the building is haunted by the spirit of Tom Peters. He comes back to watch over the business. He is said to move hats around the make the displays more appealing to customers. There is another ghost that began to make itself known after they acquired the space of a former pizzeria that occupied part of the building. According to the locals, along with the space, they acquired the ghost of the dishwasher, Jack Martin. Jack baptizes new employees with a good spray from the dishwasher.

## Schoonover House

A jeweler, James E. Mitchell, constructed the house at 600 8$^{th}$ Avenue around 1907 on the southwest corner of 8th Avenue and Pennsylvania. He hired Sanguinet & Staats to design this highly decorated and ornamented home. In 1920, Dr. Charles Simmons, a family friend, purchased the home. In 1945, the doctor transferred the ownership to his daughter and her husband, Dr. Frank

Schoonover. The Schoonovers lived in the home until 1979, when it was sold and converted over to a savings and loan and professional offices.

In 1995, Attorney Art Brender purchased the Schoonover House and did some restoration on the interior and has been using the location for his practice. However, as happens with many old houses, the renovations seem to have awakened the spirits that reside in the house. Visitors have reported experiencing cold spots, apparitions, voices, footsteps, and encountering lights that operate on their own in the basement.

## W. E. Scott Theater

The W.E. Scott Theater located at 1300 Gendy St, is a four-and-a-half level theater with main auditorium seating for nearly 500. The theater is located on Amon Carter Square adjacent to the Modern Art Museum of Fort Worth. According to the night cleaning crew, the theater is haunted by the ghost of a janitor that is said to haunt the basement of the theater. This spirit has been known to make laughing noises from the stage.

However, there are others who say that the ghost of the Scott Theater is actually a former actor named Ken Yandell who hung himself in the basement. His ghost seems to spend most of time in the strange corridor filled basement where he died. As for the laughter from stage, a wardrobe woman was so frightened one night by cackling coming from the stage that she left and never returned.

## Stockyards: General Store

The Fort Worth Stockyards is now a National Historic District comprising the area that was originally a high traffic business area in the early days of Fort Worth. In 1849 Major Ripley Arnold and a troop of soldiers were ordered to set up Fort Worth and protect the settlers in North Texas. By 1853, the frontier moved west. The fort was abandoned and the buildings that were left became the town of Fort Worth. By 1856 the citizens stole the county records from Birdville and won the county seat.

Soon Fort Worth became a frequent stop for cattlemen herding through the area. Wild longhorns that roamed the open range were free for the taking. Many cowboys herded them up, branded them, and drove them north for a large profit. By 1866, the city had earned its reputation as "Cow town," and was in the middle of the Chisholm Trail. The city now began to prosper as a leader in the cattle business. The general store located at 101 W. Exchange Ave. is little changed from when it was part of the flourishing cattle business of the 1800s/ witnesses have reported hearing footsteps and seeing fleeting figures moving about the second floor of this building.

## Stockyards: The Maverick

The Maverick Fine Western Wear, located at 100 E. Exchange Ave. was established in 1987 in the Historic Fort Worth Stockyards. The building occupied by the Maverick was built in 1905 on the corner of North Main and Exchange. Since that time, this historic old building has housed numerous colorful enterprises, but it has always been known as The Maverick and has always contained a bar. And it still does. Today, patrons of The Maverick can "belly up", relax and enjoy a cold one just like they did in the days of the big cattle drives while shopping at one of the best western boutiques this side of the Mississippi.

As for ghosts, there are man stories about a ghostly woman who leaves roses upstairs.

## Stockyards: Miss Molly's Bed and Breakfast Hotel

Miss Molly's is an historic, 8-room hotel operating in the bed-and-breakfast tradition, located at 109 1/2 W. Exchange Ave. in the Stockyards section of Fort Worth, on the second floor of a building originally constructed in 1910. The inn features shutters, lace curtains, iron beds, antique quilts and oak furniture in every room.

The building, which is said to have been a bordello in its pre-B&B days, is alleged to host more than a few ghosts. As befits a former bordello, the supposed spirit visitors at Miss Molly's are often reported to be attractive young women who materialize at the foot of guests' beds. Some guests have reported that the spirits apparently wanted to do more than just moan and generally haunt the place. The Cowboy's and Cattlemen's rooms are alleged to be the places to stay to have the best chance of encountering something supernatural.

## Stockyards: Spaghetti Warehouse

The Spaghetti Warehouse, located at 600 E. Exchange Avenue in the historic Fort Worth Stock Yards. The third floor of this old building is haunted by a woman who was killed during a fire. You can still see the fire marks. Others report that the building is actually haunted by three different ghosts. There is a small girl in the bathroom that turns on water, flushes toilets, and scatters paper towels. There is a woman in white that can be seen on the balcony late at night and then there is an old cowboy who throws glasses and knocks over stools.

## Texas Wesleyan University – Fine Arts Building

Texas Wesleyan University is a private college located in the southeast part of Fort Worth, Texas. The university opened in 1891. The college became a woman's university in 1914 but was forced to become coeducational in 1934 due to financial problems from the Great Depression. The school is affiliated with the United Methodist Church and is located in Fort Worth's Stop Six neighborhood.

The Ann Waggoner Fine Arts Building has long has a reputation for being haunted. This prestigious old building was built in 1908, enlarged in 1923, and finally, remodeled in 2002. It includes teaching studios, rehearsal rooms, offices, an electronic piano laboratory, and the Fine Arts Auditorium, which includes Martin Hall. There are a number of witnesses who claim to have seen a ghostly observer sits in the audience during rehearsals and roams the building at night. It is also claimed that she periodically plays the piano. Students call her Georgia.

## Texas Wesleyan University - Eunice and James L. West Library

The Eunice and James L. West Library, located at 1201 Wesleyan, was built in 1988. This ultramodern structure is an 84,400 square foot building housing the University library and special collections, classrooms, Media Services, computer classrooms, and the Academic Resource Center. It is also said by many that the West Library also houses a ghost. A number of witnesses have claimed to smell of smoke and be overcome with unexplainable choking sensations. Several who have had cause to be in the library late at night, have reported a feeling of being watched.

## Texas White House B & B

The Texas White House Bed & Breakfast is located at 1417 8th Ave near the historic Stockyards. According to management, there have been three ghostly experiences at the Texas White House. It is believed that the primary spirit is that of the husband of the only family who ever lived in the house; he died here and now haunts his old bedroom. All of the reported hauntings have occurred when only one lady was staying in the room.

In the first, the woman awoke in the middle of the night to the feeling that someone was lying on the bed beside her, back to back. She says that for several minutes she lay perfectly still, and then she felt the "person" start to move off of the bed. At that point she turned over very quickly to see who it was, and no one was there. The overhead light came on even though no one had turned it on.

In the second instance, the woman awoke feeling someone getting into bed with her. She turned over immediately to see who it was, and, of course, no one was there. But immediately afterwards, her cell phone, which was plugged in several feet away, began to beep and wouldn't stop for several seconds. She says that her phone had never done that before.

In the most recent, a woman returned to the room and "felt a presence" over in the corner. Later that night she felt the same presence again on the other side of the bed. This woman was not aware of any such occurrences having happened in that room until the morning she checked out; she merely stated to me that she enjoyed the "friendly presence" that had been in the room.

## Thistle Hill House Museum

Thistle Hill House Museum is located at 1509 Pennsylvania Avenue. It is said that W.T. Waggoner, one of the wealthiest of the Fort Worth Cattle Barons, paid $38,000 for the construction of an 11,000 square foot "honeymoon cottage" to keep his only daughter, Electra, from moving to Philadelphia.

In 1901, Electra had met Albert Buckman Wharton, a prominent Philadelphian, while touring the Himalayas. They were married in 1902 at her family home in Decatur, Texas-El Castile. Completed in 1904, Thistle Hill graced the crest of Summit Avenue in the fashionable residential district known as Quality Hill and quickly gained a reputation for opulence and lavish entertainment.

Thistle Hill was sold to Mr. and Mrs. Winfield Scott in 1911, longtime acquaintances of Electra's parents. Mr. Scott, a successful cattleman and prominent Ft. Worth businessman, embarked on an extensive remodeling of the mansion, converting it from Colonial to Georgian Revival. Sadly, Mr. Scott died in 1911 and Elizabeth Scott and their son, Winfield Jr. moved into the mansion in 1912. During her 26 year residency, Elizabeth expanded the gardens and added a tea house and pergola to the grounds. She was known as an elegant hostess and her dinner parties were very formal affairs.

After his mother's death in 1938, Winfield, Jr. sold the mansion to the Girls Service League. The League, founded in 1917, is still in operation today and is dedicated to the assistance of young women. In 1968, the League put the mansion up for sale. In 1974, after watching many of the mansions on Quality Hill abolished to make room for "progress", a group of concerned citizens formed a committee called "Save the Scott Home" and embarked on an all-out fund raising project. After several failed attempts, they finally succeeded in purchasing Thistle Hill in 1976 for $240,000[41].

There are two spirits said to haunt this historic old home. One is a lady dressed in white that is said to appear on the grand staircase. Shortly after she is seen, a man wearing tennis clothes is always seen at the top of the stairs as if he is waiting for her. Some visitors have reported hearing music coming form the ballroom as well as ghostly voices carrying on an animated conversation.

## The Castle

There is a castle situated near the lake. There have naturally been a number of stories told about this unusual home, but I am told on good authority that the Castle was originally a 1960's rock farmhouse purchased in the 1920s by the Whitings. After extensive renovations and the addition of the round crenulated front wing and the rear tower the rambling mansion took on the look of a castle. It was completed in 1938 and Mrs. Whiting, who mostly supervised the renovation, named it "Inverness". The residence has seen several owners in the past and at one time Gary Stewart stayed there while filming a movie in the 1950's. In the not so distant past the castle was vacant for a long period of time and was in such disrepair it was on the verge of being condemned. It is now currently occupied and restored.

---

[41] http://www.thistlehill.org/

Witnesses have reported seeing apparitions of a man around the building. According to local legend a young man built this castle for his bride to be. The wedding was to be held in the newly finished house, but on the wedding day, the bride was found floating in the lake. No one was sure if she died accidentally or if foul play was involved, however, a few months later the groom married the dead woman's sister. Now, at night, the bride can be seen running from the house, across the road and towards the lake before disappearing.

## Fort Worth Zoo

The Fort Worth Zoo is home to more than just the exotic animals, it is also the home of several ghosts. The elephant keeper was crushed and killed in the elephant yard in the 1980s, but he is still seen near the elephant and zebra areas of the zoo. There is a woman who is dressed in a white dress who carries a parasol. She has been seen to walk slowly back and forth near the spot where the zoo cafe is. She dresses in attire from the late 19th century and no one knows who she is.

## Red Lobster

The Red Lobster Restaurant on Hulen St. is said to be haunted. His particular spirit is mainly seen in the kitchen area and is said to be the ghost of a girl who seems to like to tease the cooks. At night employees have seen her walking about the restaurant.

## Wet Seal Co.

The Wet Seal Company is located in Hulen Mall. It has been said that the land was built on an old Indian burial ground and perhaps the spirits do not like living beneath a mall. Who's to say if anything has happened in other stores, but there have been a number of rumors regarding other hauntings. Several associates have worked for the Wet Seal Company for three years and all have several stories. One recent experience is the heavy wooden doors that are locked after hours open and slam on their own. The back door that opens to the outside of the mall and is locked for security reasons tends to shake mysteriously. You can watch it shake violently as if someone is trying to enter the store. People have reported being pulled across the room by their hair, with the store closed and no one around.

Voices have been heard and cool winds are felt in the backroom. There have even been sightings of figures moving about when store lights are off and store is locked. Clothes and display carts have been moved when store is empty of anyone besides employees. Several employees have reported seeing an Indian girl sitting Indian style on the floor when store is closed and lights are off.

## ALLEN, TEXAS

Allen is on Farm Road 2478 eight miles southwest of McKinney in southwestern Collin County. The town was established in 1870 by a purchasing agent for the Houston and Texas Central Railway and named in 1872 for Ebenezer Allen, former attorney general of Texas and a promoter of the railroad. In 1876 a post office opened there.

Four years later Denton outlaw Sam Bass supposedly committed the first train robbery in the state at Allen. By 1884 Allen had a population estimated at 350, three churches, a school, a chair factory, and a flour mill. In 1908 the Texas Traction Company built an electric railway through the town.

The population had increased to 550 by 1915. In the mid-1940s the number of residents declined to 400, and in 1948 train service was discontinued. Beginning in the late 1960s, however, Allen's population grew rapidly. Between 1970 and 1980 the number of residents jumped from 1,940 to 8,314. This increase was influenced by the economic growth of Dallas and nearby Plano and the construction of Dallas-Fort Worth International Airport. In 1990 Allen had a population of 18,309 and was the third largest town in Collin County.

## Eagle Stadium

Eagle Stadium, 601 E. Main, is a high school stadium with a seating capacity of 7,800. It is said that Eagle Stadium is haunted by an ex-football player that died on the field over 65 years ago. There have been a number of witnesses who have reported sightings of a shadow running down the field at midnight, but the ghost has only been seen on Friday nights after a game.

# ARLINGTON, TEXAS

Arlington is halfway between Dallas and Fort Worth in east Tarrant County. It was founded in 1876 on the Texas and Pacific Railway as a market town for the surrounding farms. From the 1840s the area had attracted farmers because of the fertile blackland in the eastern part of the region and the sandy loam, good for growing fruits and vegetables, in the western part. The place was also well watered by the Trinity River and its tributaries. Early settlements included Bird's Fort, Watson, and Johnson Station, founded by Middleton Tate Johnson.

## Chuck E. Cheese

Chuck E. Cheese is located at 2216 S. Fielder Rd. However, before the advent of this well known children's fun center, there was a grocery store at this location. According to rumor, the manager supposedly took his life inside the store. Now "Floyd", as the employees have named him, plays with the radio, switching from station to station, and rolls balls down the stairs from the second floor area where he had once maintained his office.

## **Flagship Inn Resort**

The Flagship Inn Resort, located at Hwy. 360 and Avenue K. consisting of several dozen housing structures, is being leveled. The owners, Heaven on Earth Inns, a group headed by meditation guru Maharishi Mahesh Yogi, plans to convert the 20-acre parcel into 120,000 square feet of low-rise office space. Reportedly this complex is haunted by the ghost of a disgruntled security guard, who after being fired, set the ballroom on fire, then died in the ensuing blaze. The fire also killed several homeless people who had taken shelter in the building, so perhaps they are there, as well. Investigations at the location have provided unexplainable photographs, temperature shifts and EMF spikes.

## **University of Texas at Arlington Sigma Chi**

Before the building of Greek Row, there was an orphanage located where the Sigma Chi Fraternity now stands. It burned and most of the children died. One girl named Mary still haunts the place and likes to play tricks on girls that come over to the Frat House.

The apparition of the small girl has been spotted in this frat house - but she is only seen on one side of it. "We call her Mary," President Mason Kuehl said. "I heard she wears a sun dress and a bonnet."

The finance junior said the lights in the house have flickered numerous times, and members have seen ghostly silhouettes. The ghost is just old folklore; the story has been around for a long time, he said. He said he has never had an encounter with it, and he's a very superstitious guy. "It scares me to death," he said. "I'm the type of person who doesn't walk underneath a ladder and turns the other way when he sees a black cat."

## **Arkansas Road-House**

This building that houses the Arkansas Road House was built in the 40's. The whole area around it was a ranch, and that's where the family lived that was murdered. The murders happened in the 60's or early 70's. There are two stories, the first being the family had a retarded son they kept in the cellar, but not abusively. He lived down there, had everything he need, bathroom, bed, television. There is a large walk in freezer down there too. Apparently he murdered his parents and kept the bodies in the freezer, and eventually died himself.

The second story is that the kid that lived there wasn't retarded, and after his parents died of natural causes he continued to live there. It's said he was a pedophile and a child murderer and would kill children and hide their bodies in the freezer. Right now it's zoned for commercial use, so companies keep buying the property with plans to level it and put a building there. About two or three weeks later, they'll sell it without explanation.

There is one report of a family who bought it and started to renovate it. New shingles, new windows, all the graphite on the outside was done, but about three weeks later, all work on the house stopped. Right now there is a fence around the property, and the road has been lowered, but you can still see it. It's said that if you go into the house mysterious people run out, weird noises are heard like footsteps, doors slamming, windows breaking though a later investigation will show that nothing was broken.

## Arlington High School Auditorium

A boy committed suicide in the drama room of the Arlington High School Auditorium and if you are alone in the room you can hear a boy's voice even though nobody is there. The voice is also heard in the backstage area of the stage you can hear him talk as if he is reciting something and than just stop. It is said that the boy that died, James was said to be his name, died as he was reciting a monologue. It is said that he just simply shot himself. It is said that if you do not leave him a seat on opening night to each play held in the auditorium it has been known for plays to go bad very quickly. The theatre crews always leave him a front row seat empty

## Cinemark Tinsel Town 9

Supposedly, during the construction of the Cinemark Tinseltown 9 Theater, a construction worker died while making the sixth theater. Customers say they have seen a chair move or actually see a guy sitting next to them when there wasn't anyone sitting thee before. Those who suddenly find themselves sitting beside this stranger say that he gets up, starts to walk away, and then disappears. Many employees have reported objects being moved when their back was turned and weird or banging sounds & the door shutting in the projection booth when there was nobody near the booth.

## Martin High School

Two years after Martin High School was built a boy who was in the theater department was dismissed from his duties on a play. The student felt that the punishment was unfair and he loved the theater program there so much that he hung himself from the catwalk. Another story says this student went naked to prom and as a punishment he was taken of the theater crew. Despondent at what he considered an unfair punishment he hung himself in the auditorium catwalk. It is said that if you go out on the catwalk alone you hear strange voices and footsteps along with winds that come from nowhere.

## Parklane Apartments

Residents at the Parkland Apartments have been hearing unexplained noises in the bedrooms, the sounds of babies crying, faucets turn on and off.

## River Legacy Park

Located just north of Arlington, River Legacy Parks is a 1300-acre string of parks located along the Trinity River. River Legacy Parks is an ongoing project aimed at turning the area along the Trinity River between Dallas and Arlington into public parks. River Legacy Parks is a great place to enjoy a number of recreational activities. Visitors come to the park to enjoy hiking, biking, jogging, walking, picnicking in the picnic areas, meditating in the meditation area, just relaxing or checking out River Legacy Parks many river overlooks, water fountains, playgrounds, and open areas. Currently, there are over eight miles of paved trails in the parks and an even greater number of unpaved trails. River Legacy Parks is made up of both wooded and prairie areas that are home to many species of wildlife and plant life. Many birding enthusiasts enjoy bird watching at River Legacy Parks.

Hikers have reported that if you are walking on a narrow path away from hell's gate you will come upon what was once a clearing. There have been numerous reports of moaning and several have sighted a red hair haired general clad in a Confederate uniform.

## River Legacy Park - Hells Gate

It is a long trail with swamps on either side and shaded over by large trees. At the end of the trail is a large mound of dirt and two fence posts that are all that is left of a very old gate. As it is said this was the trail walked by captured spies of the Union Army on their way to be hung. This gate, called Hell's Gate by most, was the last thing they saw before being led to the tree that stands beyond the gate where they died. Walking the trail one can still hear the sobs and whispered prayers of the men and some women who walked there last steps here.

## River Legacy Park - Screaming Bridge

One night after a high school football game a carload of kids were driving fast on a country road just outside of the park. Coming to a narrow bridge over the Trinity River they met their fate when they did not see another car coming from the other end of the bridge. The two cars hit head on. Both cars erupted into flames and plummeted into the river below. All involved were killed. Since then the road has been closed and can only be walked to through the park.

Legend has it that if you find the bridge you will see the dates of the occurrence and the names of the deceased glowing as tombstones in the water and if after that you still dare you can sit in the middle of the bridge on the night that it happened and at midnight you will witness a heavy fog coming up from the river as you see headlights approaching from either side of the bridge.

## River Legacy Park - The Hobo

Near the park are some railroad tracks that run through an area called Mosier Valley. The park is a good getting off place for the train hoppers since the train has to slow down here. One night an old hobo was staying in the park and was awoken by the sounds of screams. Wondering to the edge of the woods from where he had been sleeping he saw a car parked nearby and what appeared to be a man and a woman fighting inside the car. Walking closer he saw the man hit the woman and knock her unconscious.

Opening the door he grabbed the man but in the struggle that ensued was shot. The next day the woman was found wondering through the park delirious and half naked but the hobo lay dead next to where the car had been parked. However, lovers parked late at night still catch a glimpse of the old hobo. Legend has it that late at night if you are still in the park after closing you will hear a tap on your window and there will be an old man standing there dressed in rags.

## Six Flags Over Texas

In the Texas section of Six Flags Over Texas, next to the entrance of the "Texas Giant" is a yellow candy store. This building is the oldest building in the park and was once a private home. It was said that in the early 1900's a young girl (8 or so) who lived in the house drowned in nearby Johnson's Creek. She supposedly can be seen walking the railroad tracks or playing in what was once her room in the yellow house. Witnesses say that Annie enjoys turning the light on and off or opening the curtain and then closing it. Security guards at night also have problems locking the upstairs door because "ANNIE" feels playful.

## Bowie High School

It's rumored that a man was either killed during the building of Bowie High School or while he was a custodian there. Students have nicknamed him "Leonard." He lives on the catwalk in the auditorium, and has reportedly thrown small rocks onto the stage. Noises have been heard like machines going off in the shop room, and bells chiming on the catwalk. One student was spit on during a rehearsal for "Grease" in 2000. The left side of her face was wet, and no one was standing on that side of her.

## University of Texas at Arlington  - Theatre Arts Mainstage Theatre,

Dennis Maher, an associate professor, at the University of Texas at Arlington, Theater Arts Mainstage Theater said the apparitions are there because of the intense energy and emotion from performances[42]. "All theaters have ghosts," he said. "Most of them are attracted to the actors' emotions or are there to live out their greatest aspirations."

Maher said good spirits are in the theater studio's house left, the left wing of the stage from the audience's view, and on stage and usually show up at 10 or 11 p.m. But sometimes a poltergeist, which he said is a negative energy, will appear when a performance involves violence or religion. According to the Merriam Webster dictionary, a poltergeist is a noisy, usually mischievous ghost held to be responsible for unexplained noises, such as rappings.

---

[42] http://www.theshorthorn.com/archive/2002/fall/02-oct-31/sc103102-01.html

Many believe the ghosts are Charles Proctor, a theatre arts professor who died in 1993 and Richard Slaughter, a former theatre arts director whose memorial service was held in the theater.

## Berachah House

At the 700 block of East Mitchell Street, around the trees and through the fence, lies the Berachah Home and Cemetery, organized by the Rev. J.T. Upchurch. It holds up to 80 graves.

According to the Central Library's Web site, the home was originally established in 1894 in Waco, and nine years later a second site was opened in Arlington. It was the Berachah Industrial Home for the Redemption and Protection of Erring Girls, a safe haven for homeless girls and unwed mothers.

One of the first residents of the home was buried at the site in 1904, when it was erected. Many of the children and infants buried there died from measles epidemic in 1914. Most of the graves are unmarked, and others have only a first name or an infant number on them. In 1935, the home was shut down, but the site was used until 1942 as an orphanage run by Upchurch's daughter. Arlington State College, now UTA, purchased the land in 1963.

She's not a mean ghost. At the burial site, there is a headstone there marked "Mary," Kuehl said. "Mary's there," he said. "She may be trying to find a home." Maher agrees.

He said a little girl who haunts the Mainstage Theatre is from the grave site. He said she loves to dance around the theatre 'ghost light.' The bare bulb left on stage every night serves mainly as a source of protection, used so people can still see when all the stage lights are off. Theater lore says it is there to call to the ghosts that inhabit the theater.

"Apparently, she's quite taken with it," he said. "Several students have spotted her dancing around it after performances." The girl has been spotted wearing old-fashioned clothing and has blonde hair. She hasn't really been active since the headstones at the site were cleaned, he said[43].

## University of Texas at Arlington -Student Publications

Billy Smith II has seen a ghost at Student Publications. It was on a weekend about two and a half years ago, he said. The former Shorthorn photographer said he went in the UC's lower level to get film. When he was about to leave, he forgot to set the door alarm and had to go back down.

"I walked back down the stairs and saw something blue reflected in one of the windows," he said. "I walked around the corner and, by the advertising area, I saw a figure coming. We looked at each other." He said when she saw him, she fled the other way. She's not a mean ghost and was wearing a colonial-looking dress, he said.

---

[43] Ibid

"I never got the feeling that she was something to be afraid of," he said. "I told others at The Shorthorn, and they said they had seen the same thing."

Sports editor Jason Hoskins said he's had two encounters with the ghost. Different areas in the office are always chilled after hours, he said. He said the ghost appeared once on the security monitor, and she walked by the front reception area. Both times he saw her were in one night, he said. He didn't know if he was just tired or if he really did see it, he added. "Who knows what really happened?[44]"

## Amilio's Delicatessen.

Amilio's Delicatessen owner Amil Del Biaggo said several customers and employees in the past have claimed that they "know the house is haunted." He said he hasn't had any personal experiences with ghosts, and there hasn't been any recent talk. According to past customer accounts, a young girl who lived in the home in the late '20s hung herself there. Biaggo said he can definitely report he sometimes hears strange noises but never anything specifically. He said he believes it's all just a myth; the deli has been there for four years. He said people's minds may be playing with them. "Who knows what really happened?" he asked[45].

# ALTON, TEXAS

Alton, established by the state legislature on February 24, 1848, to replace Pinckneyville as county seat of Denton County, was less than a mile from the site of present-day Corinth in the east central part of the county. For three years the residence of W. C. Baines, the only person living in Alton, served as the legal center of the county.

On November 26, 1850, because of a lack of water at the original site, the state legislature chose a new site for the county seat, five miles south of the site of present-day Denton near Hickory Creek. This new site kept the name Alton. By 1855 at least two stores, a hotel, and a post office had been constructed there. In 1856, however, residents of the county demanded a new county seat. They argued that Alton was not in the center of the county, that the water from the standing pools in Hickory Creek had made a number of families ill, and that the development of the town had been unsatisfactory.

As a result of these complaints, in an election held in November 1856, Denton County voters accepted an offer from Hiram Cisco, William Loving, and William Woodruff to provide 100 acres of their property for a new county seat. This new site, near the center of the county, was named Denton. Soon after the establishment of the new county seat Alton disappeared.

---

[44] Ibid
[45] Ibid

### Alton Bus Crash

In September 1989 a school bus fell over the ledge of a caliche pit full of water. Twenty-one children drowned that day while struggling to get out of the bus. Now the pit is fenced in. People have claimed to hear the screams of the children coming from the pit. Though most of the locals figure it is the teens that hang around there, some people claim to have seen figures sitting on the ledge of the pit. If you should park and get out of your car in order to see everything up close, there is a definite sense of sorrow and gloom surrounding the area.

# AVINGER, TEXAS

Avinger is on the Louisiana and Arkansas railway at the junction of State highways 49 and 155, eight miles southeast of Hughes Springs in southwestern Cass County. Hickory Hill, a settlement that began in the early 1840s, was located a mile south of the site of Avinger. A post office was established there in 1848 with Thomas M. Kimball as postmaster, and at its height it had a school house, two or three churches, a store, a gravel yard, a tannery, and several residences. In 1876 the East Line and Red River Railroad was built through the area, and a station was located at the current site of Avinger. Gradually the businesses began to relocate, and when the post office was moved in 1877 it was renamed Avinger in honor of Dr. H. J. Avinger, who operated the first store at the new location.

The town became a shipping point for lumbermen and area farmers and by 1884 had two churches, a school, saw and grist mills, a gin, and a population of fifty. By 1892 the population had increased to 100, and by 1914 the town supported numerous businesses including a small bank and had an estimated population of 500.

### TJ's

The building that housed TJ's Kustom Kakes & Bakery was built by D. R. Coulter in 1928 for a drugstore. C. B. Templeton was the first proprietor. Other owners were A. V. Simpson, Joel Steed was manager and Earl Tate was the pharmacist for a few years. Tobe and Ruby Johnson were the next owners and then Tobe died in 1938 and Ruby, a pharmacist herself, operated the drugstore until 1948. Then, the drugstore was run by several others including Sam Connon, Jo Orr and Mr. and Mrs. Jessie Steward. The soda fountain was memorable.

When it ceased to be a drugstore, Charlie Powell bought the building for his tax office for himself and Mattie Jean Sharber. Mattie Jean sold the building to Herb Stark, Jr. who in turn sold it to Terry and Janice Lee who owned T J's Kustom Kakes & Bakery.  In 2004 they sold the building to Avinger Timber, LLC. The bakery has relocated just outside of town, but something from the past still occupies this old building. Witnesses have reported hearing strange sounds and seeing the lights turn on and off when no one is in the building. Most figure that these events are caused a ghost from the days this building served as a doctor's office or when it was a soda shop.

## BALCH SPRINGS, TEXAS

Balch Springs is on Interstate highways 635 and 20 and U.S. Highway 175 ten miles southeast of Dallas in Dallas County. It was founded around 1870, when the family of John Balch settled in the area and found three springs, one of which was never dry. The perennial spring was kept cleaned and bricked up and became a gathering place for families in the area to fill their buckets and talk. In 1900 the area had only a cemetery and scattered farms. Several years later a school was built and named after the springs.

### Dunston's Steak House

Many believe that Dunston's Steak House is haunted by the ghosts of not one but two men who died right after leaving the steakhouse. One was an older man who had a heart attack on his way home. The other died in a motorcycle accident when struck by a car as he was leaving the parking lot. Both apparently enjoyed the food so much, they decided to spend eternity here.

## BIG SANDY, TEXAS

Big Sandy, also known as Big Sandy Switch, at the junction of State Highway 155, U.S. Highway 80, and Farm Road 2911, fourteen miles southwest of Gilmer in extreme southwestern Upshur County, was established in the early 1870s. In 1873 the Texas and Pacific Railway was built through the area, and around 1880 the Tyler Tap, a narrow-gauge railroad, intersected the Texas and Pacific just south of Big Sandy Creek. A switch was constructed at the junction of the two railroads and came to be known as Big Sandy Switch, after the creek. By the early 1880s a small settlement, also known as Big Sandy Switch, began to grow up. A post office was established in 1875, and two merchants named Arenson and Yesner opened stores around the same time.

By 1885 the community, now known as Big Sandy, had several stores and saloons, Baptist and Methodist churches, a school, and an estimated population of 500. Several hotels and restaurants opened by 1900, and by the eve of World War I Big Sandy had two banks, a weekly newspaper named the Times, and a cotton market. The town's principal products included lumber, cotton, potatoes, and livestock. The community incorporated on June 21, 1926.

## Old Ambassador College

For many years Big Sandy, Texas was known as the location of the third campus of Ambassador College, a liberal arts institution which briefly became known as Ambassador University. It was sponsored by the Radio Church of God, which later became known as the Worldwide Church of God. Because of the size and location of the campus, the grounds were also used once a year in celebration of the Feast of Tabernacles which attracted hundreds of church members to the area. The economic impact was considerable. While some members camped on the grounds, other members booked into local motels and became patrons of local restaurants and other facilities in the area.

Many have reported feeling negative presences around isolated parts of the campus especially around the library & the guys' dorms. Campers who tried to stay the first couple of nights in either of these locations claimed that they had the feeling that someone or something was grabbing at their throat and brushing up against them.

# BRIDGEPORT, TEXAS

In 1860, Colonel W.H. Hunt and Associates built a toll bridge spanning the Trinity River, mainly for the Butterfield Stagecoach. Thirteen years later a post office was established near the toll bridge giving birth to the town of Bridgeport.

## Hells Gates

Locals tell of a brooding presence is always felt in this area and the surrounding area is always cold. Some witnesses have reported seeing a black figure of a 4 foot tall man with glowing red eyes in the area called Hells Gate.

There is an old wooden bridge which is about 30-40 ft. long. According to one witness, around midnight to 1 in the morning the witness and some companions walked across the bridge[46] and went up a small foothill covered with tree branches and finally arrived at a  dirt road covered by tall grass about 10-12 ft. high on each side. At the time it was very warm. After they had walked about 30 feet, they were past the tall grass. As they walked further down the road it got colder and colder and they could sense a presence. One of them looked to the right toward an open field just in front of a wooded area and saw a small black figure in the shape of a man about 4 ft. tall with glowing red eyes.

---

[46] Local legend says that if you have crossed the bridge you have just gone through hell's gates and entered the demons domain.

As they walked further down the road it became clear that he was pacing them from a distance. Once they got gone a good distance the bridge they came upon a log blocking the road. The log was very long and covered the entire road. Even with 10-12 people it was much too heavy to move. (Keep in mind that it was cold enough to wear a heavy jacket at this point, but the strange thing is it was the middle of the summer in Texas) so we left it there. A couple of the group decided to walk back to the bridge and the others wanted to keep walking. So the two turned around and starting heading back for the bridge.

At that point the two walking back toward the car noticed that the black figure was not following them. They started running, but the figure kept up with us the entire time. As soon as we got to the tall grass it was gone.

The two went on to the bridge and waited for the others. After about 45 minutes they returned and the group decided to leave. They got in their cars and went driving around the area. They turned down this road and that road and then they turned down the same road they had been were walking on. They reached the point where the log was across the road but to their surprise, found that it was gone. After that we drove back to the bridge and got out to talk about the missing log. Finally they decided to go back to the area where they had seen the log, but when they arrived, they were surprised to see that the log was back across the road. Not really knowing what to do, they drove back to the bridge area and discussed the matter. It was decided that one of the vehicles that had a wench would be used to tow the log out of the road. However, when they returned to the spot, the log was gone again. Taking the opportunity, they left the area quickly.

## BURKBURNETT, TEXAS

BurkBurnett was named after Samuel Burk Burnett who owned the 6666 Ranch. Teddy Roosevelt was a guest of Burnett on a 1904 wolf hunt and pulled some strings with the P.O. Department in naming the town. The discovery of oil in 1918 changed the town into one of the more famous oil boomtowns in Texas. 20 Trains a day ran between Burkburnett and Wichita Falls.

### Goat Man's Bridge

Gilbert's Creek has a bridge out past the golf course between Burk and Sheppard Air Force Base. Teens used to party down there all the time. It was nicknamed Goat Man's Bridge. There was a man who was man from head to waist and goat from waist down. People say if it's really quite you can hear him. And if you park your car in the middle of the bridge it will not start. They say you can hear children screaming. A friend of mine said he was out there alone one night and he saw someone standing by a tree. He threw his pocketknife at the man and it went right though him and stuck in the tree. I have also heard that a few miles back behind the bridge is a church. Not just any church but, a satanic church. A lot of strange things happened out at that bridge. If you're from Burk and want to go out there ask anyone from Burk they can tell you right where it is. But, don't go alone!

# CARROLLTON, TEXAS

Carrollton is on Interstate Highway 35 East fourteen miles north of downtown Dallas in Dallas, Denton, and Collin counties. The site was in the Peters colony grant. The first settlers in the area were William and Mary Larner, who came in 1842. The A. W. Perry family followed two years later and claimed their headright in the Trinity Mills area. In partnership with Wade H. Witt, Perry established a mill there. Over time he acquired extensive landholdings, which probably included the site of Carrollton. Many early settlers were related by blood or marriage. In the northeastern area of settlement, which extended into Denton County, was the English colony, where many of the large landowners, including the Jackson, Furneaux, Morgan, and Rowe families, were English immigrants. It is most likely that the settlement was named for Carrollton, Illinois, the hometown of many of the early settlers.

## Newman Smith High School

Abigail was a dependable worker in the theater department of Newman Smith High School. She reportedly died while storing boxes under the stage. Now she is sometimes seen on the catwalk high above the stage, and playing with the gels on the spots. Students need to hit the stage with a hammer three times to keep her from interfering with a show. It has been reported that sometimes, when reviewing a tape of a show, they can spot her standing in the set's shadows.

## DeWitt Perry Homestead

The Dewitt Perry Homestead is abandoned now, but local rumors say that the ones who lived there may be still around. There have been a lot of unusual happenings in the area. On different nights, the nearby railroad crossing lights will flash, but no trains would be there.

# CASON, TEXAS

Cason is on State Highway 11 and the Louisiana and Arkansas Railway, five miles west of Daingerfield in southwestern Morris County. The town grew up around a station on the East Line and Red River Railroad, which was constructed through western Morris County in the late 1870s. Many of the early businesses were transferred from Snow Hill, three miles north. When the post office, which had been in Snow Hill, was moved in 1878, the postmaster, William M. Cason, named the new town Cason in honor of his father, J. W.

By 1884 the settlement had an estimated population of 200, a church, a district school, and businesses that included sawmills and gristmills and two cotton gins. By 1892 the population had grown to 250, and a bedspring factory was in operation. The town reached its peak in the late 1920s, when the population was estimated at 500. The population declined between World War II and 1972, when a population of 160 and five rated businesses were reported. In 1986 the population was estimated at 165, and Cason had four rated businesses. In 1990 the population was 173.

## Slaton Cemetery- Blue Light Cemetery

The stories about the Slaton Cemetery are due to the various occurrences experienced by locals such as a young couple went to the cemetery to make-out one night , and were found several days later laid against a tombstone with their faces frozen in fear. It is said that if you go into the cemetery after dark, you will see a blue light floating around the cemetery. If you go in the middle of summer, you will reach places in the cemetery that are ice cold, also there are bushes planted inside that if stood in front of on a still day, one side of the bush will be moving as though being struck by a tornado. One report is of a man in his car actually being pulled inside the cemetery with his car not going into any gear but drive while something outside was calling his name repeatedly.

# CEDAR HILL, TEXAS

Cedar Hill is the oldest organized community in Dallas County and was once the temporary county seat. Located along the Old Chisholm Trail, the town was one of the first in north central Texas to be serviced by railroad. The city became a center of commercial activity for early settlers, cowboys, and nearby farming households.

Settlement began in 1841 when the Congress of the Republic of Texas authorized W.S. Peters to locate colonists in the north central part of the Republic. In 1845, new settlers from Illinois came to Peters' Colony and settled in southwest Dallas County. This area provided the settlers with cooler temperatures than neighboring Dallas as it was the highest point between the Red River and the Gulf Coast. Because of the elevation and nearby cedar brakes, the settlers named the area Cedar Hill.

In 1847 one of the first wagon trains to the Cedar Hill area brought Milton Merrifield and his five married sons and their families. They bought land from the Trinity River to Beltline Road. The earliest recorded land grant in this area is by the then Governor of Texas, E.M. Pease to E.C. Thomas to Milton Merrifield.

On October 5, 1854 Milton Merrifield and his wife, Margaret, donated 2 acres (situated north of Beltline Road on Old Cedar Hill Road) for the Cedar Mountain Church house of worship. There were five graves there, believed to be of the Hart Family. In 1856 a tornado destroyed the community, leaving only 2 houses. The Merrifield family moved into a log cabin on the Castleman property until their house was built. Other early wagon trains brought the families of Hart, Penn, Rape, Anderson, Stewart and White.

## Hangar Lowe Rd.

On the Hangar Lowe Road there is the ghost of a jogger that was run over by a hit and run driver. Today, he shows up every now and then on the side of the road, just laying there. When someone tries to call help for him, he disappears.

## Witch Mountain

It is said that there is a hill that is visible on some nights. On the crest of this hill you can see a lit up cabin, but when you try to drive to it you cannot find it anywhere. In the late 1800's there was a woman that was said to be a witch that lived there and it is said that her ghost is still there trying to attract people so she won't have to be lonely.

# CELBURNE, TEXAS

Cleburne, the county seat of Johnson County, is on U.S. Highway 67 thirty miles south of Fort Worth. Its origin and growth can be attributed to its role as a crossroads and transportation center. The site was near the earliest Johnson County road, an old wagon trail that was used by soldiers traveling from Fort Belknap to Fort Graham. The location had an excellent water source on West Buffalo Creek that attracted travelers, including cattlemen from the nearby Chisholm Trail. During the Civil War the site was used as a bivouac for Johnson County units marching off to war.

This temporary facility, known as Camp Henderson, became a permanent settlement on March 23, 1867, when it became necessary to choose a new, centrally located county seat to replace Buchanan. The town was named in honor of Gen. Patrick R. Cleburne, under whom many of the men had fought during the Civil War.

## 1896 Railroad House Hotel

The 1896 Railroad House Hotel at 421 E Henderson St has a long history. The Railroad House is a former Railroad Hotel with a clear view of active railroad with BSNF and Amtrak trains. One bedroom, dining room and deck faces track. Amtrak stop within several yards." "Historical railroad district is being established in this area. The former Santa Fe maintenance yard is only a few blocks of B&B."

The owners as well as the guests have reported hearing footsteps early in the morning moving about the house.

## Wright Place

The Wright Place is a two story building that has a restaurant that has music on the weekends occupying the first floor. According to legend, the second floor of the Wright Place is haunted by a young woman who is always spotted near the window. Whenever she is seen, the smell of oranges is reported by many. The woman, who was supposedly pushed out of the window by an angry boyfriend, has been spotted by many visitors.

## Old Foamy

When you go to this little water stream you go at night turn off your headlights and honk three times. Then a goat man will appear in front of you. Others say strange things happen to your car.

# COMMERCE, TEXAS

Commerce is at the juncture of State highways 50, 11, 24, and 224, fifteen miles from Greenville in northeastern Hunt County. It owes its origins to William Jernigin, a pioneer merchant in partnership with Josiah Hart Jackson in nearby Cow Hill, who in 1872 opened a mercantile store on the site of the northwest corner of the present town square to take advantage of a new trade route that developed with the building of a new bridge on the South Sulphur River. The community grew up around Jernigin's store and apparently received its name on one of Jernigin's business trips to Jefferson. Jernigin had his merchandise sent to "commerce," since his small community did not have a name. In 1885, the year of incorporation, Commerce had twelve businesses in addition to a hotel and livery stable, a wood shop and wagon factory, and a steam mill and gin, as well as a church and school. In 1887 the St. Louis Southwestern Railway (the Cotton Belt) connected Commerce with Texarkana, Sherman, and Fort Worth. During the 1890s Commerce gained additional rail outlets to Ennis and Paris with the arrival of the Texas Midland Railroad. Commerce has been a college town since 1894, when William L. Mayo moved his East Texas Normal College from Cooper to Commerce to benefit from the rail connections and to collect a $1,000 bonus offered by the community.

## Texas A&M University - Hubbell Hall

The male residence hall Hubbell Hall is haunted on the third floor. An older ghostly woman has been seen numerous times in the northwest lobby of the third floor. The ghost is believed to be Julia B. Hubbell the woman the dorm is named after. Hubbell Hall was once a female dormitory when it was East Texas State College.

# COPPELL, TEXAS

Coppell is on Interstate Highway 635, U.S. Highway 121, Interstate Highway 35, the Elm Fork of the Trinity River, and the St. Louis Southwestern Railway, seven miles from Farmers Branch in the extreme northwest corner of

Dallas County. The community is bordered by Irving, Grapevine, and Carrollton and is northeast of Dallas-Fort Worth International Airport. Grapevine Creek, Denton Creek, and Cottonwood Branch flow through the city. The area was on the original land grant of J. A. Simmonds. President Sam Houston and Republic of Texas troops camped on Grapevine Creek during negotiations with area Indian tribes in an effort to enlist their aid in defending the republic against attacks by Mexican troops in 1843.

The site was first settled in the mid-1800s by James Parish, from Goliad. In 1887 the community secured a post office. It was originally named Gibbs Station, after Texas lieutenant governor Barnett Gibbs, a large landowner in the area. In 1888 construction of the St. Louis, Arkansas and Texas Railway through the town was completed. In 1892 the post office was renamed Coppell, in honor of a railroad employee and pioneer settler of the region, George A. Coppell. In 1914 the settlement had two churches, two general stores, two blacksmiths, a bank, a hardware store, telephone service, a population of 450, and dealers in poultry, livestock, and lumber. However, by 1926 the population had decreased to 200, where it remained for three decades.

## Bethel Cemetery

Bethel Cemetery is a historical cemetery established in 1853. The location is just east of Moore Road just north of Beltline. There is a grave that was supposed to be haunted. It is marked with odd symbols. Apparently, the gravesite does not like its picture being taken because more than one photographer has clicked off a roll of Polaroid instant film with every picture of the headstone overexposed. However, any picture taken of anything in the area except the headstone always comes out perfectly.

# CORSICANA, TEXAS

Corsicana was established in 1849, but had very little growth until an early boom touched off in 1894 when the city was drilling for water and accidentally struck oil. One of Texas' first refineries built here in 1897. The city was the first in state to use natural gas for fuel and lighting, and crude oil for locomotive fuel.

## Navarro County Courthouse

There have long been stories of ghosts being heard on the stairs between the 2nd and 3rd floors of the historic Navarro County Courthouse. It is not uncommon for late night users of the law library or persons in the Courthouse to have heard footsteps descending from the third and second floors. Others have reported seeing figures moving about the District Clerk's Office after hours. The primary ghost is believed to be the ghost of the old District Clerk who was shot by the County Sheriff after a political dispute on the Court House steps.

## Emhouse School

The Emhouse School is an old school house that was closed in the early 1950's. It is a small two story building located in the little community of Emhouse, outside of Corsicana. Witnesses have seen lights come on inside building and then turn off. However, the building has no electricity. Others have seen apparitions moving about inside the building. All the desks, chalkboards, chalk, and pencils where left in the school from when it closed. Even the shower curtains from the showers are said to still be there.

## Old Navarro Regional Hospital

The old Navarro Regional Hospital building is now torn down, but it is said that the area where the building once stood is extremely haunted because of the many lives that were lost there. There are a number of witnesses who maintain that you can still hear voices and other hospital noises if you sit quietly, close your eyes, and listen for a while.

# DEKALB, TEXAS

DeKalb is on the Missouri Pacific Railroad and U.S. Highway 82 twelve miles northwest of New Boston in western Bowie County. It was one of the earliest settlements in the county. According to some county histories a community had begun to take shape in the winter of 1835, when David Crockett visited the site on his way to the Alamo. These sources claim that when Crockett enquired about the name of the town, residents told him it had none and then asked him to name it. He suggested the name of the Prussian Baron de Kalb, a general of the American revolutionary army.

## Crybaby Creek

It is said that on a clear night you can drive to a bridge located outside this small town and hear the screams of an infant that seems to come from every direction. The story states that a mother and her baby had a horrible accident at the bridge and the infant drowned in the near freezing waters. This child's ghost still haunts this spot.

# DENTON, TEXAS

Denton, the county seat of Denton County, is on Interstate Highway 35 where it forks to become 35E to Dallas and 35W to Fort Worth near the center of the county. Less than forty miles north of the cities, Denton has become closely associated with the Dallas-Fort Worth metropolitan area. The city was not an early settlement. It was founded in 1857 in order to become the county seat, because residents wanted one located near the center of the county. Hiram Cisco, William Woodruff, and William Loving donated 100 acres as the site for the town, which, like the county, was named in honor of John B. Denton. A commission composed of Otis G. Welch, sometimes known as the "Father of Denton," county surveyor Charles C. Lacy, and Joseph A. Carroll laid out the city. Although it was established in 1857 and a courthouse was built on the north side of the square, Denton was not incorporated until 1866. The charter provided for election of a mayor and five aldermen. J. B. Sawyer was elected the first mayor.

## Argyle Bridge

Strange lanterns and partially seen figures have been reported around old Argyle Bridge. Some witnesses have reported that their non-power locking car doors locked and unlocked by themselves as they drove near the bridge. There have also been a number of mysterious break-downs reported.

## The Old Hospital

For some reason, it seems that most hospitals have one or more ghosts. This is especially true at the old hospital site in Denton. The hospital is now closed and the building abandoned, but it has quite a history. There was a very pretty nurse that worked at this hospital known as "Betty". Betty died after a botched abortion to terminate a pregnancy caused by a fling with a prominent married doctor.

After the area was annexed to inpatient facilities, patients would often see Betty attending to them. Sometimes night duty nurses would hear something unusual coming from a patient's room and they would investigate only to find no cause for the sound. However, in each case, they would find that the patient was having a life-threatening medical crisis but had been unable to reach the call bell. Older nursing staff who knew Betty in life recognized her apparition on sight.

## University of North Texas – Bruce Hall

The apparition of a young woman has been spotted in Bruce Hall. According to legend, her name was Wanda, and she was a student at the University living in Bruce Hall. It is reported that she became pregnant during the fall semester. Unmarried, she was too ashamed and too scared to tell her parents so she hid in the attic of the building to try and wait out Christmas break. Depressed, Wanda decided to try and abort the baby herself. She died alone as a result of internal bleeding and wasn't found until the school was opened up three weeks later. Students attempting a séance in the attic area reported an unusual power outage and cold spots. Crying is often heard from the attic, and a woman wearing clothing from the 1930's or 40's has been spotted wandering the halls late at night.

Other major points of haunting are said to be in the disused elevator shaft. This shaft was used on multiple occasions by students for elevator surfing, until some were killed doing it. The bottom floor entrance to the elevator is opened every Halloween for the haunted house and each year bizarre happenings have occurred in the area, i.e., cabinets and shelving collapsing and nearly hitting people. The basement itself always fills people with dread. Also as a note, Halloween (beyond the usual pranks) has many incidents of strange phenomena in this building. For example, the power always turns off at midnight (for whatever reason) and the security lights activate. However, the security lights would blink at different rhythms, even though they were on the same circuit.

## The University of North Texas - Union Suite 324

The CSRR and SLA offices of the university have wandering ghosts. Those who have extra work to do and stay after hours report hearing the fax machine turn on and off. This ghost is "nicknamed" Brandy and likes to lock employees in copy rooms and offices, run blank pages through the copier, and turn off and then reboot computers.

# DUNCANVILLE, TEXAS

Duncanville is west of the intersection of Interstate Highway 20 and U.S. Highway 67 in southwestern Dallas County. The land on which the city lies originally belonged to the Peters Colony. Settlement began when Crawford Trees arrived from Illinois in 1845 and purchased several thousand acres south of Camp Dallas. Trees donated land in 1855 for the Little Bethel Male and Female School, which also served as a church building until 1881, when citizens constructed the Union Hall House. In 1880 the Chicago, Texas and Mexican Central Railway reached the area and built Duncan Switch, named for a line foreman. Charles P. Nance, the community's first postmaster, renamed the settlement Duncanville in 1882. The Gulf, Colorado and Santa Fe acquired the railroad in 1883 and erected telegraph poles and lines. Though a fire in 1884 destroyed most of the community's commercial buildings, by the late 1800s dry goods stores, a pharmacy, a domino parlor, and a school existed in Duncanville.

## 9th Grade School

Duncanville has long been known for its quality education system which consists of seven elementary schools, three intermediate schools, two junior highs, a ninth grade campus and a high school. This particular haunting takes place on the campus of the 9th Grade School. It is reported that in 1993, a teacher was murdered on campus and now this teacher has been spotted in the girls' locker room, usually after volleyball games.

# ENNIS, TEXAS

Ennis is on the Southern Pacific Railroad and at the intersection of Interstate Highway 45, State highways 34, 75, and 287, and Farm roads 85, 879, 1183, 1722, and 3413, fourteen miles southeast of Waxahachie in southeastern Ellis County. Bardwell Lake, a popular recreational area, is less than a mile south of the city limits. The Houston and Texas Central Railway reached the area in 1871, and the community established there was named for an early railroad official, Col. Cornelius Ennis. The David Rose survey of 300 acres and the W. H. Bundy survey of 347 acres were purchased by the trustees of a land company in 1872. Capt. W. G. Veale selected the townsite in May, and Theo Kosse mapped it in August and laid out the streets and alleys. The first train ran through the community that year, on its way from Corsicana to Dallas. Citizens of Burnham, a small town to the south, responded violently to being bypassed and attacked the new community, killing one man and wounding several.

## The Raphael House

The Raphael House, 500 W. Ennis Avenue, is located in the historic Templeton McCanless District. Witnesses are adamant that this historic old home is haunted. There are many stories of self-closing doors and windows, ghost steps upstairs, disappearing objects, as well as rumpled bed sheets. There have been a number of apparitions seen that are blamed on a pair of spirits named Raymond and Julia.

# EULESS, TEXAS

Texans are proud of their heritage and the citizens of Euless are especially proud of their founding fathers. In 1867, Elisha Adam Euless moved from Tennessee to Texas and purchased 170 acres on the present intersection of North Main Street and West Euless Boulevard. He had a cotton gin and a community center located on his property and became a very prominent figure among other settlers. The community eventually grew around his land and settlers decided to name the city, Euless, after this successful farmer and businessman. Euless has since grown from a population of 25 in 1915 to a population of 45,500 in 2000. As Euless continues to grow, City officials have strived to preserve its historical significance by restoring the Fuller House, the first brick house in Euless as a museum, obtaining a historical marker for Elisha Adam Euless from the Texas State Historical Commission and restoring the Himes Log Cabin, which dates from the 1850's.

## Midway Recreation Center

At night people have reported a strange spirit moving around inside the Midway Recreation Center turning on lights and working out to rap music. There are a number of witnesses who maintain that the grunts of his workout can be heard from inside the buildings. Some of the janitors say it looks like one of their old co-workers who had died a couple of years ago

## The Old Nursing Home

Back behind the new nursing home, and the drive through pharmacy, right off of Industrial Blvd. (Hwy 157), there exists an old nursing home in which all of the patients and doctors just up and left one night for unknown reasons. The halls are littered with the wheel chairs and medical supplies of the former residents. It is said that the moans of the elderly patients can be heard up and down the halls and if you can find the dining hall, a table stands in the center of the room stained with blood and the stench of something rotting lingers in the air.

# FARMERS BRANCH, TEXAS

Farmers Branch, located just 15 minutes from DFW International Airport, is the oldest continuous settlement in Dallas County. Although Farmers Branch has a population of 26,900 residents within its 12 square miles, its daytime population is 85,000. The cities of Farmers Branch, Addison, and Carrollton are often referred to collectively as the Metrocrest.

Farmers Branch is on Interstate Highway 35 and State Highway 77 twelve miles north of downtown Dallas in northwestern Dallas County. The Burlington Northern and Missouri, Kansas and Texas railroads serve the city. Farmers Branch was the location in 1845 of the first office of the Texan Land and Emigration Company, or the Peters colony. It was the most well-known Dallas County town during the 1840s because of its advertising throughout Europe and the United States. Thomas Keenan, Isaac B. Webb, and William Cochran all arrived in 1842 and received original land grants in the area that became the site of Farmers Branch. By 1843 settlers had established a community called Mustang Branch, named for the Mustang grapes that grew along the creek. Cochran later changed the name to Farmers Branch because of the area's rich farmland.

### Manske Library

The Manske Library is located at 13613 Webb Chapel on the corner of Webb Chapel and Golfing Green. The library is said to be haunted by a ghost that is believed to be either that of a construction worker who was killed during the renovation of the library in the 80s or it is an Indian from the Indian burial ground it is rumored to be built on. The most recent sighting was last year when a young man (who did not know the library was supposed to be haunted) reported seeing the figure of a man with red eyes pass into a wall.

# FILES VALLEY, TEXAS

Files Valley, or Files, was on Farm Road 66 and Valley Branch fourteen miles northeast of Hillsboro in northeastern Hill County. Originally the community was called Eureka Valley, but it was renamed on November 19, 1879, for David Sidney Files, who built the first house at the site in 1846. Many artesian wells in the area supplied soft but slightly sulfurous water. The community received a post office with the name Files in 1880 and by 1890 had a population of fifty, a church, a district school, a general store, a steam cotton gin, blacksmiths, carpenters, and physicians. In 1905 the school had sixty-one pupils.

The railroads bypassed the community, however. In 1906 the Southwestern Home and School for Orphans was founded in Files. It remained into the 1980s, when it was known as the Presbyterian Children's Home. In 1907 the post office was withdrawn from the community. In the 1930s Files had a population of 100 and three businesses. The population remained at this level until the 1970s, when it dropped to fifty and no businesses remained. Afterward the community has been called Files Valley rather than Files. In 1990 Files Valley remained on maps as a community, and the population was still fifty. A cemetery, a church, and the Presbyterian Children's Home remained there.

## Goat Man Tunnel

There is a tunnel located outside of town that has a very bizarre reputation. Most people called it Goat Man Tunnel. Witnesses have reported hearing unexplained footsteps, the sounds of women screaming in terror, seeing odd lights, and finding stains where blood has dripped from the top of tunnel.

# FORT HOOD, TEXAS

Fort Hood is located in southwestern Bell and southeastern Coryell counties in Central Texas. Most of the 218,000 acres owned by the United States Army is located in Coryell County. On January 14, 1942, at the beginning of United States involvement in World War II, it was announced that a tank destroyer tactical and firing center would be established near Killeen, Texas. Gen. Andrew D. Bruce was selected as the first commander. The first major unit, the 893d Tank Destroyer Battalion, arrived from Fort Meade, Maryland, on April 2, 1942. As other troops began arriving, some 300 farming and ranching families were required, on very short notice, to give up their land. Camp Hood was officially opened on September 18, 1942, and has been continuously used for armored training ever since. The installation was named in honor of Gen. John Bell Hood. The mission at Camp Hood was almost immediately expanded to include a replacement and basic training center at North Fort Hood. At times as many as 100,000 soldiers were being trained for the war effort. During the later part of the war some 4,000 German prisoners of war were interned at Camp Hood.

## Fort Hood - BLORA

A number of witnesses have reported seeing a soldier in military style PT uniform. This figure appears in the early morning hours, skipping rocks across the lake. He seems to take no notice of anyone else, and slowly fades away and finally disappears when the sun starts to rise over the horizon.

## **Fort Hood - III Corps Headquarters Building**

Personnel working security late at night in and around the III Corps Headquarters Building have reported hearing footsteps and hearing the sounds of doors opening and closing when no one is in the building.

## **Camp Hood**

Unidentified little white or green lights were seen here near Killeen Base (apparently some section of Camp Hood). This alarmed the base commander, who stated that this was not due to natural causes. These sightings took place from March to perhaps December 1948.

# **GARLAND, TEXAS**

Garland is on State highways 66 and 78 and the Missouri Pacific and Atchison, Topeka and Santa Fe railroads, fifteen miles northeast of downtown Dallas in northeastern Dallas County. Duck Creek runs through the city, and Lake Ray Hubbard lies on its eastern border. Garland was named for President Grover Cleveland's attorney general, Augustus H. Garland, in 1887, when a new post office was established between the two communities of Duck Creek and Embree. Duck Creek was a station on the Missouri, Kansas and Texas Railroad, and Embree was a station on the Atchison, Topeka and Santa Fe. They had fought over the post office for several years, but in 1887 Congressman Joseph Abbott solved the problem by submitting a bill to Congress to move the post office to a place between the two towns; the new site was called Garland.

## **Smiley's Grave**

Smiley's Grave is located off Hwy 66 at Centerville. According to one legend, Smiley was killed in a shootout nearby and walks the cemetery at night. Another legend has it that he and his entire family were killed by a tornado. That would explain the matching dates of death. Others say that he slaughtered his entire family and then killed himself.

## **Lakeview High School**

Ever since it was opened in the 1970's, Lakeview High School was always considered the "bad" school. Over the years it was given the name of "Suicide High" because sometime in the late 70's a boy shot himself in the bathroom. Later on in the 80's a girl broke the bathroom mirror and used the shards to slit her throat, two girls found her lying in a pool of blood on the tile floor. To this day there are still no mirrors in the girls' bathrooms. Later, another girl and a boy also killed themselves in the school. It has been reported that many students that attended Lakeview in the mid 90's committed suicide. In the bathrooms, sometimes you can hear footsteps when nobody else is in there. There are no windows in the school, which may be one reason that some students feel that make rooms so cold. There are cold spots in some places, and you can hear voices too.

# GILMER, TEXAS

Gilmer, the county seat of Upshur County, is on U.S. Highway 271 and State highways 155 and 154 thirty-five miles northeast of Tyler and twenty-two northwest of Longview in the central part of the county. When the county was established in 1846, provision required that the county seat be located within five miles of the geographic center and that it be called Gilmer, for Thomas W. Gilmer, who died during the test firing of a new cannon on the USS Princeton on February 28, 1844. The same explosion also killed United States secretary of state Abel P. Upshur.

On December 15, 1846, when the fifth district court first met in Upshur County, Judge Oran M. Roberts held court in a grove of six oak trees at the residence of William H. Hart and declared that site the location of Gilmer until a more permanent location could be selected. The Gilmer post office opened in 1847. In 1848 county voters selected the permanent site. The original site came to be called Old Gilmer and was gradually abandoned; a historic marker on the Cherokee Trace three miles north of Gilmer marks the original site. Bethesda Masonic Lodge No. 142 received a charter in 1853 and sponsored the Gilmer Masonic Male Academy (1854). In 1861 the lodge rented the school building to Morgan H. Looney, who established Looney School; from 1868 to 1871 O. M. Roberts taught there. In 1860 Gilmer had twenty-five businesses, seven physicians, six law offices, two churches (Methodist and Baptist), two academies, and the post office. During the Civil War Gilmer businesses provided hats and leather goods to the Confederate States of America. Shortly after the war ended, members of the Ku Klux Klan beat up Meshack Roberts, a former slave of O. B. Roberts, who had helped him to become a landowner.

## Cherokee Trace

At different locations an unexplained fog will rise up on the Cherokee Trace road, thick enough that you have to slow down. Barely seen though the thick fog are figures of people moving about including a woman and several small children have been seen crossing the road.

# GRANBURY, TEXAS

Granbury, county seat of Hood County, lies thirty-six miles southwest of Fort Worth on the shore of Lake Granbury on U.S. Highway 377. In 1854 "Uncle Tommy" Lambert and Amon Bond led a group of emigrants, mostly from Tennessee, across the Brazos River to the west bank into traditional Indian Territory. That same year, Elizabeth Crockett brought her family from Tennessee to settle on a league of land awarded by the Republic of Texas to heirs of men who fought in the Texas Revolution in 1836. In 1866 brothers J. and J. H. Nutt donated forty acres of riverfront property to form a new townsite, and Hood County was carved out of Johnson and Erath counties and named in honor of Gen. John Bell Hood. The new town was named for Gen. Hiram Bronson Granbury, who led Confederate troops from this area into battle during the Civil War. Three spirited elections were needed to make Granbury the county seat, instead of the older Glen Rose and Fort Spunky further south. The first two courthouses burned, the second one in 1875, at which time Somervell County was demarcated out of Hood County. Granbury's new three-story courthouse was built of Brazos limestone and had a lighted clock tower.

## Granbury High School

Granbury High School, 2000 W Pearl St, is rumored to be haunted. According to the story, a janitor fell from the roof and died. Since that time, he has been seen by other janitors, sweeping the floor and going about his regular duties.

## Opera House

Carpetbaggers coming in after the Civil War made a law that a county seat had to sell liquor, and before long, Granbury had six saloons and seven bawdy houses. The same year, 1886, the theatre opened as the Kerr Opera House on the second floor of the building it occupies today. It began as a stage for touring groups.

It is rumored that prevailing history errs about John Wilkes Booth being chased down and shot to death after assassinating President Lincoln. Evidence suggests he may have come to Granbury as John St. Helen, and if so, he performed Shakespeare in the Opera House. Various people working at the Opera House swear there is a resident ghost, and Ms. Van Kleek said, "You can hear footsteps pacing in the balcony. Those who have seen him say he wears a white shirt, dark pants, and tall, heavy boots.[47]"

## Driftwood Theatre 6

In Driftwood Theatre 6 staff members can hear children playing after closing. Witnesses say that these children run up and down the aisles laughing and talking. Also there have been occasions where people have seen a woman in a white dress walking through that particular theatre as well as in the projection booth and offices upstairs. Employees get a creepy feeling going in that theatre because of this. Some say that things get moved and doors open and close by themselves. No one has come up with an explanation for why only this particular theater is haunted as of yet.

---

[47] http://www.texasescapes.com/TexasTheaters/Granbury-Opera-House.htm.

## Camp El Tesoro

Camp El Tesoro is Camp Fire USA First Texas Council's co-ed resident camp and has been in operation since 1934. El Tesoro (meaning "The Treasure") is a 228-acre site in the beautiful Cordova Bend of the Brazos River, an area rich in legends and history and is located near Granbury, Texas approximately 45 minutes from downtown Fort Worth.

The campers and counselors say that the camp is haunted by the spirits of Indians. Many campers and counselors have seen visions of Indians walking about the camp grounds, crying out in grief, and riding about on horses at night. Witnesses report, "We saw an Indian in full headdress sitting on a white horse...we all saw it."

# GRAND PRAIRIE, TEXAS

Incorporated as "Grand Prairie" in 1909, the community was first recognized as Dechman in 1863. From his home in Birdville, Texas, Alexander McRae Dechman learned he could trade his oxen and wagons for land in Dallas County. In 1863, he bought 2391/2 acres on the east side of the Trinity River and 100 acres of timber land on the west side of the river for a broken down wagon, oxen team and $200 in Confederate money. He tried to establish a home on the property, but ran into difficulties, so returned his family to Birdville before joining the Civil War. In 1876 he filed a town plat consisting of 50 acres with Dallas County.

In 1876, Dechman traded half his "prairie" property to T&P Railroad to ensure the railroad came through the town. The railroad named the depot "Dechman" prompting its namesake to relocate his home from Bryan to Dechman. His son Alexander had been living in Dechman and operating a trading post and farm.

The post office was opened in 1877 under the name "Deckman" rather than "Dechman" because the U.S. Post Office couldn't read the writing on the form completed to open the post office. The name of the town changed to Grand Prairie later in 1877. Dechman sold the remainder of his Grand Prairie land in 1890 and apparently moved to Waxahachie. He is buried in historic Greenwood Cemetery in Dallas.

## Confederate Graveyard (near Joe pool lake)

This old Confederate Graveyard has a sign that says - 'posted - no trespassing' - and a local man does own this land, and lives very deep into the graveyard, but he probably wont see you, regardless. This graveyard is said to be a burial ground for dead soldiers from the civil war. If you go there late at night/early morning (from midnight to about 3 am) you will see a red light down the road in the darkness, but when you get closer to it the light goes away. When you go in the graveyard you will hear voices, feel random wind gusts, cold spots, and hear gunshots in the distance as well as screaming men.

It has been reported that a couple of teenagers who went to the graveyard came back to the car, to find all the doors unlocked even though they made sure it was locked before they went inside. There was a small child's handprint inside the car which no human hand could reach near the bottom of the windshield where it meets the dash board. When you leave the graveyard, if you look back you will see flashing lights, as if a gun is emitting a light.

## Estes Cemetery

Estes Cemetery dates from 1855 when James Estes donated an acre of his land to be used as a cemetery for his family and neighbors to use as a private cemetery. The first grave was that of James' wife Sarah, who died in 1857. His granddaughter died the same month as his wife and she is also buried here. In fact, there are over 150 graves in this private graveyard, though most of the markers have long since disappeared. Some say that mostly women and children are buried here, but it is known that at least two Civil War veterans are buried in this location. There are strange lights that have been seen hovering over the tombstones late at night and witnesses have heard a strange hollow laughter coming from nowhere.

## Grand Prairie Memorial Cemetery

The Grand Prairie Memorial Cemetery is another interested haunted location. Witnesses have reported seeing strange blue lights dancing about the headstones as well as a girl in a long white dress that runs across the road directly in front of your car and then disappears.

## Old Road Near Beltline Blvd

A number of years ago, it is said that a girl fell off the bridge at this location and drowned. Help was summoned, but in one of those bizarre instances that are rarely seen outside of movies, the police and the ambulance were going opposite directions and collided into each other almost at the spot where the girl had fallen. The paramedics were killed and the police officer was injured. It is now reported that late at night you can hear sirens and screaming.

## Palace of Wax and Ripley's believe it or not. –

Louis Tussaud's Palace of Wax and Ripley's Believe It or Not! These two names certainly generate excitement as well as a certain atmosphere of ghosts and the unexplained. These two establishments are located under one roof midway between Dallas and Fort Worth at 601 East Safari Parkway in Grand Prairie. As is only fitting, it is believed that the building is haunted by the victims of a fire that raged through this location.

Witnesses have reported feeling strange presences, as well as a number of unusual electrical malfunctions that could not be explained. Others have heard strange noises that sound like bells ringing in the distance as well as someone screaming. Security has reported that the motion detectors would go off and yet, searches have revealed that there wouldn't be any one in the building but a few staff members.

# HALTOM CITY, TEXAS

Haltom City is located northeast of and adjacent to the City of Fort Worth in the North Central Texas Metroplex. The sixteen-county extended Dallas/ Fort Worth metropolitan area has a population of over five million, according to the 2000 Census.

### Broadway St Bridge

Behind the old Haltom High School (Now its Shannon High) it is said that in the mid 1990s, a High School boy was killed and his body was thrown into the creek. A group of kids that had skipped school and gone down to the creek for a smoke found his body. Now witnesses report that there are two places that he can be heard and one where he has been seen.

On nights that the moon is not out, go under the Broadway Street Bridge you will discover that no matter what the outside temperature is, it will be very cold underneath the bridge and you will also hear heavy breathing and moaning. Also if you walk through the woods there at night you can hear breathing and get a feeling of being watched. A young man has also been spotted walking along the road that runs parallel to Broadway back into the forest but if you try to get close to him he disappears.

# HAMILTON, TEXAS

Hamilton, the county seat of Hamilton County, is at the intersection of U.S. Highway 281, State highways 22 and 36, and Farm roads 218 and 932, in the Pecan Creek valley in the center of the county. The first settlers came to the area in 1855, and the first store in Hamilton was opened the same year by James M. Rice and Henry Standefer. Hamilton became the county seat when the county was founded in 1858 and was named, like the county, for South Carolina governor James Hamilton. The post office was established in 1861, and by 1873 the population was 200. The Civil War and Indian attacks, which continued until 1876, slowed the growth of Hamilton. During the 1890s two attempts were made to establish a new county seat, on Cowhouse Creek and on the banks of the Leon River, but both failed. By 1896 Hamilton had a population of 1,100, a grocery, two saloons, and three general stores. In 1899 a flood destroyed many of the homes in Hamilton and drowned one resident.

## Pecan Creek Trail

On Highway 36 East, past the filling station and before the old antique shop, there is an old bridge. Under that bridge is a bike trail. If you follow the Pecan Creek Trail North, stop under the Highway 36 bridge and turn towards the creek you will see a drainage pipe. Go across to the pipe and crawl in on your hands and knees past two turns. Shine a flashlight down the tunnel and you should see a head look at you and then duck around the corner. Also you should hear metal banging ahead of you and grunting noises. Rumor has it that this is some sort of goat-man.

# HARKER HEIGHTS, TEXAS

Harker Heights, on U.S. Highway 190 just east of Killeen in Bell County, originated when two landowners, Pinckney R. Cox and Harley Kern, began subdividing their land and selling lots in 1957. Their 400-acre plot corresponded with the boundaries of Water Control and Improvement District No. 4, established in 1955. Purchasers of the lots demanded water, and Cox led in getting a water system completed in September 1960. Sometime before that, residents of the area, estimated at 600 to 700, had filed a petition for an incorporation election, which occurred on September 24, 1960. Voters overwhelmingly approved the incorporation and named Harker Heights in honor of Harley Kern, who had died earlier. Cox, the first mayor, held the office from November 1960 through April 1966. In December 1988 the city annexed the 2,200-acre Comanche Hills utility district, which increased the townsite from 4,400 acres to 6,600 and added almost 3,500 people to the population, bringing the total to 16,500. Harker Heights is a bedroom community; most of its residents work in Killeen, Fort Hood, or elsewhere in Bell County. A 1987 study estimated that 8 percent (approximately 4,300) of Fort Hood personnel living off base lived in Harker Heights. The city has 300 businesses but no major industry. The schools are a part of the Killeen Independent School District.

## Soccer Field

It is said that there is a cowboy with red eyes that walks across what is now a soccer field then disappears into the sewage plant. Legend has it that this figure is looking for the Indian tribe that had killed his family. Witnesses report that when the cowboy disappears into the sewage plant, an Indian runs out of the trees towards the direction of the sewage plant. However, before he gets to the sewage plant you hear gunshots and the Indian falls in the tall grass. If you run over there you can't see the Indian but long a dent in the grass like he was dragged by the cowboy we believe. And you can also hear light screams from a distance.

# HASLET, TEXAS

The City of Haslet is located on Farm Road 156 approximately 16 miles northwest of Fort Worth in extreme north central Tarrant County. The area was settled around 1880, but it is likely that no distinct community was formed until 1883 when the tracks of the Gulf, Colorado, and Santa Fe Railway were extended through the area. The first Post Office was opened there in 1887 and the community was named for the Michigan hometown of the railroad's contractor. In 1896 the community had a school with twenty-one students and one teacher. Ten years later, the Haslet school had twenty-five students. During the 1920's, Haslet had three grocery stores as well as a hardware store, dry goods store, and cotton gin. The availability of war-related employment in Fort Worth probably contributed to the growth of Haslet's population by the late 1940's.

## Blue Mound

In the 1800's as white settlers came to Texas, Indian tribes were being removed from their homelands. Blue Mound Hill was an Indian lookout for the tribe. The white settlers wanted to use the land for cattle and homes. The settlers tried to purchase the land, but the Indians did not want to sell. Finally, an incident ignited smoldering hatreds and this tribe was slaughtered by the white settlers.

Now every full moon around midnight you can see the ghosts of the Indians circling atop Blue Mound Hill, chanting and screaming for revenge. The next day ashes can be found atop the hill where the fire of the Indians anger went out. To get to Blue Mound Hill, take either North or South 287(depending on where you come from), then take a left or right onto Blue Mound Road. Follow until you get to a hill with a white shed on top of it.

# HEMPHILL, TEXAS

Hemphill, the county seat of Sabine County, is at the junction of State highways 87 and 184, thirty miles southeast of Nacogdoches in central Sabine County. The original county seat of Sabine County was Milam, in the northern portion of the county, but voters in 1858 approved a resolution to move the county seat to a more central site. E. P. Beddoe of Sabinetown was given the authority to determine the new location, lay out a town, and move the county records. When the new county seat was laid out in 1859, it was named in honor of John Hemphill. The town received a post office in July 1859, with Michael Watson as postmaster.

## Rebel Ridge

Rebel Ridge is located on the banks of the Sabine River, where the Confederate Army had a fort. Many of the soldiers stationed here died of disease, and some are rumored to still be hanging around carrying out their assigned duties until properly relieved.

## **Patriots Hill**

Patriots Hill is located on the boarder of LA and TX. Patriots from the Civil war set up camped there fearing that the Yankees would come across Sabine Lake and fight there. The patriots stayed there and guarded their posts until the end of the Civil War. Some of the men perished there from starvation and sickness. You can hear voices on the hill and see men in Civil War attire standing guard in the woods.

# HENDERSON, TEXAS

Henderson, the county seat of Rusk County, is on U.S. Highway 259, 138 miles east of Dallas near the center of the county. It was named for James Pinckney Henderson, the first governor of Texas, when the town was laid out in 1843. A post office was established there in 1846. The town grew rapidly during its first two decades, but a fire in 1860 destroyed most of the commercial buildings. The Henderson and Overton Branch Railroad was completed in 1877 and connected the agricultural center of Henderson with the Illinois and Great Northern at Overton. At that time the population was 1,500. In addition to being a shipping center for agricultural products, in the nineteenth century Henderson was also a center for education, with a number of private schools. Among them were Henderson Female College (1849-66), Fowler Institute (1850-ca. 1861), Henderson Masonic Female Institute (1864-66), and Henderson Male and Female College (1871-90). In 1990 Henderson was the home of the Texas Baptist Institute and Seminary.

## **Howard-Dickson House Museum**

The Howard-Dickinson House was the first brick home built in the county. It has three stories, consisting of two floors and a basement. Two brothers, James and David P. Howard, settlers from Virginia, erected the house in 1855. The brothers were brick masons and carpenters and were involved in building many of the buildings in downtown Henderson.

Sam Houston was a frequent visitor to the house. The first president of the Republic of Texas was also a cousin to Martha Ann (Mrs. Dave) Howard. The Texas statesman's campaign trunk is displayed in the house. In 1967, the Howard-Dickinson House was restored by the Rusk County Heritage Association and opened to the public as a living museum and meeting place for special events. The house is open by appointment only.

One of the Howard brothers was killed when a gun went off accidentally in the basement. His blood still stains the second floor flooring where he died. Lights turn themselves on in the basement, and two female apparitions have been seen in the house. There is also a lady who walks out onto the balcony at midnight. She is seen often, but the alarms never sound.

# HILLSBORO, TEXAS

Hillsboro, the county seat of Hill County, is on Interstate Highway 35, U.S. highways 81 and 171, State highways 22 and 171, Farm roads 286 and 3267, and the Missouri, Kansas and Texas Railroad, fifty miles south of Fort Worth and fifty-five miles southwest of Dallas, in the central part of the county. Katy Lake and Lake Aquilla are both partially within the city limits. When Hill County was established in 1853, three locations were suggested for the county seat, but none was near the center of the county. A 220-acre plot was donated by Thomas M. Steiner a mile from the center of the county, and the community was called Hillsborough, in honor of Dr. George W. Hill, a surgeon from Tennessee; Hill was the first settler in Navarro County, which later became part of Hill County. In 1853 the first school in Hill County opened, and in 1854 Hillsborough received a post office. Before the last courthouse was built in 1890, several courthouses served the community. The first, built of elm poles, was replaced by a frame building in 1854. In 1872 a two-story brick courthouse was constructed; it burned and was replaced by a fourth courthouse in 1874.

## Old Junior High Building

The old Junior High School building is located on Walnut Street. When this school was a college in the early 1900's, students often got into fist fights with each other in the cafeteria. One day, a fight got out of hand when a student threw a metal tray at another student's head. The tray was thrown so hard that it cracked the other student's head open. The injured student died before the paramedics arrived. People have reported seeing him roaming the halls of the now deserted building.

## Tarlton House B & B

Greene Duke Tarlton, builder the Tarlton House in 1895 as a permanent home for his family. The house was constructed with the best materials and he spared no expense creating a lasting legacy for his family. He was very much in love with his second wife and it is said that he hanged himself on the third floor after her death.

Rumor has it that Mr. Tarlton himself is said to be wondering the halls at night. Witnesses have heard the sounds of footsteps and female visitors have often felt cool brushes, like soft kisses to their brow. Eyewitness accounts can be read in the journals that are found in every room, left behind from the weary traveler or vacationer. Mr. Tarlton once surprised a maid who found him in one of the rooms looking out of the window, and the owner felt someone sit down on the bed next to her, only to look over and find an empty space. This house is currently a Bed & Breakfast Resort.

## Canterbury Villa Of Hillsboro

Canterbury Villa, 1725 OLD BRANDON RD, is an elder living facility located in Hillsboro. It is reported that there are several spirits that haunt this place. One of the best known seems to like the laundry room. If someone doing their laundry happens to be drinking a soda and puts it down, then the spirit will drink half of the contents. This has happened to a number of people.

## The Shadows

The Shadows is a rather lonely patch of undeveloped area that seems to be a magnet for lovers and children. It is said that if you go into the shadows late at night, park your car and turn everything that makes noise, you can hear voices and the sounds of people walking around your car. Apparently, those invisible residents of this area also know that you are there, because after a while rocks will be thrown at your car and something will knock on your back window. If you try to out of your car you will feel a cold presence envelope you even in the middle of summer.

# HUTCHINS, TEXAS

Hutchins is at the southern Dallas city limit and Interstate Highway 45, nine miles south of downtown Dallas in southern Dallas County. Settlement at the site began around 1860, as Hutchins became the trading place for settlers along the west bank of the river and new arrivals who crossed the Trinity River at Dowd's Ferry from the east. The town was named for William J. Hutchins, one of the promoters of the Houston and Texas Central Railway, which was completed through Hutchins in 1872. At that time the community had gins, a gristmill, several general stores, a school, and a church. Hutchins also had a post office by the end of 1872. In 1884 it had a population of 250, three general stores, three gins, two gristmills, one sawmill, three doctors, and a wagon maker.

By 1890 the population had grown to 300. It was 204 in 1904 and 500 in 1926. It remained steady until 1952, when it was 741, and then rose to 1,100 by 1961 and 2,719 by 1990. The number of businesses increased from fifteen in 1931 to sixty-seven in 1990. Most of the town's residents are employed in Dallas. In 1991 small manufacturing dominated business in Hutchins. Producers of central-air-conditioning units and parts, bronze and brass castings, and data-processing cards and magnetic tapes were the largest industries.

## Lancaster Country Club Lake

People have reported that there is a strange purple mist that has approached them while they were out on the Lancaster Country Club Lake at night. The phantom approaches from the north side of the lake and disappears a few feet from boaters.

# IOWA PARK, TEXAS

Iowa Park is on State Highway 370 five miles west of Wichita Falls in central Wichita County. D. C. and A. J. Kolp founded the community in 1888 on the Fort Worth and Denver City Railway. The settlement was called Daggett Switch and grew rapidly. After the townsite was laid out, the Texas Panhandle Company organized an immigration train from Iowa to the area. A post office opened in Iowa Park in 1888. A plan for the first addition to the community was filed in August 1889. Iowa Park incorporated in 1891, and that year a fire destroyed much of the town. The community developed into an agricultural marketing center, making use of its rail connection to ship wheat and cotton produced on area farms. Drought and the panic of 1893 ushered in difficult times in the 1890s, but by 1900 Iowa Park had a population of 792. The population level fell slightly before World War I, but the discovery of oil just south of town before the end of the war introduced a period of growth.

## Iowa Park High School

Witnesses have reported that there is a little dog that roams the campus of the Iowa Park High School before school starts, most that have seen this animal believe that he is searching for someone that he never finds. Faculty and students both have reported that the computers in the basement turn themselves on and off during early morning hours.

## Building and Bridge

If you go between Vernon and Iowa Park there is a road close to Buffalo Lake, where you can turn off of the main highway. If you take this side road, you will soon a "T" in the road where you can turn left or go straight. The road will get very narrow," by the way if you go in straight you'll have to back out backwards" but if you go left you should see an old burned bridge.

According to local legend, a girl and guy coming back from the prom ran out of gas on that bridge. The guy went to get some gas, but the closest gas station was 20 miles away. The girl waited in the car for sometime until she heard a knock on the door. She looked up to see that it was two weird looking guys looking in the window at her. She tried to lock the door but they opened it and pulled her out onto the ground where they raped her then tried to burn the car with her in it. The fire spread form the car to the bridge itself and set the bridge on fire.

Realizing that they were now in serious trouble, the two men ran into a tin building located about fifty yards away. The billowing smoke was noticed by a farmer, who called the police. The police came and found the victim's body in the burned car as well as the men hiding in the shed. There was a struggle and in the end the two men were killed. They say if you go park your car get out go underneath the bridge you will here screaming and all of the sudden a teenage girl will come out of nowhere and beg you for help before vanishing.

# IRVING, TEXAS

Irving is on State Highway 183 and the Chicago, Rock Island and Pacific Railroad, twelve miles west of Dallas in west central Dallas County. It began as a settlement called Gorbit (Gorbett, Torbit) and had a post office under that name from 1889 to 1894. In 1894 the name of the settlement and post office was changed to Kit, and the location was shifted to anticipate the route of a railroad. The line did not follow the original survey, and in 1902 Julius Otto Schulze and Otis Brown promoted a third town site, called Irving, possibly after Washington Irving, Mrs. Brown's favorite author. The post office was moved to Irving in 1904.

## Crockett Middle School

A young pregnant girl is said to have killed herself in the old ladies dressing room at Crockett Middle School. Most believe that she took her own life because she was afraid to tell her parents about the pregnancy. There have been sightings of this young girl and screams heard before and after gym class in the new dressing room

## Texas Stadium

It is said that the whole of Texas Stadium is haunted but sometimes after the game when everyone has left except workers you will see an old man and what appears to be his granddaughter walking around on the second floor. She is dressed in a cheerleaders outfit and waving a flag. If you talk to them they won't answer, but will walk pass you and disappear into the darkness.

# JEFFERSON, TEXAS

Jefferson, the county seat of Marion County, is at the junction of U.S. Highway 59 and State Highway 49, on Big Cypress Creek and Caddo Lake in the south central portion of the county. It was named for Thomas Jefferson when it was founded in the early 1840s by Allen Urquhart and Daniel Alley. In the late 1830s Urquhart, who immigrated to Texas from North Carolina, received a headright on a bend in the creek; he laid out a townsite there around 1842. At about the same time Alley obtained a 586-acre parcel adjacent to Urquhart's survey and laid out additional streets that became known as Alley's Addition. In contrast to most other town planners of the time, who arranged their plans around a central square, Urquhart laid out the town along Big Cypress Creek, with its streets running at right angles to the bayou. Alley's streets, on the other hand, followed the points of the compass. The intersection of the two plans gave the town its distinctive V-shaped layout. As the westernmost outpost for navigation on the Red River, Jefferson quickly developed into an important river port. The first steamboat, the Llama, reached Jefferson in late 1843 or early 1844. A post office was established in 1846, and the town was incorporated in March 20, 1848, though because of various delays a city charter was not adopted until 1850.

## The Claiborne House

Claiborne House, 312 South Alley, was built as a single family home in 1872 and was named after Captain V. H. Claiborne who was the original owner. It is a modified Greek Revival design with a front gabled roof. The Claiborne House features two 40 ft. porches on each side of the house.

Guests have long believed that the house is haunted by an unidentified, well-dressed man. The apparition has been seen a number of time by several of the residents and their guests.

## Excelsior House

The Excelsior House, 211 W. Austin, is an old hotel that has long had the reputation of being haunted. There have been many ghostly encounters at this old hotel. It is said to be haunted by a headless man on the second floor, as well as a woman in black who has a baby. The woman has appeared and frightened many guests, including the famous film director Stephan Spielberg. This encounter is said to have caused Steven Spielberg (yes, THAT Steven Spielberg) to gather up his group of location scouts and drag them to the nearest Holiday Inn at 2am.

The Excelsior House has been in continuous operation since the 1850s. Among is guests over the years have been President Ulysses S. Grant, railroad mogul Jay Gould and President Rutherford B. Hayes. Another room is named for Lady Bird Johnson. But we can tell you the Jay Gould Room is supposedly the most haunted and includes a rocking chair that some guests say sometimes rocks on its own! Be sure to read the guest registers in each room, especially the Jay Gould Room if you are lucky enough to spend a night.

## The Galley Restaurant

The Galley Restaurant, located at 121 W Austin St, seems to have quite a mischievous spirit. Many employees have reported that items turn up missing, waitresses bump into invisible objects and hear their names called, doors slam, and bills disappear. There is a story that a former constable in the area may have hung an innocent African-American man in the building, and the owner thinks that's who's haunting it.

## Grove Restaurant

The Grove Restaurant was built in 1861 and has long had a reputation for being haunted. The ghost stories go back through many owners - Miss Louise Young, who lived in the house from the early 1900s until her death in the 1980s used to tell her friends about the "haints" that occupied the house with her. Somewhere along the way, though, the fun little ghost stories took a dark turn. In her later years, she said that she was terrified of the spirits. She had a security light installed in the garden because she would see people outside walking around, who disappeared when she turned on the porch light. She called the police several times a week in her later years to report that someone was in the house with her, but the officers never found anyone else there. Finally, she moved into just a few rooms of the house, letting the rest of the place start to deteriorate.

Long before Miss Young's day, back in 1882, The Grove was sold to a man named T.C. Burke. He moved his family in, and they moved right back out, with the only explanation being that, "They couldn't live in that house!"

When the Grove family owned the property (the name is just a coincidence), Mrs. Grove reportedly brought a Bible to bed with the intention of praying for her and her husband, but she fell asleep. She awakened to a black swirling mass engulfing the bedroom. There were also unexplained voices, disembodied footsteps, sounds of objects being moved by unseen hands, and apparitions.

Other reports have included sudden odors that have appeared in rooms: including the scent of a woman's perfume, or the smell of body odor, as if someone hasn't bathed for a long time. When Patrick Hopkins, the former owner, was getting the restaurant ready to open, a lady dressed in white walked down the hallway, and into the ladies' powder room.

Heavy mirrors have fallen off the wall without explanation, and have landed without breaking or crushing the objects beneath them.

During its restaurant years, a waitress walked out of the kitchen into the hallway and was attacked by a black and white dog that knocked her to the ground. After quickly regaining her composure, she ran back into the kitchen, screaming for help. Patrick Hopkins searched the building and yard - there was no dog to be found. It simply had vanished.

During a Candlelight Tour, a couple visiting from Dallas took a picture of the Christmas lights on the neighbor's house to the east of The Grove. Their photo showed the Christmas lights in the foreground. In the background was a lady in a high-collared, puff sleeved white dressed surrounded by a ring of smoke.

While rehearsing a dinner theater, a light technician was on the front porch looking through the window. Suddenly she felt someone staring at her so she quickly glanced to the right. Standing on the east side of the house by the porch was a lady in white who began walking behind the east side of the house. Chasing the eerie-looking woman, the girl turned the corner of the house, and the woman had vanished. Ironically, at one time there was a door on that side of the house leading into the Blue Room.

On that same rehearsal night, the actress portraying the heroine came down the stairs. When she reached the bottom step she glanced to her right and saw a person in costume she was not familiar with, standing in the corner. When she began to ask the lady something, the woman disappeared.

Wet footprints have appeared in the middle of the hallway, even though it wasn't raining outside and there were no plumbing leaks. Drops of water have been found on the staircase, and on one particular mirror in the house, all when the atmosphere was dry.

A neighbor lady told a former owner, "Let me tell you what my sister and I have seen recently. My sister was standing on our porch one night around 9 o'clock when she called me out to see a glowing white figure across the street. She looked like she was inspecting the renovation of an old building. The figure came from the east side of The Grove!" She and her sister had witnessed this several nights in a row.

A renter lived in the garden cottage at one time, and he looked out its window to see a little girl playing out among the flowers. He went outside, and she looked at him, and then disappeared. A shadow-figure has been seen in the garden many times - striding quickly across it, or simply just hanging around.

Lights go on and off in the house, and the chandeliers have reported to sway, even with the absence of moving air in the room[48]. An unidentified male ghost and a dog haunt this restaurant (now closed). The property sits on or near several reported murder sites, and the property itself is reported to contain several unmarked graves.

## Hale House Bed & Breakfast

The Hale House Bed & Breakfast, 702 S Line St, is a 19th century Greek Revival-style home. Originally built by the Hale family sometime between 1872 and 1884, the house was a one-story structure until the great oil boom of the 1920s and 30s. At that time, a second story was added, and Hale House was operated as a boarding house by May Belle Hale, daughter of the original builders. However, after 24 years as a Bed & breakfast, it is now closed. No one seems to know the identity of the ghost that haunts this location, but a young girl's apparition has been seen near the staircase.

## Hotel Jefferson

The Hotel Jefferson, 124 W Austin St is directly across the street from the Excelsior House. At a time when steamboats plied the Big Cypress River from New Orleans and true Southern gentility was the order of the day a stately structure, now known as the Jefferson Hotel, was built. Once used as a warehouse to store cotton, this lovely building changed hands numerous times until, at the turn of the twentieth century it was transformed into a hotel and has served as a haven for weary travelers since that time. Once known as the Crystal Palace in the 1920's, ragtime music rang through these halls as couples swirled around the room.

It is also clear that this old hotel is one that has more than its share of spirits. Room 19 is considered uninhabitable. A maid has claimed to hear voices

---

[48] http://www.thegrove-jefferson.com/photos/index.htm

coming out of room 19 when not occupied. Some occupants had been known not to stay in room 19 due to the feeling of being watched.

Room 12 contains a warm, benevolent female ghost. A security guard/police officer became involved in a tug-of-war with an unseen force in room 2. Most of the staff has reported ghostly footsteps and a feeling of being watched. A "whispering woman" makes Room 14 one of the hotel's most-requested among ghost buffs.

Some of the other manifestations include: whispers from nowhere, orchestra music from a closed dining hall, knocks on walls and headboards, the smell of cigar smoke in the smoke-free building, faucets opening of their own accord, and doors pulling back when pulled shut!

People who have been the only guests in the hotel have heard the click-clack of footsteps walking the halls in the middle of the night - even though the hall is carpeted!  Children have been heard laughing and romping throughout the hotel in the middle of the night. A child calls for mama, a baby cries, but at that time, no children were staying in the hotel!

A former desk clerk named Michael was ending his shift in the middle of a slow week and there were no "paying" guests staying at the hotel overnight. Michael made his rounds upstairs, turning off lights and locking rooms before leaving for the night.  He was closing the last door in the long, dark hallway when the doors started opening and slamming shut all at once!

Lights turned on and off as Michael dashed downstairs and phoned his friend Phyllis, a desk clerk at the Excelsior Hotel across the street.  Phyllis reports that Michael was in a complete panic when he called, screaming that he was alone in the hotel but that "all heck" was breaking loose upstairs! He said he could hear doors slamming and the sound of footsteps and someone dragging furniture. Michael locked up and waited in the street for his ride that night.

Then there is the story of a couple in room 5 whose young son awakened them repeatedly, because a man, in a long coat and high boots, would not go away. Whispers and repetitive knocks are common occurrences.

At times there is a thick white cloud with a thin, long-haired blonde in the mist.  She seems to be emotionally attached to a bed that was moved from room 12 to room 14.

A ninety year old man reluctantly told his tale of wandering the hotel at one in the morning after not being able to sleep.  He saw the petite blonde woman floating down the stairs smiling at him, only to disappear before she reached the bottom step. He said he never believed in ghosts until he saw her!

Walking into some rooms, one can get the feeling of being watched. In room 19 a man told his wife to go back to sleep when she awakened him with rants about a petite woman who chilled the wife's arm with a touch of her hand. Another woman took one step into the same room and refused to stay there - stating that she could tell the room was haunted.

Directly under room 19, room 20 seems to be another very active place. Two older women staying there kept waking to the sound of running water from the bathroom. They'd turn off the spigot, only to wake to its splashing later in the night.

One night, a woman was staying with her husband in room 24 near the front of the hotel. She happened to wake up at five the next morning, so she got up and went into the hallway to make coffee. As she turned, she noticed a nice-looking man dressed in western clothes go into the entrance foyer down the hall to rooms 20 and 21. Thinking it strange that she had not heard any doors opening or closing she went down the hall to investigate. The doors to both rooms were wide open and there was no-one in either room!

On another occasion, a girl was hired to stay a few nights while the owners were away. She wanted to be next to the only guest staying that night as she was uneasy about being alone all night in the hotel. So she decided to sleep in room 23 downstairs. She was awakened about three in the morning to the sounds of scrapping and banging in the room above her as though someone was moving furniture. Needless to say, she didn't get up and check it out!

The next morning, the people in the room next to her asked if she had heard loud noises from upstairs the previous night. It seems that the scrapping and banging had also awakened them at the same time!

There are rumors that one of the hotel's specters might be Mrs. Schluter, the woman who ran the hotel during the 1890's through the roaring 20's. A story is also circulated by some tells of an 1890's bride who hung herself when the groom sent word he was not coming to marry her. Whoever it might be, the sound of someone crying has also brought people wide awake, and they never discover where the weeping is coming from.... It echoes from everywhere.

Camera crews from various local TV stations and radio stations have all had their own weird experiences while taping programs in the hotel - from cameras not working in certain areas of the hotel to recorders turning themselves off and on. Pictures after being developed showed strange anomalies in them.

## Lamache's Italian Restaurant

Lamache's Italian Restaurant, 124 W Austin St, is directly next door to the famous (or infamous) Hotel Jefferson, and connected by a couple of doors. Hotel and restaurant employees have often heard the sounds of big band music coming from the restaurant. Restaurant employees have heard knockings on the connecting doors. Guests in the hotel, with rooms above the restaurant, complain of noises coming from the restaurant even when the restaurant is empty. Candles flicker, wine glasses clink and the electrical system goes haywire on a regular basis.

## Living Room Theater

The building occupied by the Living Room Theater, 112 Vale St., was built in 1869. The Living Room Theater is a one woman repertory theater. Occupying front row seats at every performance are the ghosts that haunt this building. Footsteps are routinely heard on the stairs and items often rearrange themselves. These activities have been attributed to the ghost of a 12-year-old slave girl named Mary who was traded with the land to get the building put up.

## Maison-Bayou Waterfront B & B

Maison-Bayou started as an authentic recreation of an 1850's Creole Plantation. The Antebellum family history of owners Pete and Jan Hochenedel was the original inspiration for this unique bed and breakfast setting. After G. Michel Hochenedel first emigrated from Strasbourg, France to New Orleans in the 1830's, he worked for the Customs House, was a cabinetmaker, and owned a beer house on Bourbon Street in the Vieux Carre (French Quarter). After General Benjamin Butler commandeered the family home during the Northern occupation in 1863, the Hochenedel family moved to Baton Rouge and bought a Plantation there. While researching this genealogy, the Hochenedels discovered that a cousin, Frances Hochenedel Monroe and her family currently live in the "Big House" on the Burden Plantation in Baton Rouge. That plantation is now a part of L.S.U.'s Rural Life Museum, and is the model for the origins of Maison-Bayou in Jefferson.

Ghosts have slapped a plumber; there is an AC current in the ground that MIT could not explain, guests experience strange lights and apparitions. All of this activity is attributed to the ghost of "Diamond Bessie" a woman murdered in the late 1800s.

## McKay House

McKay House, 306 E. Delta St. was built in 1851 as a single family home. The proprietors of this stately B&B, and some of their guests over the years, have reported the kinds of things that have come to associated with "haunted" houses: footsteps in empty hallways, odd noises, odors and occurrences, a baby crying in the distance. The Sunday House, separate from the main house, is a favorite of ghost hunters.

Aside from the footsteps and rattling cookware, a smoke alarm went off in the house while the owner was standing under it with the batteries in his hand! Then his wife noticed a female apparition behind him watching them! An African-American female apparition has also offered cherry pie to guests in the middle of the night!

## Oakwood Cemetery

Oakwood Cemetery is a historic burial ground. It is also haunted. An apparition seen in the cemetery has been attributed to a former prostitute named "Diamond Bessie" who was probably murdered by her husband in 1877.

## Twin Oaks Country Inn

Twin Oaks Country Inn, 2620 FM 134 S, is also known as Twin Oaks Plantation Inn. The Inn is located on a pre-Civil War plantation site, nestled among towering trees. The antebellum home is inspired by the D'Evereux Plantation, built in the 1840s. Mr. Julien Sidney D'Evereux became a successful planter and a Texas legislator, representing the East Texas region of the state. This site was once a large sugar plantation situated between two major arteries of commerce, the Big and Little Cypress Rivers. Another interesting feature of Twin Oaks is the Civil War-era water well lined with a double wall of slave-made bricks. "The Belle", the Victorian guest house, has five bedrooms and the poolside cottage suite. Guests are invited to stay in one of the two suites in the antebellum main house, as well.

After the pre-Civil War cistern was uncovered, guests and staff began to hear the sounds of music and see fleeting shadows moving about the house. The cistern is now under a wishing well.

## White Oak Manor

White Oak Manor is a Greek Revival home that was built around 1928 and now welcomes Bed & Breakfast lovers and, some say, spirits. The ghost of a young girl has been reported by some guests, and one guest claimed to have watched the mischievous spirit pull the covers from the bed in the room known as Miss Clara's Room. Apparitions and moving quilts are attributed to the spirit of a young blonde-haired girl who may have died of pneumonia in the house.

## KELLER, TEXAS

The Texas and Pacific Railroad between Fort Worth and Texarkana was completed in April 1881, and the first train ran on this track on May 9, 1881. With the advent of rail service, new villages were established all along the line. The Keller of today was one of them.

On July 19, 1881, H.W. Wood, a druggist of Tarrant County, set aside 40 acres out of the north end of the 62 acres deeded to him by A.C. Roberts (being a part of the Samuel Needham Survey) for a town site to be known as Athol, situated 14 miles northeast of Fort Worth. The land was dedicated to the public for street and alleyways, but title to the remainder of the 62 acres was held by Mr. Wood.

Settlers migrated to the new village, and before a year had passed the name of the town was changed from Athol to Keller, honoring John C. Keller, a foreman on the railroad. Streets were named and those in the original 40 acre site still carry the names given to them in 1881. Streets going north and south are Lamar, Main and Elm; those running east and west are Price, Taylor, Hill, Vine, Bates, Olive and Pecan.

## Old Stone Recreational Building

This building that is used as a municipal recreational facility seems to have a history that is not known by too many people. Guests and staff have both reported hearing footsteps. There have been many report of hearing unexplained footsteps made by the nightshift janitors. Also, a number of witnesses have heard the sounds of splashing water at night, but the pool is empty.

# KILGORE, TEXAS

Kilgore is on U.S. Highway 259 and State highways 31, 42, and 135, 120 miles east of Dallas in south central Gregg County. The area was first settled before the Civil War by planters from the old South, but the city was not founded until 1872, when the International-Great Northern Railroad built a line between Longview and Palestine. The railroad bypassed New Danville, and the company platted a new town, which they named for Constantine Buckley Kilgore, who sold the 174-acre townsite to the railroad and urged many of the businesses of New Danville to move there. A post office opened in 1873, and by 1885 Kilgore had two steam gristmill-cotton gins, a church, and a district school; the estimated population was 250. The Kilgore State Bank opened in 1906, and an independent school district was formed in 1910.

## Danville Cemetery

During the 80's a woman was killed by radiation while working at a power plant in Oklahoma. She is buried in the Danville Cemetery and it is said that her grave glows green at night.

## Kilgore College

Kilgore College, in Kilgore, was established in 1935 through the efforts of citizens of Kilgore Independent School District. From 1935 to 1946 the college operated under the direction of the school district's board of trustees; W. L. Dodson was superintendent. In January 1946 invitations were issued to neighboring school districts to join a union district for junior college purposes. Seven districts accepted: Sabine (1946), White Oak (1946), Leverett's Chapel (1946), London (1947), Overton (1947), Gaston (1948), and Gladewater County

Line (1951). A board of nine trustees from the union district directed the affairs of the college after 1946, and B. E. Masters served as president.

Like many colleges across the country, Kilgore also developed a reputation for being haunted. It is said that several years ago, a girl committed suicide on the eighth floor of Stark Hall, which was the girls' dorm at that time. The college closed that floor for several years after the incident because people complained about strange noises, finding footprints on their bed, extremely cold spots, and the feeling of being watched.

The floor has been reopened ever since the dorm was remodeled. The residents of the eighth floor still complain however of strange happenings, such as knocking and scratching on the walls along with cold spots.

## Pirtle Cemetery

Pirtle Cemetery is located in the tiny community of Pirtle, Texas. In 2000, the only thing left of Pirtle was the church and this cemetery. The story is told that a boy died and was buried in the cemetery. His mother knew that he was terrified of the dark, so his mother sat at his grave every night for the next year holding a lantern. Then she died and now passersby still report that every night the lantern light will still appear. From time to time the lantern will appears in the far corner of the cemetery.

## Sabine River

In the 1800's an old lady named Annie lived deep in the woods near the river bank. A local religious leader accused of being a witch and with typical mob mentality, a group of men took it into their minds that she needed to be killed to protect the women and children of the area. So one night, this group went to her small shack to kill her. They drug her outside, chained her to a tree and beat her to death with whips. Now, it is said that if you can find the remains of the old shack, you can hear chains dragging across the floor, screaming, and the sounds of whips.

## Tywhiskey Creek

In the bottoms of Tywiskey Creek there is said to be a chicken man. Many sightings occurred during the late 60's and 70's. If you go into the bottoms at night you can hear loud sounds as if whole trees are snapping in half and loud strange sounds deep in the woods.

# KILLEEN, TEXAS

Killeen is on U.S. Highway 190 in western Bell County about forty miles north of Austin. In 1881 the Gulf, Colorado and Santa Fe Railway, planning to extend its tracks through the area, bought 360 acres some 2½ miles southwest of a community known as Palo Alto, which had existed since about 1872. Soon afterward the railroad platted a seventy-block town on its land and named it after Frank P. Killeen, the assistant general manager of the railroad. When the first train passed through the new town in May 1882, about forty people lived there. Before the end of that year the town included the railroad depot, several stores, a saloon, and a school. Many of the earliest residents of Killeen moved to the site from smaller communities in the surrounding area, while others were attracted by a national promotional campaign sponsored by the railroad. By 1884 the town had grown to include about 350 people, served by five general stores, two gristmills, two cotton gins, two saloons, a lumberyard, a blacksmith shop, and a hotel. As it became an important shipping point for the cotton, wool, and grain produced on local farms, Killeen continued to expand. By 1896 it included six general stores, three cotton gins, three blacksmiths, two hardware stores, and a jeweler; around this time telephone service was introduced. Some 780 people lived in Killeen by 1900; virtually all of them white Protestants, since the community openly discouraged blacks and Catholics from living there. The First National Bank of Killeen was incorporated in 1901, and the town's first electric-light system and power plant was installed in 1904 and 1905. About that same time local boosters helped to convince the Texas legislature to build bridges over Cowhouse Creek and other streams, effectively doubling Killeen's trade area. A public water system began operating in 1914, and by that year the town had two banks, and its population had grown to about 1,300.

### Randall's Food Store

Randall's Food Store, 2200 E Veterans Memorial Blvd, has long said to be haunted. It was felt by many managers that there was a ghost roaming the manager's office and the store aisles. This ghost would knock off magazines from the check stands onto the floor. Also, it was said that the ghost would make pyramids by food cans on the aisles. There was also a door leading to the catwalk of the store in the manager's office, late at night many times the manager would feel a cold chill and wind blow papers off the desk. It would be discovered that this door would be open. Randall's Food Store is now a Hastings.

## LINDALE, TEXAS

Lindale is on the Missouri Pacific Railroad and U.S. Highway 69 ten miles north of Tyler in northwestern Smith County. The site, originally part of the Thomas Burbridge survey, was settled as early as 1873, when the Lyndale post office opened with John M. Davis as postmaster. The next year the spelling was changed to Lindale, and in 1875 the settlement became a station on the new International-Great Northern Railroad. Five years later the population had reached 300. By 1884 residents had begun shipping cotton and fruit, and the businesses included seven general stores, two groceries, a hotel, two drugstores, a gristmill, and a cotton gin, as well as the services of a gunsmith, a physician, and an undertaker. There were also two churches and a school. Citizens numbered

500 in 1892, when seven flour mills, the East Texas Canning Factory, and a high school had all been constructed. The J. S. Ogburn and Company Canning Factory, specializing in peaches, was established in 1895. On November 1, 1898, the Lindale City school system was established. Two years later fruit and truck farming had become the major sources of income.

## Old Grade School Gym

It is said that while playing basketball in the old Grade School Gym that you can hear kids' voices coming from the underground classrooms that haven't been used in many years. If you go downstairs you could hear the voices even stronger and when you leave, the lights will turn on behind you and the dangling light fixture will be shaking as if someone had just pulled the cord. Some who have visited the lower levels have reported that they have even heard chains rattling.

# LONGVIEW, TEXAS

Longview, the county seat of Gregg County, is on Interstate Highway 20 and U.S. highways 80 and 259, about 125 miles east of Dallas in eastern Gregg and western Harrison counties. In the early 1990s it was the largest city in Gregg County. Its current boundaries include three leagues of land granted to Anglo-Americans late in 1835. There was no significant settlement of the area, however, until the 1840s and 1850s. What became Longview consisted of mostly hilly land in the southeast corner of Upshur County, devoted more to small farms than to large plantations. Before the Civil War there were, within what are now the Longview city limits, two rural communities with United States post offices: Earpville in the east and Pine Tree in the west. A Methodist congregation at Earpville, dating back to 1846, later became the present First United Methodist Church of Longview. Today's Pine Tree Cumberland Presbyterian Church was chartered in 1847. What is now Longview was founded in 1870.

## Refinery

Witnesses have reported that sometimes a man is seen in the Refinery standing on a pressure vessel. Some believe that he was a victim of the explosion, or one of the victims of the gas leak. Others are said to have reported that people are sometimes seen walking around or sitting at desks, even though the plant has been shut down for years since the second toxic gas leak.

## Old Caddo Indian Museum

The Caddo Indian Museum off Farmed Market Road, also known as loop 1845, has been closed down for many years. The museum displayed artifacts that were found in burial sites in East Texas. Several people have seen a little ghost girl standing beside the road or in front of the museum during the night and strange sounds can sometimes be heard while driving down the street in front of the museum late in the evenings. The ghost girl is said to be that of a little Indian girl that was killed from a head injury. Her skeleton was on display in a glass case inside the museum for many years.

## LUTHER, TEXAS

Luther, on Farm Road 846 in north central Howard County, was named for its first postmaster, Luther F. Lawrence. The town's post office dates from 1909. Between 1936 and 1947 the population grew from five to ninety and the number of businesses from one to three. By 1966 the population had risen to 335. In 1980 Luther had lost its post office, but the population remained steady at 335 in 1990. One of Howard County's oilfields, the Luther Southeast, is located near the town.

### <u>Old Gay Hill School</u>
The Gay Hill School is located just outside of Big Spring, Texas. Supposedly the school's ceiling collapsed and killed students in the auditorium. The principal knew about the safety hazard concerning the ceiling, and didn't do anything about it until it was too late. He felt guilty and went home and hung himself (his house is just down the road from the school). The principal haunts the house, and the children haunt the school. Strange lights, sounds, and apparitions can be observed at both the house and the school. The school was also reported to be a place for devil worship after the disaster occurred. Feelings of being watched and stalked occur at the school.

Another story is, is that a young girl had hung herself in the girls' bathroom. Reasons floating around are that she had failed a class, had been rejected by her boyfriend, or was murdered by a jealous rival. After her death the school, then town, began to fade away. With the town in repression, the school was in trouble. Press and families were putting a lot of heat on the school, and it was too much for the principle. He shot himself in his office. After these events, the school was shut down, and the town no longer exists. But you can still visit this school.

It is said, that the bathroom and the principle's office are very cold. Those who enter then report a sense of being watched, almost breathed on, it feels, on the back of your neck. In the bathroom, with no lights, if you can stand it, as you stand in the bathroom, unable to see anything else , you can almost see a girls face, RIGHT in front of your face, LOOKING you right in the eyes!

# MARSHALL, TEXAS

Marshall is located on Interstate Highway 20 approximately thirty-nine miles west of Shreveport, Louisiana, in central Harrison County. Harrison County was marked off in 1839. Two years later, in an effort to influence the commissioners who were choosing a site for the county seat, Peter Whetstone offered land for a courthouse, a church, and a school. The offer was accepted, and the town, named by Isaac Van Zandt in honor of Chief Justice John Marshall, became the county seat in 1842. It was incorporated by the Texas legislature in 1844 and enlarged in 1850 to include an area of one square mile with the courthouse at the center. Marshall was the first town in Texas to have a telegraph; by 1854 the local paper had a telegraph link to New Orleans, which gave it quick access to national news. By 1860 Marshall was one of the largest and wealthiest towns in East Texas, with a population estimated at 2,000. The community had an outstanding group of lawyers and political leaders including the first and last governors of Confederate Texas, Edward Clark and Pendleton Murrah.

## Maplecroft

Maplecroft is the name of the Starr Family Mansion in Marshall. The first Starr family member associated with Texas, Franklin J. Starr, moved here from Ohio in 1834. For a while Starr partnered in the practice of law with William Barret Travis. He ended up in Nacogdoches as a result of the Runaway Scrape, or the hasty departure to the east in front of Santa Anna's Mexican army during the Texas Revolution in the spring of 1836.

James Harper Starr joined his brother Franklin and soon was involved in public affairs. He served as land commissioner in Nacogdoches County and as President Mirabeau B. Lamar's secretary of the treasury before relocating in Marshall.

Starr purchased Rosemont, the home of the Rev. A.F. Wagner, for his residence, and over time the property became a family compound. His son, James Franklin Starr, helped manage the family's business interest. He purchased a portion of the estate for his own residence, Maplecroft -- now known as the Starr Mansion. James Franklin Starr and wife Clara had six daughters. As each daughter married, Starr built a home for her new family on the estate. Several of these buildings are still standing: a portion of Rosemont, three of the houses Starr constructed for his daughters, a school house, and proud Maplecroft.

Maplecroft is said to be haunted by the unidentified ghost of a young female. No one is sure who she is or why she haunts this historic old home, but she has been seen a number of times.

## Marshall Pottery - HWY 31

Marshall Pottery Inc. is the largest manufacturer of red clay pots in the United States and one of the oldest pottery manufacturers in the world. Marshall Pottery operates a 100,000 ft² (9,000 m²) retail store adjacent to its headquarters in Marshall, Texas, which attracts over 500,000 tourists each year.

Marshall Pottery was founded by W. F. Rocker in Marshall in 1895. Rocker located the business in East Texas because of its abundant water and white clay deposits. In 1905 Marshall Pottery was acquired by Sam Ellis. With the invention of the glass canning jar and other new competing products in the 1920s, the business almost folded. Prohibition led to a thriving moonshine industry and a need for inexpensive jugs to store the liquor. If not for the sale of jugs during Prohibition, Marshall Pottery would likely have gone bankrupt[49].

Along with pottery, Marshall Pottery would seem to give birth to ghosts. A patron of the business reported seeing an apparition of a head. It was looking up towards the ceiling, long curly black hair, pale face, and no expression at all; only at second glance it was gone. Strange cold and warm spots are felt in the plant as well.

## Marshall Pottery - HWY 59

When Marshall Pottery decided to expand and build a new plant, they apparently found one of the workers dead, lying by a tree, when the construction first started. No cause of the death was ever determined. That tree was located in what is now the center of the warehouse. The second reason that people give for the hauntings here is that the plant was built on ancient sacred Indian grounds, it may be both. Workers will very clearly hear their name called, even with the roaring of machinery.

## Stagecoach Road

Stagecoach Road ran from Karnack to Marshall. This route saw a lot of Texas history. There have been reports of a spectral stagecoach seen driving along the route. Other witnesses have reported seeing apparitions of men carrying a coffin.

# MAYPEARL, TEXAS

Maypearl is on Farm Road 66 ten miles southwest of Waxahachie in western Ellis County. The settlement, originally called Eyrie, had a post office from 1894 to 1903. The name was changed to Maypearl on June 25, 1903, in honor of the daughters of two officials of the International-Great Northern Railroad, which had recently reached the settlement. Maypearl incorporated in 1910 and had a population of 417 by 1920. That year the community's

---

[49] "http://en.wikipedia.org/wiki/Marshall_Pottery"

elementary and high schools served 300 students from the town and its environs, and the town had two banks, a weekly newspaper, four churches, and twenty-five businesses by 1914. The population remained at 350 to 400 from 1925 through the mid-1960s. The business community declined from twenty-eight to twelve establishments during the same period. Afterward, the population again began to increase, from 462 in 1977 to 626 in 1986, when some fifteen businesses operated in the community. In November 1988 federal officials selected Ellis County as the intended location for the Superconducting Super Collider. In 1990 the population was 781.

## Greathouse Cemetery

Archibald and Mary Greathouse, who settled in this area in 1848, gave their name to a creek and rural community that grew up here. The church, school, and cemetery that formed the focal point of community life were located on land deeded in 1881 by Ezekiel M. Brack, and on property deeded later by Martin Judy Dawson and George W. Whitefield. John Edward Dawson hauled lumber from Waxahachie by oxcart to erect the Greathouse Missionary Baptist Church Building.

The community is gone and the Greathouse Graveyard is no longer in use. However, something still prowls the area. Witnesses have reported hearing a loud, strange heartbeat sound coming from the cemetery.

# MAXDALE, TEXAS

Maxdale is on the Lampasas River eight miles southwest of Killeen in southwestern Bell County. It was established sometime before 1883, when a post office was opened in the community. In 1884 Maxdale had a population of twenty, two churches, a district school, and a cotton gin. It had a general store by 1914 and reached a peak population of fifty in 1925. The post office was closed the next year. In 1948 Maxdale had three businesses and two churches. The community declined in the 1950s and 1960s and had a population of only fifteen by 1968. By 1979 many of its houses were empty, though a new focus for community life, the Maxdale Community Center, had been built a mile east of the old townsite. The population of Maxdale was reported to be four in 1988 and 1990.

## Maxdale Cemetery

It is believed that the very old Maxdale Cemetery is haunted by an old man with a limp; some say he was the caretaker of the cemetery. There is also a small old iron bridge you have to cross to get to the cemetery which is also believed to be haunted. It is said that if you go at night to visit the cemetery and you stop on the bridge turn, off your headlights and count to ten, then when you turn them back on there will be a man hanging from a noose. This unfortunate fellow is said to have hanged himself when he could not save the life of his girlfriend who had drowned in the river under the bridge.

Another story is that a man committed suicide by driving his truck off a small bridge on the road to the right side of the cemetery. Witnesses report a phantom old truck appearing behind them and chasing them for a short time. Most also report feeling a sad presence felt through out the entire cemetery.

# MCKINNEY, TEXAS

The history of McKinney, one of the oldest towns in North Texas, dates back over one hundred and fifty years to 1841, when the first settlers arrived in the region from Kentucky, Arkansas, and Tennessee. Collin County got its name five years later, when the state's first legislators, meeting under the Constitution of the State in 1846, created Collin, Denton, Hunt, and Grayson counties out of the territory that had been named Fannin County, an area that encompassed most of Northeast Texas.

The original county seat was established in Buckner in 1846, but just two years later, the seat was moved three miles eastward to a more central location, and was renamed McKinney. Both the county and its seat were named after Collin McKinney. The town was originally incorporated in 1849, and was re-incorporated on May 28, 1859.

## Buffalo Joes

Buffalo Joes, 100 N. Tennessee Street, is a fine dining restaurant located in downtown McKinney on the east side of the old city hall. The restaurant has four areas: the lower level, the main dining room upstairs, the private banquet room, and the storage area behind the banquet room.

A mischievous spirit occupies the storage area. Sometimes the toilet paper would be strung out, other times forks would be pinned into walls. All the employees left at the same time just because they were easily freaked out being by themselves with the spirits. The restaurant used to be a brothel when McKinney was first founded.

## McKinney Court House

The Old Collin County Courthouse is a three-story courthouse built in the Neoclassical Revival Style. Neoclassical Revival architectural movement is based on the use of Greek and Roman architectural forms. Architects of the times were inspired by the World Columbian Exposition in Chicago in 1893, which had a classical theme as well as the classically inspired architecture of Andrea Palladio who inspired many of the English and American architects of the 18th and 19th centuries. Neoclassical architects of the early 20th century designed monumental classical style buildings using giant pedimented porticoes, columns, and elaborate cornices. It has been stated that no other style carries so well the elements of dignity, simplicity and monumental repose essential for public buildings.

This historic old courthouse also has a ghost. A number of people have seen the mysterious lady in white looking out of a window of the courthouse after it is closed. According to legend, she hung herself inside the building in 1896.

## McKinney Public Library

The McKinney Public Library, 101 E. Hunt Street, is home to another very active ghost. Staff has reported that many books in the library are misplaced, bookcases are being knocked over, and money being taken out of the register. Others have reported that books are being found in purses and that other personal belongings are vanishing only to appear in out of the way places.

# MESQUITE, TEXAS

Mesquite, on Interstate highways 20 and 30 and Loop 635, between Dallas, Garland, and Balch Springs in east central Dallas County, was established by the Texas and Pacific Railway in May 1873 and named after nearby Mesquite Creek. Station agent William Bradfield was the first settler in the town, which attracted residents from the surrounding farm communities of Long Creek, New Hope, Haught's Store, and Scyene. A post office began at Mesquite in 1874, and Dallas County's longest-running newspaper, the Mesquiter, was established there by R. S. Kimbrough in 1882. Citizens incorporated the town in 1887 and selected J. E. Russell as mayor. Early industries included cotton gins and a brick factory. During these years outlaws Jesse James, Cole Younger, and Belle Starr lived in the vicinity. Sam Bass held up a Texas and Pacific train as it passed through town, escaping with $30,000.

## Eastfield College

Eastfield College has been serving the Mesquite, Garland and East Dallas community since 1970. Eastfield College works to provide educational opportunities through high-quality instruction, services and programs in an environment conducive to student success in academic, technical, occupational, and continuing education.

Eastfield was built in the early '70's on the site of the old Motley Mansion. The Motleys donated the land for the school after the house was burned down by vandals. The family cemetery is still there and includes a grave for a severed arm! The theater of the school is said to be haunted by a man who watches practices of plays. He has been reported several times in the past twenty years or so.

## Galloway Elementary

Several stories are told by employees to visitors who went through personal experiences at Galloway Elementary School. Children are heard running up and down the halls at night by janitors that work there. Chairs are heard moving in the lunch room. A women dressed in 19<sup>th</sup> century clothing was spotted by a janitor walking down the hallway one night. There is also the gym where children have been spotted in the daytime that don't exist. There is a story of a gym teacher that told his children they couldn't use the restroom in the gym without permission. He glanced over at one of the children that were standing in front of the restroom. At that moment, she darted into the restroom. He called after her but she didn't answer, so finally he entered the restroom. To his surprise, there was no one in the restroom. On the last day of this teacher's job he said out loud in the gym, "you can have it I don't have too deal with you anymore? As he was walking out of the gym, a hockey stick was thrown across the gym and no one was in there. This was after school hours. Witnesses there at night have heard children on the playground, but they are unable to see them.

## Old Holloman's Road

Holloman's Road is a small dirt road that curves between Lawson Rd. and Bruton Rd. There is a solitary home that has sat for many years abandoned on this small street. It is the only structure on the road. Brave teenagers have tried to walk the street at night only to disappear and never to be seen again. The road became such a danger that the city closed the road off. Witnesses who try to walk through the area report that they become overwhelmed by a sense of dread and of being watched, even in broad daylight. In the 80s, a Dallas man killed a young woman and her young son and dumped their bodies on that dark and brooding road.

## Trail Dust Steak House

It is said that there was a man working on the upstairs railing above the dance floor when the Trail Dust Steak House was being built. He was adding something to the railing, when he slipped and fell to his death on the left side of the dance floor. Local history reports that the dead man's name was John Brown. The owners have given him his own table in the upstairs dining area. His table is Table #218 that sits between the entrance to the kitchen and the grill window.

The upstairs lights are on a timer, set to go off at exactly 1am, but John likes to keep the light above his table lit till way after that time. Also, managers and employees have quit their jobs there because around 4am, some nights, they have seen lights turn on and off, phones ring off the hook, printers spit out whole rolls of gibberish, doors swing by themselves. As if this was not enough, some have also reported hearing footsteps on the dance floor.

He is also known to haunt the men and women's restrooms upstairs, no matter what the lights find a way to mysteriously turn themselves on in the restrooms. There have also been reports of cold spots felt in the women's restrooms.

# MEXIA, TEXAS

Established 1871, named for Mexican General Jose Antonio Mexia whose family donated townsite. The general first served under Santa Anna, but later joined an uprising against the Mexican dictator. The rebellion failed, and the city's namesake died before a firing squad.

Natural gas discovered nearby in 1912; oil gusher blew in nine years later. Resulting boom brought rowdy period marked by violence and martial law. As in most cases, the boom faded quickly, and Mexia today is a small, quiet city devoted to modern agriculture, oil and gas production.

## Battery Road

Legend is you can go drive down Battery Road at midnight and turnoff your car and lights you will see a ball of fire. As you watch this ball of fire it seems to come right at you and flashes real bright.

## Wal-Mart

At this Wal-Mart there is a ghost that keeps unstocking the shelves as fast as employees can stock them. The new super center opened up a short distance from the old store and it still is happening. If the employee involved tells "Oscar" to leave you alone and stop tearing the place up, he will stop and sometimes, he just may go bother some other stocker.

# MINERAL WELLS, TEXAS

Discovery of medicinal qualities in waters made the city of Mineral Wells nationally famous in late 19th-early 20th Centuries. It was said that waters of the Crazy Well (discovered in 1885) could cure mental illness and a long list of other maladies. Today modern health seekers, conventioneers, retired persons, hunters and fishermen enjoy mild climate and surrounding Palo Pinto Mountains. Several outfitters provide canoe rentals and trips on nearby Brazos River.

## Crazy Water Hotel

By the early 1900's Mineral Wells was on its way to becoming a national health resort as bath houses and spas popped up all over the valley. People were coming by the hundreds every week to bath in or drink the healing waters. Many accommodations such as hotels and boarding houses were springing up everywhere. In 1912 the city saw the need for a luxury hotel and decided to build one on the sight of old well No. 3, hence; the "Crazy Water Hotel" was born. The four-story structure was completed in 1914 and operated until March 1925 when a tragic fire completely destroyed the hotel.

Two Years later, two Dallas businessman, Carr and Hal Collins, rebuilt a new seven story structure on the sight of the old one, keeping the same name, the new structure had two complete bathhouses located in the basement, electric elevators, a huge and lavish lobby, 200 rooms, and a spacious enclosed pavilion of semi Moorish design.

The Crazy Water Hotel was a beautiful sight during the 1920's and 1930's as over 100,000 people a year visited the city for the mineral waters. At the end of the 1940's the days of the mineral waters were numbered and Mineral Wells would never enjoy the fabulous times that it saw earlier in the century. By the 1980's many of the old hotels and boarding houses had either burned down, fallen down, or were simply tore down but the old Crazy Water survived and was converted into a retirement center and remains so to this day.

Ever since some kitchen remodeling in the early 90's, the ghost of a small girl in a pink dress has been seen in the kitchen and basement, and a man in a trenchcoat has shown up in the kitchen. It is now a retirement home.

An employee of the Crazy Water reported that one morning in 1994, she was in the kitchen panning bacon for the residents at breakfast when suddenly, just to her left, stood a little girl in an old fashioned pink frilly dress with white stockings standing with her hands perched on the side of the table watching Amy at work. The employee said the girl was there for just a few seconds and suddenly disappeared. Then at Christmas, 1999, this same employee was entering the kitchen area from the dining room when she was suddenly overcome with a cold chill as if something "passed right through her".

Then there is Isabel Hernandez, another Crazy Water employee stated that a little girl's spirit, who has called her "Dizzy", a nickname that only her family knows, frequently follows her around in the kitchen. On another occasion she felt someone touch her while she was serving food in the serving line. She said at first the little ghost scared her but over the years she has gotten use to it.

Another employee by the name of Walter has reported hearing the little girl sobbing in the basement and then upon investigating the cries felt a cold spot in the area where he heard the sounds originating from. Joyce Landon, another Crazy Water employee, claims she too has seen a little girl playing in the kitchen area, as has Linda Ruiz who reported in April 2000 saw a man in the kitchen wearing a long trench coat as if he walked out of the 1930' or 1940's. He too was there for just a short time and then vanished.

Several of the employees have heard the sounds of voices and of the little girl in the basement area located just under the kitchen. Curtis, the maintenance man reported seeing the little girl near the elevators in the basement. The basement area is part of the old Crazy Water Hotel that burned down in 1925 and the old brick walls still bear the charred remains of the original building.

## Ft. Wolters

Fort Wolters, established as Camp Wolters in 1925, is four miles east of Mineral Wells in Parker and Palo Pinto counties. It was named for Brig. Gen. Jacob F. Wolters, commander of the Fifty-sixth Brigade of the National Guard, and designated a summer training site for his units. Mineral Wells donated fifty acres, leased 2,300 acres, and in World War II provided land to increase the camp's area to 7,500 acres. The camp became an important infantry-replacement training center with a troop capacity that reached a peak of 24,973. Six months after the end of the war the camp was deactivated.

A number of people have seen the ghost of a WWII soldier who is said to have committed suicide to prevent him from going to war walking around his old barracks.

## Mineral Wells Mansion

Mineral Wells Mansion is located on Silk Stocking Row 415 NW 4th Street. Most believe that this historic home is haunted by the ghosts of a young man and an old man.

## Old Baker Hotel

Once a very lavish hotel, the huge Baker Hotel was the site of many wonderful times. Set in the backdrop of the bustling early twentieth century, the Baker was a reflection of all that America was. The hotel, born at the beginning of the great depression, survived the financial hardships of the era to witness the greatest war mankind has ever seen.

Becoming one of the state's most lavish resorts, the Baker built a magnificent reputation that attracted people from all walks of life for one reason or another. One may find the history of the grand old hotel very interesting. That history could well be a key to some of its permanent guests.

In 1914 the Crazy Water Hotel was erected and became the center of activities, but a devastating fire in March 1925, destroyed most of the building. It was then that a man by the name of T. B. Baker, a wealthy hotel businessman, decided to build a grand hotel in Mineral Wells based on the Arlington Hotel in Hot Springs, Arkansas.

Baker owned several hotels throughout Texas at that time, including the St. Anthony, the Gunther, and Menger in San Antonio, the Stephen F. Austin in Austin, the Texas Hotel in Ft. Worth, the Baker in Dallas, the Goodhue in Port Arthur, the Galvez in Galveston, the Edson in Beaumont, and the Sterling in Houston.

Construction began in 1926 and was it was completed in 1929, at a cost of $1,250,000.00. The facility magnificently reflected the spirit of the "roaring twenties". Its fourteen stories towered over the small town of 7,000 residents like a brown brick giant. It had 460 rooms, two complete spas, and what is said to be the first Olympic-size swimming pool in the United States. It rivaled any hotel in New York or Chicago.

Many celebrities visited or performed at the Baker, according to old hotel registers. The Baker hosted the Three Stooges, Clarke Gable, Judy Garland, Will Rogers, Marlene Dietrich, General Pershing, L.B.J., Jean Harlow, Sammy Kaye, Jack Dempsey, Sam Rayburn, Helen Keller, Ronald Reagan and Mary Martin, just to name a few.

The stories of ghosts and hauntings began in the Baker long before it ever closed. A porter who worked there during the 1950's and 1960's was the first known to witness the ghost of the woman on the seventh floor. She was possibly the mistress of the hotel manager. Distraught from her affair she jumped to her death from the top of the building. The year of the incident has not been verified but the room she stayed in, apparently quite comfortably, was a suite on the southeast corner of the seventh floor. Many have reported smelling her perfume and her spirit is said to be quite flirtatious with men she may fancy.

Recently a woman, who worked as a maid in the hotel, reported that on several occasions she found glasses in the room with red lipstick stains on the rims. This took place at times when no one was staying in the room.

Jane Catrett who is assisted by Ronny Walker now manages the building. Ronny manages tours of the building on weekends when time allows and is quite knowledgeable on the history of the hotel as well as the reports of a few sightings of disembodied guests.

Ronny reported one night he was near the main lobby on the first floor when he heard the distinct sound of a woman in high heals walking across the lobby. Thinking the footsteps to be those of Jane Catrett he yelled out her name; however, the footsteps faded away and upon further inspection, Ronny found himself all alone. Later he discovered that Jane had not been in the building that day.

On another occasion, Ronny reported being on the 7th floor re-setting an electrical breaker to the Christmas lights, which continuously tripped every night during display. As he was inspecting the fuse box, attempting to locate the breaker switch, he heard the footsteps of an unseen person walking up to his left - quietly - as if not to bother him. A bit startled, he turned to look and saw no one. Ronny spoke to the possible ghosts and assured them he meant no harm. After that night the lights never tripped off again.

Another incident occurred during a tour of the hotel by a group of W.W.II veterans and their spouses. As the group entered the "Brazos Room" on the first floor, which was the main dining room and dance area, a couple suddenly stopped. The woman looked at her husband and asked, "Do you hear that?"

He replied, "Why, I certainly do". About that time several other people in the group began to hear sounds of dishes and silverware clanking as well as people talking with orchestra music in the background. Most of the people there reported this event. It has never happened before nor since - according to the source - but the witnesses were sure they were experiencing the ghostly echoes of a time long past.

The most eerie story of the old Baker would have to be the tragic tale of the death of a young elevator operator by the name of Douglas Moore. The original story was told that in 1948, Douglas went to work at the Baker and quickly began to earn a lot of money - perhaps too much - for an elevator operator.

After a period of gainful employment, Douglas confessed to his mother that he had become a minor part of an illegal prostitution racket in the hotel. His mother insisted that he quit. Douglas went a step farther and reported the happenings to the local authorities not knowing that some were actually involved in the ring.

Douglas was laid off but was suddenly called back to work two weeks later. Upon returning to his job he found himself in the basement playing around in the service elevator late one night with two other bellboys. This particular elevator had a call button that would send it rapidly from the basement to the top elevator room without stopping.

It was reported by the other two boys that one of them accidentally depressed the call button when Douglas was not completely inside the elevator - suddenly trapping his body halfway out and severing him at the waist. Many believed the two boys were paid to kill Douglas. Some have reported seeing the ghost of Douglas lurking about in the basement area. Some say that only the upper portion of his body and his head can be seen, the lower portion is of course, missing.

A young woman who worked at a local drive-through bank in the early 1990's reported that she and other tellers had their workstations facing the huge hotel. During slow times they noticed hotel windows open on various floors. Later they would notice these windows closed and others would be open. After awhile they began to take note and count which were opened and closed. The pattern changed.

One of the girls told the others "it must be the man who lives in the building and takes care of it". After that, the interest ceased and they stopped noticing. The strange thing is, no one has ever stayed in the Baker at any time since its closure in 1970. There never was a caretaker. So just who was opening and closing the windows?

Then there are the stories about the small child that haunts the hotel. A little boy, about six to eight years old, was the only one to communicate with her. He told her he died in a hotel apartment in 1933 when his parents were seeking medicinal treatment for his leukemia. The witness, a local psychic, reported a large shaggy dog always accompanied the child. He also bounced a ball to get her attention and he was watched by an unknown older woman who was always near him.

The psychic also reported that one of the ghosts of the hotel was a helicopter pilot who attended basic flight training at Ft. Wolters in the 1960's. He was killed in a helicopter crash while at Ft. Rucker, Alabama. He had returned to the Baker with his body in the same traumatic state that resulted from the crash.

## City Park

While sitting in the bleachers, you can see figures in old style baseball uniforms walking across the baseball field. Orbs have been photographed by the jungle gyms.

# MINEOLA, TEXAS

Mineola is at the crossing of U.S. highways 69 and 80, eighty miles east of Dallas in southwestern Wood County. Before 1873 the place was called Sodom. According to some, Maj. Ira H. Evans, an International-Great Northern Railroad official who laid out the townsite, named the town for his daughter, Ola, and a friend, Minnie Patten. Others say the name originated when Major Rusk, a surveyor for the I-GN, combined his daughter's name with that of Minna Wesley Patten. The town came into existence when the railroads built lines through this part of the state.

## Beckham Hotel

The Beckham Hotel, 115 Commerce Street, is a genuine railroad hotel, built to house passengers as well as railroad employees lying over between runs. Located on Commerce Street in the downtown area, the hotel sits directly across the tracks from the Amtrak station. Several rooms overlook the tracks, and are favorites of guests who find Mineola's railroad heritage particularly appealing. The present brick structure was completed in 1927 after a fire razed the first (ca. 1880s) hotel. Big bands were said to have played in the upstairs ballroom during the 1920s and 1930s, and there are stories of bootlegging, ghosts and late night poker games interrupted only by the passing of trains.

When the Beckham Hotel is mentioned, most mention the apparition of a lovely woman that was spotted descending the staircase. It is reported that this ghostly figure has been identified as "Elizabeth", a woman who died in the end of the 19th century when she fell down the stairs.

## Cry Baby Bridge

The story goes that when the American Indians roamed the hills of East Texas they were being massacred by the white man. The chief learned of a planned attack and had separated the women and children from his men. The white man planned for the split and killed the chief and his men by the huge trees by Cry Baby Bridge. The women and children were slaughtered right by the bridge. There is a couple of the original old trees that are still there and with the leaves & branches are shaped like a Chief's head gear with the shape of a face. If you go to the bridge at night and turn your engine off right on top of the bridge, roll your windows down, you can still hear the cries of the women and children that were massacred.

# MOODY, TEXAS

Moody is an incorporated community at the intersection of State Highway 317 and Farm Road 107, ten miles from McGregor in McLennan County. It was established in 1881, when the Gulf, Colorado and Santa Fe Railway built the section of track between Temple and Fort Worth; the community was named in honor of William Lewis Moody, a director of the railroad company. The Moody community grew rapidly, drawing many of its early residents and business interests from nearby Perry, which had been bypassed by the railroad. The Moody post office was established in November 1881 with J. H. Morrison as postmaster. The first newspaper in the community, the weekly Monitor, began publication in 1883. By 1884 Moody had four churches, four cotton gins, two steam gristmills, a school, and 250 residents. It became the focus of an independent school district in 1889. By the early 1890s its population had increased to 800, and it had a variety of businesses, including a private bank (established in 1893).

## Moody High School

The new Moody High School going towards Temple, Texas is "said" to have been built on an Indian burial ground. Teachers would tell of times they would be up there at night alone, and they would hear lockers slam or glass break. The night cleaning crew will also tell of footsteps being heard and the sound of voices that can never be found.

# NACOGDOCHES, TEXAS

Nacogdoches, the county seat of Nacogdoches County, is on State highways 7, 21, 59, and 259, fifty miles west of the Sabine River and 100 miles north of Beaumont in the central part of the county. It was named for the Nacogdoche Indians, a Caddo group. Archeological research has established that mounds found in the area date from approximately A.D. 1250, when the Indians built lodges along Lanana and Bonita creeks, which converge just south of Nacogdoches and continue as a single stream to the Angelina River. The mounds were found to contain human bones and pottery. The expedition of René Robert Cavelier, Sieur de La Salle, visited the area in 1687. Louis Juchereau de St. Denis was sent by the French governor Sieur Antoine de la Mothe Cadillac to establish trade with the Indians in Spanish Texas. St. Denis marked a trail through Nacogdoches to the Rio Grande, along part of the route later known as the Old San Antonio Road, and was briefly arrested. In the summer of 1716 he accompanied Domingo Ramón back to East Texas to found Nuestra Señora de Guadalupe de los Nacogdoches and five other missions. The Franciscan Antonio Margil de Jesús had charge of the missions.

Guadalupe Mission was abandoned briefly two years later due to fears of a French invasion but was reestablished by the Marqués de Aguay in 1721. It operated more or less continuously until 1772, when Viceroy Antonio María de Bucareli y Ursúa promulgated the New Regulations for Presidios, which recommended the recall of all missions and settlers to San Antonio. The following year Governor Juan María Vicencio de Ripperdá sent soldiers to force the removal of all Spanish subjects to San Antonio. Antonio Gil Ibarvo, from the Lobanillo Creek area southeast of Nacogdoches, became the leader of the settlers. He petitioned successfully for the group to be allowed to return part of the way to East Texas. They established a community named Bucareli on the banks of the Trinity River, where they remained for four years until floods and Indian raids caused Ibarvo to lead them in 1779 to the abandoned mission site at Nacogdoches, possibly the only building of European origin then standing in East Texas. Later Ibarvo was commissioned commander of the militia and magistrate of the pueblo of Nacogdoches, the first official recognition of civil status for the community.

## La Hacienda Restaurant

La Hacienda Restaurant, 1411 North St, has long had a reputation for fine Mexican food. The building is reportedly haunted by the ghost of a little girl who died of smallpox. Odd things happen in the kitchen and people trip over unseen obstacles. Location now closed.

## Tol Barret House

The Tol Barret House, Rte. 4, Box 9400, was the homestead of Captain Lyne Taliaferro ("Tol") Barret, QM, C.S.A., who, in 1866 drilled the first producing oil well in Texas, at Oil Springs in southeast Nacogdoches County. The Barrets moved into the house in 1848, and lived there until their deaths in 1913 and 1920. The house is typical of early Texas; a basic center hall is flanked by two large and two small rooms and fronted with a long wide porch. It is unique in that the vertical exterior and interior wall boards are two inches thick and the two 12 over 12 pane front windows are unusual in farm homes of the 1840s. This house withstood a tornado which flattened most of Melrose about 1854, and it became a storm shelter to neighbors.

Witnesses have heard unexplainable footsteps and knocking on the front door. Some have also seen the apparition of a woman in a gold dress walking past the front windows.

## Stephen F. Austin State University - Griffith Hall - 3rd Floor

When Griffith Hall was a female dorm, a female resident assistant jumped out of her window after playing with a Ouija board. Her spirit is said to haunt the floor. The lights in the community shower flicker at the same time every night which is said to be the time she died. Residents have reported seeing a girl at the end of the hall in tattered clothes and when they look back she is gone. Also, around 2AM every night, people on the South wing hear footsteps running down the hall. One resident has reported watching out the peephole and seeing no one but feeling a gust of air rush under her door as if someone had ran by.

## Stephen F. Austin State University - Mays Hall 11

Before Mays Hall was a dormitory, it was a hospital, with a morgue in the basement. On the other end of the building is a deep, ruined bomb shelter from the early 40s or 50s. In the basement is a very negative feeling that is very hard to describe. The basement area is usually locked, but occasionally residents break in and wander around. The bomb shelter has been locked for years but last year was broken into. Recently students discovered what appears to be a false wall in there, because the lining on the wall ends (no one noticed before because of the lighting and the junk all over the floor).

The negative feeling from the basement is present in the bomb shelter too, but grows as you near the false wall. Dorm residents are curious to explore but don't want to get caught. No one knows any specific stories, but the students all speculate it would have to deal with someone dying in one of the hospital rooms. Further research reveals that the first floor of the original wing was the campus clinic which did have a couple of overnight observation rooms, but the city hospital was (and still is) less than half a mile away and the campus clinic was never used for long term care.

The clinic closed when the "short wing" was built in the 60's, and the clinic was renovated into individual rooms (which is why those rooms resemble the short wing rooms more than the rooms above. The false wall in the bomb shelter covers an alcove designed to hold air filtration gear. A shaft behind the wall runs into the main basement.

## Stephen F. Austin State University - The Theater

Some think "Chester", said to be the ghost of the Theater, at Stephen F. Austin State University is the ghost of the architect of the fine arts building, or a former student. Research indicates that neither of these is likely, but he may be the ghost of a foreman who died, a combatant in the Texas Revolution, the Civil War, or any number of battles the Caddo Indians fought on the site. Regardless, he haunts the theater building and has been known to show up as a ghostly extra during plays. He has also been blamed for odd noises, cold spots, and a weird face that showed up on a stage curtain. It has been said that in the construction of the theater a worker died and has been haunting the place since. The spirit is said to have killed a professor there.

## Stephen F. Austin State University - Wilson Hall building # 13

Reports from Wilson Hall tell of stereos will turn themselves on, speakers that will increase in volume until they blow, chairs that will move themselves, books that will re-arrange themselves, and apparitions that have been seen.

## Sterne-Hoya House

The Sterne-Hoya House, 211 South Lanana Street, was built in 1828 by Adolphus Sterne as a home for his new bride.  The pioneer merchant was active in the ill fated Fredonia rebellion of 1826-27 and also helped with founding of Texas Republic. Sam Houston baptized as Roman Catholic here, because Mexico required landholders to be Catholic. Legend has it that Sam Houston remarked, "Texas is worth a mass".

A former housekeeper reports feeling a gentle pressure on every inch of her body and suddenly felt like the room was spinning. She could feel a happy presence. It went away as she descended the stairs but she seldom entered the attic after that and didn't clean the house much longer. Possibly the children of the house were responsible for this incident. But in the cellar the feeling was more negative.

## Stephen F. Austin State University - Turner Fine Arts Auditorium

"Chester" haunts the theater in the Turner Fine Arts Auditorium on the Stephen F. Austin University campus. Reputed to be the ghost of the architect who died before the building's completion--some think the blueprints were misinterpreted and the building was erected backwards. Other people believe that "Chester" is the ghost of a former drama student. He has been seen as a face on a stage curtain and even once appeared onstage as an extra ghost in a play in the 1960's. Students have reported cold spots and strange noises in the halls of the building.

Further research has shown that Chester was, in fact, the architect of the building. When learning his plans were set backwards, he killed himself in disgrace. Chester was seen originally in a photo of the original theatre cast of Hamlet. With the actor playing the "ghost" in Hamlet called in sick, the director found the only person who knew the lines to play the part that night. When the cast picture was taken that night, only a faint glow comes from where the ghost portraying the character was standing. Members of the cast were dumbfounded.

# NORTH RICHLAND HILLS, TEXAS

North Richland Hills is on State highways 26, 183, and 820, eight miles west of the Dallas-Fort Worth International Airport and eight miles northeast of downtown Fort Worth in northeastern Tarrant County. The town is part of the Fort Worth-Arlington Metropolitan Statistical Area. The area was agricultural until 1950, when Clarence Jones developed his farm into a residential area and named it North Richland Hills, in imitation of an adjacent successful development to the south. The city was incorporated by election on April 25, 1953. During the 1980s North Richland Hills had a broad business base, manufacturing everything from computers (Tandy Advanced Products) to mattresses (Ohio Sealy). Other businesses included Walker Construction Company, Sanger Harris (Foley's retail), Graham Magnetics (magnetic tape), Bates Containers, Allied Northeast Bank, Interfirst Bank, and the Bank of North Texas. The Mid-Cities Daily News and the North Hills News were the local papers. In 1990 the Birdville Independent School District had six elementary schools, one junior high, and one senior high in North Richland Hills. In addition, there were several denominational schools, and twenty-two churches representing ten faiths. The city boundary ran through the northeast campus of Tarrant County Junior College. A municipal complex built in 1960 and expanded in 1987 housed the police department, the water department, and the city administration. A second civic center of 87,000 square feet housed the city library and the Parks and Recreation Department; the theater in the building was home to the North East Fine Arts League. In 1958 North Richland Hills had an estimated population of 7,000. Its population increased steadily, until by 1970 it was estimated at 15,735. In 1978 the population was 23,265, and by 1990 it had risen to 38,959. In the early 1990s North Richland Hills had a council-manager form of city government.

### Knob Hill

People have reported seeing dark figures moving through the trees late at night at the top of Knob Hill. Residents also report shouts and hollers early in the morning before dawn. It is reported that a local outlaw Known as Sam Bass took two men up to the top of the hill in 1870 and shot both of them in the head. Some residence have reported over the years of seeing men with old cowboy hats walking around by their fences, but when they go out to investigate no one is there.

## OAKALLA, TEXAS

Oakalla is at the confluence of Rocky Creek and the Lampasas River, off U.S. Highway 183 in far northeastern Burnet County. The first settlers arrived in the area in the 1850s. Oakalla officially came into being on May 19, 1879, when its post office was opened. By 1881 the community had a cotton gin, a drugstore, a blacksmith shop, a general store, and a doctor; by 1890 it included Baptist and Methodist congregations, a cotton gin, a gristmill, eight other businesses, and a population of 100. The settlement supported fourteen businesses by 1896, and its population had risen to 175. Schools in the area were private until a cooperative was built with classrooms on the second floor. The two-acre school site was deeded in 1890. The school also functioned as a place of worship until 1908, when the Oakalla Baptist Church erected a meetinghouse. Methodists met in the schoolhouse until March 1923, when C. W. Tedder and his mother, Mary, deeded land for a Methodist church; it was constructed in 1925. Both churches were still active in 1990. In 1920 the wooden school building was torn down, and a two-room structure was built of stones from the old Rock School on Gregory Branch. In 1929 two more rooms were added. The Oakalla post office was discontinued sometime after 1930. In 1946 Oakalla high school students were transferred to Briggs, and in 1956 the elementary students followed. The local district was consolidated with that of Lampasas in 1958. Oakalla's population was estimated at 180 in 1925 and at 250 in 1931, when ten local businesses were in operation. From 1940 to 1970 the population level hovered around 100, then decreased to forty-five by the late 1980s. In 1990 Oakalla had a general store and a population of forty-five, and the 1920 school building was in use as a community center and county library branch.

### The "OZONE"

It a long winding road with lots of sharp curves, hills and bridges. It is said that the headlights of a truck will just appear out of no where and chase you till you run off the road, which is said to be the reason that so many people have died on that road. There is also an old bridge that is still there, but condemned now, where a school bus full of kids fell over side down into the river killing them in the process. Since then, they have a new road and bridge near an intersection by a white church leading away from the old creepy one, which is in the vicinity of east of the new bridge. You will see a large metal road block next to a Historical Marker.

In the mist of the trees you can see the metal beams of the bridge. You can still walk over the old bridge which base road is made out of wood planks; and you're quiet and listen, you will hear the cries of the screaming children. There is also a grave yard across the road from the bridge which has been rumored to have a witch's grave in it. The headstone glows a shimmering orange color like the reflection of flames from a fire when there is a full moon.

## OLNEY, TEXAS

Olney, at the intersection of State highways 132, 114, 251, and 79 and Farm roads 210 and 3329, in north central Young County, was settled in 1879 and 1880 by Boone McCarty, L. Pankonon, and the Neely brothers. Pitts Neal formed a partnership with the Neely's to establish a site for annual roundups held by local ranchers. In 1889 John W. Groves donated two acres for a townsite, and J. M. Brisco built the first store. A post office was established when pioneer G. W. Hutchings agreed to carry the mail there from the Farmer post office. The name Olney came either from a news article noticed by Hutchings and the Farmer postmaster concerning Senator Roger Q. Mills's activities at Olney, Illinois, or from Richard Olney, secretary of state for President Cleveland. The first school opened in 1891. The town was incorporated in 1909 when rail service started with the Wichita Falls and Southern Railway. Olney was moved a mile north to gain access to the line, and in 1910 the Gulf, Texas and Western began providing service. Rail service was discontinued in 1942. Oil was discovered in 1923. With the production of the Swastika Pool in 1924 Olney became a leading oil town; it had three refineries and a population of 5,000 by 1930. In 1951 a tornado struck, killing two, injuring seventy-five, and causing $2 million in property damage. Olney had a population of 3,872 in 1960; 3,624 in 1970, when the town supported 116 businesses; and 4,060 in 1980. Olney is an agri-business center and manufactures apparel, recreational vehicles, aluminum products, rubber hose, and agricultural airplanes. It has an airport, a hospital, a library, and a nursing home. In 1990 the population was 3,519.

## Hamilton Hospital

The old part of Hamilton Hospital is said to be haunted by the spirits of those who once worked there. Many workers have experienced hot and cold spots throughout the halls and even have tricks played on them such as lights coming on when they have just been turned off, and files missing from the file cabinets. Some witnesses have reported seeing nurses in old style uniforms walking down the hallways.

## Johnson Road

It is said that if you drive down this road and turn you lights off that bright orbs will start flying and swarming around your vehicle.

## Padgett Cemeteries

In the little town of Padgett there are two Padgett Cemeteries. However most people only know of one as the second is usually impossible to get to due to terrible road conditions and the weather. It is said that if you drive to the road of the second cemetery and leave your lights on with your keys on the roof of your vehicle that walk to the cemetery, that when you get back your vehicle will be started with the keys in the ignition, and the doors locked. No one knows exactly why this happens.

The other cemetery is haunted by the grounds keeper that used to tend to the cemetery. He still tends to the cemetery at night like he used to, to keep kids from destroying things in the cemetery. Many people have seen him raking leaves. Others have taken pictures near or around a certain tombstone in the center of the cemetery however when the pictures develop the tombstone is not in the picture.

## Cemetery at Springcreek and Ave. M

The cemetery located on Springcreek and Avenue M. is said to be haunted be some kind of unknown source. Many claim that in the back of the cemetery there is a statue of Jesus. In the day if you drive by or go look at it. His hands are facing up. But at night if you go and see it his hands are facing down with his thumbs broken off.

# POSSUM KINGDOM, TEXAS

Possum Kingdom Reservoir, popularly known as Possum Kingdom Lake, is on the Brazos River in Palo Pinto, Stephens, Jack, and Young counties (its center is at 32°52' N, 98°26' W). It has a capacity of 724,700 acre-feet, a surface area of 19,800 acres, and a shoreline of 310 miles. Here Morris Sheppard Dam impounds 1,500,000 acre-feet of water annually for municipal, industrial, mining, irrigation, flood-control, recreational, and power-generation uses. Area hills and valleys, post oaks, and cedars make a "veritable paradise" for possums around the lake. The dam, named for Senator John Morris Sheppard and authorized by the United States Congress in 1935, was the first erected by the Brazos River Conservation and Reclamation District. It was begun on May 29, 1938, under general contractors C. F. Lytle and A. L. Johnson and completed on March 20, 1941.

## Camp Constantine

Those who have stayed at Camp Constantine have reported seeing the apparitions of two cowboys standing there staring, off into the distance as if searching for something. Others have reported hearing screams and yelling.

# PRINCETON, TEXAS

Princeton began in September of 1888, when Missouri, Kansas and Texas Railway extended its line from Greenville to McKinney and created a railroad switch on the land (known as Wilson's Switch). When the post office was established, Wilson could not be used since there was already a town named Wilson, so Princeton was chosen in honor of Prince Dowlen, a promoter of the townsite.

## County Road 400 at 447

Two people were killed at this intersection when the motorcycle they were riding collided with a horse trailer. Now, the young man is seen walking shirtless down 447.

## County Road 400

There is a barn on this road that is rumored to be the sight of "devil worship". People who have approached it at night have reported seeing two black shapes that chase them off the property.

## County Road 392 (AKA Airport Road)

At or near the intersection of 447 (near the equestrian center), two skydivers were killed in separate accidents in the mid-80's, one about a year after the other. A woman's chute failed to open, and a man got wrapped up in some power lines. Now you can hear the woman screaming for help at the top of her lungs, even from a couple of blocks away.

## Water Tower

Park next to the tower and you can see what looks like a girl's legs dangle over the side. Honk 3 times and she'll appear on your hood, and the next day, she'll show up somewhere that you go. There have also been reports people seeing an apparition of a woman falling from the Water Tower.

# RICHARDSON, TEXAS

Richardson, a residential and electronic manufacturing suburb of Dallas, is on U.S. Highway 75 and the Atchison, Topeka and Santa Fe, the Southern Pacific, and the St. Louis and Southwestern railroads, ten miles north of downtown Dallas in northern Dallas and southern Collin counties. The twenty-eight-square-mile area of Richardson has an uneven boundary surrounded by other communities, including Dallas to the northwest and south, Garland to the east and south, Plano to the north, and Murphy and Sachse to the east. The 159-acre city of Buckingham is entirely within the city limits of Richardson. Spring and Duck creeks and Cottonwood Branch run through the community. The area of Richardson was settled by the Peters colony in the 1840s and 1850s. The area of waving grass and numerous springs was popular with early settlers, who formed the community of Breckinridge in the 1840s and 1850s. Breckinridge flourished until 1873, when the Houston and Texas Central Railroad bypassed it. Richardson was founded on the Houston and Texas Central Railway tracks. After it was built, the residents of Breckinridge moved to Richardson. William J. Wheeler, a local ginner, and Bernard Reilly donated 101 acres of land for the townsite and right-of-way for the railroad on June 23, 1873. Wheeler refused to have the community named after him, so it was called Richardson when it received a post office in 1874. There are several suggestions for the origin of the name. One is A. S. Richardson, a secretary on the H&TC. Most likely the town was named for E. H. Richardson, a contractor who built the Houston and Texas from Dallas to Denton. By 1881 Richardson was a thriving community with several stores, including general stores, groceries, and drugstores, four doctors, several cotton gins, and churches. In 1886 a train accident in the community killed one man, and when the sugar car overturned, spilling sugar on the tracks, residents took it home in buckets.

## Shopping center at Yale and Beltline

When the business at this location was Herman's Sporting Goods back in the late 80's an ex employee was let in after hours where he killed almost every one still working in the store. People who have worked in the store since that time claim that they can boxes moving, people laughing and than an eerie dead silence.

# SCOTTSVILLE, TEXAS

Scottsville, on Farm roads 1998 and 2199, four miles east of Marshall in east central Harrison County, was named after its founder, William Thomas Scott, who moved to Texas from Louisiana in 1840. In 1840 Scott's slaves built his lavish plantation home, reputedly identical to Jefferson Davis's Mississippi mansion. Scottsville's white schoolchildren attended classes in the small schoolhouse that Scott had built; it was staffed with the Scott family governess. The Scotts also established the first church in the community, a Methodist congregation. During the Civil War the Scott plantation provided provisions for Confederate troops. On August 4, 1869, Scottsville was granted a post office. Its population was reported as 300 in 1929, as 50 during the Great Depression, and as around 260 by 1950, a total that remained fairly steady into the 1980s. In the early 1990s Scottsville, which still had its post office, was an incorporated community and reported 287 residents and eleven businesses.

## Scottsville Cemetery

The Scottsville Cemetery dates from before Texas was a state. The haunting is actually on the grounds bordering the west of the cemetery and church. There is a covered spring house at the foot of a hill just outside the fenced off area leading to the cemetery parking lot. Stairs lead up the hill from the spring house to the top, where a large, two story house once stood. This house burned in the 50's, but was reputed to be haunted. Old-timers told of standing outside this old home, in their youth, and listening to voices and furniture being moved in the empty rooms inside. Youths of today say that if you stand at the top of the stairs, you can hear a woman weeping several hundred feet away, down at the spring house.

# SHERMAN, TEXAS

Sherman is in central Grayson County seventy-five miles north of Dallas on U.S. Highway 75. The city is also intersected by U.S. Highway 82, State highways 11 and 56, and the tracks of the Missouri, Kansas and Texas, Southern Pacific, and Burlington Northern rail lines. The community, which is in the center of the county, was designated as county seat by the act that established the county on March 17, 1846. Thomas J. Shannon was one of the first settlers in the area. The town was named for Gen. Sidney Sherman, a hero of the Texas Revolution and one of the state's earliest railroad promoters. A log courthouse was among the first buildings constructed in Sherman, and settlers soon began moving into the new community, which grew rapidly as a merchandising center.

A post office began operating in 1847. The town originally was on a hill just west of its present location. In 1848 Sherman was relocated to a site three miles east of the original location. By 1852 400 people lived in Sherman, which "consisted of a row of clapboard business buildings along the east side of the public square," and, among other things, two saloons, a district clerk's office, a doctor's office, and a church. By the end of the decade the town had incorporated and was a stop on the Butterfield Overland Mail route through Texas.

## Woodman's Circle

The Woodman's Circle Building is located at the intersection of hwy 56 & 1417 on the west side of Sherman Texas. It was built by the Supreme Woodmen's Circle and established 25 Jun 1930. The Woodmen's Circle merged with the Woodmen of the World in 1965 and closed down over the next few years. By early 1980's no one lived on the property and today it sits terribly vandalized and empty. It was the scene of much activity over its years and was a beautiful building. It has been used to house orphans and the elderly over the years and for a period was also used as an asylum. A scrapbook kept about the Woodmen's Circle Home is in the Rare Books Room of the Sherman Library.

Witnesses have reported seeing the apparition of a woman wandering the grounds, as well as strange noises ranging from voices, cries and screams.

# SOUTHLAKE, TEXAS

Southlake is at the intersection of State Highway 114 and Farm Road 1709, on Southlake and the St. Louis Southwestern Railway seventeen miles north of Fort Worth in northern Tarrant and southern Denton counties. It is bordered by Grapevine, Keller, and Dallas-Fort Worth International Airport. By the 1960s the scattered community had incorporated. The estimated population was 1,250 in 1966 and 2,031 in 1970. People moving from cities to the rural atmosphere of Southlake caused phenomenal growth in the 1980s, when the population grew from 2,808 in 1980 to 7,065 in 1990. Most of the population (6,823) was in Tarrant County, and the remaining 242 were in Denton County. By 1990 six manufacturers in the community produced engines, concrete products, and food packaging. Southlake had become the third largest community in Tarrant County, after Fort Worth and Arlington.

## Southlake/ Timmeron

A number of witnesses have reported that if you walk down the street by the pool, you will feel a sudden feel of cold energy and be overcome with a feeling you are being watched all the time. When you are on the bike trails you can occasionally hear something walking near to you. People's dogs always bark out as if at an intruder, but if you check, there is nothing there. Lights will flicker, you can hear loud noises outside and many people have reported seeing ghost.

## SPRINGTOWN, TEXAS

Springtown is on State Highway 199 twenty-seven miles northwest of Fort Worth near the northern border of Parker County. In 1856 Joseph Ward of New Jersey settled on the site, on a creek fed by numerous springs seventeen miles northeast of Weatherford. Three years later Ward designed the town square and named the place Littleton's Springs after a pioneer family. In the mid-1870s the name was changed to Springtown following a petition by a majority of the 200 residents. The town's post office has operated continuously since its establishment in June 1875. In 1884 Springtown was incorporated, and the community elected J. A. Graves its first mayor. Springtown Male and Female Institute opened that year and served the northern part of the county for a decade. Public schools eventually developed, and in 1936 Springtown High School was incorporated in the Parker County school system. The first town newspaper, established in 1881, was the Springtown Sentinel. Newspapers that followed included the Pilot, Local, and Journal. By 1890 the community had four churches, two cotton gins, one steam corn mill, a daily stage to Weatherford costing one dollar, and a triweekly stage to Decatur. Springtown grew from a population of 500 in 1890 to nearly 800 in 1940. From the Great Depression through 1960 the population growth slowed. Afterward, primarily because of an increase in the Springtown-Fort Worth commuter population, the number of residents nearly doubled. Springtown had a population of 1,658 in 1986. In 1990 the population was 1,740.

## <u>Veal Station Cemetery</u> (just North of Springtown)

It is said that there is a glowing tombstone in the Veal Station Cemetery. There was even a news story about the glowing tombstone and the ghost of a woman walking around her own grave. The cemetery is chained off at night now because of so many people going there.

## SULPHUR SPRINGS, TEXAS

Sulphur Springs, the county seat of Hopkins County, is at the junction of Interstate 30 and State highways 11, 19, and 154, in the central portion of the county. The town was originally known as Bright Star when stores and a hotel were first built at the site, which had become a popular camping place for teamsters hauling commodities west from Jefferson. A Methodist church was organized in 1852 and a Baptist in 1859. A post office named Bright Star was established in 1854, and the Odd Fellows' Lodge continued to bear that name until 1949. Bright Star was incorporated possibly as early as 1852. Dr. O. S. Davis deeded the public square to the county when the town was rechartered and became the county seat in 1870. The name was changed to Sulphur Springs in 1871, when the mineral springs in the area were being advertised to make the town a health resort.

## Dead Mans Run

Dead Mans Run got its name around 1890 because of a man who was working on the railroad tracks that were being laid through town. About 2 miles off of highway 19 on hwy. 11 to the right on a little black top road is a desolate patch of railroad tracks. Now this man who was working on it was having a bad time with his wife. So one night he took her out there for a "romantic interlude" and instead he beat her badly and tied her to the tracks. Well, thinking she was unconscious he sat down beside her to rest and without him knowing, she tied his boot laces to the track. He felt so guilty that he sat there on the tracks and never moved until he saw the train barreling down on him. When it was almost there he got up to move and couldn't. He looked down to see his wife grinning up at him and his laces tied in multiple knots. He tried to untie his laces, but to no prevail, and was killed with his wife on the tracks.

Now if you go to those tracks on November 12 at about 2 to 3 am you can get out of your car and sit on the tracks and you will witness the entire scene. You can hear the man screaming and the woman laughing.

## SUNNYVALE, TEXAS

Sunnyvale is on U.S. Highway 80 between Mesquite and Garland twelve miles east of Dallas in far eastern Dallas County. The site is on about forty-five original land grants, the largest four being those of J. Johnson, P. Green, M. A. Freeman, and T. D. Coats. Sunnyvale was incorporated on February 26, 1953. The town incorporated the communities of New Hope, Tripp, Hattersville, and Long Creek. New Hope and Tripp each had several stores, a church, and a school at the time. The area of old New Hope along Beltline Road became Main Street in Sunnyvale, and in 1965 the old New Hope school served as the Sunnyvale town hall. By 1982 the building served as the city library. Around the time of incorporation Sunnyvale was named by the students of the Tripp-Long Creek School in a contest initiated by area officials. The students originally chose Sunnyville, but that name was already claimed by another community. Sunnyvale had a population of 1,000 and an industrial-equipment factory in 1958. By 1982 the population began to grow, and by 1991 the community had five construction-related industries and one drilling-equipment manufacturer. The population in 1990 was 2,228. On October 4, 1994, a 105-year-old landmark store, Lander's Mercantile-E. E. Kearney, Dealers in Everything, burned.

## Barns Bridge

One night in 1974 and lady and her daughter were driving on Barns Bridge and flipped into the creek where they both died. Legend is that at midnight if you stop on the bridge, turn your car off and roll down the windows and drop your keys onto the road. Wait for 3 minutes and get your keys and they say that when you get home you will have a set of 3 finger prints all over your car.

## TEXARKANA, TEXAS

Texarkana is at the junction of Interstate 30 and U.S. highways 59, 67, 71, and 82 in extreme northeastern Texas on the Texas-Arkansas border. It was named for its location on the state line between Bowie County, Texas, and Miller County, Arkansas, only a short distance above the Louisiana boundary. The three parts of its name honor the three states. There is some debate about the actual origins of the name, which was in use some time before the town's founding. According to one tradition, the name was derived from a steamboat known as the Texarkana, which plied the water of the Red River as early as 1860. Others claim that a man named Swindle, who ran a general store in Red Land, Bossier Parish, Louisiana, manufactured a drink called "Texarkana Bitters." Yet another story claims that when the St. Louis, Iron Mountain and Southern Railroad was building its line through the area, Col. Gus Knobel, who made the survey, coined the name and erected a large sign at the site. The strategic position of Texarkana is the keynote to its history and development. The Great Southwest Trail, for hundreds of years the main line of travel from Indian villages of the Mississippi River country to those of the South and West, passed by a Caddo Indian village on the site that later became Texarkana. Seventy Indian mounds, reminders of Caddo occupation and culture, are within a radius of thirty miles of Texarkana.

## Spring Lake Park

For a long time Texarkana was known as the town that dreaded Sundown. Right at the end of World War II, a mysterious killer was roaming the city, killing at will. One of the murders took place at Spring Lake Park where a couple was making out. The killer surprised them and both of the young people were murdered. Rumor is that the girl was tied to a tree and stabbed to death. Now if you stand by that tree, you feel rope being tied around you.

## THURBER, TEXAS

Thurber was once the largest city between Fort Worth and El Paso, as was the case with Indianola. Thurber was also the first city in Texas to be completely electrified and amenities included refrigeration and running water. It did, however, have an abnormally high child mortality rate that still puzzles historians.

Thurber was built by the Johnson Coal Company that was later bought out by The Texas and Pacific Coal Company in 1888. Its mining operation provided the fuel for coal-burning locomotives of numerous railroads, including the Santa Fe, the Southern Pacific, the Texas & Pacific and the "Katy". At one time the coal deposits were thought to be inexhaustible. There are still millions of tons left.

## Smokestack

She has been seen near the smokestack a number of times, but no one has been able to catch her. She is a pretty young girl that is rumored to sing opera tunes as she walks the streets of Thurber at night.

Another young girl sits atop the smoke stack. She supposedly died of pneumonia and was buried. Her fiancé dug her body up to retrieve the ring - but he had to cut her finger off to do it.  When she started bleeding, he realized that she was still alive, but he buried her again anyway to cover his shameful deed. Now she searches for the man who betrayed her.

# TYLER, TEXAS

Tyler, the county seat of Smith County, is one of the leading cities of East Texas. It is ninety-nine miles southeast of Dallas at the junctions of U.S. highways 69 and 271 and State highways 14, 31, 64, 110, and 155. The city was authorized on April 11, 1846, when the Texas legislature voted to establish Smith County and a corresponding county seat. The townsite, located near the geographic center of the county, was selected by a panel of commissioners appointed by the legislature and was named for President John Tyler in recognition of his support for admitting Texas to the United States. On February 6, 1847, commissioners purchased a 100-acre site from Edgar Pollett for $150, and a townsite was laid out in twenty-eight blocks around a central square. A log courthouse on the north side of the square served as the meeting hall and church. Another log courthouse was built in 1847 on the center of the Tyler square; it was replaced in 1852, when a new, larger brick courthouse was constructed on the same site. A Methodist church was organized in 1846, and the First Baptist Church was established in 1848. Tyler was incorporated on January 29, 1850.

## Tyler Junior College - Wise Auditorium

Witnesses have reported that Wise Auditorium is haunted by a little boy who screams as you leave the building at night.

# WAXAHACHIE, TEXAS

Waxahachie, the county seat of Ellis County, is on Interstate Highway 35E and U.S. Highway 287, thirty miles south of Dallas in the central part of the county. The name comes from an Indian word meaning "cow" or "buffalo" and is also the name of a local creek. Waxahachie was established as the seat of the new county in August 1850 on land donated by Emory W. Rogers, a pioneer settler. Rogers, J. D. Templeton, W. H. Getzendaner, B. F. Hawkins, and J. H. Spalding were among the first settlers in the community, which began with just over 100 residents and grew rapidly from the start. In 1850 the first county courthouse was built, and a general store and the post office opened. Waxahachie was incorporated on April 28, 1871,

## Becky Rd.

The site of the last Confederate hanging by Union Army soldiers is on Becky Road. The victim, Pvt. John Hemerich, still hangs around the site of his death as his apparition has been seen standing on the side of the road.

## BonnyNook Bed & Breakfast Inn

The Bonnynook Inn is located at 414 W Main St. This 1887 Victorian home is located near Square, in a historic national district. Each room is a different experience. Mrs. West, the ghost of a former owner, has been experienced in the Morrow Room. Guests have reported singing, and seeing something floating near the ceiling.

## Catfish Plantation

The Catfish Plantation is located at 814 Water Street, Waxahachie, TX. There are a number of stories about the hauntings of this historic old house. According to one version it is haunted by benevolent Elizabeth Anderson who was murdered on her wedding day, a farmer named Will, and grumpy Caroline Mooney.

Others say that the spirits are those of Eliza Herrod Richards, who died 14 October, 1925, and her son, Jesse Thomas Richards, who died in the house on 9 October, 1937. Although Eliza was 77 years old at her death, she appears as a young woman of 20, close to the age she was at her first marriage in 1867. She apparently had an unhappy second marriage, to a man in Kentucky, whom she left. She moved to Texas with her eldest son, and returned to using her first married name, Richards. The "old farmer, Will" is her son J.T. Richards, who was the local meat cutter and grocer from the early 1900s until his death in 1937. Then there is the spirit known to be Carrie Jenkins Mooney, who lived in the house from the 1950s until her death in 1970.

There have been a number of formal investigations into the ghosts that haunt this historic location. During the course of the investigation investigators reported hearing footsteps and tapping noises on the tables. One investigator reported the feeling of someone brushing up against him. Several investigators reported sounds of footsteps from attic area. Investigators also noticed the clock in a photo was set to midnight when the first arrived on scene. Investigators also noticed at some point in the investigation the time changed to 5 o'clock. None of them touched the clock. One of the investigators heard a loud chime as if the clock was ringing the hour, however, further investigation revealed that the clock did not work and had not worked in some time.

Waitresses and customers are always reporting strange things that happen, such as rude patrons having plates dumped on them and cold spots in the bathroom. Pictures have been taken that show a slender young woman in outline form. One is a farmer, one is an old woman who lived there, and one is a young girl who was murdered on her wedding day in the house. Supposedly a burglar attempted to burglarize the safe one night and seemed to leave in a hurry. The Catfish Plantation was partially burned on June 29, 2003, but is now back up and open for business. The owners say that the three ghosts (Elizabeth, Will, and Caroline) are still present.

## Courthouse

The Ellis County Courthouse was built from architectural plans created by J. Riely Gordon. The building incorporates the Richardsonian Romanesque architectural style originally created by Boston architect Henry Hobson Richardson and made popular in Texas by J. Riely Gordon.

Ellis County's courthouse is without a doubt one of the grandest old county courthouses in the Southwest. To make it even more interesting the county recently spent about eleven million dollars restoring the building. After years of restoration work, the courthouse was reopened in the fall of 2002. The restoration was so detailed that they matched the colors of the interior to those used when the building was originally built, and the county bought red sandstone for repairs from the same query that produced the stone used for construction in 1895. This is truly a good time to go see the Ellis County Courthouse!

While J. Reily Gordon often incorporated small ornamental faces on some of his buildings, none was as populated (or infested) with faces as the Ellis County Courthouse in Waxahachie. As the faces started appearing they caught the attention of the sidewalk superintendents and before long the entire town was speculating on their meaning - or trying to identify individuals.

Since no one was willing to come forward and explain the carvings, speculation turned to legend. A few names are repeated in most accounts - nationalities of the stone carvers vary. All agree she was the landlady's daughter.

A series of intricately carves stone faces grace each of the four porch capitals, ranging from the sublime to the grotesque. Legend has it that German itinerant stone carver Harry Herley fell in love with the local girl Mabel Frame, whose grandmother operated the boarding house where he resided while sculpting of all of the courthouse's exterior ornamentation. Herley loved Mabel Frame dearly, but she did not return his love. The beautiful likenesses of Mabel portrayed on the stone porticoes soon turned into demons. Time and the dwindling love affair are portrayed as one walks around the courthouse.

Perhaps you will be able to see a manifestation of its resident spirit said to be Mabel Frame. The strange voices, cold spots and other "materializations" that have been reported by witnesses are blamed on the ghost of Mabel Frame.

## Rose of Sharon Bed & Breakfast

The Rose of Sharon is located at 205 Bryson was built in 1892 as the family home for the E.P. Powell Family. In 1912, Powell, a lawyer took a job in Austin as his family had to leave their beloved home. After the Powell family left, the home had a series of owners, until it finally sat empty. At this point, Sharon Shawn purchased it.

Shortly after purchasing the house, the owner took a tour before renovations started. She had left her purse at the front entrance and when she returned to reclaim it, she discovered a pair of earrings lying near her purse, earrings that she had lost a year before.

In the former master bedroom, now called Kathleen's Room, a family of four has been spotted, dressed in the style of the late 1800s and standing as if posed for a picture. These figures have been seen a number of times and they always exude a sense of peace and happiness, not ear. Witnesses have also heard the sounds of stringed music echoing throughout the house as well as the sounds of footsteps going up the stairs to the second floor.

## Waters St.

A little boy is said to be haunting the streets late at night in his bike. The story goes as is. One day late at night, he was riding his bike, when a car of drunken teenagers shot him for no reason. It is said that he still rides his bike late at night, and if you approach him he takes out his revenge on you.

# WEATHERFORD, TEXAS

Weatherford, the county seat of Parker County, is at the intersection of U.S. highways 180 and 80, thirty miles west of Fort Worth in the center of the county. Interstate 20 passes the southern edge of the city, and Farm roads 920, 2421, 51, 1884, and State Highway 171 serve it too. Parker County held an election to select the site for its county seat. Of three eligible sites, the present location was selected and named Weatherford in honor of Jefferson Weatherford, a member of the Texas Senate who coauthored the bill establishing the county. On the crest of a divide between the Trinity and Brazos valleys, Weatherford, for its first decade, was the principal frontier settlement in North Texas. The town was incorporated in 1858, and a post office was opened in 1859.

## Law Office

This law office was formerly the home of a prominent family Weatherford family. When the law form moved into this space, they had no idea that they were also moving in with a ghost. A number of members of the firm, as well as clients have reported music that is heard in the building (no source), radios that change stations, as well as footsteps and doors slamming. Invisible hands have touched visitors, and paint cans have turned themselves over.

## Rural Area

Between Wichita Falls and Dallas on 287 (Closer to Wichita Falls) A ghost train disappears as it approaches cars crossing the tracks. Nearby, witnesses have reported that a burned down house has strange lights and those bold enough to enter the ruins have reported encountering "eerie" sensations.

## Baker Mansion

The Baker Mansion was originally built in 1894 and it is said to be haunted by Charles Baker, a son of the original owner JD Baker. JD Baker died before the house was completed and in 1908, another tragedy struck the family. A strange tale that remains unsolved to this day. Charles Baker, who grew to be an intelligent man and business wise, became a buyer for the Baker Company. In the early spring of that year he embarked on a buying trip for the stores and was last seen leaving San Francisco en route to Seattle where he was to order goods. He was never seen nor heard from again. A short time after the disappearance of Charles Baker, his brother, Harry was on a business trip to Chicago where he was suddenly struck with a ruptured appendix and tragically died.

The last of the Baker children, Mary, married and moved to Oklahoma City. Mrs. Baker continued to live in the Baker home until she got too old to take care of herself and moved to Oklahoma City with her daughter to live out the remaining days of her life, keeping the home in Weatherford until her death in 1942.

Mrs. Mary Baker Rumsey, the remaining Baker child, sold the huge home to Mr. & Mrs. George Fant, in the early 1940's. Mr. Fant happened to be the President of the First National Bank of Weatherford, the bank that backed the $5,000.00 reward for the whereabouts of young Charles Baker in 1908. The Fants owned the house until the late 1970's, long after the death of Mr. Fant.

When the Fants moved into the home, nothing seemed out of place for about a year. Then their teenage niece came to visit. She is the one that reported most of the encounters that people had with the resident spirits. She, out of fear of what others would think of her, never told anyone of the strange happenings until many years later.

She reported that her encounters one summer during World War II when she was staying with her aunt and uncle in the Baker Mansion. The reporter and one of her aunts were sleeping in the easternmost bedroom downstairs. This bedroom had a door leading to the southern side of the verandah. Only the screen door was latched and she remembered all was quiet and everyone was asleep. She was awakened by the sound of someone very quietly and slowly walking down a small hall on the south side of the house that connected an inner bedroom with the bedroom she and her aunt were sleeping.

She said that she closed her eyes, afraid to look up. When she finally got the nerve to open them, a figure was standing at the foot of the bed. She screamed loudly enough to wake the dead and the figure immediately disappeared. Naturally, everyone in the house descended upon her bedroom and the consensus of opinion was that she was merely having a nightmare, but she knew it was not a nightmare because she was very much awake when she heard him."

That incident was the only time the ghost ever appeared when anyone else was around and the last time that she screamed in terror. She didn't spend the night in that house again for a long while. Her family out of town and she didn't return to the big house until the early 1960's. In the meantime, her aunt built a smaller house near by leaving a gate between a brick wall for easy access to the big house, which stood empty for a short while.

Her next encounter with the spirit was one night in the mid 1960s when she was reading in her second floor bedroom. Her aunt was still living there at that time and was in her bedroom-den downstairs. It was again, a warm night but not warm enough to turn on the window air conditioning units so my aunt had turned on the huge exhaust type fan in the upstairs window over the stairway. She suddenly heard a loud cry-not like crying actually-more like someone wailing or moaning.

She ran out of her bedroom to the top of the stairs thinking that her aunt had fallen and was crying out for her but her lights were out and she could see nothing. She then realized that the crying was not coming from her part of the house. It seemed to be emanating from the area near the front of the house close to the dining room. The wailing went on for at least five minutes. Afraid of what she might find, after the wailing stopped, she went back to her room, locked the door and tried to sleep. The next morning at breakfast her aunt said nothing and she decided that she had best keep her mouth shut.

After breakfast, her aunt went on to work and she was getting ready to do the same when the maid started yelling at her to come down to the dining room. In the downstairs part of the house, between the dining room and the hallway are heavy wooden sliding doors. Lying next to one of the doors was a huge dead bat. They were never able to determine where the bat came from or how he got into the house.

The front of the house was always kept closed off and locked from the back of the house because they had plenty of room in the back after her uncle had added a huge den so it was easier to cool and heat by closing it off from the front. The maid, however, inspected and cleaned the front of the house every day and the bat was not there the day before. Even though she knew what she had heard the night before was certainly no bat, she still tried to write it all off as a vivid imagination.

Most of the strangeness occurred in this house when she was alone, which is probably why she never mentioned it to anyone. There was always a pocket of cold, not cool, but extremely cold air in the downstairs hallway close to the living room. No matter how hot the day, when she would walk down that hall, there was about five feet of cold, cold air. She was always startled by it. Yet if someone was with her and we walked down that hall, the air was always normal, cool or warm, depending on the time of year.

One day, in the mid 60's, she was with her aunt shopping at stores on the Weatherford Square. They were in a boutique called "Sturges-Allen". The elderly owner of the store, Mrs. Bozelle and she were having a conversation about the old house. She told the niece that sometime during the 1920's, her aunt attended a party at the house given by Mrs. Baker. At some time during the festivities a loud noise emanated from a large armoire, located on the first floor that had belonged to Charles Baker. The door of the armoire slowly opened and an old starched collar fell out and rolled down the hallway to near the large wooden sliding doors and came to a stop. She said the party goers were more than mystified by the event. She realized that the collar stopped in about the same place the dead bat was found.

In 1970, she and her husband moved into the house with plans to purchase it. Her husband worked a lot at night and sometimes traveled so she was in the house alone for five to seven days at a time. After living there for about a year, the visitations started.

She reported that their bedroom was upstairs on the south side. One night, while alone in the big old house, she woke up sure that she heard something on the stairs. The dogs were outside and one of them started howling. Then she saw a shadow along the wall of the stairwell rising toward her bedroom. She was absolutely terrified. She couldn't reach the phone, she couldn't say anything - just lay there. Once again she closed my eyes and kept them closed. She heard the footsteps enter my bedroom and approach her bed then she felt a hand gently touch my shoulder.

She opened my eyes and jumped up very quickly but nothing was there. She didn't know what the neighbors thought but she immediately got up and turned on every single light in the house and left them on until daylight. In the bright light of day she did my best to convince herself that she had had another nightmare like the one 30 years earlier.

This event happened to her at least six or seven times during their years in the house, always with the same result. Someone came upstairs, walked into her bedroom, put his hand on her shoulder and then disappeared. It was unnerving to say the least, but she never told anyone, not even her husband.

There were times when she reported that she felt someone was watching her. She felt what ever it was, it wasn't exactly friendly. She did not feel potential violence as much as plain malice. This almost became a daily feeling. Anywhere she went in the house, she felt that someone was watching her and she became extremely edgy and frightened, afraid to leave and afraid to stay. Then, for a period of months to a year there would be no feelings of being watched and I would relax.

The worst incident of all happened one night about 1976. It was in the spring of the year and she was alone in the house late one night. One of those Texas spring storms blew up with its usual violent winds, rain, hail, lighting and thunder. At that time there was an electric transformer on a pole about 20 yards east of Lamar on Columbia Street. The transformer would blow every time there was a drizzle and of course, it blew in this storm. She had no lights.

She was upstairs in the bedroom, thunder crashing, lightning flashing, and the wind was blowing something fierce. Suddenly, she heard loud pounding on the door from the basement to the hallway downstairs. This door was always securely locked and there was no way out of the basement except through the hallway downstairs and likewise, there was no way to the basement from the outside except through the house and hallway.

She first tried to tell herself that the wind was causing the door to rattle, but a rattle didn't sound like that. Someone was loudly and furiously pounding on that door from the basement side. Every time she thought about it, it sent chills up and down her spine. She managed to get to the telephone and contact her aunt next door. She immediately knew that her niece was frightened out of her wits and said she would meet her at the gate".

She ran downstairs in her nightgown not even stopping to get her raincoat or shoes. The second she passed the basement door, the pounding stopped. She went through the kitchen, locked the kitchen door and started across the screened-in porch to leave the house. By the time I got to the screen door to leave, the pounding on the basement door started again, louder and angrier than ever. She ran across the parking lot to the gate where her aunt was waiting for me. She still didn't say anything about the ghosts, only that the storm unnerved her.

She was never again comfortable there. A year later, she and her husband divorced and she left that house for good. She truly believed that the ghost, or spirit, figure that appeared to her in 1942 was that of Charles Baker and she don't think he liked her even one little bit. Since no one else, that she was aware of, ever saw him, she could only assume that she was the catalyst that aroused his ire.

The present owners of the home, Rhonda and Michael Lasely report they have had no strange encounters and have lived in the beautiful Victorian home for over 16 years. Of course, there was that time that their maid, who spoke little English, was very upset, and assured them that a "ghost" or "something" tried to push her from the stairs on the second floor.

## Diamond Oaks Trail

Late at night if you come around a curve in the road on Diamond Oaks Trail there will be big rocks lying in the middle of the street. When you stop to get out of your car to move the rocks, then you will hear little kids laughing, and playing. This has been reported many times.

## Horseshoe Bend

There is an old Victorian home sits off on a little country road that is said to be haunted by a little girl and her mother.

## Lake Weatherford

There have been reports of a bull like creature with eyes like fire having been encountered around Lake Weatherford. Native Americans that used to live in the area called it the "Demon Water Cow".

## WHITEHOUSE, TEXAS

Whitehouse is on Farm Road 346 and State Highway 110, six miles southeast of Tyler in southeastern Smith County. In 1818 a Quapaw Indian camp was located in the vicinity. Travelers from Tennessee, Alabama, Georgia, Virginia, and North and South Carolina first came through the area in 1836 en route to San Antonio to help Texas defend the Alamo, but arrived after the fort had fallen. Impressed with the countryside, they returned home, collected their families, formed a covered wagon train, and moved back to settle in the area. By 1850 local farmers raised cotton, tomatoes, peaches, watermelons, and vegetables on land purchased in the Emmanuel Gutierrez survey, and the town had sawmills, gristmills, and cotton gins. By the early 1870s the International-Great Northern Railroad made it practical to ship produce from Whitehouse, and a post office was established in 1873. Whitehouse is said to have gotten its name from a whitewashed building near the railroad tracks that served as a school, church, and place for business meetings and social gatherings. Steam locomotives going through stopped to take on water near the "white house," and soon the community itself became known by the term. By 1885 the town had a population of seventy-five. The New Hope Baptist Church, organized in 1869 by area settlers, moved to Whitehouse in 1901 and was renamed the Whitehouse Baptist Church. A local fair was held in 1912, and the community's oldest business, the Whitehouse Mercantile Corporation, began in 1913.

## Bascom Road

It has been reported that some nights you can see a woman dressed in white crossing the Bascom Cemetery Road. Most have reported that the woman appears to be carrying a large knife in her hand. It is believed that she is possibly the ghost of a local woman who, in a fit of rage, stabbed her husband then stabbed herself. He lived but she died of her stab wounds. The husband did die sometime after that and now she is said to be searching for him to finish what she started.

## WICHITA FALLS, TEXAS

According to tradition, the land where the city of Wichita Falls is presently located, in southeast Wichita County, was acquired in a poker game by John A. Scott of Mississippi in 1837. In fact, Scott acquired the tract by purchasing Texas land certificates, which he packed away and promptly forgot. Years later the certificates were rediscovered by Scott's heirs, who commissioned M. W. Seeley to map out a townsite on the tract on the Wichita River. As platted by Seeley in July 1876, the townsite included the location of a small waterfall on the Wichita River that was later washed away, several named streets, and a town square. In a fanciful drawing that accompanied the plat, Seeley also included an imaginary lake, a steamboat on the river, and warehouses laden with cotton and other goods. The town never became a steamboat shipping center, although railroads were very important to its later development.

At the time of Seeley's plat there were already a few settlers living in the area. Tom Buntin and his family had been there since the 1860s, making their living hauling buffalo hides, and John Wheeler settled there in 1875, as did John Converse, who built the first store. Seeley himself built a small house at a site now at the corner of Sixth and Ohio streets, and Alexander Craig built a cabin nearby. All of these early settlers eventually moved on. The first permanent settlers were the Barwise family of Dallas. They first came to the townsite on an exploring trip in 1878 and returned to stay the following year.

## Whites Sanitarium

The F.S. White Sanitarium, also known as the Asylum, is located at the corner of California and Olen roads. This facility opened in 1926 under the direction of Frank S. White, a man who had been superintendent at the state asylum in Austin before the turn of the century. He first advocated providing a non-institutionalized lifestyle for his patients to diminish the effects of the asylum itself on their sanity. He ran the facility for just five years before retiring for health reasons.

In 1939, the building was abandoned after it was damaged due to severe flooding. The building remained a local haunt for daring teens until 2002, when Gilbert Rios, who was 70 years old at the time and retired, purchased the building for $15,000, a measly price for such a vast estate. There were so many tales of horror and hell associated with the asylum that most investors wouldn't touch it.

A group of Houston ghost hunters contacted Rios in August, 2002, requesting a visit to the asylum. They set up shop in the White building, monitoring it for any signs of supernatural activity. The results were inconclusive at that time. Rios is not a superstitious man nor does he believe in ghosts. His purpose for the asylum is to repair and refurbish it into an apartment complex. The building now possesses a fresh coat of pink paint, a well-manicured lawn, and attractive landscaping.

Though Rios does not believe in ghosts himself, that doesn't mean they aren't there. Witnesses have reported that an unseen woman calls for "Susan".

Others talk of hearing water dripping in the basement although the place has been vacant and no utilities for over 30 years. When up on the second floor we heard heavy footsteps coming up the stairs, but no one else was in the building. One MSU student told a tale of high school friends discovering abandoned manacles in the asylum's basement. Local residents tell stories of ghosts seen playing cards, as well as unexplained screams heard, coming from the direction of the asylum, in the dark hours of the night[50].

## Dirt Mound on Fairway Blvd.

Way out on south Fairway Boulevard, right at the end of the road, there is a huge dirt mound that has been there for several years. It was dug up for some work around the lake. When it was dug up the body of a child was found. This child had been missing for years. The child was murdered and was secretly buried there. This huge dirt mound that is about two stories high is there and has been there for five years. It has not been washed away by rain and no grass grows on it, even after all this time. The spirit of that child is said to be on that mound.

## Drunk Tom

Outside of Fallstown there is a place in between the North Texas State Hospital and Southwest parkway, where a young college bound man, Drunk Tom, was walking along the Holliday Creek reservoir. Drunk Tom had been drinking heavily that night and either tripped or was pushed into the reservoir. It is said if you go there at night and stand in the exact spot where he died, you will hear a whiskey bottle breaking against the concrete, and see something in the corner of your eye, which immediately disappears.

## Barn on Highway 79

In this old barn, it is said that three men who raped and killed a woman. The three were caught, tried and hung for their crime. Now it is said that if you go to the barn you can still see the woman and the three men wandering around.

## Lucy Park

In the cemetery behind Lucy Park there is a statue that's called "Little Sister". It's a statue of a young women and it is said that she died from a fever she caught in England when she went there to purchase items for her home after her marriage. If you go there at midnight and you truly feel sorry for her it is said that the statue will cry.

## North Texas State Hospital -Administration Building

In 1917, the State of Texas created the Northwest Texas Insane Asylum. It was located on 940 acres seven miles south of Wichita Falls. The first patient

---

[50] http://wichitan.mwsu.edu/2004-1027/features.asp

was admitted to this new facility in 1922. In 1925, the name was changed to Wichita Falls State Hospital (WFSH). It had a modern surgical operating room, radiology, laboratory, electrotherapy apparatus, and hydrotherapy equipment. By 1930, the census was over 1500 patients with a staff of 235, including seven doctors and 93 attendants. During the height of the Depression, the hospital was virtually a self-sustaining community. It had an agricultural enterprise that included farming, hogs, chickens, and cattle. Most of the staff lived on the campus.

The Administration Building is an old building, built in the 1920's. This building was originally used to house the insane, and many deaths occurred within its walls prior to it being turned into offices. Employees have reported lights that go on and of without human hands and others have reported that on quiet evenings that they can hear moans and wails coming from the third floor. Security reports occasionally hearing chains rattling and the sounds of doors opening and closing. Employees have even reported seeing vague shapes at the ends of the hallways at dinnertime.

## North Texas State Hospital "M" Building

The 67-year-old, 39,788 square-feet building, known as the "M" building, housed the then-called insane asylum's mentally ill patients, Jerry McLain, the hospital's chief information officer, said. Although the rest of the hospital still operates, the M Building, which is now used as storage, shut down in the early 1980s, indicating the hospital's decreasing number of permanent residents and the transformation of mental health care, he said.

From the 20s through the 70s, doctors used almost inhumane treatments to cure the mentally ill because of the lack of mental illness information. They heated towels to about 106 degrees and wrapped the patients in them until the patient went into convulsions. They also used a technique called a frontal lobotomy in which they jammed an ice pick-like device into the inner corner of a patient's eye until it reached the brain. Then, the doctor wiggled the pick until the patient went into shock. They also used electroshock therapy, which uses a short pulse of high-voltage electricity to shock the patients into "mental wellness," Mr. McLain said.

Even though patients haven't roamed the long, eerie corridors of the building for about 20 years, evidence of their presence still remains. Some patients' nametags remain below the five-by-eight grated door windows. Note cards displaying patients' black-and-white photos and personal information peppered hallways and nurses' stations. Fingernail marks on doors and door frames inside residents' rooms scream the occupants' desperation to leave. The few furniture pieces left on the second and third floors lie scattered, as if a tornado lifted and threw them.

As if the patients' traces aren't haunting enough, time and intruders have weathered the building. The paint on the walls cracked and chipped over time, leaving what looks to be horizontal scratches throughout the building. Peeling paint droops from the ceilings. Rust eats away at metal pipes. Sporadic, cold drafts spurted from the buildings broken windows, rattling bars and shafts.

Dirt and animal feces and remains blanket the third floor, causing a putrid smell and each step to crunch and echo throughout the morbid building. One owl died facing the ceiling with its wings spread out, leaving a skeleton complete with feathers. Other intruders left signs of their trespasses. Someone marked a peace sign about three feet in diameter in an oil stain on the floor in the second-floor ward. Another intruder drew a red, devilish head in a first-floor office window.

Those brave enough to spend the night inside this building have reported hearing doors opening and closing and footsteps in the hallways. An apparition of a "nurse in a white dress with the old nurse's cap on" has been seen going from room to room checking on the patients, Security guards have reported a hand on their shoulder but when they turned to look, no one was there. Cold spots were also noted in a number of areas.

## Screaming Sheila Bridge

There is a faded and abandoned bridge, generally referred to as Screaming Sheila Bridge, eight to ten miles north of Electra, which is no longer used because a girl named Sheila died there. There are varying stories as to what actually happened to her.

An Electra resident known just as "Hollywood" said that, when he attended Electra High School in the 1980s, the legend was that Sheila had been hung off the side of the bridge, swinging over the river as she gasped for her last breath. Another version of the tale is that Sheila was burned alive on the bridge, evidenced by a large hole burnt completely through it. "Hollywood" disproved this story when he confessed that he and some buddies had, during high school, had a party on the bridge and accidentally set it on fire. This means, however, that the bridge was shut down prior to the fire, when its framework and steadiness were still sound. So what happened to a girl on that bridge so many years ago to cause the area's citizens to close down a perfectly good, and often used, road?

Were a person unfamiliar with the bridge to set out in search of it, they would have great difficulty locating it. Past the town of "Punkin Center," there is a road, Wolf Road, which runs east toward Iowa Park. Were some adventurer to follow the road past where its pavement ends, he or she would find themselves at the unusual intersection of Wolf and Moeller roads.

In one direction, Moeller road extends farther than the eye can see a packed dirt road that leads back toward Electra and civilization. In the opposite direction, after just a few hundred yards, Moeller road becomes overgrown with grass and weeds. The line of an electric fence stretches across the road, barring entry or exit. The line belongs to a local rancher who put it in place to hold his cattle. The road is still a public road, though, and as long as explorers re-connect the fence, there is no problem with going through to investigate.

This is actually in the edge of the town of Clara was established in the 1800's. Another story is that sometime in the mid 1800's there was a woman put on trial and convicted of practicing Wicca. She was burned alive on the bridge. The whole bridge is burned but in one particular spot, there is a perfect circle burned all the way through. The victim of public hatred can still be heard screaming at night.

## Witches Gate

Witnesses have taken to calling this ruined house Witches Gate. According to its history, two armed intruders, at least one in blackface makeup, killed Jim Keith, 61, in this Clay County ranch home and trussed his brother, Kenneth, 70, before ransacking the house of a valuable collection of guns and antique jewelry.

According to the front-page story titled "Clay County Rancher Murdered" which was printed in the July 14, 1975 issue of the Wichita Falls Record News, the newspaper at that time, about 9:30 p.m. on July 12, Kenneth Keith was getting ready for bed when he heard voices coming from his brother's room. As he stepped into the hall, he heard a gunshot. When Kenneth reached his brother's room, he found him, shot in the back, in a pool of blood.

An armed man with a painted face pushed Kenneth back into his room at gunpoint and bound him. Some time later, two armed men returned to release his bonds, in order to force him to open the house safe. They then retied him. The thieves made off with several vintage and collectible firearms and antique jewelry, leaving the house at about 3 a.m. after disabling the telephone. Kenneth Keith worked himself free of his bonds and drove to the Jolly Truck Stop, from where he reported the murder-burglary.

Twelve years after the incident, in the October 31, 1987 issue of the Times Record News, Judith McGinnis did a follow-up piece concerning the Keith murder. According to her article, the four men involved in the murder-burglary were Clyde Theron Burns, Lonnie Dale Lloyd, Alton Woodruff Fanchier, and William Leon Pinson Burns.

Pinson Burns was the man who pulled the trigger. Special prosecutor for the case, Howard Martin, said the robbers had gone to the ranch that night in search of a valuable coin collection reportedly worth $200,000. Another criminal who had seen the collection advertised in a magazine tipped them off. However, Kenneth Keith had donated said coins to a museum in Denver, CO more than a year prior to the robbery.

Jim and Kenneth lived in the Keith home together and continued the work of their father, raising Herefords. Jim never married; Kenneth married and divorced. Neither man had any children. After the murder, Kenneth moved into a neighbor's home.

In February, 1976, just eight months after Jim's gruesome murder, arsonists destroyed all but the stone shell of the home. Because the blaze occurred just days after Clyde Burns was arrested, many people believed there was a connection. Though it was determined to be purposefully set, there was no formal investigation into the fire.

Burns, Lloyd, and Fanchier pled guilty to murder and each was sentenced to 20 years in prison. Evidence produced during the trial proved that Pinson Burns pushed the barrel of a shotgun through a screen at Jim's bedroom window and shot him in the back as he tried to escape.

On Jan. 30, 1970, the jury deliberated for a mere six minutes before returning with a guilty verdict. They sentenced Pinson Burns to life in prison, to be served in Kansas's Leavenworth Penitentiary.

In April, 1980, Pinson Burns was released from Leavenworth due to health reasons and fled to New Mexico. Officers there arrested him on unrelated charges and he was sent back to prison in Huntsville, where he died three years later.  On June 19, 1977, Kenneth Keith died; just five months after the last of his brother's killers were convicted.

The gutted house stands off of US Hwy 287, between Wichita Falls and Henrietta.  There are many local tales of Satanists performing rituals and sacrifices there. Residents exploring the site claim to have found human bones. And sometimes, as it nears dark, the home appears to be on fire.

# WINNSBORO, TEXAS

Winnsboro (Winnsborough), an incorporated city, is at the junction of State highways 11 and 37, fifteen miles northeast of Quitman in northeastern Wood County and extends into Franklin County. The town, first settled in the early 1850s, was named for John E. Wynn, an Englishman who settled in the area. Originally the settlement's name was spelled Wynnsborough, but when a post office was established in 1855, it was changed to Winnsborough. By 1861 the community had, in addition to the post office, two general stores and a church. After the Civil War it grew rapidly; in 1876 the East Line and Red River Railroad built a narrow-gauge road west from Jefferson, and Winnsborough developed into an important local shipping center.

### Oaklea Mansion & Manor House

Starting with the name "Oakley" Norma Lea Wilkinson set out to make Oaklea Mansion & Manor Houser Bed and Breakfast something out of the ordinary. "I've always been a romantic and I wanted to make this a romantic get-away." The name came from a novel by Robert Penn Warren, but everything else is a credit to Norma who has done, and continues to do the bulk of the work. She has one assistant Jim Freeman and hires part-time workers for special events.

Originally built in 1903 by Marcus DeWitt Carlock, Sr., the grand home stayed in the Carlock family until 1996 when Ms. Wilkinson bought it. "That's quite an interesting story," she said. But then everything about Oaklea is an interesting story.

Rhea Carlock, widow of Marcus DeWitt Carlock Jr., called Norma and asked her if she would consider buying the house. Ms. Carlock was very near the end of her life and she wanted to insure that the house would be taken over by somebody who would treasure it the way she had. She had made that same call to a few other people, but Norma ended up buying the mansion with the intention of making it a Bed and Breakfast.

The home had been lovingly cared for by Rhea Carlock, and she had restored most of the beautiful old wood, including a unique curled-pine staircase. Even as her life slipped away, she continued to advise Norma on the décor and made arrangements for Norma to purchase pieces of furniture from the estate. The result is an assortment of period pieces that add authenticity to the atmosphere of early Twentieth Century.

One of the greatest treasures is a hand-carved Rosewood square Grand Piano from Steinway & Sons. There were only a hundred of these pianos built during a ten-year period in the late 1800s. This one was built in 1873. "So many things have come from someone contacting me to say they have something that is meant to be here," Norma said. "And that's how I acquired the piano. A lady called to say she had this piano and it would be perfect for Oaklea. It belonged to a man named Phillips, and he and his wife grew up in the area. Since he passed away the piano had not been used, and his widow thought it should be here for people to enjoy."

Among the guests who have played it is Virginia Mancini, wife of the late Henry Mancini. She came to visit grandchildren who live in the area, and they made reservations for her to spend a night at the Oaklea. She fell in love with the piano and left a standing offer to buy it if Norma ever decides to sell it.

The twenty-two room Mansion has luxurious suites and guest rooms, and one of the most popular is the "Angel Suite." Couples request that suite to celebrate an anniversary or other special occasion, and it is also a first choice for newlyweds. Recent guests were a couple from Longview who spent two days here. "This was a second marriage for both of then," Norma said. "So they had a simple ceremony then came here for their honeymoon. What was really special is that he called and made all the arrangements. He asked for a dinner by candlelight, so we did that in the dining room. We also had champagne, flowers, and baskets with fruit and candy in their room."

In addition to the main house, there is also a three-story Manor House where the rooms and suites offer a panoramic view of the beautiful grounds which host a gazebo, koi ponds, dove cotes, stone patios and a Spa House with a hot tub. Since Ms. Wilkinson has owned the Mansion, she has established it as a "premier" Bed and Breakfast, and she also hosts weddings, receptions, concerts, author signings, church and business meetings and retreats.

As every historic house should, Oaklea has it own ghosts, named "Mr. Shelton". He is periodically heard to pace the floor in the Angel Room, and open the bedroom door.

**PART EIGHT**

**GHOSTS OF SOUTHEAST TEXAS**

# HOUSTON, TEXAS

Houston is a strange blend of past and future. Within view of the Houston Ship Channel is the battlefield where, on April 21, 1836 General Sam Houston defeated Santa Ana and won Texas' independence from Mexico. South of that point are the Johnson Space Center (NASA's Mission Control) and Space Center Houston. Houston's Medical Center is home to the greatest minds in Medicine.

## Ale House Pub

The Ale House Pub, 2425 West Alabama, is an English-style pub that is said to have two spirits: a mild-mannered maid who is fond of light switches and a less-congenial sea captain who likes to break glasses and throw lighted candles. The current owner has indicated that the source of their activity may be the former madam (the structure is a former speakeasy/"house of ill repute"). Unfortunately, on June 3, 2001, the Ale House Pub and Eatery was torn down to make way for a new book store. The owner fought the developer until the end - and did not sell it out.

This English-style pub is located in a building that was once a farm house and has supposedly been used as an inn, a brothel and a speakeasy through the years. The place has several well-documented "occurrences," many linked to the third floor, which was once the apartment of a woman who owned the building and allegedly operated an illegal drinking establishment on the first floor and a house of ill repute on the second. The woman is said to have died in her rooms, which today are decorated like an English pub.

Employees who work on the third floor report being overwhelmed with feelings of grief. They say lights and air conditioners turn themselves on -- even when they're not plugged in. Throughout the building, mugs swing and chairs squeak of their own volition, and people hear the sounds of women talking when no one is in the building. Photographs of the stairway taken when the woman was supposedly descending show strange orbs of light -- which "ghost hunters" believe indicate a supernatural presence.

## Alief Cemetery

The Alief Cemetery is located on the southwest corner of Bellaire Blvd. and Dairy Ashford. Alief is a former farm community that was incoporated into Houston in the 70's. In some areas it has managed to retain that farm community feel. The cemetery is about a century old and is bordered on one side by Bellaire Blvd, on another by Dairy Ashford, and by an apartment complex on the remaining two sides. In the 1980's there was a plan to widen Dairy Ashford at that point, but the plan had to be abandoned when it was discovered that the cemetery extended beyond the marked boundaries. A white cross in front of the entrance marks the location where a previously unmarked grave was discovered. The point is, nobody knows just what the true boundaries of the cemetery are, and the apartment complex has units that are directly outside of the fence. One girl lived in one of those units, and she experienced nightly poltergeist phenomena, and her neighbors complained of similar problems. A note to ghost hunters: due to the extremely busy nature of Bellaire Blvd. even at 3am, this may not be a very good location for a ghost hunt.

## Alley Theater

The Alley Theater at 615 Texas Ave. is believed to be haunted. It is believed that the spirit of managing director Iris Siff has never left the site where she was murdered.

## Barnard Street

Barnard Street is located in the Montrose area. The former owner of a house on Barnard Street, Mr. Cowen was murdered by a friend. New owners have reported cold-spots, strange animal behavior, and "Old Hag"-type experiences.

## Battleship Texas

The Battleship Texas is located in San Jacinto State Park. The Battleship TEXAS is the last dreadnought in existence in the world, a veteran of Vera Cruz (1914) and both World Wars, and is credited with the introduction and innovation of advances in gunnery, aviation and radar. Having been designed in the first decade of the 20th century, (keel laid in 1911 and completed in 1914), and having seen action in some of the most intense and critical campaigns of WWII, she is an important piece of our naval and maritime history.

The Battleship Texas is the only such surviving vessel to have taken part in both world wars. It was the first ship in the U.S. Navy to have anti-aircraft guns and commercial radar. It fired on Nazi defenses on D-Day in 1944 and was later hit by German artillery near Cherbourg, France. Now retired, the Battleship Texas is moored near the San Jacinto Battlefield east of Houston and is open to the public.

The ship is reportedly haunted by a red-headed sailor who appears on one of its decks. Reports indicate the apparition is seen dressed in a white sailor's suit and standing near a ladder, smiling. Also, a caretaker in the trophy room (located on the same deck) claims she entered a space/time slip that sent her to the cemetery at Normandy. The room is used to display guns and other military equipment.

## Blue Light Cemetery

There are nearly half a dozen cemeteries in the Houston area that have been identified as "Blue Light Cemetery"; all of them are old and suffering from vandalism. One explanation for the blue light that emanates from the tombstones is that the material used in making the markers has phosphorescent properties, causing the stones to glow in the dark.

## Bookstop

The most charming of the four Houston-area locations of this chain, now owned by Barnes & Noble but still operated under the Bookstop brand. The one on Shepard is located in what used to be the old Alabama Movie Theater, and most say that it's a fairly good general bookstore, particularly popular non-fiction. When the building was converted to a book store, all they took out were the seats; they kept the entire architecture of the theatre intact, and in fact, have maintained it much better than the theatre owners did. There is lovely carpeting, murals, high ceiling, stairways, etc. Customers purchase their books at what used to be the concession stand. There are stories of apparitions and hauntings dating back to when the Alabama Theater was showing such cutting edge features as Alien and Rocky Horror Picture Show. Several apparitions have been seen moving about the old theater and are now, perhaps, rubbing elbows with readers.

## Cactus Moon

The Cactus Moon is actually located in Humble, North of Houston. A number of witnesses have reported seeing the ghost of a pretty woman who often sits on patron's laps. Additional reports indicate that there may be a second spirit of a man who enjoys playing pool, moving chairs, and shaking the beer cooler cage.

## Esperson Building

The Esperson Building, 808 Travis St # 102, was once the crown jewel of Houston's skyline. Today is the only full-blown example of Italian Renaissance architecture left in the downtown area. It is wonderfully detailed with columns, great urns, terraces, and a grand tempietto at the top similar to one built in 1502 in the courtyard of San Pietro in Rome. It is lit up at night.

Because of its history, this structure is properly referred to in the plural. Mellie Esperson had the building constructed for her husband, Niels, a Texas real estate and oil tycoon. His name is carved on the side of the building in large letters at street level. The name "Mellie Esperson" is carved on her accompanying structure, known as the Mellie Esperson building. It is really just a 19-story annex to the originally building, and the reason the two are termed collectively. The Esperson buildings have the curious habit of popping up when you least expect it in photos of the Houston skyline. Because of its central location and lack of any taller next-door neighbors, this architectural ghost of the Espersons is able to haunt millions of people daily from its lofty perch.

There are many who have reported that Mellie has come back to check out her building. When Mellie is on the premises, the elevator has been known to malfunction, and employees report feeling watched.

## First Pagan Church of Houston

Located at 903 Welch St., for years this lovely house was reputed to be the scene of animal sacrifices. In 1974 the cult inhabiting the building and had converted it into the First Pagan Church of Houston was evicted. During the subsequent renovation, one worker was struck by an unseen force, another had strange recurring nightmares, and others walked off the job because they were "spooked". The cult mentioned above was not connected in any way to any known religion, polytheistic or otherwise.

## Jefferson Davis Hospital

This Jefferson Davis Hospital off Elder Street is an unused hospital building that was built on top of an old Confederate graveyard. During the excavation for the basement, which was used as the morgue, several human bones were unearthed. It is rumored to be haunted by angry Confederate soldiers, doctors, nurses and patients. The building is the property of the Harris County Hospital District and is off-limits. During the excavation for the basement (the morgue), several human bones were unearthed. Other witnesses have heard things being thrown about and the sounds of glass shattering, but found no evidence of any damage. It is rumored to be haunted by angry Confederate soldiers, doctors, nurses and patients. The building is the property of the Harris County Hospital District.

A few months ago, I was given a report about a group of teenagers who had gone ghost hunting inside this old building. They went into the attic and the windowless room contained only a baby crib that was rocking by itself. They also explored the crematory is located, where they were surprised to see the shape of a face in one of the top windows.

In the basement of the hospital, there were dark red stains on one of the walls but they had no way to determine if the stains were blood. It was that this point that they heard a door slam and decided it was time to leave.

On another trip, a second group of teenagers saw something pass in front of the window one of the rooms and quickly go toward the stairs. When they entered the building, debris began to fall down the empty elevator shaft. Deciding that there were less scary places to investigate, the group left, but once outside, saw a figure in one of the windows watching them.

The hospital has spirits such as nurses, doctors, and patients that still roam its halls. Many have gone into this establishment and have had their own personal experiences such as being watched, seeing shadows, and smelling sterilization solutions in certain spots. The spirits are restless and have been agitated from all of the visitors they've been receiving. It was built upon a site of about 3,000 graves of Civil War and yellow fever victims, from when it was a cemetery in the 1800s.

## Julia Ideson Building

The downtown library's Julia Ideson Building, 500 McKinney Street, is reportedly the home of Mr. Cramer, a spectral violin-playing janitor. Mr. Cramer began working in the building when it opened in 1926 until his death in 1936. At night, after the library had closed, he often practiced his violin while wandering its rooms and corridors. Many visitors have reported hearing his ghostly music, especially on overcast days. Cramer died in the Ideson Building's basement in 1936, and since then, he has made his presence known with ghostly violin playing, particularly in the rotunda and the Texas Room.

## KLOL

The KLOL studio is located on Lovett Boulevard in Montrose. It is the former site of one Jones family (as in Jones Hall) residence, reports of phenomena include apparitions, telephones jumping off the hooks, stuffed animals moving of their own accord, anomalous shadows, and elevator malfunctions. Some have also seen the apparition of a Hispanic Cleaning lady.

The station's modern building is located on the site of the Jesse Jones mansion (the Joneses were one of the wealthiest families in early-20th-century Houston). A Houston Paranormal Investigation Group, Lone Star Spirits, reports that at least one murder and one assault have taken place on the premises.

When the investigators first visited the location last year, they found that the elevator doors opened and closed for no reason. One of the members rode the elevator to the second floor, and when the door opened, he caught a glimpse of a Hispanic woman in a denim shirt.

During the team's second visit, just before Halloween last year, it brought along a camera crew from KPRC-TV. While the reporter was interviewing one of the station's employees, a camera bag fell off a table for no apparent reason, and the room temperature reportedly dropped. Later, the reporter, the camera man and four members of Lone Star Spirits were near the elevator when the door began to open and close repeatedly with no explanation.

## La Carafe

La Carafe is located in a pre-Civil War building on Houston's historical Market Square. The second floor seems to be the seat of the haunting. Employees have reported hearing footsteps and the sound of heavy objects being dragged across the unoccupied second floor. The figure of a large black man has also been seen standing in the second floor window after closing time. A former bartender has also been spotted on several occasions.

## Lovett Hall

William Marsh Rice was born in Springfield, Massachusetts on March 14, 1816. He was the third of ten children born to David and Patty Hall Rice. Little is known about Rice's childhood but records indicate that he worked for a while as a shopkeeper in Springfield before deciding to move to Texas in 1838.

Rice started out in business as a merchant in Houston, Texas. His first business partnership with a Barnabas Haskill was formed in 1840 but dissolved by 1842. In 1844 Rice became a commission and forwarding merchant in partnership with Ebenezer B. Nichols, a successful Houston businessman. By 1850 Rice's siblings began to follow him to Houston and assisted in his ventures. On June 29, 1850 Rice married Margaret Bremond whose father Paul was one of Rice's many business partners. In the census of 1860, Rice is listed as having $750,000 in real and personal property, making him one of the wealthiest men in Texas at the time.

On August 13, 1863 Margaret Rice died, possibly from cholera or yellow fever. Shortly after his wife's death, Rice went to Monterrey, Mexico and stayed there until August of 1865 when he returned to Houston. Later in that summer, he went to Massachusetts for business and did not return to Houston until 1866. On June 26, 1867 Rice married for a second time. His second wife was Julia Elizabeth Baldwin Brown, a widow and a daughter of Horace Baldwin, one of the early mayors of Houston. Elizabeth's sister Charlotte was the wife of William's younger brother Frederic.

During one of the Rices' visits to Houston, he was approached by Cesar Maurice Lombardi, who was interested in building a high school in Houston. Rice had been interested in endowing an educational institute of some kind, having revised his will twice previously to include a school for needy boys, first in New Jersey, then in New York City. After the meeting with Lombardi, Rice decided to fund an institute of higher learning in Houston. On May 19, 1891 the charter for the William M. Rice Institute for the Advancement of Literature, Science and Art was incorporated in Austin, Texas. Captain James Addison Baker, William's brother Frederic, Houston businessmen Emanuel Raphael, Cesar Lombardi, James E. McAshan and Alfred S. Richardson were named as the first board of trustees.

Lovett Hall was the first building constructed for the new school in 1911. Perhaps the murder and tragedy that surrounded the founder help give rise to the hauntings. But for a number of years, ghostly voices and typewriters have been heard at night inside this building. In one reported incident an apparition hurled a chair at a janitor twice!!

## Milby High School

People report to have seen a janitor walk in the second floor hall of Milby High School. Students hear footstep walking down the hall and sounds of a door slamming shut. In the library people claim to see a ghostly figured of a librarian

## Neiman Marcus

The Neiman Marcus store located in the Town and Country Mall is the only Neiman Marcus store that can lay claim to having a ghost on the premises. There have been reports that merchandise falls from the shelves, and cold spots have been reported. A customer reported that he even spoke to the ghost was said that his name was "Frank".

## Office Building 1011

The building, referred to only as Office Building 1011, is said given rise to reports of ghostly footsteps, elevators that operate on their own, disembodied voices and items that move on their own have been reported. One possible cause is a man who worked there and committed suicide in the early- to mid-nineties. Suite 217 had a hard time keeping tenants, and is now used for storage. One employee reports that the first-floor ladies room has a stall on the far end from the door that slams open and shut violently.

## Peck's Bar

Peck's Bar is located at 2395 Hwy 6 South, in the West Oaks area. Two spirits said to be named Ava and Mad Dog make lights flicker, dishes fly, TVs turn on and off, etc., after closing. Per the General Manager, the activity is experienced day and night, and has been going on since before the death of Mad Dog (a customer who was killed in a motorcycle accident).

## Rice Hotel

The Rice Hotel is said to be where President John F. Kennedy spent his last night on earth. The room in which John F. Kennedy stayed that night has been home to cold spots, rattling doors & beds as well as balls of light. Perhaps the ghost of the late President is making himself known. Ghostly dancers have been seen in the ballroom, and one witness is said to have seen a lady in white pacing where the balcony USED to be. The Rice is an apartment building now, but Sambuca, the restaurant, is open to the public.

## Slainte Irish Pub

A female homeless woman was raped and murdered in the building and her spirit roams the Slainte Irish Pub. The silhouette of a brunette woman can sometimes be seen behind the textured glass, near the Golden Tee game in the back of the pub. She only comes out when females employees are around and the males haven't experienced her presence. She moves objects, turns on lights and has been known to lurk in the larger, handicapped stall in the women's restroom when no one is on the second floor and keep whoever uses that stall company while they are using the facilities. It's a little creepy, but the women who work here have realized she means them no harm[51].

## Southpoint Cinema 5

It is rumored to have ghosts of three former patrons that have died at the Southpoint Cinema 5. A little girl murdered in a robbery, and two others who died of heart attacks in the same theater same row/same seat - different years. Cast members of the Rocky Horror Picture Show report hearing odd noises in the prop room and feeling like they' were being watched.

## Spaghetti Warehouse

The Spaghetti Warehouse is located downtown at 901 Commerce St in a historic building that has been a cotton storage facility and a pharmaceutical warehouse in its 100-plus-year history. Legend has it that the owner of the pharmaceutical company was killed when he fell down an elevator shaft while working late one night.

Most of the reported activity takes place on the second floor, where employees have said table arrangements change and flatware flies off racks in the kitchen. Night crews say they feel like they're being watched from the second-floor stairs, and others have reported seeing a lady in white on the premises. I have also heard a story about a waitress who went downstairs to grab some beverage napkins for a party she was setting up. She was gone all of two minutes and when she got back, all of the tables were against one wall, and the chairs against the other. All of the menus and silverware were piled in the middle of the floor. There are reports of salt and peppershakers being moved, and even visions of full or disembodied apparitions, strange feelings of not being alone, and photos of orbs and mists throughout the building.

It is said that when elevator operators were still common that one worked there and died one night during his shift. The spirit haunting the place is that of his wife who, every night, turns up the tables and moves things around looking for him.

## Theater Suburbia

Theater Suburbia, 1410 W 43rd St. is a not for profit member of the Gay and Lesbian Bisexual & Transgender Pride Organization. Gurden McKay has been known to put in an appearance from time to time

## The Vatican/The Abyss

This building once housed a theater, but has also been home to two clubs, The Vatican and the Abyss. Footsteps and slamming doors are heard

---

[51] http://www.slainteirishpub.com/index.html

coming from the old projection room on the second floor of this near-downtown club.

## Treebeard's Restaurant

Treebeard's Restaurant, 1117 Texas St., is a popular Houston eatery. However, it is also haunted. Witnesses have reported hearing phantom footsteps and cold spots are reported everywhere.

## University of Houston- Cullen Library

The University of Houston–University Park is the central campus and research-oriented component of the University of Houston System. It offers undergraduate, graduate, and professional education as well as basic and applied research for area corporations and government on projects relating to the Gulf Coast and public-service programs. The university began in 1926 with Houston school superintendent Edison E. Oberholtzer's plans for a local institution of higher education. The campus grew out of Houston Junior College, which was first housed at San Jacinto High School and was authorized to operate as a junior college on March 7, 1927, with 230 students and twenty-five faculty members.

There are a number of witnesses who feel that the Cullen Library is haunted. In addition to feeling as though they are being watched, visitors experience dimming lights, hear whispers, movement out of the corners of their eyes, and one student felt as though she was touched on the shoulder on the 5th floor of the Brown Wing. Some say that books have been known to spontaneously fall off the shelves, as well. The activity seems to occur around midnight and closing time.

## Wunsche Bros. Cafe

Wunsche Brothers Café, 103 Midway in Spring (on the north side), has quite a reputation as being haunted. Witnesses have reported that "Old Man Wunsche" haunts the upstairs balcony. The building has served many purposes including rail station, brothel and restaurant. Many have seen an apparition of "Old Man Wunche" on the upstairs balcony.

## Austin High School

Most of the times when students at Austin High School are walking alone they feel the presence of some one following them, but only on the third floor. Many students have said they have seen a young girl running down the halls who vanishes if approached.

## Bellaire - Episcopal High School

There is a ghost that walks the halls of Episcopal High School. People have claimed to hear her walk across the hallways and slam doors shut, sometimes even locking them, though it takes a key to lock these doors. Some of the school faculty does not stay after 10:00 pm for fear of running into this phantom of the night.

## C.E. King High School

It is said that a woman roams the halls of the C.E. King High School looking for her lost love that was said to have killed her after a terrible argument.

## Cinemark Tinsel Town 17

There have been a number of witnesses to report seeing ghostly figures moving about the Cinemark Tinseltown 17. Many years prior to the building of this Cinemark, a trailer part sat on this site. According to legend, there were two deaths in this park, a little boy and man. One was murdered and the other died with the entire trailer park was consumed in a terrible fire. Now staff and patrons report doors opening and closing; voices being heard at night, and lights that turn on by themselves.

## Cypress Springs High School

Cypress Springs High School is a fairly new school, built about 7 years ago in 1998. They say that a construction worker died while building the school and his body was not recovered, but rather left in the schools foundation. The reason for leaving the body was that searchers were unable to find it. Strange noises are heard in the bathrooms as if someone is trying to escape from the walls.

## Edison Middle School

There have been a number of reports students at Edison Middle School hearing hysterical screaming coming from the girl's locker room. Subsequent investigations reveal no explanation.

## Episcopal High School

Episcopal High School has expanded greatly in its 20 year existence; however, many other schools have stood on this site. The Convent, the oldest building on the campus, has four stories, but students are only allowed on the first three because one of the nuns living on the fourth floor of the Convent almost a century ago hung herself. The Catholic Church would not perform a service for her funeral, and out of respect, no classes of Episcopal High School are held on the floor where she supposedly still resides. Witnesses have reported hearing her moving about on the empty floor.

## Federal Court Building 515 Rusk

The 10th floor of the Federal Court Building is believed to be haunted by the spirit of U.S. District Judge Woodrow Seals, who died after surgery in October 1990. The judge's former chambers are said to always be colder than the rest of the floor and the smell of smoke from his cigars still lingers in the air late at night. Janitors and security guards report being touched and hearing voices and doors rattling when no one else is around.

## Fiesta Elementary School

An old teacher who was accused of abusing children was reported to have killed herself in the bathroom of Fiesta Elementary School. At night, janitors and teachers staying after hours have seen the bathroom door opening and closing on its own and there have been reports of staff members hearing someone walking the halls and messing with the bulletin boards.

## Gilleys

Gilleys is an old indoor rodeo ring that burned to the ground many years ago. Supposedly a few people died in the raging inferno. Those who have entered the ruins report that they got the eerie feeling that someone was watching them. A number reported hearing footsteps from the catwalk.

## H.E.B on Harrisberg

Many people have seen an image of a little girl walking in the back warehouse. According to local legend, before the facility was purchased by H.E.B., this little girl was kidnapped and killed. Now she haunts the site.

## Hogg Middle School

In the mid 30's or 40's a famous gangster of the Heights Area was dug up and hung up on the Hogg Middle School flag pole as a practical joke. Apparently, the gangster didn't get the joke, since now janitors and Librarians who work late, have been said to have seen his shadow and heard his footsteps.

## Jackson Middle School

Jackson Middle School is another site that is said to be haunted. There have been reported that two girls drowned in the pool and now haunt the place where they died.

## Kingate Village

The Kingate Village apartment complex has been the sight of much misery and violence. A girl was killed because she saw her boyfriend cheating on her. Her boyfriend killed her and threw her in the bayou on Halloween. They say she came back to get revenge on her the person who killed her. She found him with his new girlfriend and killed him because of what he did.

In building 1501 is the site of another haunting. This one involved a girl that wonders around in the rooms. Some people who lived there said that they spotted her in the dark wandering as if she were lost. When they tried to call out to her she disappeared. They said that the stroke of midnight that a soldier walks with in with an arm cut off and a twisted neck. As he passes the homes they say he breaks all the windows as if someone was shooting out bullets and when morning comes everything is back to normal.

## Klein Collins High School

Klein Collins High School is a brand new school that was built in the middle of the woods recently which is said to have been built over a burial ground. Most students have been mentioning how they hear and sometimes see two 5 year old children holding hands and running down the hallways. Whenever anyone tries to catch them, they vanish.

## Mendel Elementary School

The Mendel Elementary School is also said to be built on top of an old graveyard. Footsteps and whispers can be heard in the halls and in the restrooms faucets turn on and off and stall doors open and shut on their own.

## Northshore High School

Many witnesses working late at night have seen a girl wearing high school gym clothes in the hallway leading to the girls' locker room at Northshore High School. Whenever anyone tries to approach this girl, she mysteriously vanishes.

## Old Greenhouse Road

The ghost of an old woman who died in a car wreck appears here. If you turn off your headlights and drive around the corner to the bridge VERY slowly, a mist forms over the bridge and comes together to form the shape of a person. They say if you stick around long enough, the apparition will begin to approach your car. The ghost seems to prefer warm or cold clear nights or nights just after it has rained.

## Old Park

A little girl wanders this area at night saying where's my mommy? She has a white dress, and looks around from behind trees at witnesses. Witnesses generally report that if she is about, you can she her behind a tree or walking parallel to your own path as if pacing you.

## Old Woman Hollerin' Creek

Located off of Interstate 10 between San Antonio and Houston, this forest-surrounded creek is said to be haunted by the spirit of a woman who drowned her two children in the creek, and now walks along the bank searching for them. Many have claimed to hear and see her, and it is said that if you get too close to the creek, her hand will reach out and pull you in.

## Patterson Road

Patterson Road is located between Highway 6 and Eldridge in Houston. This place is rumored to be the site of a Civil War battle and the bridge closest to Eldridge is haunted. If you park in the center of the bridge and turn your engine off you will begin to hear tapping noises all over your car. They aren't just the sounds of your car settling. They are mostly on the sides and the back of the car. It is said to be the spirits of the soldiers who died. Be careful, this road is absolutely pitch black at night; however you can see cars coming from either direction at quite a distance.

## Patterson Street

While driving down the narrow road slowly, black objects start to chase the car. Handprints start to appear on windows and cold spots are felt in the car. Sometimes the black object runs right next to the passenger side of the car.

## Robert Louis Stevenson Elementary School

An old custodian who worked at Robert Louis Stevenson Elementary School in the 1980's died in his sleep. He was an older man who loved his job. On many occasions he has been heard and felt by the staff. He often opens and closes closet doors and will sometimes call out in a whisper using the person's name.

## Valley Oaks Elementary School

A former worker at the Valley Oaks Elementary School reported that she had always felt an eerie presence in the girls' bathroom and many of the kids told the worker that the school used to be a cemetery a long time ago. As a cost saving device, instead of moving the bodies, they just took out the engraved cements. There's a legend that a girl was accidentally decapitated on the playground merry-go-round a long time ago, decapitated, on the bottom of the merry-go-round. Since that time, witnesses have heard toilets flush by themselves! Some students have reported that when they turned off the bathroom lights, and chanted "La Llorona" (Bloody Mary) 40 times, the dead girl would appear.

## Fort Sam Houston

Fort Sam Houston has a playful spirit entertains itself with typewriters and by playing ping-pong by itself. It is so common a phenomenon that the spirit has been named Harvey. The building is open to enlisted military personnel only.

Service Club Number Two at this Army training center is haunted by a playful ghost. Since 1960, employees and guests have heard the mysterious presence clearing its throat and watched as it opened and closed windows. The ghost tampers with unmanned typewriters and plays solitary ping-pong.

Unexplained noises and musical sounds similar to a flute have been reported. The ghost is such a regular part of activities here that patrons have named it Harvey. In 1951, a young trainee committed suicide by hanging himself in a small storage room in the building, but there is nothing to connect him to the manifestations that occur in the clubhouse.

# GALVESTON, TEXAS

After San Antonio, I must say that Galveston is the place to visit. The main street is lined with stately old homes, a few blocks away is The Strand historic district. One block off of The Strand you can step aboard the Tall Ship Elissa which is a floating museum. If you are looking for more modern fare, you can visit Moody Gardens which is constantly expanding (and currently contains a 3-D IMAX, a ride film, and a rainforest among other things...) or one of the many beaches.

## Ashton Villa

The Ashton Villa on Broadway doesn't have a particularly sad or tragic background but it is one of the houses that survived the hurricane of 1900. This Italianate mansion was built in 1859 by James Moreau Brown. His lovely daughter, Bettie Ashton Brown, is said to haunt her old home to this day. Bettie was a free spirit even when alive. She traveled alone throughout the world, smoked in public, and never married, though she picked her escorts from a long list of admiring suitors. Until Bettie's death in 1920, Ashton Villa was the scene of many parties and gala dinners. Today, her presence is sensed most strongly on the center stairway and in the hallway on the second-floor landing. In the Gold Room and near an alcove in the living room, furniture moves and clocks stop for no apparent reason. An employee saw Bettie's ghost on the landing in 1991. She was wearing a turquoise evening gown and carrying an ornate Victorian fan in one hand. According to Ashton Villa's manager Lucie Testa the ghostly activity intensifies on February 18, Bettie's birthday. It is said that it's one of the most haunted houses in America.

There have been a number of reports of apparitions, both male and female dressed in old style clothes, being seen here. Others report feelings of not being alone and there are witnesses who have heard strange noises of movement when no one else is around. The ghost is believed to be that of one of the Brown daughters, Bettie, who is said to visit the Gold Room and the second floor landing.

## Boarding House

The Boarding House is located at Ave K and 23rd. Several people have died of natural causes in this house, and now visitors report poltergeist activity. The current owner appears to be proud that the house is one of the Island's most haunted.

## Bolivar Lighthouse

The original lighthouse, which was identical to the original Matagorda Island Lighthouse, was established in 1852. During the Civil War, Bolivar Lighthouse was completely dismantled and the parts removed. The current tower was constructed and was lit in November of 1872. It is constructed of cast iron with brick lining. Although in its early days the lighthouse had red and white bands, it is now black in color. The tower has a height of 116 feet. Point Bolivar light was deactivated in 1933 and is now privately owned. The lighthouse is located on and is easily visible from Highway 87, just across the ferry from Galveston, Texas.

According to local legend, a young man killed his parents inside the lighthouse. His ghost has been seen through the windows, and he has been known to chase visitors away.

## Fire Station #6

Fire Station #6 is located on Broadway in Galveston. The local legend is that Captain Jack returns to look over his former duty location, even though the building is no longer a fire station. Occupants have reported encountering unusual smells, noises of movement in empty rooms and occasional paranormal activity.

## Menard House

The Menard House, 1605 33rd St, was built by one of the founders of the City of Galveston, Michel B. Menard who arrived in Texas in 1829. He was born near Montreal in 1805 and entered the fur trading company of John Jacob Astor at the age of 14. Menard arrived in Nacogdoches in the 1830s and began speculating in Texas land. Because land was only granted to Mexican born Texans at that time, many of Menard's land deals were made by Juan Seguin, a Mexican citizen who eventually fought under Sam Houston at the Battle of San Jacinto. Seguin purchased 4,600 acres at the eastern end of Galveston Island on behalf of Menard in December 1836. With this claim, Menard formed the Galveston City Company with Samuel May Williams and other prominent Texas businessmen in 1838. Galveston was incorporated a year later.

The house, built in 1838 and the oldest on the island, is in the Greek Revival style. The furniture and furnishings, with few exceptions, all date from the first half of the 19th Century (1800-1850s). They are of the Federal, Empire, Regency, Beidemeier, William IV- American, English, French, and German periods. Carpets, drapes and upholstery fabrics, are reproductions appropriate for the period 1830-1850.

Michel Menard died in 1856 and his descendants occupied the house until 1879. In 1880, the house was bought by Edwin N. Ketchum. Mr. Ketchum was police chief during the 1900 storm. The Ketchum family owned the home until the 1970s. During the early 1990s, the house was in such disrepair, it was threatened with demolition by the City of Galveston. The current owners purchased the home and spent years researching, repairing, and reconstructing the house.  There have been a number of reports of the apparition of a woman that has appeared in the entry hall. Most believe that this is the ghost of Clara Menard who fell down the steps and died at the foot of the stairs from a broken neck.

## Old Skinner House

The Skinner House at 1318 Sealy was built in 1895. This delicate Queen Anne style house, with original iron fencing enclosing the yard, has a lacelike exterior. It also has one or more spirits. Apparitions and strange noises have been experienced throughout the house. An antique cane bearing the inscription, "J.D. Skinner, Nov. 6, 1895," mysteriously showed up in the empty attic.

## Queen Anne B & B

The Queen Anne, located at 1915 Sealy, was built in 1905. This historic old home features original stained glass windows, twelve-foot ceilings; exquisite inlaid wood floors, pocket doors and has many fine antiques throughout.

The ghost that haunts this Bed & Breakfast periodically scares the daylights out of some of the employees in the kitchen by suddenly rummaging loudly around in the Butler's Pantry. One or two of the staff maintain that they saw the figure of a man inside this alcove that vanished when the entered. He also seems fascinated by new technology, and can frequently be seen watching closely as someone uses the keyboard. Others have heard heavy footsteps walk up the stairs.

## Samuel May Williams Home

The Samuel May Williams Home, 3601 Avenue P, is a rare combination of Creole-plantation and New England architectural styles. The home was built in 1838 for Samuel May Williams, secretary to Stephen F. Austin and founder of the Texas Navy.

Williams played an important role in early Texas history. The son of a ship captain, he was born on October 4, 1795, in Providence, Rhode Island. He learned the trades of bookkeeping and international commerce while employed by his uncle in Baltimore.  After working in Buenos Aires and New Orleans, Williams arrived in Mexican Texas in 1822, settling in San Felipe de Austin.  In 1838, Williams, along with Michel B. Menard and other early Texas businessmen, helped found the Galveston City Company. A year later the city of Galveston was incorporated. Other business ventures included a partnership with

Thomas F. McKinney, resulting in a successful commission house and Texas' first bank.

Williams died on September 13, 1858, at the age of 63, without a will. The four surviving Williams children divided the property and sold the house to Philip Tucker. The Tucker family lived in the house until 1953, when it was sold to the Galveston Historical Foundation

Some historians have described Williams as the "most hated man in Texas." The man refused to give up his ill-gotten gains even after his death in 1858. Within weeks of his demise, his former slaves reported seeing him sitting in his rocking chair on the L-shaped front porch. Tourists and employees have sensed his dark spirit in his upstairs bedroom, and neighbors report seeing a light in the window late at night or a mysterious figure walking on the narrow balcony that surrounds the third floor observation room. A number of people have heard his heavy footsteps, but when they investigate there is no one there. Perhaps he is still watching over the State that he helped build.

## Stacia-Leigh

The Stacia Leigh, Pier 22 and Harborside Drive, is a unique bed and breakfast as this lodging in actually on board a ship. It is also unique in that it is a haunted ship. A former owner claims to have met the ghost of Benito Mussolini's mistress on board.

## Stewart Beach

An unidentified spectre of a man has been seen running across Stewart Beach after dark. He is generally seen just after a storm has hit the area.

## Trinity Bay

The smoothly curved sides of Trinity Bay have been sculpted by the scouring action of successive hurricane storm surges and runoff events (floods). The sediment plume streaming out of the bay into the Gulf of Mexico flows straight for only a short distance before it is washed westward by the long shore current.

Jean Lafitte, the notorious pirate, was known to have used this area as an anchorage from time to time and was said to have buried treasure here. There have been a number of reports that he is still lurking about, guarding his ill gotten gains. His spirit has been accused of attacking treasure hunters - they've seen an apparition, resembling Lafitte, choking them in the middle of the night.

## University of Texas Medical Branch - Old Red

The building, also called Ewing Hall, is a fairly modern one with a grid type pattern on one side. The building is concrete with sandstone like finish. The old man's face appeared on one of the grids (there were nine total) the face is a lot like a shadow picture but is quite clearly visible. The story is that the grid where the face appeared was sandblasted to remove the face, only a few days later the face reappeared in a different grid. It is possible that the sandblasting was repeated at least one time with the face appearing yet again in a different spot. The building is quite close to the bay edge of the island and the site is very difficult to see without being on the actual grounds of the building. Someone might be able to see it from the water.

## Virginia Point Inn

The Virginia Point Inn Bed & Breakfast has a long reputation of being haunted. Witnesses have reported hearing ghostly footsteps moving about the house. The poltergeist activity has been attributed to the original owner of the building, Sarah Hawley.

## Wal-mart

There are rumors that a cemetery may be beneath the foundation of this Wal-Mart. Full trash bags have been found dangling from the rafters, neatly "zoned" aisles will be trashed within moments, and an 18-wheeler was mysteriously unloaded and re-stocked when no one was on duty.

Another possible cause for the haunted may be that the site is supposed to be where an orphanage run by nuns was destroyed during the storm. The nuns had tied themselves and the children together to keep from being separated, but they ended up drowning together.

## Witwer-Mott House

The Witwer-Mott House is located at 1121 Tremont. Built in 1884 by Captain Marcus Mott, this house has been in the Witwer family for the last forty years. Neal Witwer, born in the house in 1947, blames a ghost in the attic for destroying his first marriage. It all started when a new tenant moved in. The man strongly resembled the captain's son, who was rumored to have murdered his father. For whatever reason, the boarder's arrival coincided with the emergence of a ghost. Every night at 3:00 AM, loud voices and banging sounds came from the attic. Then, the ghost of a bearded man started to appear to Witwer's wife and call out to her in the middle of the night. For two weeks, regular séances were held to try to placate what was assumed to be Mott's spirit. Instead, another presence emerged, a female ghost who focused her attention on the new boarder. Before long, neither the boarder nor Witwer's wife could stand to live in the house. Neal Witwer's wife divorced him, and his tenant moved away. Strangely, the ghosts moved on as well.

## The Hotel Galvez

This hotel is located at 2024 Seawall Blvd. and is the oldest hotel on the island. When the Hotel Galvez opened in 1911, this hotel was called the "Queen of the Gulf". One room, room 505, is supposed to be haunted and most people how stay in that room, do not stay overnight. Most just feel incredibly uncomfortable there. You can also smell Gardenias in and around the room at times. There are two other ghosts there but no one seems to know much about them.

## Luigies Italian Food

Luigies Italian Food is located at 2328 Strand, Galveston. Northern Italian cuisine is served in this converted 1895 bank building. The muted sienna walls, fruitwood-paneled bar, and mural-size replicas of classical Italian artists create a warm atmosphere, making it so inviting that some guests have never left. Many workers have seen the figure of a lady who is softly crying and walking down the stairs.

## The Bishop's Palace

The building known as Bishop's Palace, 1402 Broadway St, was originally known as Gresham's Castle. The home was erected in 1886 at an estimated cost of $250,000 by Colonel Walter Gresham, a wealthy Galveston attorney. Designed by a well-known architect, Nicholas Clayton, it is built from native Texas granite, white limestone and red sandstone, all cut and shaped on the premises. Many rare woods, like rosewood, satinwood, white mahogany, American oak and maple were used for the interior, hand-carved woodwork. Massive sliding doors are unique in that the wood surface on each side of the door matches the room it faces.

It was later purchased for Bishop Christopher Byrne in 1923 by the Galveston-Houston Diocese. It is said by the locals that this historic old home is still haunted by the family that was forced to give it up. The house is now open to the public and there is a tour. On one occasion a group of young people tried to sneak into the house by an unlocked side door and take their own tour. The ended up in a room that was closed to the public and were unable to join the actual tour group. As they tried to leave, they saw a young girl, about their own age, standing by the back door. She just stared at them. This figure was described as being dressed in Victorian-style clothing, which would have been current during the time in which the house was used as a home. Suddenly the figure vanished and the room suddenly went ice cold. Needless to say, the teens left rather quickly. Later they discovered that there is a local legend that when the people were forced to leave, the girl hid because she didn't want to go, and they couldn't find her. A week later, they found her body in a corner of one of the old rooms. She was dead. They didn't know how she died though. She was only 16 or 17.

## ALVIN, TEXAS

Alvin is twelve miles southeast of Houston in northeast Brazoria County, on land originally granted to the Houston Tap and Brazoria Railroad. In the

1860s the Santa Fe Railroad established a flag station near the head of Mustang Slough on its Galveston-to-Richmond branch line. Santa Fe hired Alvin Morgan in 1872 to supervise the loading and shipping of cattle at the stock pens. Morgan built the first house in the area in 1879 and persuaded many travelers to settle there. In 1881 the settlement acquired a post office, and the residents named the community Morgan but renamed it Alvin upon learning of another Morgan, Texas. City folklore recalls Morgan's inseparable companions-a dog, a goose, and a white buzzard. Alvin was incorporated in 1891 and again in 1893.

Alvin had a population reported at 3,087 in 1940 and 3,701 by the mid-1950s. The community's economic growth was based on livestock, poultry, dairying, agriculture, jasmine, oil, natural gas, and petrochemicals. During World War II businessmen persuaded the United States government to place an internment camp in Alvin. About 500 Germans from the camp worked in the local canning factory and rice fields for two years.

### Harby Jr. High

Harby Junior High School is said to be teeming with weird things. During the Galveston Hurricane of 1900, some bodies were buried where the school was later built. Teachers have reported seeing the faces of people in windows. Also showers in the locker rooms will turn on without anyone in the locker room.

## ANGLETON, TEXAS

Angleton, on State highways 288, 35/227, and the Union Pacific Railroad, was founded in 1890 by Lewis R. Bryan, Sr., and Faustino Kiber near the center of Brazoria County and named for the wife of the general manager of the Velasco Terminal Railway. The founders deeded one-half interest in the original town site to that railroad in 1892 for $1,000, with the stipulation that the rail line be routed through the town and a depot be built on Front Street, between Mulberry and Myrtle streets. An Angleton post office was established in 1892.

### Brazoria County Historical Museum

The Brazoria County Historical Museum was designed to showcase the past. However, Lavinia Perry, wife of William Joel Bryan (for whom the town of Bryan, Texas is named), is still haunting her old home. Visitors have heard footsteps and unexplained banging inside her old room. Her furniture rearranges itself, and a portrait of her changes expression.

## BANANA BEND, TEXAS

The area of Banana Bend is a subdivision off of the San Jacinto River.

## Banana Bend

One of the stories is that a man was murdered on Grace Lane and he could be seen and felt in the vacant lot where he used to live in his fifth wheel trailer. Witnesses claim when going to the vacant lot and entering the trailer that they felt cold and despair and had to get out of there fast. Another version of this story is that the man was not murdered, but that he committed suicide.

# BATSON, TEXAS

Batson is on State Highway 105 and Farm Road 770 in southwestern Hardin County. It had a post office from 1891 to 1898 called Otto, for settler R. Otto Middlebrook. The community was settled before 1840 by the Batson brothers and others, who lived in mud houses. They later built a church that also served as a school. Two schools known as Batson Prairie operated in the area in 1897 with twenty-four and forty-four students, respectively. With the discovery of an oilfield a half mile north of Otto in October 1903, the town and post office were moved to a site just south of the oilfield, and a city of 10,000 sprang up overnight. This new community was named for pioneer Eli Batson.

## Batson/Moss Hill Cemetery

There have been a number of strange things happen in the Batson/Moss Hill Cemetery. Officials have found a number of open graves dating from the late 1700's to the early 1800's that appear to have been broken open form the inside. Wrought Iron fences encircling some of the old tombstones have been found all mangled up. Some have said that if you try to mess with the graves weird things will happen like ants crawling all over you coming out from nowhere.

# BAYTOWN, TEXAS

Baytown, a highly industrialized city of oil refining, rubber, chemical, and carbon black plants, is on Interstate Highway 10 and State Highway 146, thirty miles east of downtown Houston in southeastern Harris and western Chambers counties. Among its first settlers were Nathaniel Lynch, who in 1822 set up a ferry crossing at the junction of the San Jacinto River with Buffalo Bayou that is still in operation, and William Scott, one of Stephen F. Austin's Old Three Hundred, who received a land grant in 1824. His two leagues and one labor of land, over 9,000 acres, covered most of the area of present Baytown. Near his home on San Jacinto (Scott's) Bay, a settlement grew to include a small store and a sawmill. It was called Bay Town.

## Premiere Cinema 11

Staff members at Premiere Cinema 11 have reported that on the night shift, during the week, around 10 or 11 or at a later time they will start getting an eerie feeling that somebody is watching them. In the ticket box, sometimes the computers will go crazy, and start printing tickets. In the Projectionist room when they are threading the last movies before going home they can hear people talking and feel somebody walking behind them. They have even had the little windows open by themselves as well as movies start and stop by themselves mysteriously without any reason. CD ROMs open and speakers turn up by themselves with no reasonable explanation. At other times all the breakers are shut off in projection. Others workers have reported that someone they could not see tried to have a conversation with them.

# BEAUMONT, TEXAS

Beaumont, the county seat of Jefferson County, is in the northeast part of the county, at 30°05' north latitude, and 94°06' west longitude, on the west bank of the Neches River and Interstate Highway 10, eighty-five miles east of Houston and twenty-five air miles north of the Gulf of Mexico. With nearby Port Arthur and Orange, it forms the Golden Triangle, a major industrial area on the Gulf Coast. Beaumont developed around the farm of Noah and Nancy Tevis, who settled on the Neches in 1824. The small community that grew up around the farm was known as Tevis Bluff or Neches River Settlement. Together with the nearby community of Santa Anna, it became the townsite for Beaumont when, in 1835, Henry Millard and partners Joseph Pulsifer and Thomas B. Huling began planning a town on land purchased from the Tevises. The most credible account of how the town was named is that Millard gave it his wife's maiden name, Beaumont. At Millard's urging, the First Congress of the Republic of Texas made Beaumont the seat of the newly formed Jefferson County and granted it a charter in 1838. Under a second charter municipal government was organized in 1840, but it was soon abandoned. Another attempt at municipal government in 1860 was short-lived. Continuous municipal government dates from incorporation under a general statute in 1881.

## Forrest Lawn Memorial Cemetery

If you go to the Forrest Lawn Memorial Cemetery at night and find the statue of a young man and women, take the driveway that goes behind them and shine your bright lights on them and they will turn and start kissing. You can see the girls face moving and the guy's arms moving all over her back.

## Saratoga Road

Hundreds of people have witnessed a ghostly light that appears and hovers along Saratoga Road and then zooms past and even has sat on the hoods of cars. This story is so amazing because so many people have witnessed it and it can be viewed with almost a 100% probability of appearance.

### Lamar University

Sigma Phi Epsilon House at Lamar University was built by a farmer to be his dream house. After the man passed, it was supposedly a whorehouse. The fraternity bought it in the late 80's. The house sits on old farmland. There is the main house in the front and also a huge house in the back (just a structure with two bathrooms and a small bar). Everyone that has lived in the house knows about "Chester". He likes to knock on the guys' doors when no one else is home. He has been heard opening and closing doors, and walking on the stairs. This ghost is very friendly with the guys and protects them from strangers.

## BOLD SPRINGS, TEXAS

Bold Springs is on Farm roads 350 and 942 eighty-five miles north of Houston in west central Polk County. One of a series of small communities known collectively as the Louisiana Settlement, Bold Springs was established during the 1840s and named after the springs in the area. A Baptist church was organized there in 1849. The community subsequently had a small turpentine distillery. The Bold Springs post office was known as Nettie, after the postmistress, Nettie Burgess, and operated from 1903 to 1923. A few scattered residences and a church remained in 1984. In 1990 the population was 100.

### Bethel Baptist Church

Vigilantes severed the leg of a rapist who managed to struggle into the Bethel Baptist Church and died of blood loss in the sanctuary. The sounds of his step-drag can still be heard if you put your ear to the door.

## BRAZORIA, TEXAS

Brazoria, on Farm Road 521, State Highway 36, and the Brazos River eight miles southwest of Angleton in west central Brazoria County, was established in 1828, when John Austin laid out the town on land granted by Stephen F. Austin. Austin chose the name "for the single reason that I know of none like it in the world." Six Masons met in March 1835 under a giant oak in the town, the "Masonic Oak," to organize what was reportedly the first Masonic lodge in Texas. Brazoria was virtually deserted in the Runaway Scrape. H. M. Shaw opened a school at the community in April 1838. A post office was established there in 1846, and by 1884 Brazoria was described as a "stirring village" of 800. It had several steam cotton gins and grist and sugar mills, twelve general stores, three hotels, five churches, and "excellent schools." Area farmers shipped crops on the river.

## Bailey's Prairie

During the 1800s, Brit Bailey died a natural death. His widow arranged his burial according to her wishes and let out a few of his requests, namely the jug of moonshine he wanted to be buried with He is said to return every 7 years in search of his jug in the form of a large fireball. He is even said to have caused a gas well blowout when they drilled too close to his actual grave. His resting place is a little off State 35 between West Columbia and Angleton. This is and remains a very old haunting, as this area is quite active in the paranormal sense.

## The Hanging Tree

Two men were found hanged at this spot. It is said that you cannot ride past it in a car, a carriage, or on horseback.

## Mansion

This house was never occupied by its original builder - his bride-to-be died before she arrived from Tennessee, and he was killed in the Civil War. The doors of the house would open constantly with no explanation. It eventually feel into ruin, and may be long gone by now.

## Rural County Area

Lily Brown was the daughter of a white man and black woman who lived as man and wife (it was illegal for them to formally marry at that time), she and her trademark Palomino pony disappeared. Nobody suspected foul play until her spectre was spotted riding through rural Brazoria County. Her murderer or murderers were never found.

# BRAZOSPORT, TEXAS

Brazosport is on State Highway 288 where the Brazos River meets the Gulf of Mexico, sixty miles south of Houston in southern Brazoria County. It is a 214-square-mile urbanized industrial and port area. According to some sources the popular name was first used in eighteenth-century nautical charts. Brazosport shares a chamber of commerce with local economically linked municipalities—Clute, Freeport, Lake Barbara, Richwood, and Lake Jackson—and small towns—Jones Creek, Oyster Creek, Quintana, Surfside, Gulf Park, Bryan Beach, Perry's Landing, and Bastrop Bayou.

## Brazosport Little Theater

The Brazosport Little Theater is said to be haunted by a female spectre that has been possibly identified as Tallulah Bankhead. She is said to walk the theater searching for "Ruth".

# BRYAN/COLLEGE STATION, TEXAS

Bryan, the county seat of Brazos County, is located in west central Brazos County and is crossed by State highways 6 and 21, U.S. Highway 190, Farm roads 158, 1179, 1687, and 1688, and the Missouri Pacific and Southern Pacific railroads. Along with College Station, the home of Texas A&M University, which adjoins Bryan to the south, the city is the urban center of Brazos County. The area around the future site of Bryan was settled by members of Stephen F. Austin's colony in the 1820s and 1830s. In 1859, when the Houston and Texas Central Railroad graded a railroad bed through the area, a nephew of Austin, William Joel Bryan, donated land for a townsite to the railroad company. The townsite was named in his honor and was platted that same year. Construction of the railroad was halted at Millican, eighteen miles southeast of Bryan, during the Civil War, but a community of some 300 inhabitants grew up at the townsite. A post office was opened in Bryan in 1866, and that same year the county voted for Bryan to replace Boonville as the county seat.

## Corps Dining Hall

The Corps Dining Hall on the Texas A & M main campus is said to be scene of poltergeist activity.

## Old Animal Sciences Building

The Animal Sciences Building is located on the Texas A & M main campus. There are a number of reports of a haunted elevator that operates of its own free will. There had been a number of rumors that a murder had taken place in this building, but research determined that the building housed the location where deceased animals were disposed of (A & M has a world-famous veterinary school) and one of the workers whose job was to cut them up, well, he missed and severed a major blood vessel. He died of blood loss in the building.

## A&M Consolidated High School

Rumors abound of a very nasty metaphysical presence that walks (or rather floats) in the career technology wing of the newly renovated A&M Consolidated High School. This presence is supposedly named Toby and several young students have tried unsuccessfully to document this scary and mysterious hauntings.

## Plantation House

This old home seems to be the site of several hauntings. Doors have slammed shut in the middle of the night and footsteps have been heard in the attic and in the dead space between the rooms.

## Schulman Theater

The upstairs projection rooms of the Schulman Theater are said to be haunted by the ghost of a young man. The man was supposedly closing alone one night when he heard a knock on the door. The theater was closed but he went down stairs to see his partner at the door He let his partner inside, where they began to fight. The partner fled in anger, only to return to kill the man.

The opening crew discovered the body the next day. The haunting is said to take place upstairs, which consist of projection rooms and an office. The man will appear behind you and whisper. He is also seen standing next to projectors. The partner/killer is said to currently be serving his sentence for the murder.

# CALDWELL, TEXAS

Caldwell was founded 1840 and has been seat of two counties. Before Burleson County organized in 1846, it was seat of Milam County. Caldwell, Texas was named for Mathew "Old Paint" Caldwell, noted frontiersman and signer of Texas Declaration of Independence. In 1850s the town was rendezvous for west-bound immigrants, and had one of finest hotels on Old San Antonio Road. One of state's best country inns is still located in Caldwell.

Today city is primarily a rural trade center for surrounding farms and ranches with diversified industry, including manufacturing service and technology. Town has been named "Kolache Capital of Texas" by state legislature.

## Caldwell High School

Located on Highway 21, basically in a field of cows, sits Caldwell High School, a fairly new building (less than 30 years old). The spotlight projection room in the auditorium and the sound booth is haunted by an unknown spirit the theatre troop refers to as "George". The soundboard and light dials will move and the lights will dim or flicker during rehearsals (but never during actual shows) despite the electrical wiring being checked repeatedly. Folks working in the spotlight room have reported chills and strange noises.

# CARTHAGE, TEXAS

Carthage is at the intersection of U.S. highways 59 and 79, forty-two miles west of Shreveport, Louisiana, near the center of Panola County. Carthage is Panola County's second county seat. When an act of the Texas legislature delineated the county in 1846, the temporary county seat was Pulaski, a settlement on the east bank of the Sabine River. In 1848 the county commissioners selected a site at the county's geographic center as the permanent county seat. Jonathan Anderson, who owned the proposed site, agreed to donate 100 acres for the town. Spearman Holland is credited with naming the community in honor of Carthage, Mississippi. A post office was established in 1849.

### Carthage - Marshall Hwy 2792 –

On 2792 you take a right and a little ways down the road there is an old broken down house partially hidden by high bushes and overgrown weeds. The story behind the house is in the mid 1980's a young woman lived there with her husband and newborn daughter. On Halloween night her brother came to her for money (possibly for drugs) she told him no. He turned violent when she told him no.

He picked her up and slammed her on the hot stove then shot her. It was rumored that he even broke the gun and stabbed her with it, but after she was already dead he drowned her in the bathtub. The police found him wandering the streets all bloody. The child was unharmed. Those who have visited this sport have reported strange feelings, not being able to breathe. Others have reported seeing a light come on in the attic and a white figure appear in the window. Some have said that they have seen the face of the dead woman in the hallway of the house.

# CONROE, TEXAS

In 1881, Houston lumberman Isaac Conroe established a sawmill on Stewarts Creek. A Post office was established under the name Conroe's Switch because of its site on the I-GN railroad in 1884. In 1889 the population reached 300 and Conroe replaced Montgomery as county seat. In 1891 the Courthouse was constructed In 1904 Conroe was incorporated with a population of about 1,000

### Huntsman Chemical Plant

Witnesses have heard doors slamming and opening, voices, and the apparition of a tall pale man wandering about the Huntsman Chemical Plant. Most have heard unexplained footsteps. Some employees always get a strong feeling that they're being followed or watched as they patrol through the company's training building, which was used as a makeshift hospital during a plant emergency about 4 years ago where 2 people lost their lives in an explosion.

# CROSBY, TEXAS

Crosby is on Farm Road 2100 near the Southern Pacific tracks two miles north of State Highway 90 and just outside the Houston city limits in eastern Harris County. The town was named for G. J. Crosby, a railroad construction engineer. Charlie Karcher opened the first store there in 1865, and the town quickly became a retail and shipping center for lumber and agricultural products from between the San Jacinto River and Cedar Bayou. A post office opened at the community in 1877, and in 1884 Crosby reported a population of fifty, a school, a Baptist church, and a general store. By 1891 it still had fifty inhabitants, as well as a Methodist church, two livestock stables, and a general store. Local legend reports that the community had received the nickname Lick Skillet by 1898. In 1905 it had one school with four teachers and 122 students.

## Newport Subdivision

Built on top of a "potters field" type cemetery, residents of this subdivision have reported apparitions, poltergeist activity, and a general impression that whatever was there was "evil". The phenomena was the subject of the book, The Black Hope Horror and the movie Grave Secrets

This haunted neighborhood has been written about in the novel, "The Black Hope Horror". The neighborhood was constructed over an old slave cemetery and many of the residents were terrorized by the angry spirits that dwelled below. No one had a clue as to what was causing it until a couple, while digging a swimming pool, unearthed the remains of a couple who had been buried in their backyard. It is a story that is very similar to the movie "Poltergeist", but it is frighteningly real. Most of the activity is centered at the east end of Poppets Way and the side street that connects at the east end. According to the book, people would rent a house on the street and abruptly leave within a month...and this was a very regular occurrence.

# DIBOLL, TEXAS

Diboll, on U.S. Highway 59 three miles north of the Neches River in southern Angelina County, was founded in 1894 when Thomas Lewis Latane Temple built a sawmill on the Houston, East and West Texas Railway. Temple came to East Texas in 1893, purchased 7,000 acres of pine timberland from J. C. Diboll, and began operation of his sawmill at Diboll in June 1894 under the name Southern Pine Lumber Company. By 1908 Temple had added a second sawmill at Diboll and enlarged his timberland holdings to 209,313 acres. In its early days Diboll was a company town. Many of its homes, built from lumber produced by the Southern Pine mills, were owned by the lumber company and rented to employees. Between the early 1900s and the 1950s the lumber company also maintained a large commissary, which included a drugstore, a post office, a grocery, and a feed store. Adjoining were doctors' offices, the railroad station, and lumber company offices. Diboll received a post office in 1897 with William P. Rutland as postmaster. The town's first school opened in 1894.

## The Diboll House

Owners of the Diboll House would have coinciding nightmares, smelling bad odors that seemed to come from nowhere, feelings of being watched, strange banging noises, apparitions, and report being physically attacked (smacked, thrown).

# EAST BERNARD, TEXAS

East Bernard is on the west side of the San Bernard River at the intersection of State Highway 60 and U.S. Highway 90A, fifteen miles north of Wharton in northeast Wharton County. The community was originally on the east side of the river, where Jethro Spivi built the first residence around 1850; hence the name East Bernard. Settlement was slow until 1859 and the arrival of the Buffalo Bayou, Brazos and Colorado Railway. A bridge was built, and the depot, Bernard Station, though originally located on the east bank of the river, was moved by 1869 to the west side, to the site of East Bernard's future Main Street. The rest of the town grew up around the railway. The first post office was established in 1866, but the community was probably not officially named East Bernard until 1874. After the Civil War the community began to grow rapidly, as new settlers arrived with British surnames.

## East Bernard High School

There is an old High School in the small town of East Bernard that is called East Bernard High School. In the gym there are orbs and spirits everywhere. If you go down to the girls' weight room the punching bag will start and stop moving

# EAST COLUMBIA, TEXAS

East Columbia (originally named Marion) is one of the oldest Angelo settlements in Texas. It was established in 1824 by Josiah H. Bell on the third land grant issued by Stephen F. Austin. Beginning as a major river port and commercial center for Austin's original colony, Marion (or Bell's Landing as it was called) continued as a major business around 1900.

The Republic of Texas was born at Columbia (now called West Columbia) on October 3, 1836 with the inauguration of Sam Houston as the Republic's first President and Stephen F. Austin as Secretary of State and the Swearing in of the Republic's first congress. Columbia was established in 1826, also by Josiah H. Bell.

## The Woman in Grey Taffeta

A woman dressed in gray taffeta wanders the grounds where the Sweeney house once stood. She was murdered there by her husband and dumped into the cistern. When the Sweeney's moved in soon afterward they found her body. The house has since burned to the ground, but some say she can still be seen in the rubble.

# EGYPT, TEXAS

Egypt, on Farm Road 102 eleven miles northwest of Wharton, is the oldest community in Wharton County. John C. Clark was there in 1822, and Egypt is located on his league. Robert Kuykendall's land was below Egypt, and Thomas Rabb's was above. These three men were among the first of the Austin colony settlers. The land along the Colorado River was the favorite hunting ground of the Karankawa Indians, and Clark, Kuykendall, and Rabb were noted Indian fighters. The area soon became safe enough for others to move into because of the efforts of these men. The original settlement was started in 1829, when Eli Mercer established a plantation and ferry on the Colorado River at the San Felipe-Texana crossing. The road from Matagorda to Columbus crossed the San Felipe-Texana road a mile or so from the river, and the community developed at this junction. The town was originally called Mercer's Crossing, but during a severe drought the area supplied corn to surrounding settlements, and people began to refer to it as Egypt.

## Captain Heard House

The Heard House is also known as Egypt Plantation. The Heard's fostered their home as a center of commerce, religion, social life & military strategic planning. By 1849 the existing, story and a half, dormered, Georgian Revival red brick home was built from sun-dried, local clay replacing the log, dog-trot home. Later owners, George and his brother, William A. Northington, amassed a fortune in land development in Wharton and Glen Flora. Today Egypt Plantation is still owned by Northington descendents who raise cattle & operate numerous businesses on this historic property.

Visitors have reported hearing ghostly voices and unexplained footsteps. There is a backwards-running clock, balls of fire that shoot through the house, and a headless ghost has been seen riding about the property.

# ELWOOD, TEXAS

Elwood is near Farm Road 47 thirteen miles northwest of Canton in northwestern Van Zandt County. Its Baptist church was started as early as 1898. The name Elwood was formed by a combination of the nearby Ellis Chapel and Woodall schools in 1917, when the local church moved and became known as the Elwood church. In 1904 the Ellis Chapel school enrollment had reached fifty and the Woodall School, forty-eight. In 1936 the Elwood community had the school, a cemetery, and scattered dwellings. Its school had been consolidated with the Edgewood Independent School District by the early 1950s. In 1981 scattered dwellings remained near the Woodall cemetery.

## Allphin Cemetery

In the old Allphin Cemetery, there is an unkept grave that is marked with the year 1870. No one knows who is buried there and no one seems to pay any attention to the grave site, but once a year there will be a single fresh rose laid upon it.

# FREEPORT, TEXAS

Freeport, on the Missouri Pacific tracks some sixteen miles south of Angleton in southern Brazoria County, is a deepwater port three miles from the mouth of the Brazos River on the Gulf of Mexico. The community's post office has been in continuous operation since 1898, but the town itself was officially founded by the Freeport Sulphur Company and formally dedicated in November 1912. Freeport was at the site of the world's largest sulfur mines and was the home of the Houston and Brazos Valley Railway. The community also provided storage tanks for the Freeport and Mexico Oil Company. A one-room school was in operation there by 1913, and by 1914 the community had a hotel, a bank, a fish and oyster plant, and a church.

## Mary Ann

There is a ship called the Mary Ann has been known to guide hapless boats caught in storms into safe harbor. The only problem is that the Mary Ann sank decades ago.

# HEMPSTEAD, TEXAS

Hempstead, the county seat of Waller County, is on U.S. Highway 290 at its junction with State highways 6 and 159, fifty miles northwest of Houston. Dr. Richard Rodgers Peebles and James W. McDade, founders of Hempstead, organized the Hempstead Town Company on December 29, 1856, to sell lots in the new town at the terminus of the projected Houston and Texas Central Railway. The doctor named the town for his brother-in-law, Dr. G. S. B. Hempstead of Portsmouth, Ohio. Peebles and his wife, Mary Ann Groce Peebles, contributed 2,000 acres from the Jared E. Groce, Jr., estate for the townsite, which Mary Ann Peebles helped lay out. The Houston and Texas Central was extended to Hempstead on June 29, 1858, and the town became a distribution center between the Texas interior and the Gulf Coast. Hempstead incorporated on November 10, 1858, and its importance as a transportation center increased with construction of the Washington County Railroad from Hempstead to Brenham.

## Liendo Plantation

Jose Liendo received the original Spanish grant for this land, but then sold it in 1849. In the early 1870s, what is known as Liendo Plantation was owned by Elizabeth Ney, a renowned German sculptress. She, her husband, and the ashes of their only son, Arthur, are buried in a family plot on the ranch. When little Arthur died of diphtheria, his parents cremated him in the living room fireplace and placed his ashes in an urn on the mantel. Ever since his death, the boy's gasping ghost has been seen in the white guesthouse that is located next to the ranch house. It was there the child lay quarantined, struggling for a deep breath, his lonely cries filling the crisp night air.

## HOCKLEY, TEXAS

Hockley is thirty-six miles northwest of Houston on State Highway 6, U.S. Highway 290, and the Southern Pacific line in northwestern Harris County. The earliest settler in the vicinity was Sam McCurley, who in 1829 lived a few miles from the site of present Hockley. The community was established in 1835 by George Washington Hockley. The Texas army  camped near the settlement in April 1836. The Houston and Texas Central Railway began service to the community in May 1857. A post office was established there as Houseville in 1858, but the name was changed to Hockley before the end of the year.

### Schultz Middle School

Students of Schultz Middle School report that a girl hung her self in the girls' bathroom and now she haunts the site of her death.

## HUDSON, TEXAS

Hudson is on State Highway 94 just west of Lufkin in north central Angelina County. The largely residential community grew up as a suburb of Lufkin in the 1960s and was incorporated in the latter part of the decade. The population of Hudson was 695 in 1980. After that time the community grew rapidly, and in 1990 it reported 2,374 residents.

### Largent Cemetery

Many reports of paranormal activity revolve around Largent Cemetery and its surroundings. It is also rumored that the ghost of Robert Faigen goes from house to house looking for his family. He is reported to be a rather mischievous ghost.

## HUMBLE, TEXAS

Just before the Civil War, a wandering fisherman named P.S. (Pleasant) Humble brought his family into the area. They settled on the banks of the San Jacinto River and operated a ferry near the present U.S. 59 crossing. A flood drove his family away from the river in search of higher ground. Soon a small community began forming in the area.

## 1960 Over Pass Area/Train Track

The East 1960 overpass is built over what was once a cemetery. The overpass was built to cross a set of train tracks. Workers dug up the cemetery and moved it to the woods beside the tracks. Most say that this is now an extremely evil area. Several businesses along the tracks have reported violent disturbances. There was a Putt-Putt Golf Course along the tracks in the area that became a church. When the church would be closed in the night demonic screams could be heard from inside. The woods are very active as well, There are images seen floating through the woods as well as red lights, which are believed to be a gateway into pure evil.

## Old Golf and Games

The area of the old Golf and Games is now a church but was abandon for years only a haven to cults and ghosts. The ghosts here are the result of being disturbed by men moving their graves. About 97 percent of every sighting in this area the ghost appears as a rotting corpse. There's a bench just outside the building where every night there a white figure that sits on the far side of the bench. The figure is that of a human. The corpse like ghosts can also be seen in the woods across from the building wandering through the turned over gravestones and fallen church.

## Old Dollar Theater

The Dollar Theater is located along an area believed to be haunted by demons and demonic forces. It is part of the 1960 overpass haunting. The workers of the theater would be attacked by the evil entity. It would throw things at them and corner them with shadows. The theater was once blessed with holy water and a cross was put in the projection booth, but everyday the cross was moved from one booth to another with no explanation. Some mornings the person who was opening would hear voices from the projection rooms, and footsteps outside the hall. There was one morning when the projectionist went in and found the word "SATIN" carved in the wall of projection booth 2, this booth was where most of the bang and violent attacks occurred.

## HUNTSVILLE, TEXAS

Huntsville, seat of Walker County, is at the junction of Interstate highways 45 and 75, U.S. Highway 190, and Texas highways 19 and 30 at the approximate center of the county. It was founded in 1835 or 1836 by Pleasant and Ephraim Gray as an Indian trading post and was named for Huntsville, Alabama, former home of the Gray family. The city originally lay within the northeast section of Montgomery County, which was organized in 1837. It was designated the seat of Walker County when the county was organized in 1846. Huntsville acquired a post office on June 9, 1837, with Ephraim Gray as the first postmaster. The Grays' trading post was well situated to trade with the Bidai,

Alabama, and Coushatta Indians. Relations between these groups and the early settlers around Huntsville appear to have been peaceful.

## Sam Houston State University

The old Music Building at Sam Houston State University, which is now classrooms and offices, has a ghostly audience that once interrupted a class by breaking out in applause. Some of the residence halls also have reports of apparitions and televisions that turn on by themselves. The park across the street also has a ghost of a little girl that leaves hand prints on windows in the steamboat house.

## Walls Unit

The Walls Unit of the Texas Department of Criminal Justice is the oldest prison in Texas, built in 1848. Many apparitions have been reported here, apparently all are former inmates. There have also been reports of ghosts and unexplained noises on the original death row (first floor of the South Building, not used since the 1950s), the East Building, and the catwalk connecting the two. One Halloween a correctional supervisor put a voice-activated tape recorder on the now abandoned old death row. When he played it back later for several correctional officers, they heard the clanging of cell doors and at the very end an unidentified voice saying "Hey captain, Hey captain." Source: Austin-American Statesman, October 29, 1999, pp. A1, A8.

## Oakwood Cemetery

Oakwood Cemetery is where General Sam Houston is buried, and also where the statue college kids call black Jesus is located. It's a bronze statue on the far north edge of the cemetery. It is in a gorgeous spot with palms and it is recessed into the woods a bit, with benches. All the graves in the cemetery are laid out with the feet facing east, this family's graves are the only ones where the feet face west. This family erected the statue when their 5 year old son died and the bronze soon weathered to a black color that could not be cleaned. The Jesus is a classic pose with the hands out stretched and palms up, except sometime when you go out at night the hands are turned down!

## Sam Houston Memorial Museum

When you're in the loft of The Woodland Home at the Sam Houston Memorial Museum, you can hear people walking around underneath you, and see their footprints in the gravel leading up to the house. You can also see things fall off of Sam Houston's desk sometimes in his law office.

## Bellaire Theatre

It was rumored that a projectionist passed away due to a heart attack in the Bellaire Theater. Other spirits floating around this building include a young girl and a not so nice guy named Neil. Strange sounds, doors closing and actual interaction with the young girl have all been witnessed.

## JACKSONVILLE, TEXAS

Jacksonville is an incorporated town on Interstate Highway 69 in northeastern Cherokee County. It began on the east bank of Gum Creek in 1847. That year Jackson Smith built a house and a blacksmith shop in the area; he was appointed postmaster when the Gum Creek post office was authorized in 1848. Soon after, Dr. William Jackson built an office near Smith's shop. In 1850 Smith had a townsite and square surveyed near his home. Since the townsite was on Jackson Smith's land and Dr. Jackson was among the first to build inside the boundaries of the survey, the name Jacksonville was chosen by local citizens for the new town. The post office name was changed from Gum Creek to Jacksonville in June 1850.

### Killough Monument

The history of Killough Monument involved the Killough Family who settled there and built a home. Eventually Indians came along who wanted to take over their land and massacred the family, and destroyed their home. The monument was supposedly built in the same place the house was located, with the graves of the family members surrounding it. The monument itself is a brick pyramid formation on a concrete foundation. The foundation is approximately 4 feet tall and the pyramid is about 15-18 feet from the ground to the top. On top of the foundation there is 4-5 inches from the edge, to where the bricks begin. On the south side of the monument, the second layer of bricks from the top, which was 3 bricks side-by-side, with bricks surrounding the top and bottom, the center brick is missing. Since this monument is the same formation on four sides, not sure if it is hollow or not, it is believed to be nearly impossible for any human to remove that brick.

The Killough Monument is a native stone monument that commemorates victims of East Texas's worst Indian depredation. It was erected on the spot where a massacre rook place on October 5, 1838. The monument is seven miles northwest of Jacksonville near community of Larissa. There have been a number of reports that you can see a Native American in full headdress riding on a white horse at this spot. If you draw attention to yourself, he will look at you and ride away.

### Jacksonville City Cemetery

Inside the Jacksonville City Cemetery, there is a statue by the name of Mother Templeton. It is said that during full moons she changes her positions. Some have seen her holding one hand over her heart and her left hand down by her side, some have seen her holding a bible in the palms of her hands, and some have seen her holding flowers in her hands.

## Lon Morris College - Craven-Wilson Dorm

Lon Morris is an accredited, church related, two-year College of the arts and sciences with a core curriculum emphasizing the liberal arts. It is also the oldest two year college in Texas. It is also said to be haunted as the result of a suicide.

The Craven-Wilson Dorm is haunted by a supposedly female ghost and each year she chooses a resident to live with. Sources say the ghost is apparently the former dorm director Ms. Brown who died of cancer before her term as director was completed. Sources say her spirit feels the need to complete her stay as the dorm director. Harmless activities are noticed by residents in the chosen room such as: things being moved on shelves, drawers being opened, electronics turning on and off, radio stations changing on their own, noises being heard from the room while the occupants were away for the weekend, clothes moving in closet, dishes being re-arranged, items jumping off shelves as if pushed from behind, unexplained steaming water from the cold water pipes, and the shower curtain would be pushed in with great force towards the occupant while showering. It is also said to be haunted as the result of a suicide. Witnesses have reported opening doors and other strange phenomena.

# JASPER, TEXAS

Jasper, the county seat of Jasper County, is on U.S. highways 96 and 190, State Highway 63, and Sandy Creek in north central Jasper County. The site was settled around 1824 by John Bevil. Thirty families occupied the settlement as early as 1830, when it was known as Snow River or Bevil's Settlement. In 1835 it was renamed for William Jasper, a hero of the American Revolution. Jasper became the county seat in 1844 by an act of the Texas Congress. A post office was established there in 1846, and travelers reported a population growth from forty to 400 in the decade from 1848 to 1858.

## Bishop Family House

The Bishop Family Home is said to be haunted by several apparitions, including one female.

## Maund House

The ghostly voices, unexplained footsteps and odd manifestations experienced in the Maund House are blamed on Lacy Merritt. Even though the house in which she committed suicide in has been demolished, witnesses say that the new house is haunted, too.

## Mill House

Inside the Mill House, bloodstains mark the spot of a 1974 murder. In spite of major cleaning efforts, these tell tale stains keep showing up in the tile.

Mysterious mourning sounds and voices, and a female apparition wearing a dress from the 1920s are also reported

# LA MARQUE, TEXAS

La Marque, also known as Highlands and as Buttermilk Station, is an incorporated residential community on Interstate Highway 45, State Highway 3, and Farm roads 519, 1765, and 2004, some twelve miles northwest of Galveston in northwestern Galveston County. The community was originally known as Highlands, probably for its location near Highland Creek, and was renamed in the 1890s when residents learned of another mainland community of the same name. Madam St. Ambrose, postmistress, chose the new name, which in French means "the mark."

## Weller Home

The ghostly noises, poltergeist activity and apparitions in the Weller Home have been attributed to the ghost of 15-year-old Elvie Weller.

## LaMarque High School

When people go up to the cat walk, in the auditorium at LaMarque High School they can hear voices. It is said that someone was climbing the ladder, slipped and fell and was killed instantly. If you go further down, there use to be an elevator shaft in which people say the line broke and the elevator fell while people were in it.

# LAMPASAS, TEXAS

Lampasas is presently a small town of about 8,000 people nestled in the rolling hills of Central Texas, and surrounded by seven mineral springs; two of which produce more than 3,000,000 gallons of water daily. There are several theories on how the name Lampasas came to be. The Texas Almanac states the word came from a Spanish word for "lilies" that are found in nearby streams. Another source states the word comes from the Spanish word "Lampazos", the name given to the river by the Spanish Aquayo Expedition in 1721. It is believed the name was inspired by a Mexican town that also had beautiful springs. Tonkawas, Apaches, and Comanches were frequent visitors to these medicinal springs long before the first white settler came. Flowing springs, rivers and streams filled with fish and a countryside teeming with game made the area a popular spot for the Indians to camp.

## Sulpher Springs

In the 1800's the only daughter of the richest man in the town fell in love and got pregnant by one of their slaves. She told her father and he had the slave hung. After she had the baby she jumped into the Sulpher Springs with her newborn baby and drowned. But the body mysteriously floated up to the top of the springs 15 years later. It is now said that the ghost walks around the grounds where her house used to be but. The site of her old home is now an Intermediate school and a number of students have seen her. They say that she is actually wandering around where the old slave house stood with her baby looking for her lost love to show him the baby.

# LAKE JACKSON, TEXAS

Lake Jackson is an incorporated residential community ten miles upriver from the mouth of the Brazos River in south central Brazoria County. The 3000-acre sugar and cotton plantation of Abner Jackson occupied the site from 1843 to 1845. It originally used as many as eighty-two slaves to produce cotton, sugar, and corn, and later used convict labor to cultivate sugar after Jackson's death in 1861. As the plantation declined, the area became a black community, which had a single school and one teacher as late as 1937. In 1942 the plantation was purchased for use as a townsite for employees of the Dow Chemical Company.

### Jackson Plantation

One night the two Jackson brothers had a fight at Jackson Plantation. One ended up decapitating the other and throwing the head into the lake (Lake Jackson). The head was never found and the body had to be buried without it. To this day residents say that you can hear the sounds of someone wading into the lake and asking, "Where is my head?"

### Lake Jackson

The lake for which the town was named, Jackson Lake is a slave-built structure with a strange history. The Lake was made to serve the Jackson Plantation, owned by two brothers. During a particularly ugly spat, one of the Jackson brothers murdered the other and threw his head into the nearby lake. From that day, apparitions have appeared as well as sounds of the headless brother searching for his head. The plantation was moved decades later to make way for a new subdivision. People who live in the now-called "Lake Jackson Farms" have reported apparitions outside their homes, strange noises, and in at least a few cases, full hauntings. All that remains on the site of the original plantation house is the fireplace, made of mud brick.

# LEAGUE CITY, TEXAS

League City is on Clear Creek and Magnolia Bayou, State Highway 3, and U.S. Highway 75, equidistant from Houston and Galveston, in northwestern Galveston County. It was formerly the site of a Karankawa Indian village. George W. Butler, the town's first resident, arrived from Louisiana in 1873 and settled at the conjunction of Clear Creek and Chigger Bayou; a brickyard was the first local business.

The community was known as Butler's Ranch or Clear Creek until 1893, when J. C. League acquired the land from a man named Muldoon who, on entering the priesthood, relinquished his property rights. League laid out the town site on the Galveston, Houston and Henderson Railroad, which built through the area in 1854, and also provided land for the town's first school, known as the Little Green School. The railroad depot and Straw Hall or Straggler's Hall, which first housed guests were soon supplemented by general stores and a saloon. Early settlers raised cattle but turned to farming after 1890, when the Clear Creek Development was organized to sell lots to farmers.

## Clear Creek High School

On several occasions, people have witnessed spectral forms sitting in a small gazebo outside the band hall and auditorium at Clear Creek High School. The gazebo was set there along with a stone, commemorating students that have died while attending school there.

## Nasa Road 1

This part of Nasa Road 1 was completely within the last couple of years, and runs through two sets of neighborhoods. On the new road, witnesses have seen several shadow forms crouching at the edge of the trees, seen more shadows crossing the road and felt presences watching them. At the end of Nasa Road 1, there is a neighborhood that has been there for several years. Within that neighborhood, first is a large tree that radiates a dark presence. There is house next to it that is almost constantly lit, but that tree remains dark. A cemetery near by is reported to have demonic looking creatures roaming it.

# LIBERTY, TEXAS

Liberty, the county seat of Liberty County, is on State Highway 146 and U.S. Highway 90 in the south central part of the county. The site is in a major oil and gas production area served by the Southern Pacific Railroad. Liberty once stood at the head of navigation on the Trinity River. The town was founded near the sites of a Spanish settlement called Atascosito (established in 1756) and Champ d'Asile, a French colony established in 1818. The area was first occupied by American squatters as early as 1818, when it was still under Spanish law; settlers along the Atascosito Road, which crossed the Trinity three miles to the north, petitioned unsuccessfully to be included in Stephen F. Austin's colony. Subsequently, under Mexican law, land commissioner José Francisco Madero established an office in the settlement and on May 5, 1831, granted thirty-six land titles there, thus forming a new municipality, Villa de la Santísima Trinidad de la Libertad. Hugh B. Johnston was made Alcalde. In this Anglo-American colonization period, according to some sources, the town shortened its name to Liberty, after Liberty, Mississippi, whence many of the early settlers had come.

## Hardin House/Seven Pines

In 1839, Franklin Hardin built a house, called Seven Pines, in Liberty and moved his family from his plantation north of town to the now historic site. In addition to his own family, which consisted of his four daughters and two sons, Aunt Harriet and her children also resided at Seven Pines behind the main house. While Harriet called herself Harriet Evans, her children called themselves by their fathers' surnames-Henry Rowe, and Calvin and Melinda Green. There is no record of Harriet's having married. She remained a servant at Seven Pines before, during, and after the Civil War. By the 1870s one of Franklin Hardin's daughters, Camilla, had married George W. Davis, and they took up residence at Seven Pines, where they enjoyed the continued services of Aunt Harriet. Their daughter Geraldine married George Humphreys and eventually took over Seven Pines, also retaining Harriet as their servant. In March 1916, when a chimney fire almost destroyed the house, Harriet rescued all of the family's letters and documents and stored them in safe cupboards. Having served six generations of Hardens, she became the family historian because she lived to be nearly 100 years old and could always recall how the people in the area were related. She was responsible for written notes concerning the history of the family and the Liberty community, which were recorded by two of Franklin and Cynthia Hardin's children. The house is said to be haunted by the son of the builders, "Christy", who died at the age of 24.

## Witches Grave

Supposedly in the 17-1800s, a black slave was accused of being a witch. She was hung in a nearby tree (which is still there) and buried in the cemetery. Her grave marker says something like "whoever passes over this grave, shall die as I died". The words are so worn off that you can hardly read them. On Halloween night, people claim to hear the "witch" and sometimes see her hanging in the tree.

# MONTGOMERY, TEXAS

Montgomery is the official birthplace of the Lone Star flag. Designed by Dr. Charles B. Stewart in 1839 for the Republic of Texas, the flag and seal were adopted by the State of Texas, which inspired the slogan "Lone Star State". Dr. Stewart was the first to sign the Texas' Declaration of Independence. He lived and worked in Montgomery and is buried in the New Cemetery that was founded in 1868.

Montgomery began in 1826 as an Indian trading post at Town Creek, about a mile north of the center of town. It was chartered in 1837 and remains a small historic Texas town with shady trees and friendly people. You're invited to stroll back in time, browse through antique and gift shops and enjoy our restaurants.

## Community Building

The Community building is a historic building where the town used to hold all meetings, to include trials. There are two cages located in front of the building were they used to hold prisoners awaiting trial. It is said if you walk inside the doors of the cages at night you can hear moaning and other sounds of pain.

# MOUNT PLEASANT, TEXAS

Located on a broad hill in the heart of Northeast Texas, Mount Pleasant has served as the county seat of Titus County since 1846; just a few months after Texas became a state. A few remaining members of the Caddo Indian Tribe were probably in the area as the first pioneers from the United States began to settle Northeast Texas during the 1830's. The Caddos were known as builders of large burial mounds. Legend has it that they spoke of a "Pleasant Mound" in the central part of what is now Titus County. It is believed that the early Anglo settlers modified this Caddo name and referred to the broad, oak and hickory covered hill as Pleasant Mount. When the county was organized, the small village that would become the seat of government was given the name Mount Pleasant.

## Pizza Hut

In the 1980's, four people were murdered at this Pizza Hut after closing one night. Witnesses have said that they have seen a girl who worked there at the time walk past the front windows. There are still bullet holes in the windows and back freezer where one guy was stabbed and another shot. Employees have reported that when they put silverware on the tables after close for the next day, with no one there, they leave then come back 5 minutes later, all the silverware is slid to the opposite side. The intercom phone rings which it's not suppose to do in the first place and when it is picked up, there is a whisper but it is impossible to tell what they are saying.

# NEDERLAND, TEXAS

Nederland is on Farm roads 365 and 366, State Highway 347, and U.S. Highway 69/96/287, seven miles southeast of Beaumont in eastern Jefferson County. The site was developed by the Port Arthur Townsite Company and the Port Arthur Land Company as part of Arthur E. Stilwell's effort to make his newly built Kansas City, Pittsburg and Gulf Railway profitable. Stilwell, who had received much of his financial backing from Dutch investors, wanted a community for Dutch immigrants to Southeast Texas. The first such settler at Nederland was George Rienstra; forty others arrived in November 1897.

## Nederland House

It is said that Nederland House is haunted by a spirit named Joe Lee. It is said that he shakes beds, has shattered a glass chimney, and make ghostly footsteps. He has also been known to materialize.

# PASADENA, TEXAS

Pasadena, off State Highway 225 between Houston and Deer Park in southeastern Harris County, was founded in 1893 by John H. Burnett of Galveston. Because of its lush vegetation the site was named for Pasadena, California. The La Porte, Houston and Northern Railroad was built through the townsite in 1894 and opened the area for development as a farming community. Retired Kansas banker Charles R. Munger and land promoter Cora Bacon Foster were instrumental in organizing the early community. After the Galveston hurricane of 1900qv Clara Barton, of the American Red Cross, purchased 1½ million strawberry plants for Gulf Coast farmers. Pasadena quickly established itself as the strawberry capital of the region.

## Old Hospital Building

Witnesses have reported the sounds of a woman screaming and a baby crying inside this old hospital building. Figures are seen in the windows and going through the front doors when no one is present, and the elevators operate by themselves. The old building is now used as a municipal building.

## Deepwater Junior High

There have been rumors that a girl drowned in the swimming pool when Deepwater Junior High School was first built and now she haunts the girls' locker room by opening lockers and turning on the showers

## First Line Apartments

Residents of the First Line Apartments have reported hearing strange noises during the day and also at night. Several have heard footsteps coming upstairs and the sound of keys in the door, but when they look who had arrived, no one would be there. Several have also reported seeing the apparition of a woman coming from one of the bedrooms, walking past the small hallway and continue to the next room and disappear. While she was walking down the hallway, she would pause for a short time and turn and stare into the living room as if looking for someone.

## Pasadena High School

It is said that a janitor who was fixing the light in the catwalk at Pasadena High School fell to his death in auditorium. He fell in about the 6th row and if you sit there during a production or in the sound room you will get chills. If you walk up the stairs to the sound room there is a door to the roof and sometimes you can hear it slam. Also there is a girl who hung herself because she did not get the lead role in a play and she is said to play tricks on the students putting on a production.

## PORT NECHES, TEXAS

Port Neches, once known as Grigsby's (or Grigsby) Bluff, is located in eastern Jefferson County on Farm roads 365 and 366 and State Highway 347, ten miles southeast of Beaumont. The area was formerly the site of an Atakapa Indian village, relics of which were excavated in 1841. Thomas F. McKinney located his land claim there during the 1830s and went so far as to survey a townsite to be called Georgia. His plans, however, never materialized, and he sold two-thirds of his league to Joseph Grigsby in 1837. Grigsby and his family, who established a plantation and boat landing on a bluff overlooking the Neches River, were the earliest Anglo settlers of the area.

### Sarah Jane  Road

Sarah Jane was reportedly a union sympathizer during the Civil War who was betrayed and drove her wagon off the bridge into the water trying to escape from Confederate soldiers. She was shot by a soldier while trying to save her baby, who was in the wagon with her. People have reported hearing Sarah Jane and also the babe cry while standing on the bridge at night. Here is another explanation of the Sara Jane Haunting... A woman left her abusive husband, so to get back at her the man took their 5-year-old girl, and jumped of the side of a bridge. The woman searched for the girl for years, and finally got so distraught that she hung herself off the side of the same bridge that her daughter and husband jumped off of. It is said that at midnight, if you drive across the bridge, you can see the noose on the side on the railing and you hear a woman's voice saying, "Sara Jane, Sara Jane, where are you my Sara Jane".

## RICHMOND, TEXAS

Richmond, the county seat of Fort Bend County, is on the Brazos River fifteen miles southwest of Houston. The city's transportation links include U.S. highways 90A and 59, the Southern Pacific Railroad, and the Atchison, Topeka, and Santa Fe Railway. In early 1822 a group of twelve to fifteen men led by William W. Little camped in the vicinity of the present city and were soon followed by other members of Stephen F. Austin's Old Three Hundred. A log fort built at the bend in the Brazos River became the nucleus of a settlement, which came to be known as Fort Bend, or the "Fort Settlement." The community was evacuated in 1836 during the Runaway Scrape. In early 1837 the town of Richmond was established by Robert Eden Handy and his business partner, William Lusk, and as early as April the partners were advertising to sell lots in the town. Named after Richmond, England, the town was first incorporated by the Republic of Texas in May 1837; in December, when Fort Bend County was formed, Richmond became its seat of government.

## Jail House

This old jail house is located on Preston Street and is currently the local police department. It used to be a killing place for slaves and is now said to be haunted. Police officers now housed there have reported seeing ghosts thought to be those of slaves killed on the location.

# SARATOGA, TEXAS

Saratoga is at the junction of State Highway 105 and Farm Road 770, thirty-eight miles northwest of Beaumont in west central Hardin County. One of the earliest Anglo settlers in the area, J. F. Cotton, discovered a spring at the site during the 1850s. By the 1880s P. S. Watts had begun promoting the spring's medicinal value and had established a hotel, cottages, and campsites to serve visitors. The settlement's name was changed from New Sour Lake or Friendship to Saratoga, after the New York health resort.

## Big Thicket Light

The Big Thicket Light (or the Saratoga light) is a ghostly light that periodically appears at night on the Old Bragg Road that runs through the heart of the Big Thicket in Hardin County. Bragg Road was originally a seven-mile bed for a Santa Fe branch line from Bragg Station, on what is now Farm Road 1293, to Saratoga. The rails were laid in 1901 and pulled in 1934, but the bed remained and became a well used road through some of the densest woods in the Big Thicket. The Big Thicket light was reported while the tracks were still down. In summer 1960 Archer Fullingim, editor and publisher of the Kountze News, began running front page stories speculating on the nature of the light; these stories were picked up and carried in metropolitan newspapers in Texas and elsewhere. Light seers visited Bragg Road by the hundreds. They described the light, disagreeing as to its color or characteristics, but agreeing that a ghostly light of some sort frequented the road. The lights were variously rationalized as the reflections of car lights going in to Saratoga, patches of low-grade gas, a reflection of foxfire or swamp fire, or the figment of hysterical imaginations.

More romantic explanations produced stories about local history. The light was a mystical phenomenon that typically frequented areas where treasure was buried, and some early Spanish conquistadors had cached a golden hoard in the thicket but had failed to return for it. The light was a little bit of fire that never was extinguished after the Kaiser Burnout or the ghost of a man shot during the burnout, when the Confederate soldiers fired part of the thicket to flush out Jayhawkers who did not choose to fight for the South. Another story tells of a railroad man who was decapitated in a train wreck on this part of the Saratoga line; they found his body but never could locate his head, and the body continues to roam up and down the right-of-way looking for the lost member. And one tale tells that the light comes from a spectral fire pan carried by a night hunter who got lost in the Big Thicket years ago. He still wanders, never stopping to rest, always futilely searching for a way out of the mud and briars.

The story of the Mexican cemetery tells of a crew of Mexicans who were hired to help cut the right-of-way and lay the tracks. But, rumor has it that the foreman of the road gang, rather than pay them a large amount of accumulated wages, killed the men and kept the money. They were hurriedly interred in the dense woods nearby, from whence come their restless, uneasy souls, clouded in ghostly light to haunt that piece of ground that cost them their lives. And there is the story of a man who sold his farm and parted with everything that he couldn't pack in a suitcase, to work on the railroad. He was devoted to the line and became a brakeman on the "Saratoga." When the Santa Fe began to cut down on its runs, he found himself without a job or prospects. He died soon after, and his lonesome and troubled spirit still walks the road bed with its brakeman's lantern, the Big Thicket light, looking for the life that left him behind.

## SEABROOK, TEXAS

Seabrook is on State Highway 146 twenty-five miles from Houston near the Lyndon B. Johnson Space Center on the north side of Galveston Bay in Harris, Chambers, and Galveston counties. It was founded on the site of the Ritson Morris league, which became Elmwood Plantation, and was named for Seabrook Sydnor, son of John Sydnor of the Clear Creek Development Company, who with E. S. Nicholson platted and promoted the town in 1900. The settlement first housed summer residents who arrived on the Suburban, a commuter train that ran twice daily. The town had a post office by 1895.

### List Mansion

The List Mansion was located on Toddville Road. Mr. List was in the habit of taking in young run-away boys and taking advantage of them. Eventually some of his young wards had had enough and ambushed him when he came home. They killed their erstwhile captor and spent the evening ransacking the house and left. For a while it was a popular place for teenagers to go for "Truth or Dare" and there have heard reports that some visitors experienced some paranormal activity. The mansion has been demolished, but perhaps Mr. List is still hanging around.

### Camp Casa Mare

This site was formerly a privately owned mansion, but now it is Girl Scout Camp "Casa Mare". Years ago, a young woman who lived in the home near the shore with her father was said to be very distraught over the loss of a lover. She waited, watching for him to return from the sea from her balcony every night until she met her untimely death and collided with the ground below.

The mansion was since torn down, and a mess hall built where it once stood. Some say if you stand in a circle around the spot where she died (it remains uncovered by buildings, but now lies under a tile mural of a star), she will pull at you from the center of the circle, so that everyone "leans" inward.

Two campers supposedly died after falling in a well and being trapped. It has since been covered, but many report they still hear them screaming and clawing to get cut. Also, the dorm nearest to the shore is supposedly haunted (the dorm for those campers taking sailing). There are 3 showers, and when the first two are turned on, the third mysteriously turns on. Lights turn on and off and campers report hearing things.

## SPRING, TEXAS

Spring is off Interstate Highway 45 twenty miles north of Houston in north Harris County. The area was originally inhabited by the Orcoquiza Indians, who were first visited by Spaniards in 1746. In the 1820s some of Stephen F. Austin's colonists settled nearby. In 1836 the General Council of the Provisional Government included the area in the municipality of Harrisburg. William Pierpont established a trading post on nearby Spring Creek in 1838, and by 1840 Spring had a population of 153. In the mid-1840s German immigrants, most notably Carl Wunsche, settled in the area and began farming the land.

### The Hanging Tree

In the 1940s a young black man crossed the tracks to the white part of town at night. A group of drunken rednecks, thinking to teach him a lesson, decided to stage a fake hanging. Something went terribly wrong and the young man was actually hung and died. When the rednecks backed their Ford pickup up underneath the tree, they backed up too far and too fast. Their license plate became embedded in the trunk of the tree where it remained for decades until what was outside the bark finally rusted off about 10 years ago. You can still see part of the plate embedded in the tree. The nearby businesses and fire station have reported apparitions and other ghostly occurrences and attribute them to the ghost of that young man.

### Old Bank Building

The former bank building is just down the street from Wunsche Bros. and you can't mistake it for anything else. The architecture is distinctively that of a 19th century bank. Legend has it that it was once robbed by Bonnie and Clyde. During one attempted robbery, the would-be robber fled across the street and tried to take shelter behind a tree. The teller still managed to shoot him dead and from time to time his spirit has been reported lurking in the area of that tree. The marks where the bullets scored the facade can still be seen in the masonry today.

## Puffabelly's

This old train depot was imported in 2 pieces from Lovelady, Texas. During its early days a signal man was killed when he went out to the tracks to warn an oncoming train of another train on the same tracks headed the opposite direction. He slipped, fell on to the tracks, and was decapitated. For years his lantern was seen running down the tracks in Lovelady. Now it seems he has accompanied the depot to Spring. There is even a police report on file regarding one sighting of his spirit lying on the tracks that run by Puffabelly's and Wunsche Brothers.

After the restaurant burned down in 1999 (being approximately the umpteenth building to burn on that lot), the owners began rebuilding it. Puffabelly's is back in business, though most (if not all) of the original building has been lost to the fire. The food is still as good as it was before the blaze, highly recommended.

## Rose's Cafe

There is a rocking chair placed up against a wall in one of the dining rooms of Rose's Cafe. Witnesses have reported that this chair rocks on its own and scares the dickens out of patrons. Staff members report that if you sit in the chair and place your hands under the arms (just about an inch below); you can usually feel a temperature difference. A friend of the owner passed away in this chair and he saved it from destruction, restored it, and kept it in his house for a while.

When ghost investigators[52] arrived to examine the building, both times the owner had to go around back and unlock the front door from the inside because his resident spirit had locked the keyless deadbolt. This particular style of lock could only be locked form the inside. There was no one in the building during these visits. The owner reported that he will turn off all the lights and shut all the doors before he leaves, and frequently has to go back in and turn the lights off and shut the doors again.

## Spring Souvenir/Shirley's Cat House

Shirley's Cat House began life as a barn that originally belonged to Judge Doering. According to legend a friend of the Doering children, Sarah, was playing in the loft when she fell and broke her leg. She later died of complications from that injury. The current tenants have heard the sound of children running in the loft when no one was up there. Psychic Lorraine Ross read the building, and although she didn't detect a child who died by accident, she detected the spirit of a young woman who was murdered in the building. Perhaps it is this woman that they hear, trying to run from her assailant.

---

[52] Lone Star Spirits

## Thyme Square

In the back of Thyme Square there is a Civil War Museum that contains several artifacts. When re-enactments are done nearby the square becomes very active. During an investigation Lorraine Ross detected the displaced spirit of a Vet who was missing a leg. When she pointed to where he was standing, I took a picture and got an orb. To see the photo, visit our photo gallery.

## Wunsche Brothers

The building is in its original location and is over 100 years old. It was built by the Wunsche Brothers to cater to railroad workers. The tracks run right across the street. It was a saloon/restaurant/boarding house in its early days. Charlie Wunsche fell in love with a young woman who didn't love him in return. She jilted him and he ended up a rather crusty old man, who in turn has become a crusty old ghost. The restaurant was recently remodeled to add extra dining space and we are told that Charlie has been on a rampage on the second floor. The current manager prefers not to discuss Charlie as he has done some nasty and uncalled for things to her and other workers, such as lock them out of the building. Shortly after Charlie's death a young artist stayed in the room that he died in. The man was awoken in the middle of the night to see an old man staring at him from across the room. The artist drew a charcoal sketch of the old man and asked the owner of the building who it was he had drawn (wanting to identify the man who had interrupted his sleep). The old man was immediately identified as Uncle Charlie Wunsche.

## Zwink House

The Zwink House is not being used at the moment and is sitting on the same lot as Puffabelly's, between the restaurant and some shops. The house was brought from a few miles away and is an old farm house. You can look at the house, but you cannot enter. The story is that for one reason or another a man shot and killed his wife on the front porch. Lorraine Ross did a reading on the house for Lone Star Spirits and did detect a murder on the porch, but not of a woman. She detected a man stumbled onto an illicit affair between his wife and a college man, and shot the man on the porch. She also detected the death of a child from a snake bite.

A subsequent investigation by Lone Star Spirits revealed several spirits active in the house. Infrared footage has caught several orbs moving about the house, still photos have caught orbs in motion on the side of the house, and several members of the team witnessed 2 shadow apparitions in an upstairs window. One apparition was a child and the other was an adult. The structure was damaged in the 1999 fire that destroyed Puffabelly's, but the owners are making progress on restoring the first floor and modifying the second.

## TEXAS CITY, TEXAS

Texas City, on the southwestern shore of Galveston Bay seven miles from Galveston and eleven miles from the Gulf of Mexico in Galveston County, is a deepwater port on the mainland. In 1891, while on a duck-hunting trip to the marshlands of a community known as Shoal Point in Galveston Bay, three brothers from Duluth, Minnesota-Jacob R., Henry, and Benjamin F. Myers, saw that the area had potential as a major port. Other Duluth shippers joined the Myers brothers in buying 10,000 acres of Galveston Bay frontage, including Shoal Point, and renamed the area Texas City. On May 17, 1893, the Texas City Improvement Company filed the first townsite plat. The same year the post office was established.

### Cinemark Movies 12

All the employees of the Cinemark Movies 12 are scared to death to go into one of the auditoriums alone. Most workers have had some kind of an encounter with the ghost that haunts this particular auditorium. It makes some people feel freezing. Others became very hot. One employee said that every time she went in it, her knees would become very weak...but when she left the room, she was fine. Some employees have even seen this spirit.

## THE WOODLANDS, TEXAS

The Woodlands is a community west of Interstate Highway 45 and eleven miles south of Conroe in southern Montgomery County. In 1972 the Mitchell Energy and Development Corporation, as a response to the growth of nearby Houston, began to build, on 23,000 acres, a planned community called The Woodlands. The first homes were ready for purchase in 1974, and by 1980 the community had a population of 11,197, six schools, six parks, five churches, and a public library. About 160 companies had opened offices there by 1981. In 1990 The Woodlands numbered 29,205 inhabitants.

### The Woodlands - Walgreens,

Walgreens is located at 485 Sawdust Rd. The store is haunted by the ghost of John Cedars, a manager who was killed execution style during a robbery in 1996. Though it wasn't at the time, the location is now 24 hours and employees say that at nights Mr. Cedars can be heard walking the store or playing jokes (he likes to knock over the stacks of diapers like he did when he was alive).

Several people have reported incidents while alone in the stockroom at night, such as toys turning themselves on and off. Occasionally things have been known to fly off shelves and break without anyone nearby. The activity calmed after the convictions of the perpetrators in 1998, but he is still a presence in the store.

# TOMBALL, TEXAS

Tomball, Harris County's northernmost town, is thirty miles north of downtown Houston. It is at a higher elevation than most of Harris County and encompasses nine square miles. Before 1850 the area was the site of a farming community on a land grant given to the heirs of William Hurd in 1838. The settlement was named Peck, after a prominent civil engineer, in early 1907 and was one of forty train stations between Fort Worth and Galveston on the Trinity and Brazos Valley Railway. Peck had a freight terminal, a telegraph office, a water station, two section houses, stock pens with water and chutes, and a five-stall roundhouse. These facilities made the settlement an agricultural trade center for the area. On December 2, 1907, Peck was renamed Tomball in honor of Thomas Henry Ball, who had been instrumental in routing the railroad to the community.

## Spring Creek Park

In the Civil War era, a munitions factory existed in what is now the back portion of Spring Creek Park. It was destroyed when something touched off an explosion, which killed approximately 200 men. If you visit the sight today, even on a hot day, you will get chills. Some say that they can still smell burnt powder.

# WEST COLUMBIA, TEXAS

West Columbia, an incorporated town on State highways 35 and 36 between the Brazos and San Bernard rivers in west central Brazoria County, was founded as Columbia in 1826 by Josiah Hughes Bell, who laid out the town two miles west of Marion (now East Columbia). It was known as Columbia during the Texas Revolution and when it served as the capital of the Republic of Texas from September to December 1836. There the First Congress of the Republic of Texas convened, and Sam Houston was inaugurated president on October 22, 1836. The House of Representatives met in a two-story frame house and the Senate in a smaller house, at the site of which a state historical marker was later placed. On November 30, 1836, Congress met in joint session and decided to move the seat of government to Houston because Columbia did not have adequate accommodations for government personnel.

## Orozimbo Plantation

The original owner of the Orozimbo Plantation, Dr. Phelps, had three very good hounds of which he was very proud. It was rumored that he was killed at the Goliad Massacre during the Texas Revolution; however, this was not true. After Santa Ana was captured, Texas President Burnet ordered that the prisoner be moved around a lot before his return to Mexico.

During Santa Ana's stay at Orozimbo, Dr. Phelps managed to prevent his prisoner from committing suicide and Mrs. Phelps stopped a hoard of bloodthirsty Texans from killing the Mexican leader by throwing herself between him and the mob. One another occasions, Santa Ana's supporters managed to break him out, but nearby Texas troops were alerted to his escape by the three dogs. After Santa Ana was re-captured, the dogs could not be found. It is said that because their master did not order them back to the kennel, they must roam and prowl the area for all time. They have been known to appear and suddenly vanish without a trace.

## Palmetto Thickets & Woods

This immediate area in and around West Columbia and the old settlement of East Columbia and the surrounding woods and palmetto thickets abounds in ghost tales. There is the lady in the gray taffeta dress, and the ghost hounds of Orizimbo Plantation where Santa Ana was detained, who still waits for the return of the deceased owner of the plantation. They were reported to have been seen recently. Many other stories also float like wisps in the wind. This is one of the oldest parts on Texas to be settled, originally a part of Austin's Colony, so these are old "haunts".

# WHITE OAK, TEXAS

White Oak is on Farm Road 2152 near White Oak Creek nine miles northwest of Mount Pleasant in northwestern Titus County. It was originally a black farming community. Piney, two miles southeast of White Oak, was the first black settlement in the area. Gradually Piney became two communities, divided by Piney Creek. Those who lived east of the creek were considered to be part of the Piney community, and those who lived west of the creek were considered to be part of the White Oak community. George Baker, a prosperous landowner, was probably the first settler in what became White Oak. White Oak residents built their own church and school, so that they need not travel to Piney for education or worship. The school at White Oak was still open as an elementary school in 1964. In 1984 White Oak had two churches and a town hall.

## Shilo School

Shilo School is an old school that was an all black school in the early 1900's. The school was burnt down by the KKK and several black kids died. There are charred remains of the school still standing and a historical marker in front of it. At night it is reported that you can hear voices, cries of fear and the air gets cold. Others claim to still be able to smell the burning building and singed flesh.

# WOODVILLE, TEXAS

Woodville is on U.S. highways 190, 69, and 287 and the Texas and New Orleans Railroad, near the geographical center of Tyler County. It was established in 1846, when Tyler County was separated from Menard District. In the same year Woodville won the election for county seat from Town Bluff, the temporary seat, and from another proposed site on Wolf Creek in the northeast part of the county. The town was laid out on 200 acres in the Turkey Creek area donated to the county by Dr. Josiah Wheat. Wheat, the first physician of record in the area, moved with his family to Tyler County from Alabama as a settler. The town was named in honor of George T. Wood, second governor of Texas. In 1847 Woodville received a post office with James H. Fulgham as postmaster. The Lea Inn, erected in 1847, later became the Eden Hotel. The first Tyler County courthouse was a two-story log house completed in 1849. The Woodville Academy was established that year, and classes were held in the new courthouse building.

## Foster Hill

On Foster Hill, witnesses have reported a ghostly figure of a man and the sounds of Indian drums that can heard echoing in the distance and foot steps that can be heard but never a person seen to make them. At the end of the road a number of shadowy figures can be seen.

# TRINITY, TEXAS

Trinity is at the intersection of State highways 19 and 94 and Farm roads 230, 256, and 1617, in southwestern Trinity County. It was founded in the winter of 1872-73 on land purchased from the New York and Texas Land Company. A previous settlement in the vicinity had been called Kayser's (Kyser's) Prairie. Millican's Chapel, built in the 1850s on nearby Bell's Creek, is the first known church in the area. The new town was a station on the Houston and Great Northern Railroad, which built through Trinity County in 1872. The community was originally called Trinity Station, after the Trinity River, two miles southwest. The name was later changed to Trinity City and finally to Trinity. When the H&GN bypassed Sumpter, the county seat, many residents of that community moved to Trinity, which became the county seat on May 20, 1873.

## Parker House B & B

In historic Trinity, there is a stately old home that was once filled with the spirit of its owners, but is now operated as a bed-and-breakfast. It has also gone from being filled with the spirit of a family to having actual spirits that walk the halls almost a century after the death of the one that is believed to now haunt this home.

Built in 1888, the Parker House was once the home of Isaac Newton Parker, his wife, Mary Ashley Parker, and their children. Parker, who came to

Texas in 1822, served as a delegate from the Sabine District in the Convention of 1832.

During the Civil War, "Ike", as he was known to his friends served as a private in Company D of Hood's Fifth Texas Infantry through the war. He was one of the original members of Hood's Brigade Headquarters. After the war, Parker returned to his home in Walker County where he farmed for the next 10 years, before starting what was to be-come a very successful mercantile career in the Dodge community.

In late 1889, he and his wife moved to Trinity where they purchased the home that now bears his name. When Mary died in 1905, Parker, then age 65, remarried to a much younger 40-year-old store clerk name Lou Palmer, who reportedly was quite beautiful. Miz Lou, as she was known, lived at the Parker House until her death in 1955. Since that time, the house has been owned and lived in by several people, including Steven and Mary Ann Tyler, who bought the house in 1988 and converted it into a bed-and-breakfast.

The Tylers also purchased as their own home a house across the street from Parker

**Figure 19: The Parker House**

House that was once the domicile of Isaac and Mary Ashley Parker's daughter. While their home seems to be a haven from the cares of this world or the next, according to Steve Tyler, a number of strange occurrences in the Parker House indicate the presence of spirits.

According to those who seem able to communicate with the spirit world, Tyler has learned the presence inhabiting the home is likely a woman, possibly the spirit of the late Mary Ashley Parker.

"We knew things were going on around here, like doors being opened and closed, lights being turned off and on and people being touched," he said. "But when this particular friend of ours came in the house, she immediately said the spirit is a woman." Subsequent events have confirmed it, Tyler said. "She (the ghost) tends to communicate with very small children and new or expectant mothers," he explained.

On one occasion, a friend of the Tyler's came for a visit. With her she brought her 3-year-old son. "Everyone else was in the other room and our friend heard her son talking to someone," he said. "When she found him she asked him what he was doing and he said he was talking to the lady in the wall."

Other guests to the home have been awakened by the spirit. "One morning, a young mother from Seattle came to breakfast. She was obviously puzzled and asked me if we had spirits in the house," Tyler said. "Never knowing exactly how to respond, I asked her what happened."

The young mother recounted to Tyler what had taken place. "She awoke to the feeling that someone was stroking her fore-head and saying, 'Good mom, good mom", Tyler said.

According to Tyler, Mary Ashley Parker may have been made uncomfortable by the presence of Ike's second wife, Miz Lou.

"The thinking is that Mary was upset about this other woman being in her house," he said. Tyler also believes Mary's spirit may have lingered following her death, which occurred at the home. "Back in those days, people didn't go to a hospital or a nursing home to die. They often died at home," he said. "After Mary's death and before her funeral, her body would have been kept in the house."

It seems to be a regular occurrence for doors to open and close, ghostly voices heard in empty rooms, and there are a number of people that believe that they have seen the apparition of Mary Ashley Parker.

# INDEX

# C

## Q



## R





## S

## T